Lecture Notes in Computer Science 2252

Edited by G. Goos, J. Hartmanis, and J. van Leeuwen

Springer

Berlin
Heidelberg
New York
Barcelona
Hong Kong
London
Milan
Paris
Tokyo

Jiming Liu   Pong C. Yuen Chun-hung Li
Joseph Ng Toru Ishida (Eds.)

Active Media Technology

6th International Computer Science Conference, AMT 2001
Hong Kong, China, December 18-20, 2001
Proceedings

 Springer

Series Editors

Gerhard Goos, Karlsruhe University, Germany
Juris Hartmanis, Cornell University, NY, USA
Jan van Leeuwen, Utrecht University, The Netherlands

Volume Editors

Jiming Liu
Pong C. Yuen
Chun-hung Li
Joseph Ng
Hong Kong Baptist University
Department of Computer Science
Kowloon Tong, Hong Kong, China
E-mail:{jiming/pcyuen/chli/jng}@comp.hkbu.edu.hk

Toru Ishida
Kyoto University, Department of Social Informatics
Sakyo-ku, Kyoto 606-8501, Japan
E-mail: ishida@i.kyoto-u.ac.jp

Cataloging-in-Publication Data applied for

Die Deutsche Bibliothek - CIP-Einheitsaufnahme

Active media technology : proceedings / 6th International Computer Science
Conference, AMT 2001, Hong Kong, China, December 18 - 20, 2001. Jiming
Liu ... (ed.). - Berlin ; Heidelberg ; New York ; Barcelona ; Hong Kong ; London ;
Milan ; Paris ; Tokyo : Springer, 2001
  (Lecture notes in computer science ; Vol. 2252)
  ISBN 3-540-43035-0

CR Subject Classification (1998): H.5, H.3, H.4.3, I.2.11, C.2.4-5, K.4.2-4, I.4

ISSN 0302-9743
ISBN 3-540-43035-0 Springer-Verlag Berlin Heidelberg New York

Springer-Verlag Berlin Heidelberg New York
a member of BertelsmannSpringer Science+Business Media GmbH

http://www.springer.de

© Springer-Verlag Berlin Heidelberg 2001
Printed in Germany

Typesetting: Camera-ready by author, data conversion by PTP Berlin, Stefan Sossna
Printed on acid-free paper   SPIN 10845981   06/3142   5 4 3 2 1 0

Preface

The past few years have witnessed rapid scientific and technological developments in human-centered, seamless computing environments, interfaces, devices, and systems with applications ranging from business and communication to entertainment and learning. These developments are collectively best characterized as Active Media Technology (AMT), a new area of information technology and computer science that emphasizes the proactive, seamless roles of interfaces and systems as well as new digital media in all aspects of human life. This volume contains the papers presented at the Sixth International Computer Science Conference: Active Media Technology (AMT 2001), the first conference of its kind, capturing the state of research and development in AMT and the latest architectures, prototypes, tools, and fielded systems that demonstrate or enable AMT.

The volume is organized into the following eight parts: I. Smart Digital Media; II. Web Personalization; III. Active Interfaces; IV. Autonomous Agent Approaches; V. Facial Image Processing; VI. AMT-Supported Commerce, Business, Learning, and Health Care; VII. Tools and Techniques; and VIII. Algorithms.

We would like to thank all the program committee members for their excellent, timely service and great efforts in reviewing and selecting papers. We would also like to express our gratitude to all the invited speakers of AMT 2001 for their inspiring contributions. The invited speakers include: James L. Crowley, Toshio Fukuda, Toru Ishida, Takeo Kanade, and Oussama Khatib. We are grateful to the AMT 2001 congress chair, Ernest Lam, and general chair, Toshio Fukuda, for their strong support and valuable suggestions. The AMT 2001 conference would not have been possible without the team work of the organizing committee under the supervision of the organizing committee chair, Kelvin Wong. In particular, we would like to express our gratitude to the publication chairs, C.H. Li and M.W. Mak, for their efforts in setting up on-line tools and handling manuscript submissions, and the registration and finance chair, K.C. Tsui, for keeping a good financial balance, and the local arrangement chair, William Cheung, for coordinating conference logistics. Special thanks also go to Alfred Hofmann of Springer-Verlag for his vision and help in publishing this very first volume of AMT proceedings. Last but not the least, we would like to acknowledge the generous sponsorships from Hong Kong Baptist University, Croucher Foundation, IEEE Hong Kong Section Computer Chapter, and Joint Chapter of the Robotics and Automation and Control Systems Society.

We hope that you enjoy and benefit from the papers in this volume.

October 2001   Jiming Liu, P. C. Yuen, C. H. Li
                                                      Joseph Ng, and Toru Ishida

Organizing Committee

Congress Chair: Ernest C. M. Lam

General Chairs: Toshio Fukuda
                                     Joseph Ng

Program Chairs: Jiming Liu
                                     P. C. Yuen
                                     Toru Ishida

Organizing Chair: Kelvin C. K. Wong

Local Arrangement Chair: William K. W. Cheung

Registration and Finance Chair: K. C. Tsui

Publications Chairs: C. H. Li
                                     M. W. Mak

Workshop Chair: Samuel P. M. Choi

Publicity Chair: C. S. Huang

Program Committee

Keith Chan	Hong Kong Polytechnic University
David Cheung	Hong Kong University
Jeffrey Cohn	University of Pittsburgh, USA
Stefan Decker	Stanford University, USA
Dieter Fensel	Vrije Universiteit Amsterdam, The Netherlands
Myron Flickner	IBM Almaden Research Center, USA
Barbara Hayes-Roth	Stanford University, USA
Toru Ishida	Kyoto University, Japan
Tomonari Kamba	NEC Internet Systems Research Laboratories, Japan
Juntae Kim	Dongguk University, Korea
David Kinny	University of Melbourne, Australia
Sarit Kraus	University of Maryland, USA
Jiming Liu	Hong Kong Baptist University
Helen Meng	Chinese University of Hong Kong
Hideyuki Nakanishi	Kyoto University, Japan
Hideyuki Nakashima	ETL, Japan
Wee-Keong Ng	Nanyang Technological University, Singapore
Toshikazu Nishimura	Ritsumeikan University, Japan
Sun Park	Rutgers University, USA
Terry R. Payne	Carnegie Mellon University, USA
Eugene Santos	University of Connecticut, USA
Carles Sierra	CSIC-Spanish Scientific Research Council, Spain
Yasuyuki Sumi	ATR Laboratory, Japan
Takao Terano	University of Tsukuba, Japan
Hong Yan	City University of Hong Kong
Yiming Ye	IBM T. J. Watson Research Center, USA
Dit-Yan Yeung	Hong Kong UST
Tetuya Yoshida	Osaka University, Japan
Eric Yu	University of Toronto, Canada
P. C. Yuen	Hong Kong Baptist University

Sponsors

Hong Kong Baptist University
Croucher Foundation
IEEE Hong Kong Section Computer Chapter

Table of Contents

Keynote Presentations

Intelligent Adaptive Interface 1
Toshio Fukuda

Digital City: Bridging Technologies and Humans 2
Toru Ishida

Detection, Recognition, and Expression Analysis of Human Faces 3
Takeo Kanade

Digital Interactivity: Human-Centered Robotics, Haptics, and Simulation . 4
Oussama Khatib

I. Smart Digital Media

Smart Media: Empower Media with Active Data Hiding 5
Hong Heather Yu, Peng Yin, Samuel Cheng, Xiangyang Kong,
Alexander Gelman, Robert S. Fish

Congestion Prospect of Network Traffics by Fluctuation
of Internet Transmission Time 17
Hiroto Takahashi, Yasuo Yonezawa

Naturalistic Human–Robot Collaboration Mediated by Shared
Communicational Modality in Teleoperation System 24
Yukio Horiguchi, Tetsuo Sawaragi

II. Web Personalization

Web Personalization Techniques for E-commerce 36
Suwimol Sae-Tang, Vatcharaporn Esichaikul

A Shopping Negotiation Agent That Adapts to User Preferences 45
Runhe Huang, Jianhua Ma, Qun Jin

Combining Meta-level and Logic-Based Constructs in Web Personalization 57
Sofie Goderis, Gustavo Rossi, Andres Fortier, Juan Cappi,
Daniel Schwabe

Web Personalisation – An Overview 65
San Murugesan, Annamalai Ramanathan

Business-Oriented Web Personalization: A Decision-Making Approach 77
Carlos Alberto Odorico de Moraes Filho, Francilene Procpio Garcia

A Personalized Interface Agent with Feedback Evaluation 83
   Weihua Li, Xiaodong Fu

III. Active Interfaces

VHML – Directing a Talking Head 90
   Andrew Marriott, Simon Beard, John Stallo, Quoc Huynh

Believable and Interactive Talking Heads for Websites: MetaFace
and MPEG-4 101
   Simon Beard, Donald Reid, Russel Shepherdson

Building Multi-modal Personal Sales Agents as Interfaces
to E-commerce Applications 113
   Yasmine Arafa, Abe Mamdani

Feature vs. Model Based Vocal Tract Length Normalization for a Speech
Recognition-Based Interactive Toy 134
   Chun Keung Chau, Chak Shun Lai, Bertram Emil Shi

A Genetic Algorithm Based Approach to the Synthesis
of Three Dimensional Morphing Sequences 144
   Stephen Wang-Cheung Lam, Kelvin Yuen-Hin Ho

IV. Autonomous Agent Approaches

A Comparative Study of ANT-Based Optimization for Dynamic Routing.. 153
   Kwang Mong Sim, Weng Hong Sun

What Kind of Cooperation Is Required by Situated Agents? (The Principle
of Situated Cooperation) 165
   Angélica Muñoz-Meléndez, Alexis Drogoul

A Fault-Tolerant Scheme of Multi-agent System for Worker Agents 171
   YunHee Kang, HoSang Ham, ChongSun Hwang

Decentralized Control of Multi-agent Systems Based on Modal Logics and
Extended Higher Order Petri Nets 182
   Osamu Katai, Kentaro Toda, Hiroshi Kawakami

V. Facial Image Processing

An Improved Foreground Extraction Approach 191
   Erdan Gu, Duanqing Xu, Chun Chen

Object Detection Simulating Visual Attention 199
   Xingshan Li, Chunwei Yuan

Fast Face Detection Using Neural Networks and Image Decomposition 205
   Hazem M. El-Bakry

Modeling of Facial Expressions Using NURBS Curves 216
Ding Huang, Wei Lin, Hong Yan

VI. AMT-Supported Commerce, Business, Learning, and Health Care

Evolutionary Negotiation in Agent-Mediated Commerce 224
Samuel P.M. Choi, Jiming Liu, Sheung-Ping Chan

Optimizing Agent-Based Negotiations with Branch-and-Bound 235
Andy Hon Wai Chun, Rebecca Y.M. Wong

Engineering Fuzzy Constraint Satisfaction Agents for
Multi-user Timetable Scheduling 244
Chi Kin Chau, Kwang Mong Sim

An XML-Based Distance Learning System Capable of
Conveying Information on "LECTURE EVENT" 255
Naoaki Mashita, Hiroshi Shigeno, Yutaka Matsushita

An Authoring Tool for Building Adaptive Learning Guidance Systems on
the Web 268
José A. Macías, Pablo Castells

A Framework of Caring Interaction by a Network Model of Client's
Concepts Based on a Nursing Theory and Naive
Psychological Approaches 279
Akira Notsu, Osamu Katai, Hiroshi Kawakami

VII. Tools and Techniques

Parallel Design Based on Neural Network 291
Shaobai Zhang, Xiefeng Cheng, Zhiquan Feng

Fair Play Protocol 297
Tak-Ming Law

Collaborative Filtering Methods for Binary Market Basket
Data Analysis 302
Andreas Mild, Thomas Reutterer

An Implementation and Design of COMOR System for OOM Reuse 314
Young-Jun Kim

Automatic Aircraft Recognition Using Maximum Likelihood Ratio Test ... 321
Wei Yi

VIII. Algorithms

A Machine Learning Algorithm Based on Supervised Clustering
and Classification 327
    Nong Ye, Xiangyang Li

Visualization of a Parallel Genetic Algorithm in Real Time 335
    Xiaodong Li

The Rise and Fall of Napster – An Evolutionary Approach 347
    Bengt Carlsson, Rune Gustavsson

On the Elaboration of Hand-Drawn Sketches 355
    Saul Simhon, Gregory Dudek

The Introduction of Three Methods Generating Stereoscopic Image 365
    Guoying Zhao, Xinyuan Huang

Kansei-Oriented Image Retrieval 377
    Shangfei Wang, Enhong Chen, Jing Hu and Xufa Wang

ICSPACE – An Internet Cultural Space 389
    T.A. Tavares, A.S. Araújo, G.L. Souza Filho

Author Index 401

Intelligent Adaptive Interface

Toshio Fukuda

Department of Mechanical Engineering
Nagoya University, Japan

Abstract. Artificial or machine intelligence is quit low compared with human intelligence. Most machines, which have no autonomy, are controlled by human so that they could work properly and effectively under a complicated environment. In such a situation, intelligent adaptive man-machine interface is the key technology in order to assist operator work and to decrease human error. I introduce some key technologies and some applications, e.g. a crane operation system, a medical system and an information assistance robot. I also discuss future technologies for an enhanced man-machine interface.

Biography. Toshio Fukuda graduated from Waseda University in 1971. He studied at Yale University from 1973 to 1975. He received his Doctor degree from the University of Tokyo in 1977. During the same year he joined the National Mechanical Engineering Laboratory in Japan. From 1979 to 1981 he was a Visiting Research Fellow at the University of Stuttgart in West Germany. He worked for the Science University of Tokyo in 1981, and then joined the Nagoya University in 1989. He is presently Professor of the Center for Cooperative Research in Advanced Science and Technology at Nagoya University. He is mainly engaging in the research field of intelligent robotic systems and he is an author of six books, editing five books and has published over 1,000 technical papers in micro system, robotics, mechatronics and automation areas. He serves as Vice President of the International Fuzzy System Association since 1998. He was awarded IEEE Fellow, and SICE Fellow in 1995, both the city of Grenoble Medal and the Banki Donat Medal from the Polytechnic University of Budapest, Hungary in 1997.

J. Liu et al. (Eds.): AMT 2001, LNCS 2252, p. 1, 2001.
© Springer-Verlag Berlin Heidelberg 2001

Digital City: Bridging Technologies and Humans

Toru Ishida

Department of Social Informatics
Kyoto University, Japan

Abstract. This talk presents future technologies for digital cities as a social information infrastructure for urban life (including shopping, business, transportation, education, welfare and so on). We propose the three layer architecture for digital cities: a) the information layer integrates both WWW archives and real-time sensory information related to the city, b) the interface layer provides 2D and 3D views of the city, and c) the interaction layer assists social interaction among people who are living/visiting in/at the city.

We recently started the research project of "the Universal Design of Digital City," a five year project established in 2000, under the Core Research for Evolutional Science and Technology (CREST) of the Japan Science and Technology Corporation (JST). The objective of this project is "to construct digital cities as an infrastructure used and participated by all people, including the disabled and the aged." The universal design - useable for all people- for digital city is indispensable to create the information space for daily life. In this project, we will develop basic technologies for the universal design, subject to 'sending information,' 'receiving information,' and 'participation.'

This talk introduces various experiments including security, learning about the natural environment by experience, and crisis management, based on the future technologies including 3D, animation, agents, distributed vision and mobile computing.

Biography. Professor of Department of Social Informatics, Kyoto University, Kyoto, Japan. B.E., M.Eng. and D.Eng. from Kyoto University, in 1976, 1978 and 1989. Associate editor of IEEE PAMI from 1996-1999. General co-chair of the first international joint conference on autonomous agents and multiagent systems, AAMAS2002. Research scientist of NTT Laboratories from 1978 to 1993. Visiting research scientist at Columbia University, Guest Professor of Technische Universitaet Muenchen and Invited Professor of de Paris 6, Pierre et Marie Curie. Prof. Ishida has been working on community computing from 1995, and edited two books: community computing: collaboration over global information networks (John Wiley and Sons, 1998), and community computing and support systems (Springer-Verlag, 1998). He is currently working on digital cities: experiences, technologies and future perspectives (Springer-Verlag, 2001) and initiated Digital City Kyoto with his colleagues.

J. Liu et al. (Eds.): AMT 2001, LNCS 2252, p. 2, 2001.

Detection, Recognition, and Expression Analysis of Human Faces

Takeo Kanade

Robotics Institute
Carnegie Mellon University, USA

Abstract. Automated processing of facial images is a problem of interest since the beginning of computer vision. Recently the interest has revived for biometrics and human-computer interaction. I am going to talk about our recent progress in face image analysis: detecting faces in an image with arbitrary size, pose and background, understanding facial actions units of FACS to understand facial expression, and recognizing people by face images. Also, I will talk about "recovering" a higher resolution image of the face from an extremely low resolution image (the process we nicknamed "hallucination"). Common to these methods is a combination of probabilistic approach and critical care of registration in order to obtain better results than previous attempts.

Biography. Dr. Kanade received his Ph.D. in Electrical Engineering from Kyoto University, Japan, in 1974. After being on the faculty of the Department of Information Science, Kyoto University, he joined the Computer Science Department and Robotics Institute in 1980. He became an Associate Professor in 1982, a Full Professor in 1985, the U. A. and Helen Whitaker Professor in 1993, and a University Professor in 1998. He was the Director of the Robotics Institute from 1992 to Spring 2001. He served as the founding Chairman (1989 - 93) of the Robotics Ph. D. Program at CMU, probably the first of its kind in the world. Dr. Kanade has worked in many areas of robotics, including manipulators, sensors, computer vision, multimedia applications, and autonomous robots, with more than 200 papers on these topics. He has been the founding editor of the International Journal of Computer Vision. Dr. Kanade's professional honors include: election to the National Academy of Engineering, a Fellow of IEEE, a Fellow of ACM, a Fellow of American Association of Artificial Intelligence; several awards including C & C Award, the Joseph Engelberger Award, Yokogawa Prize, JARA Award, Otto Franc Award, and Marr Prize Award.

J. Liu et al. (Eds.): AMT 2001, LNCS 2252, p. 3, 2001.
© Springer-Verlag Berlin Heidelberg 2001

Digital Interactivity: Human-Centered Robotics, Haptics, and Simulation

Oussama Khatib

Department of Computer Science
Stanford University, USA

Abstract. A new field of robotics is emerging. Robots are today moving towards applications beyond the structured environment of a manufacturing plant. They are making their way into the everyday world that people inhabit. The successful introduction of robotics into human environments will rely on the development of competent and practical systems that are dependable, safe, and easy to use. The discussion focuses on models, strategies, and algorithms associated with the autonomous behaviors needed for robots to work, assist, and cooperate with humans. In addition to the new capabilities they bring to the physical robot, these models and algorithms and more generally the body of developments in robotics is having a significant impact on the virtual world. Haptic interaction with an accurate dynamic simulation provides unique insights into the real-world behaviors of physical systems. The potential applications of this emerging technology include virtual prototyping, animation, surgery, robotics, cooperative design, and education among many others. Haptics is one area where the computational requirement associated with the resolution in real-time of the dynamics and contact forces of the virtual environment is particularly challenging. The presentation describes various methodologies and algorithms that address the computational challenges associated with interactive simulations involving multiple contacts and impacts with complex human-like structures.

Biography. Oussama Khatib is Professor of Computer Science at Stanford University. His work is on autonomous robots, human-centered robotics, human-friendly robot design, dynamic simulations, and haptic interactions. The emphasis of his research is on methodologies and technologies that address the intricate dynamic nature of these systems, provide the capabilities needed for their action and interaction with the environment, and cope with their real-time requirements. This research spans a variety of topics ranging from the autonomous ability of a robot to cooperate with a human to the haptic interaction of a user with a virtual prototype, an animated character, or a surgical instrument. Professor Khatib was the Program Chair of ICRA2000 and a co-editor of "The Robotics Review." He is a "Distinguished Lecturer" of the IEEE Robotics and Automation Society and a recipient of the JARA Award.

J. Liu et al. (Eds.): AMT 2001, LNCS 2252, p. 4, 2001.
© Springer-Verlag Berlin Heidelberg 2001

Smart Media: Empower Media with Active Data Hiding

Hong Heather Yu[1], Peng Yin[2], Samuel Cheng[3], Xiangyang Kong[1],
Alexander Gelman[1], and Robert S. Fish[1]

[1] Panasonic Information and Networking Technologies Lab, Princeton, NJ ,USA
[2] Princeton University, Princeton, NJ, USA
[3] Texas A&M University, College Station, TX, USA

Abstract. The seamless development in computing, networking, communication, and signal processing is making media a more and more important part of our daily lives. The passive nature of media, however, limits the capability of it. In this paper, we introduce the notion of 'smart' media which carry additional active information imperceptibly in the media content itself for added interactive-ability. With smart media, traditional information access -- from single medium to multimedia -- can be enhanced with new, two-way communication abilities. Active data hiding, endowed with perceptual intelligent high capacity data hiding techniques, is used to embed an agent imperceptibly into a medium. It infuses mobility to the passive data stream by introducing personality and controllability into the medium. The design of active data hiding system for smart media shall be discussed, along with a variety of applications.

1 Introduction

The advent of modern computing and networking technologies brought multimedia closer to us. Consequently, media, in various forms, are used to enhance our lives in numerous aspects, notwithstanding, passively. One disadvantage imposed by this passive nature is its zero controllability over the use of itself. This is because current technology specifies only single-ended, single-control use of media. That is, a user can control the use of media and protect herself from bad media, but a medium can not specify the use on itself to protect itself from bad use, such as abusive handling and illegitimate client. This passive nature makes it vulnerable to any misuse.

1.1 Motivation

The smart media study at Panasonic is aiming at the application of next generation multimedia information access. Modern technologies introduce mobility, interactability, and intelligence into information access. On the receiver end, from the traditional passive watching and listening state to the new active responding state (Figure 1(a)), interactive media technology brought intercommunication capability, and hence more flexibility and usability, to the user. At the presentation end, though, the passive state of media is kept motionless in the conventional action space. This one way communication phenomenon is illustrated in Figure 1(a). To impose two way

J. Liu et al. (Eds.): AMT 2001, LNCS 2252, p. 5–16, 2001.
© Springer-Verlag Berlin Heidelberg 2001

communication capability (Figure 1(b)), we propose smart media in leading the active feedback and interaction into this space. Figure 2 vividly illustrates the idea of smart media, to infuse mobility to the passive data stream by introducing personality and controllability into the medium. More specifically, a medium with added capability to 'think' and 'take actions' on itself via an agent binding to it is named a smart medium. It can 'think' and 'act' on behave of itself for its own benefit, and therefore brings two way communication into the problem space. Furthermore, it provides new ways to attain media-to-media communication.

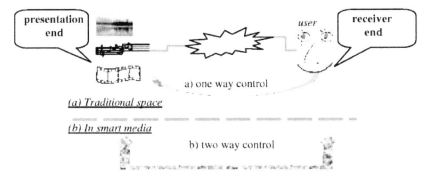

Fig. 1. Media presentation

1.2   Our Proposed Scheme

The technique we propose for smart media is Active Data Hiding (ADH). ADH is a subset of data hiding. It is to hide an active data stream, such as an applet or an executable file which can actively perform certain tasks by itself, into the host data stream, whereas Data Hiding (DH) is defined as imposing a meaningful and extractable but perceptually indistinguishable signal onto a host signal (host data stream), such as audio, image, video, or multimedia. The hidden information can be extracted and used for information retrieval, copyright protection, and other purposes.

It is easy to imagine, putting the agent into the media file header would be technically much easier. Though, the advantage of having the active agent embedded imperceptibly into the media, as we proposed using ADH, lies in binding and addition security. Unlike the file header which may be lost in transmission or be easily cut, the embedded data shall be coupled with the host data stream, the host medium, wherever the medium goes in the pre-designated position

Previous work on data hiding. In recent years, many data hiding schemes have been proposed and discussed mainly for the copy and copyright protection and access control applications. The basic idea is to embed a sequence of bits imperceptibly into the host media, such as an image. This embedded sequence can be a copy mark for access control, a signature for copyright protection, or an ID for tracking. For this kind of applications, it is often called digital watermarking as well. In other words, digital watermarking problem space is a subspace of the data hiding problem space. It is to hide data for the copyright protection and copy identification applications, whereas data hiding refers to the process of hiding a sequence of data into a host data stream imperceptibly for any applications. In the past fewer years, most of the research works have been concentrated on passive data hiding (PDH) and designing passive data hiding schemes for various applications. PDH is a complement of ADH set, which is to hide a passive data stream that can not perform any task actively by itself but acted upon, into the host data stream. In contrast to PDH, ADH can provide an active data layer to interact with the medium receiver, which helps to introduce active feedback capability to media. With ADH, an active agent can be bound to a medium imperceptibly to generate the smart medium, provide with it an intelligent dynamic data layer for various actions the medium may want to take for itself.

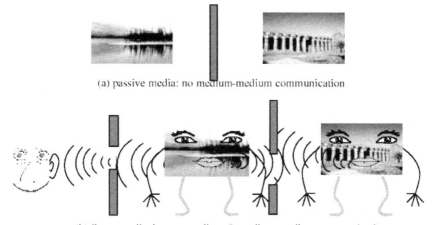

(a) passive media: no medium-medium communication

(b) Smart media: human-medium & medium-medium communicative

Fig 2. A vivid illustration of smart media: adding personality and controllability into media

1.3 Paper Organization

The paper is organized as following. Section 2 investigates the problem of ADH. Several application scenarios along with a smart media demo system are presented in Section 3. Conclusion remarks and future work direction are given in Section 4.

2 Active Data Hiding (ADH)

2.1 Notations

- i, j, k, l, n, x, z, J, K, L, M, N, X, and Z are integers.
- Denote host data stream as HDs and host data bit with HDb. For example, 1bit/HDs means 1bit/host data stream while 1bit/HDb stands for 1bit/host data bit.
- Let I represent an original host medium which, when viewed as a data stream, is called host data stream in the following discussion.
- Also define $I(i)$ to be the ith bit of the host data stream with the length of it $|I|$ being Kbits, $i \in [1,K]$. $|.|$ denotes cardinality.
- Assume W is a set of meaningful data streams for data embedding, with $aW \vee W$ a set of active data streams, such that $\forall aw \in aW$ is an active data stream sufficient

to perform certain tasks. Also assume when the embedded data stream is for authentication use, w_{au} denotes the data stream that contains authentication value.

- Define $w^0[j]$ to be the jth bit of the embedded hidden data stream w^0 and $w^1[j]$ be the jth bit of the extracted hidden data stream w^1, with the lengths being $|w^0|=J$ and $|w^1|=J$, i.e., $j \in [1,J]$.

- An embedded medium is denoted I'=Enc(I, w). Similarly, I'=Enc$_{ADH}$(I, aw) represents a medium with active data stream aw hidden inside the medium. Imperceptible data hiding implies I' equivalents to I perceptually. If we denote perceptual equivalence as $=^p$, then I' equivalents to I perceptually would be denoted I' $=^p$ I.

- Denote transformation $\tau: I \mapsto I''= \tau(I)$.

- Let JPD(I) represent the upper bound of the host signal just perceptible difference and D(I) stand the difference between I and $\tau(I)$, i.e., D(I)= $\tau(I)$- I,

2.2 Criteria and Challenge

Compare to conventional PDH, ADH bears an additional layer of difficulties which include high data hiding bit rate and low probability of extraction error requirements in addition to the imperceptibility and extractability criteria for PDH. Next, we shall discuss the challenges in detail, pose the problem, and propose feasible solutions using imperceptibility and extractability as a thread.

2.3 Transparency and the Triangular Tradeoff

We are particularly interested in hiding the active data stream imperceptibly such that visible distortion is under the upper bound of the tolerable visual distortion zone, i.e, D(i)≤JPD(i), for i∈[1,K], D(I) is smaller than the host signal just perceptible difference JPD(I). The tradeoff between transparency — data hiding capacity and between transparency — hidden data strength determine that higher transparency will yield lower capacity and lower robustness. Previous study on data hiding techniques [1, 2, 3] shows that the human perceptual model used for data compression can be adopted, with minor modifications, to guide how much data to hide. In our study, the JND (Just Noticeable Difference) function used in JPEG and the perceptual model used in MP3 and AAC compression are adopted for media data hiding[2,3].

2.4 Data Hiding Bit Rate

Data hiding capacity (DHC) defines how many bits can be embedded into a host data stream imperceptibly. It is often measured with data hiding bit rate. Mathematically, data hiding bit rate is defined as the number of bits hidden per host data stream unit, or alternatively, per time interval when it is a temporal data stream. For clarity of discussion, we shall use #bits/sec = #bps for temporal domain data stream and #bits/HDb = #bpHDb otherwise in this paper. We thus denote $Rt(I)$ and $R(I)$ to be the DHC of I in temporal and spatial domain respectively.

Requirement of host data stream capacity for ADH. Suppose the host data stream has a length L, i.e., L units in length. If an active data stream of J_A bits is hidden in it, the data hiding bit rate shall be $r(I) = J_A/L$ bits/unit $= J_A/L$ bpu. That means, the host data stream DHC needs to be at least J_A/L bpu, i.e., $R(I) - J_A/L$.

The first technical challenge of ADH. The first technical challenge of ADH is high embedding bit rate requirement. PDH, such as digital watermarking for access control, may have a low data hiding bit rate of $m$bits/medium, or alternatively, $m$bits/data stream, with $r_m(I) = \min(r(I)) = 1$bit/HDs $= 1$bpHDs. The size of an applet or an executable file, however, is usually at least several hundred bytes: $r_{mA}(I) = \min(r_A(I)) = m \times 100$bpHDs. According to our study, the smallest active data stream would be a Java agent with at least 450bytes in size. That is equivalent to 3600bits in length. That is, an active data stream has length J_A—3600bits with $r_{mA}(I) = \min(r_A(I)) = 3600$bpHDs. This requires techniques for imperceptible high bit rate embedding. The difficulty of the problem thus rises. Using music as an example. A typical song is about 2-4mins long ($L = 2 \times 60 \sim 4 \times 60$sec). To hide a smallest Java applet into it, we need a bit rate of at least $J_A/L = 3600$bits/(2×60)sec $= 30$bps $\sim$ 3600bits/(4×60)sec $= 15$bps, i.e., the lower bound of DHC requirement is $Rt_{mA}(I) \geq r_{mA}(I) = \min(r_A(I)) = 30$bps. This suggests the necessity to explore as much DHC as possible.

Notice that a smart medium may need to perform more than the simplest task. That means, the Java agent needed may be tens or hundreds of times larger then 450bytes for a practical application. However, it is impossible to have a several K bps data hiding bit rate for a 44kbps audio. To solve this problem, we used software partition. Certain parts of the software are static. For instance, the MD5 one way hash algorithm used for authentication can be made public accessible. On the other hand, the access key is often desirable to be kept secret and renewable. Our solution is to put the static segments of the software in library saved outside the agent. The embedded agent only has the console part of the software, the dynamic segments. In our demo system presented in Section 3, Java is used to implement the active agent where the total size of the library files is more than 200KB whereas the size of the embedded agent is only < 5KB for the first demo system.

2.5 Hidden Data Strength

Suppose there is a set of transformation $T = \{\tau \mid X \mapsto_\tau X'\}$ that maps a data stream X to another data stream X'. If X constructs a medium I, a transformation T that preserves the perceptual quality of the original medium I is denoted pT. A data hiding scheme V is said to be robust with reference to transformation T iff $pT(I) =^p I \mid V$. V is said to be strong if for $\forall T_n \in T_v = \{T_n, n \in [1,N], N > \beta$ (a predefined threshold)$\}$, $pT(I) =^p I \mid V$ holds. In other words, if w survives all the transformation in a predefined transformation set T_v, the data hiding scheme V is accepted as strong data hiding with reference to T_v. A hidden data stream w is said to have survived a transformation T iff w^1 is equivalent to w^0, that is, $w^1 \cong w^0$, where w^1 and w^0 are said to be equivalent iff $w^0[j] = w^1[j]$ with $|j| \geq \gamma$, where γ is a predefined threshold and $|.|$ denotes cardinality.

The second technical challenge of ADH. The second technical challenge of ADH is the low probability of extraction error requirement. Unlike passive data stream, even one bit error in an active data stream may result in failure. Clearly, this is due to the sensitivity of error in executable files, such that the extracted hidden data stream has to be virtually errorless. In PDH, $\gamma < J$ may be acceptable for certain applications. However, in the case of ADH, $\gamma = J$ has to hold. This motivated us to propose multi-layer data hiding for ADH[5]. That is, a secondary hidden data layer that includes some error correction (EC) bits for the active data stream is hidden inside the host data stream in addition to the primary hidden data layer that contains the active data stream.

The question is 'does this additional layer of hidden data increase the data hiding bit rate significantly?' Using our demo system 2 in Section 3 as an example, the embedded agent aw has length of J_A =585Bytes=4680Kbits. A song of two channels in 1 minute and 25 seconds long is used as host medium, thus L=2×85sec=170sec, and $r_{maw}(I)$ = 4680bits/170sec ≈ 27.5bps. Suppose a simple 2D checksum EC is used. Then the EC stream length L_E satisfies $J_A=(L_E/2)^2$, which yields L_E = 137, $r_{mLE}(I)$ = 137bits/170sec < 1bps, and therefore the total data hiding bit rate including the EC layer $r_{maw}(I)$ = (137 + 4680)bits/170sec ≈ 28.3bps. If we further add authentication layer using MD5 one way hash algorithm, an additional $|w_{au}|$ = 128bits of capacity increase will be needed. Subsequently, it yields a $r_{maw}(I)$ = (128 + 137 + 4680)bits/170sec ≈ 29bps. That means the total DHC needed before and after adding the secondary data hiding layer is only about a 1.56bps increase over the 27.5bps base capacity in this case. The tradeoff is clear.

Furthermore, our study in the data hiding algorithms strength and capacity tradeoff[6] show that by selecting a high capacity region with an algorithm that provides high DHC for the primary hidden data layer and then a high robustness data hiding region with an algorithm that supports high robustness for the second hidden data layer, we can expect to get a better tradeoff for large capacity data hiding with applicable low probability of error. Thus it is more suitable to use for ADH into smart medium.

Data hiding schemes are often classified into fragile and robust two categories based on the strength and survivability of the hidden data over signal processing and other attacks. Different applications, including those for smart media applications, often have different robustness requirement. Therefore, the development of both fragile and robust ADH techniques is useful. In a multi-layer data hiding system, fragile techniques can be applied to the primary hidden data layer and robust techniques can be applied to the second hidden data layer. In the following two subsections, we will use audio as an example to discuss techniques for fragile and robust ADH. The detail of the multi-layer data structure is provided in Appendix A.

2.6 Fragile ADH

We define a fragile ADH system as following.
An ADH scheme **v** is said to be fragile if

$$\begin{cases} w^1 = aw^0 \ \& \ w_{au}^{\ 1} = w_{au}^{\ 0} \ \text{when} \ I'' = I \\ w_{au}^{\ 1} \neq w_{au}^{\ 0} \ \text{when} \ I'' \neq I, \text{i. e.,} \ \exists i, \text{ such that } I''(i) \neq I(i) \end{cases} \tag{2.6.1}$$

An ADH system is said to be a fragile ADH system if it only supports fragile ADH.

Our fragile ADH system[4] has a three-pass architecture. First, the meaningful active agent data stream aw is mapped into a sequence of binary data $aw^0 = aw^0[1]$, ..., $aw^0[J]$ of length J which are inserted imperceptibly into the host data stream, $I* = Enc(I, aw)$. Then, the EC bits, $w_{EC} = w_{EC}[1]$, ..., $w_{EC}[L_E]$, are generated and embedded into the host signal $I** = Enc(I*, w_{EC})$. In the third pass, cryptography techniques are used to authenticate the embedded data stream, $I' = Enc(I**, w_{au})$.

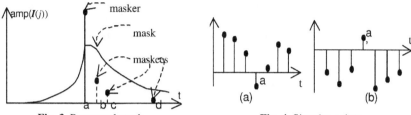

Fig. 3. Perceptual mask   **Fig. 4.** Singular points

In the decoding process, the authenticity of an input audio I'' is first checked with key $\mathcal{K}^I$. If I'' is verified to be authentic, the active agent data stream aw" can further be extracted (notice here there may be multiple keys involved). At last, an EC pass kicks in and generates $aw^1 = \tau_{ec}(aw'')$. Agent data stream $aw^1 = aw^0$ can then be invoked.

The hidden data imperceptibility is ensured with proper usage of perceptual model. It takes advantage of human auditory system's inability to distinguish noise under conditions of auditory masking. Our empirical study also shows that human ear can not distinguish the differences when a minor change is made on a singular point or maskee point (under the condition it is still a maskee point before and after the modification). In the base domain, the masking ability of a given sample depends on its loudness; while in the spectrum domain, it depends on the frequency position and loudness. Empirical results also show that the noise masking threshold at any given time is solely dependent on the signal energy within a limited temporal neighborhood. Since we are focusing on total fragile system here, we shall introduce base domain embedding only. Compare to the spectrum domain embedding, one advantage of it lies in the decoding performance in terms of speed. The disadvantage, however, is its low survivability over compression. Thus, it is not suitable for robust data hiding. The definition of singular point, masker point, and maskee point are given below.

A masker point $I(i)$ is defined as a point with a intensity value larger than a threshold δ, i.e., $amp(I(i)) \geq \delta$, whereas a maskee point $I(i^k)$ is defined as a point that is under the mask of a masker point $I(i)$, i.e., $amp(I(i^k)) \leq mask(amp(I(i)))$ (see Figure 3 where sample a is a masker point and sample b, c, & d are maskee points).

Define $I(i)$ to be a singular point iff $sign(I(i)) = - sign(I(i-1))$ & $sign(I(i)) = - sign(I(i+1))$. Figure 4 illustrates two singular points a in (a) and a' in (b).

Jointly using the singular and maskee embedding, the DHC requirement $R_A(I) \geq r_{mw}(I)$ can be reached in our fragile ADH system. For instance, the demo system presented in the Section 3.1 can embed an agent of 5KB into an 85s long, 2 channels, 44.1kbps music. Together with the bits required for authentication and EC, it has an $r_{mw}(I) \approx 238.4$bps. Whereas the system has a $R_A(I) = 151274$bits$/170s = 889.8$bps $\gg 238.4$bps$ = r_{mw}(I)$ in our test.

Several methods can be used to embed bits into the singular and maskee feature points. Interested reader can reference our paper on ADH[4].

Error correction. An EC layer shall require additional DHC. Therefore, the smaller the EC sequence is, the more desirable it is. One simple way is to use 2D or multi-D checksum EC. The book by Pless[7] gives many EC codes that can be used here.

Authentication. We can simply place the authentication value into the least significant bit of each sample as suggested in [4] Alternatively, the authentication value can be embedded into the same feature together with the rest embedded bits. In our system one way hash algorithm MD5 is used for authentication. The details of our authentication algorithms can be found in [4].

2.7 Robust ADH

We define a robust ADH system as following.

An ADH scheme **v** is said to be robust with reference to transformation **τ** if

$$aw^1 = aw^0 \text{ when } I' = T(I) =^P I | V \text{ for } \forall \tau_n \in T_v = \{ \tau_n, n \in [1,N], N > \beta \text{ (a}$$

predefined threshold)}.An ADH system that supports robust ADH is called robust ADH system.

A scheme **v** that is robust with reference to **τ** implies the feature extracted for data hiding is invariant under **τ**. We are interested in having the hidden data robust, i.e., the feature invariant, to common signal processing transformations. Denote our targeted transformation set as $T_{v=CSP}$, then $T_{v=CSP} = \{\tau \mid \tau \text{ IJ CSP set} = \{ \tau_c, \tau_f, \tau_e, \tau_t,$ $\tau_j, \dots \dots\}$. We propose parametric representation for robust audio ADH system that is robust to synchronization structure retainable processes T_{u1}, such as MP3 compression τ_c, low pass filtering τ_f, and echo τ_e, as well as synchronization structure alterable processes T_{u2}, which include time scaling τ_t, jittering τ_j, and pitch shifting τ_p. Here, $T_{u1} = \{\tau_c, \tau_f, \tau_e, \dots \} \subset T_u$ and $T_{u2} = \{\tau_t, \tau_j, \tau_p, \dots \dots\} \subset T_u$. In specific, cepstrum representation coupled with statistical mean manipulation data embedded strategy is used in our robust audio ADH system.

Denote the Fourier transform of $f(x)$ to be

$$F(f(x)) = F(u) = \int_{\infty} f(x)e^{-j2\pi ux}dx \qquad (2.7.1)$$

and the inverse Fourier transform of $F(u)$ to be

$$F^{-1}(F(u)) = f(x) = \int_{\infty} F(u)e^{j2\pi ux}du \qquad (2.7.2)$$

Then the cepstrum is defined as the inverse Fourier transform of the log-magnitude Fourier spectrum.

$$Cept(f(x)) = F^{-1}(log|F(f(x))|) \qquad (2.7.3)$$

That is $T(I) = F^{-1}(log|F(I)|)$.

The embedding procedure is as following. The host data stream is first cut into segments $I_1, I_2, \ldots I_j$, .For each segment I_j, a cepstrum transformation is performed on it and a single bit is embedded in it using statistical mean manipulation with the strength of each embedded bit controlled by the perceptual model. Suppose the feature for data embedding is $C[i]$. $C_j[i]$ is the ith feature point and $\overline{C_j}$ is the statistical mean of segment j. We use the following to embed a 1 bit.

Let $C'_j[h] = C_j[h] + \alpha_j[h]$, if $C_j[h] < 0$, if $\overline{C_j} \leq 0$, for g=1 till $\overline{C_j} > 0$, generate random number h[g] with seed SD.

To embed a 0 bit, $C'_j[h] = C_j[h] - \alpha_j[h]$, if $\overline{C_j} > 0$, generate random number h[g] for g=1 till $\overline{C_j} = 0$, with seed SD.

We assume the noise $\{w^0\}$ introduced by embedding the active data stream w^0 observes guassian distribution with zero mean, variance s^2, and therefore probability of error Pe(|B1|/2s). To ensure imperceptibility, the perceptual model used in MP3 compression is inherited with some modification suitable for data hiding. a is therefore controlled by this perceptual model.

Robustness. Cepstrum transformation provides a more canonical representation of an audio. This form of power spectrum on log scale has the property of having the shape of the log power spectrum preserved when the gain applied to a signal varies. The statistical distributions of the log power spectra have properties convenient for statistical analysis that are not shared by linear power spectra. In log-power domain, the excitation and vocal tract are often easier to be separated. That is, cepstral analysis can clearly separate out the vocal tract information from the excitation information and frequency components containing physical spectral characteristics of sound. Therefore, it can provide higher level of robustness against a wide range of signal processing including most challenging ones like jittering, time-scaling, pitch-shifting and sampling-rate changes. Our test result shows a good survivability over $\tau_c \in T_{u1}$ as well as $\tau_c \in T_{u2}$. On T_{u2}, our test gives a 100% survivability of $\leq$10% jittering τ_j or a time scaling τ_t of $\geq$0.8 factor, as oppose to the traditional base or frequency domain embedding which can only survive $\tau_n \in T_{u1}$[3].

3   Demo Smart Media System

As we addressed in Section 1, when two way control is necessary, smart media can be put to use. Here we present our demo system for smart media with access controllability in the next subsection.

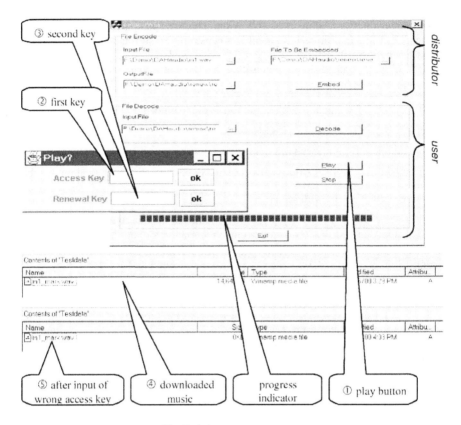

Fig. 5. A demo system at `PINTL`

3.1 Application in Secure Electronic Media Distribution

The idea of smart media with access controllability is to help prevent illegitimate use of media by bringing interactability and controllability into the media.

Generally speaking, there are two kinds of hidden data, private and public. A private hidden data is one that has to be extracted with the knowledge of the original host data stream. On the contrary, public hidden data is embedded in such a way that it can be extracted without the knowledge of the original host data stream. Considering our application in this study, for electronic media distribution application, where the original host media is not accessible at the receiver end when data extraction is conducted, a public hidden data has to be adopted. Our introduced schemes in Section 2 satisfy this criterion. Figure 5 shows the interfaces of one of our smart media demo systems. It uses two access keys. When a first time user downloaded the music from the Internet, the smart media player invokes the media agent embedded in the music during the first operation requested by user (① in Figure 5). The user would be asked for proper key, key 1, also called access key. When the user fails to provide the medium with a valid key in three tries, the agent simply deletes the music from the user storage (④➔⑤). Otherwise, the smart medium gives a preview play to the user. When the user successfully submits both keys (②&③) to the smart medium, it grants her the right to listen to it infinity number of times. Notice here the rules and responses are made depending on the smart media's preference. In this particular case, it often depends on the content distributor's preference and access rules.

3.2 Other Sample Applications

The initial interest of our study in smart media is to have the media immune to user mishandling and to provide also renewability so that different medium at different place or different time frame may have different access controllability, which is also upgradable, based on its own interest. However, the application domain is not limited to content protection. Other applications, such as to provide easier access, to support intelligent media authoring tools, and uses in virtual reality may also apply.

From the communication point of view, the application scenarios described in the last section belong to the media-to-user communication problem space. Media-to-media communication is another application domain to deploy. This may be put to use in TV-centric applications as well as in networked electronic multimedia applications. Media-to-network communication is another possible application. For example, in active network, smart media may route itself to the target.

4   Summary

Despite the fact that multimedia plays one of the most important roles in the new information era, a medium can only passively perform various tasks. In another word, media have a beautiful face but not personality. We proposed smart media with ADH in this paper in introducing added capability of 'thinking' and 'taking actions' to media. The technical challenge of ADH along with our proposed solutions for smart media applications is presented. We used audio as an example in Section 2.6, 2.7, and 3.1. However, the basic technique is also applicable to video and other forms of media, including multimedia (more than one form of media are presented simultaneously.) Currently, we are deploying applications in the media-to-media communication domain. We are also investigating real time smart media interaction in video. The study of smart media application in virtual reality is just started.

References

1.   C. Podilchuk, W. Zeng, Image-adaptive watermarking using visual models, IEEE Journal on Selected Areas in Comm., 16(4):525-539, 1998
2.   M. Wu, H. Yu, Refined human visual model for data hiding, US patent pending
3.   X. Li, H. Yu, Transparent and robust audio data hiding, in Proc. IEEE ICME'00, 2000
4.   H. Yu, A. Gelman, R. Fish, Active data hiding for secure electronic media distribution, ACM Multimedia'99 security workshop.
5.   H. Yu, M. Wu, A. Gelman, X. Li, Multi-layer data hiding, US patent pending
6.   M. Wu, H. Yu, Multi-level data hiding for video, in Proc. IEEE ICME'00, 2000
7.   V. Pless, Introduction to the Therory of Error-Correcting Codes, John,Wiley&Sons, 1998

Appendix: Multi-layer Data Structure for Data Hiding

Host data is defined as the original data stream.
Embedded data designates a modified version of the host data stream that has secondary meaningful data embedded into it.
Primary hidden data refers to the hidden data for user use. For instance, an embedded active agent data stream.
Secondary hidden data refers to the hidden data for control use. For instance, EC bits. This kind of data can be used to govern or control the use of the *primary hidden data*. Hence, are also called *governing data*.

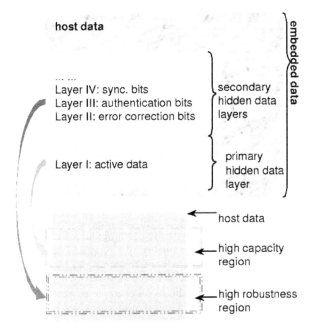

Fig. A. Multi-layer data structure

Congestion Prospect of Network Traffics by Fluctuation of Internet Transmission Time

Hiroto Takahashi and Yasuo Yonezawa*

Complex adaptive system Laboratory, System Engineering Division,
Graduate school of Science and Engineering, Ibaraki University,
4-12-1, Nakanarusawa, Hitachi, 316-8511, Japan
hiroto@life03.dse.ibaraki.ac.jp
yonezawa@life01.dse.ibaraki.ac.jp*

Abstract. In this research, we proposed a new prospect technique for a congestion problem has cased deterioration in response at the practical computer network. Since aim at effectively using the network resources, this new technique prevent the congestion problem not by improvement of processing capability but to accept new intelligent prospect methods for the congestion. In this research, we suppose network state of just before the occurrence of the congestion is state of maximum throughput. And we investigate, at the practical computer network, a relationship between the traffic and fluctuation analysis (DFT results) of the Internet transmission times. examine a possibility of a congestion prospect to prevent the congestion problem.

1 Background

At recently, the Internet system has grown greatly at worldwide with Self-reproduction by flexible connectability based on TCP/IP protocol as shown at developments of World Wide Web (WWW). With growth of the Internet, the network congestion problem has arisen as deterioration in response of the network and wasting the network resources. So it is satisfactory to consider as prevent technique of the network congestion problem have been essentially needed.

The major techniques of prevent the network congestion are to improve processing capability and some network protocols. But the improvement technique is not effective permanent, since the network traffic must over capability of processing quickly, for also users job must increase with improvement, and developing the improvement technique and hardware take costs. Some network protocols are effective and take low costs comparatively, but there is no more effective and useful protocols than the techniques to improve processing capability. It is effective to control the network traffic before the occurrence of the heavy congestion, because the congestion is apt to spread among neighboring nodes. But

---

* To whom correspondence should be addressed. Yasuo Yonezawa (FAX: +81-294-38-5208)

J. Liu et al. (Eds.): AMT 2001, LNCS 2252, pp. 17–23, 2001.

the current major hardware and protocols dose not executes. So it is satisfactory to consider as control new methods of the network traffic more effective by congestion prospect must be needed.

To prospect for the occurrence of congestion, this research accept characterization as criticality property $1/f$ fluctuation of the Internet [1]. The considerable number of works have been made on the computer network congestion by $1/f$ fluctuation as shown at the observing $1/f$ fluctuation at the congestion network [2], and theoretical works on the simulation model of the structure of the network [3]. Furthermore, Takayasu ed al reported [4] [5] [6] [7] the observation of $1/f$ fluctuation at congested network by ping packet under the Internet. These works have made Fourier transform on time series of the network transmission time to observe the state of the congestion qualitatively, and evidence a power spectrum inclination angle of time series of network transmission times is $1/f$ at the critical region of capability of the network. But yet not only few attempts have been made on the practical technique as the congestion prospect of the computer network based on the practical observation of the network traffic adopt the criticality property $1/f$ fluctuation of the Internet.

In this research, we suppose network state of just before the occurrence of the congestion is state of maximum throughput. And this research investigates by experiments, at the practical computer network, a relationship between the traffic and the power spectrum inclination angle of time series of Internet transmission times by DFT (Discrete Fourier Transform) analysis to examine a possibility of a congestion prospect to control the congestion has cased deterioration in response. Furthermore based on the experiments, we discuss congestion prospect methods at the practical network traffic, that adopt the criticality property $1/f$ fluctuation of the Internet and useful in real time.

2   Network Experiment

In this experiment, we measured the practical network traffic to investigate a relationship between the traffic and the power spectrum inclination angle at time series of Internet transmission times. Typically, there is two methods to observe the practical network traffic as described following.

1. Observation directly of the network traffic on routers and circuit of the network; this method can observe the accurate network traffic through the network hardware, but this method is difficult to spread the observation point, since must need agreement with each administrator of network machines.
2. Observation of the round trip time with *ping-command* at UNIX; This method cycle observe the round trip time of the ICMP echo packets to any hosts. It is satisfactory to regard the round trip time as the amount of the traffic, since the round trip time is considered to be effected by the network congestion. This method observes the network traffic indirectly, but this method is very simple to spread the observation point.

In this experiment, by *ping − command*, we measured the network traffic. Because necessity of agreement with each administrator must prevent adaptable of the propose congestion prospect technique to the current system at the practical network. But this method has a problem that the packet not always through the same route. Therefore, by the *traceroute-command* of UNIX that can examine routers through packets, we identify the packet through same route in round trip and select a fixed route in this experiment. It follows from what has been said that this experiment is measurement upon practical condition of the network system.

In this experiment, an observation route is Local Area Network (LAN) with constituted TCP/IP in a Hitachi campus of Ibaraki University as the practical network (Fig. 1). There is 3 routers between a terminal that is UNIX machine ($S-7/400Ui$ model $270D$, 270MHz $UltraSPARC-IIi$) send ICMP echo packets and running program and a target router connected to Wide Area Network (WAN). A cycle of sending ICMP echo packets is 1 second to not make the network congestion by itself and to improve the accuracy of the observation of the network traffic. The observation is continued for 24 hours during 7:00 a.m. to next 7:00 a.m (86,400 steps).

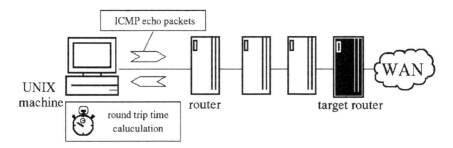

Fig. 1. Network architecture of network communication experiment; in the Hitachi campus of Ibaraki University. The target router is connected to WAN

3   Result of Experiment

The time series of the network transmission time is depicted in Fig. 2 of the network experiment. There is marked high and low region of the transmission time as shown by region I and II, that is the network traffic. The enlargement on region I and II are displayed in Fig. 3A and Fig. 3C (both 9,000 time steps).

We DFT transform on time series of Fig. 3A and Fig. 3C to analyse qualitatively. The power spectrum $P(f)$ of DFT analysis are depicted in Fig. 3B and Fig. 3D. The $P(f)$ is calculated with C program compiled by GNU C compiler (version 2.8.1) as the following equation;

$$P(f_n) = \sum_{k=0}^{N-1} h_k e^{-j2\pi kn/N}. \tag{1}$$

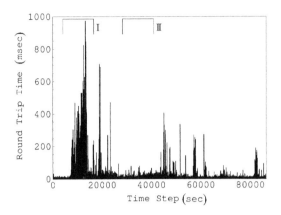

Fig. 2. Time series of the network transmission time of experiment

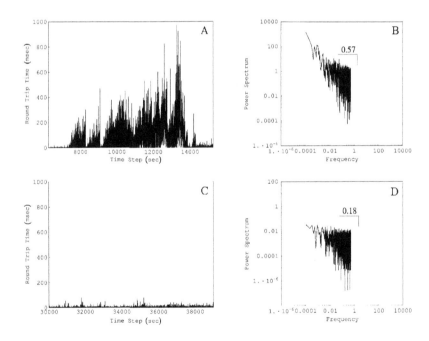

Fig. 3. Time series of the network transmission time and the power spectrum; at the *I* and *II* region of Fig. 2

where,

$$f_n = \frac{n}{N\Delta}, \quad n = -\frac{N}{2}, \cdots, \frac{N}{2}, \quad h_k = h(k\Delta),$$

N is the number of sampling data, Δ is the sampling time, and h_k is the sampling data.

At the high network traffic region, scales as $P(f)\approx f^{-k}$ with k=0.57 (Fig. 3B). At the low region, k=0.18 (Fig. 3D). The k of the power spectrum inclination is calculated by least-squares method built into $MATHEMATICA$. The some relation between the traffic and k of the power spectrum inclination angle is anticipated from Fig. 3B and Fig. 3D. This anticipation is confirmed by Fig. 4 that depict time series of k that calculated with Fig. 3A at 100 time steps sampling data shifting 10 time steps. It can be seen from Fig. 4 that k approach -1 as increase of the network traffic, and at the highest point of the network traffic, k over -1.

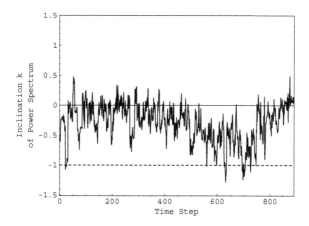

Fig. 4. Time series of k of the power spectrum inclination angle of the traffic of Fig. 2A

4   Discussion

In the recent works of $1/f$ fluctuation at DFT analysis of the Internet and simulation of the theoretical network, that is the point of k=-1 in this research, $1/f$ fluctuation of the power spectrum of the network traffic appear at critical region of capability of the network. From result of the experiment and recent works, the relation between the working state of the network and k of the power spectrum inclination angle is displayed in Table 1.

In $k > -1$ case, the working state of the network is low. In $k \approx -1$ that is $1/f$ fluctuation case, the working state is maximum throughput of network capability. In $k < -1$ case, the working state is hard congestion as over capability.

From these result, it is satisfactory to consider k is representation of working state of the network, and we obtain working state pattern to occurrence of con-

Table 1. Relation between working state of the network and k

k	working state
$k > -1$	inner capacity
$k \approx -1$	critical region of traffic
$k < -1$	outer capacity

gestion. Using working state pattern as indication of congestion, it is possibility of congestion prospect technique as effectively using.

We propose the outline of intelligent control system for the network traffic as Fig. 5.

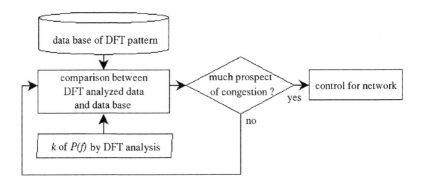

Fig. 5. Outline of future plane system

In this system, k of the power spectrum inclination angle is use as indication of congestion to effectively control the network traffic. The database is made by sampling working state pattern through occurrence of congestion at many type structural networks. In real use, this system prospect the congestion by compare the database to the k calculated from the observed actual network traffic. This system use comparison with pattern matching to control the traffic without large delay at actual computer network. In much prospect of occurrence of congestion case, the system controls the traffic by some method.

This research investigates by experiments, at the practical computer network, the relation between the traffic and the power spectrum inclination angle k of network traffic by DFT analysis. These experiments confirmed characterization of actual network traffic is indicated on network working state. The result revealed the value of using k as indication of congestion to effectively. And we proposed the outline of the network traffic control system based congestion prospect without delay.

This characterized property is able to recode at very simple as the power spectrum inclination angles [8]. And so on, estimation of the network working state is carried out by compare with the power spectrum inclinations angles in database. Namely, our new methods are used the power spectrum inclinations angles as indication of traffic control. Already, we confirmed that we carried out the control for neural networks of optimization by used $1/f$ noise effects at previous research [9] organization from by cell proliferation simulation in biological system [10] [11]. At present time, we are going to investigation for the elucidate of more detail characterization of transmission delay by the power spectrum under various network environments. Furthermore, we are in progress the construction for intelligent control system used on the traffic estimation for the Internet traffic delay in according to these research results.

Acknowledgements. The authors would like to thanks Dr. Takayasu for helpful knowledgements. And we thank to Prof. Tsutsumi and Prof. Agu at Ibaraki University for the support of research environments. Also, Y. Yonezawa thanks the member of our Complex Adaptive Systems Laboratory at Ibaraki University for helpful and collaboration, Mr. Nagano, Mr. Nishinomiya and Mr. Onodera. This work has been partially supported by a grant of SVBL (Satellite Venture Business Laboratories) in our university.

References

1. Tretyakov, Yu., Takayasu, H., Takayasu, M.: Phase transition in a computer network model. Phisica **A 253**, (1998) 315-322
2. Takayasu, M., Takayasu, H.: $1/f$ noise in traffics model. Fractals **1**, (1993) 860-866
3. Takayasu, M., Takayasu, H., Sato, T.: Critical behavior and $1/f$ noise in Information traffics. Phisica **A 233**, (1996) 824-834
4. Fukuda, K., Takayasu, H., Takayasu, M.: Spatial and temporal behavior of congestion in Internet traffic. Fractals **7**, (1999) 23-31
5. Fukuda, K., Takayasu, H., Takayasu, M.: Observation of Phase Transition behavior in Internet traffics. Advances in performance **2**, (1999) 45-66
6. Takayasu, M., Fukuda, K., Takayasu, H.: Statistical physics to the Internet traffics. Phisica **A 274**, (1999) 30-49
7. Takayasu, M., Fukuda, K., Takayasu, H.: Dynamic phase transition observed in the Internet traffics flow. Phisica **A 277** (2000) 248-255
8. Haken, H: Information and Self-Organization. Springer, Berlin (1988)
9. Saito, T., Yonezawa, Y., Agu, M.: Influence of the Complexity of Configuration of the Performance of a stochastic analog Neural Network for the Travel Salesman problems. Neural Networks, (to be submitted)
10. Yonezawa, Y., Ohtomo, K.: Structural Properties of Generative form by Hormonal Proliferation Algorithm. Forma **15**, (2000) 103-107
11. Monma, M., Yonezawa, Y., Igarashi, T.: Circulated Transport Phenomena Involving the Interaction between Arterial and Venous Vessel Systems Based on a Simulation Using Fractal Properties. Complex Systems, **12**, (2000) 457-464

Naturalistic Human–Robot Collaboration Mediated by Shared Communicational Modality in Teleoperation System

Yukio Horiguchi and Tetsuo Sawaragi

Graduate School of Engineering, Kyoto University,
Yoshida Honmachi, Sakyo-ku, Kyoto, Japan 606-8501
t60x0141@ip.media.kyoto-u.ac.jp, sawaragi@prec.kyoto-u.ac.jp
http://www.prec.kyoto-u.ac.jp/sawaragilab/

Abstract. This paper presents a new style of human–robot collaboration in a teleoperation system where the robot has the autonomy to control its behavior. Our model provides the "shared communicational modality" between the human operator and the robot autonomy to promote their mixed-initiative interactions. This paper describes the results of experiments using our developing system to evaluate our model, and discusses the interactions between the two autonomies based upon the Lens model framework known as a judgment analysis method.

1 Introduction

There proposed an idea of "shared autonomy" as a new concept of human–machine collaboration, which stresses that a human- and a machine-autonomy should collaborate with each other as *equivalent* partners [1]. And this idea mainly focuses into the aspects of the flexible role-allocation among them. This point of view is very important to couple a human user and a machine with highly advanced automation facilities, and to establish their good relationships. However, this idea still remains at the conceptual. In order to provide their naturalistic collaboration in such a human–machine system, we have to consider how to share recognition of situations among them. Especially it is significant how to let the human operator recognize the intervention of the machine-autonomy into his/her manipulations. This is a problem on the interface design.

As a design principle of human-friendly interface, K. Vicente et al. have proposed an idea of an "ecological interface design" (EID) [2]. Wherein the key issues of the interface design must be coherent with the ways of human thinking and/or perception performed under their bounded cognitive resources. Concerning with this idea, there is an important fact that action plays not only a *performatory* role but also an *exploratory*, or knowledge-granting one. The latter aspect of action is called "epistemic action." It is necessary to the flexible and skillful performance of a human in the complex world because it is an efficient strategy to reduce his/her cognitive burden such as inference and reasoning [5]. But in conventional designs of human–machine systems, actions of the operator

J. Liu et al. (Eds.): AMT 2001, LNCS 2252, pp. 24–35, 2001.

are extremely restricted in the control loop of the highly automated system because of its stability, reliance, security, and so on. In order to provide their naturalistic and intuitive relationships, such systems should allow the operator's variable actions including his/her epistemic actions.

In regard to this, "mixed-initiative interaction" is an interesting idea. It represents the style of interaction between the subjects collaborating with each other, where their roles and initiatives not fixed in advance are appropriately assigned depending on the situation they are facing. We consider that this redundant role-allocation allows the operator's epistemic actions to recognize his/her partner and the whole system. Based on this ideas, we've proposed a new style of human–machine collaboration in a teleoperation system[7]. The essence of our proposition is to provide the "shared communicational modality" between the operator and the machine autonomy to promote their mixed-initiative interactions. We have developed a mobile robot teleoperation system embodying our proposing model. This paper describes the results of experiments to evaluate our system and discuss the interactions between a operator and a robot autonomy in it based upon the Brunswik's Lens model framework [3,4] known as a method for judgment analysis.

Hereafter, we introduce our proposing model of human–robot collaboration in section 2. Then the results of experiments held to evaluate the model are referred after the development of the robot teleoperation system embodying our model in section 3. In section 4, the results of experiments are analyzed based upon Brunswik's Lens model framework, and we discuss the utility of our proposing model. And finally we conclude this paper in section 5.

2   Our Proposing Model of Human–Robot Collaboration

This section describes our proposing model on a human–robot collaboration style in a teleoperation system. We first mention about the Lens model [3,4,5] before introducing our model since it is based on the analysis using the Lens model framework.

2.1   The Lens Model as Analysis Method

Brunswik's Lens model is a functional representation of human perception and judgment [3,4] that can describe their causal relationships without separating his/her internal and external state. As shown in Figure 1, this model provides dual symmetric models of the human judge (*subject*) and the environment (*ecology*). The *judgments* and the environmental *criterion* to be judged are described as combinations of *cues*, or available information in the environment. In this way, both the judgment policy and the environmental structure in terms of the cue–criterion relationships, are captured as the *cue utilization validity* and the *ecological validity*, respectively.

This model makes the *proximal versus distal* distinction in human perception. The "proximal" refers the direct accessibility by the judge, while the "distal"

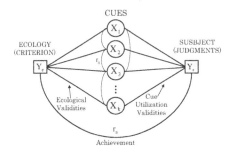

Fig. 1. Brunswik's Lens models

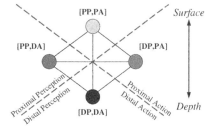

Fig. 2. The generalization of the Lens model by Kirlik

Table 1. The four different types of variables in the generalized Lens model

Variable type	Definition
[PP,PA]	a variable that is proximal for both perception and action.
[PP,DA]	a variable that is proximal for perception but distal for action.
[DP,PA]	a variable that is distal for perception yet proximal for action.
[DP,DA]	a variable that is distal for both perception and action.

represents the indirectness and is accessed through the proximal information. Hence the criterion is distal because the judge cannot directly perceive it and has to infer it from the proximal cues directly measured. As this distinction is only about perception (i.e., the proximal/distal structure of perception) but about action, the model describes the view of the subject without any control over the environmental structure. It is insufficient to deal with the proactive human–machine interactions including epistemic actions.

Therefore, A. Kirlik has proposed to add the proximal/distal structure of action into the Lens model as his *generalized Lens model* in [5]. Figure 2 illustrates this model. With this extension, variables in the environment are classified into the four different types as shown in Table 1. In addition, there is a potential of constraint relationships among these classes of variables, as indicated the six lines connecting the four variable types in the figure.

2.2 Mixed-Initiative Interactions Mediated by Shared Communicational Modality

After the generalized Lens model framework, we classified variables in a teleoperation system which have two autonomies of a human operator and a robot autonomy, and described their relations as shown in Figure 3. In this case, the large interaction loop in the figure is used for the operator to make sure of the partner's intent, or judgment policy. The collaboration by the two independent autonomies needs some shared information to establish coherent and consistent

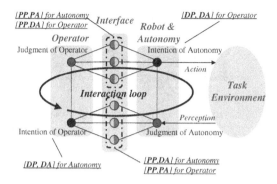

Fig. 3. The analysis of a teleoperation system

judgments among them. This style of interaction, however, has no such information, and a success of their collaboration depends on the individual interpretations about the other's judgment policy. In addition, the large time-lag involved until getting some responses to certain operations can make it more difficult to take epistemic actions ensuring those interpretations, because the operator has to associate actions with the asynchronous changes of perceptions. Hence, it is necessary to design a kind of shared information with smaller and more frequent interaction loops for their naturalistic and intuitive collaboration.

For the reason mentioned above, we have proposed a new model of human–machine interaction style by adding some constraints of their actions depending on the other's conditions. As shown in Figure 4, our model has mutual constraints between [PP,PA] variables for the operator and those for the robot autonomy, which are enclosed by a broken line in the center of the figure. The operator's action is restricted by the autonomy's intention as well as the autonomy's action is done by the operator's intention. These constraints make their interaction loops more compact, and both the operator and the autonomy become to share their respective [PP,PA] variables *virtually*. In addition, we also make the robot's behavior only reflect the interactions on those constraints between the two, in order to allow and promote their mixed-initiative interactions. Wherein, the initiative to control the robot is dynamically changing through their actions onto the constraints, with which their relationships are probed. Therefore, these constraints can be regarded as the "shared communicational modalities" for their collaboration.

3 Development and Experiments of Our Teleoperation System

We have developed a mobile robot teleoperation system embodying our proposing model. This section introduces that system and mentions about experiments we had for evaluation of our model.

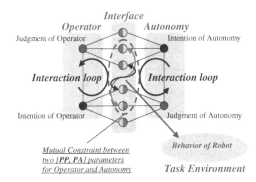

Fig. 4. The collaboration style in our model

3.1 Experimental Settings and System Configurations

The operator navigates the robot in corridor environments by a joystick whose forward-backward and right-left inputs are translated to the robot's behaviors of translational and rotational velocities, respectively. The robot has a CCD camera capable of panning, tilting and zooming (i.e., a PTZ camera) on the front, and seven super sonic range sensors to measure distances from obstacles. Basically, the operator comprehends the surroundings of the remote robot using the real image from the camera in the display information of Figure 5. It is, however, difficult for him/her to understand the environmental state around the robot completely because of a large blind spot the camera has. From this point of view, we have equipped the robot with a *obstacle-avoidance* mechanism as its autonomy.

Robot Autonomy with Obstacle-Avoidance Behavior. The autonomy's obstacle-avoidance behavior is realized after a potential field method composed of repulsive forces from obstacles that are caught by the range sensors as illustrated in Figure 6. The robot's *velocity* and *steering* commands are computed as below:

$$F_{R_i} = e^{-C_i \times d_i} \qquad (1)$$

$$velocity_{AT} = V_{max} \times \sum_{i}^{7} F_{R_i} \cos \theta_i \qquad (2)$$

$$steering_{AT} = S_{max} \times \sum_{i}^{7} F_{R_i} \sin \theta_i \qquad (3)$$

where

i : an obstacle caught by a range sensor,
F_{R_i} : magnitude of a repulsive force from the obstacle i,
C_i : a variable that defines the gradient of the field by the obstacle i,
d_i : a distance to the obstacle i, and
θ_i : a relative angle from the robot's current heading to the obstacle i.

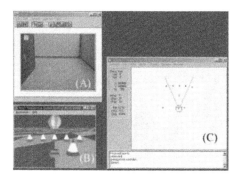

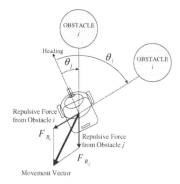

Fig. 5. A screen shot of the display information

Fig. 6. The way to calculate the potential field for generating the robot's movement commands

Wherein, V_{max} and S_{max} are constants to translate the virtual forces into the actual commands, defined as $V_{max} = 300$ mm/sec and $S_{max} = 20$ deg/sec, respectively.

As this potential field has parameters each of which determines the incline of the cone representing the effect of a particular obstacle (i.e., C_i), the autonomy can learn and change its behavior by adjusting these parameters based on the robot's behavior. That is, if $\mathbf{F_{R_i}}$ gives a good effect upon the robot's behavior, corresponding C_i will be increased, but it will be decreased otherwise.

Implementation of Shared Communicational Modality. The joystick we adopt has a mechanism to generate the force-feedback effect, which is used to "embody" our model of the shared communicational modality. By letting the intentions of the robot autonomy transfer onto the joystick using the feedback force, the autonomy can also manipulate the joystick as well as the operator. Therefore, the operator's and the autonomy's input actions are mutually restricted through the joystick, since both of them can manipulate it and effect the other's judgment policies. And the initiative to control the robot can dynamically change according to the strength of their inputs to the joystick.

3.2 Experiments

Figure 7 summarizes an overview of our developing teleoperation system including the components mentioned above. Using this system, we made some experiments to evaluate and consider our proposing model of the shared communicational modality. In addition, we also prepared an another experimental setting without the force-feedback effect of the joystick for comparison purposes. This system display the autonomy's judgment (i.e., the velocity and steering outputs of the potential field) on the monitor the operator cannot manipulate its status directly. This is denoted as No-MII style while the implementation of our

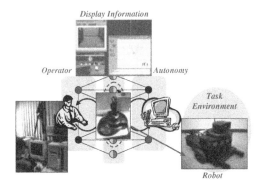

Fig. 7. An overview of our teleoperation system

Table 2. Comparisons of average execution time in the *zigzag* corridor environment

	MAN	No-MII	MII
exec time [sec]	70.95	75.49	56.35

proposing model as MII (Mixed-Initiative Interactions). In both cases, operators are informed of the autonomy's behaviors before their experiments start.
And MAN is an abbreviation for the complete manual operation without the
autonomy's intervention.

The first experiment used the "zigzag" corridor shown in Figure 8(a), and
we had three different operators as our subjects. Each of them performed trials
of MAN, No-MII, and MII styles in turn, and repeated this set of experimental
trials five times. As the result of this experiment, Table 2 lists the average values
of execution time for the three different experimental settings, and we've gotten
the better performance of MII style than the others. In order to consider the
cause of this result, we made another experiment using the "L-formed" corridor
environment of Figure 8(b), which has narrower width to detect a small mistake
of handling as a robot's collision with a wall. And its simple form is easy of
capturing the operator's and the autonomy's judgment policies to control the
robot.

Figure 9 shows profiles of execution time we got from one subject's operations
in both experiments of No-MII and MII styles. In this graph, the two-dimensional
approximate curves for each are superimposed on the plots to roughly capture
the tendencies of these profiles. There observed improvements of performance in
both of the two profiles along accumulation of trials, but those improvements are
different in their processes between No-MII and MII, especially in the beginning
of experiments. Concerning with this, some statistics are computed from the data
in the first half of trials, which are given in Table 3. From comparisons of these
values, $\bar{T}_F$ and $\bar{N}_{cw}$ are the apparent indexes to distinguish the performance

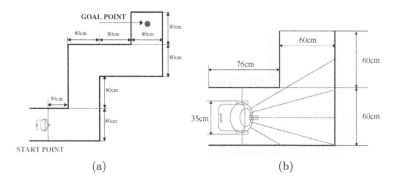

Fig. 8. The corridor environments for experiments: (a) the *zigzag* type and (b) the *L-formed* type

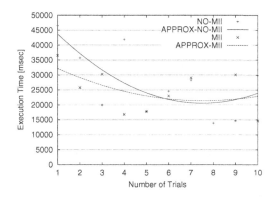

Fig. 9. Profiles of execution time in the *L-formed* corridor environment

of No-MII and MII, referred to average execution time and average number of "cut-the-wheel" operations in the *unsuccessful* trials where some collisions are made, respectively. Both of the two statistics represent the worse performance of No-MII style in the recovery operations after the robot collides with a wall for some mistakes. We consider the above result as following: the autonomy's *indirect* intervention into the operator's judgment can work well when their task execution is progressing smoothly, but otherwise it may affect and confuse his/her judgment due to the larger separation of the robot's actual behavior and the his/her estimate of it. That is, it is necessary to *directly* inform the operator of the autonomy's intervention in order to share their intentions enough in an unsuccessful state.

Table 3. Comparisons of statistics between the two different experimental settings of No-MII and MII

	P_{suc}	$\bar{T}$	$\bar{T}_S$	$\bar{T}_F$	$\bar{N}_{cw}$
No-MII	0.4	32.26	18.88	41.35	3
MII	0.4	25.41	17.25	30.85	1.33

where

P_{suc} : a rate of successful (i.e., no-collision) trials in the whole,
$\bar{T}$: average execution time in the whole trials [sec],
$\bar{T}_S$: average execution time in the *successful* trials [sec],
$\bar{T}_F$: average execution time in the *unsuccessful* trials [sec], and
$\bar{N}_{cw}$: average number of *cut-the-wheel* operations in the *unsuccessful* trials.

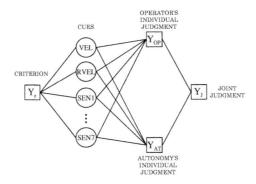

Fig. 10. Description of the operator–autonomy cooperative task using the Lens model

4   Analyses and Discussions

Irrespective of their interaction styles, the collaboration performances by the operator and the autonomy were gradually improved along with the experimental trials. There was, however, a difference in their processes of improvements between No-MII and MII in the beginning of experiments. This difference can be regarded as the result of changes in relationships between the operator's and the autonomy's judgment policies, because, in order to achieve the better performances, it is necessary to develop the adequate role-assignment between the two after enough understanding of the partner's policy. This is due to their redundant sharing of the part to control the robot in the system's default settings. Concerning with this, we analyze the correlations between the operator's and the autonomy's judgment policies to consider their relationships.

4.1   Description of Judgment Policies Based upon the Lens Model

For our analyses, a description of the operator–autonomy cooperative teleoperation task is done using the Lens model expression, which is illustrated in

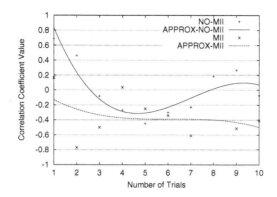

Fig. 11. Correlations between the two different judgment policies in the experiments of No-MII and MII

Figure 10. This model represents the relationships where the operator's and the autonomy's judgments on the robot control, denoted as Y_{OP} and Y_{AT} respectively, are made on the basis of available cues such as the robot's translational (VEL) and rotational (RVEL) velocities, and distances to walls measured by the range sensors (SEN1, SEN2, ..., SEN7). Their individual judgments of Y_{OP} and Y_{AT} are jointed into the judgment of Y_J that corresponds to the actual velocity and steering commands given to the robot. And Y_e means the criterion of operations.[1] The approximate models of those judgments are computed by multiple regression analysis (MRA) that is a popular method in the judgment analysis using the Lens model. Therefore, $\hat{Y}_{OP}$ and $\hat{Y}_{AT}$ usually have linear expressions of the sum of weighted cue variables.

4.2 Significant Property of Joint Judgment for Intent-Sharing

Figure 11 shows the profiles of correlation coefficients between $\hat{Y}_{OP}$ and $\hat{Y}_{AT}$ in both cases of No-MII and MII. A linearly regressed judgment model can be referred to the intuitive aspect of a judgment policy. Therefore, the correlation between those models' outputs deals with the similarity of judgments every moment. From these profiles, we can observe the changes of the correlation coefficient in the case of No-MII, that moves from the positive high value to the absolutely low value along the number of trials. The positive high value of the coefficient means that the two policies resemble with each other, and that their roles to control the robot overlap each other. Their good collaboration needs adequately revise their policies from those in isolation to differentiate their parts, because the integration of $\hat{Y}_{OP}$ and $\hat{Y}_{AT}$ with high correlations should generate too large amount of operations than the operator's estimates. Therefore, it

---

[1] In our teleoperation task, it is hard to define the criterion in the strict sense of the word. Therefore, we use the profile data of matured operators to extract a criterion model of $\hat{Y}_e$.

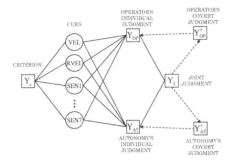
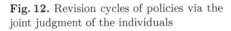

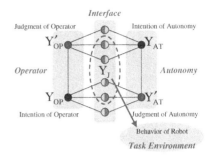

Fig. 12. Revision cycles of policies via the joint judgment of the individuals

Fig. 13. Relationships between the five different judgments superimposed on our model

can be said that the operator cannot understand and deal with the intervention of the autonomy. However, along the accumulation of experiences of collaboration, the operator became to understand the autonomy's behavior gradually, and their roles changed into the better assignments. In the case of MII with the shared communicational modality, the correlation between $\hat{Y}_{OP}$ and $\hat{Y}_{AT}$ is low in the whole trials, and there are some differences of the role to control the robot between them in the beginning, in contrast to No-MII.

We consider one of possible causes for the differences of their collaboration performance and their policy relations among the operator–autonomy interaction styles, as the accessibility to the joint judgment Y_J. Figure 12 illustrates the processes of revising judgment policies by expanding the Lens model expression in Figure 10. In this model, there are two *covert judgments* for the operator and the autonomy, referred to Y'_{OP} and Y'_{AT}, respectively. The operator revises and updates his/her judgment policy of Y_{OP} based upon understanding of the partner's policy (i.e., Y_{AT}). The covert judgment of Y'_{OP} is regarded as the *meta-level* cognition, which can infer the actual Y_{AT}'s state from their coupled behavior of Y_J corresponding to Y_{OP}, and can reorganize Y_{OP} on the basis of the Y_{OP}–Y_{AT} relationships recognized. And Y'_{AT} also plays the same role in the Y_{AT} updating as Y'_{OP}. Therefore, Y_J is significant for revisions of both of their policies. If this joint judgment isn't directly accessible, these revision cycles does not progress naturally because of uncertain recognition of the partner's judgments. In MII interaction style, the operator can directly acquire the key component of Y_J for their collaboration through the shared communicational modality as shown in Figure 13, while the interaction loop in Figure 3 is forced for that in No-MII style. But, the autonomy's behavior in our experimental settings is so simple that some amount of experiences of the task enables the operator to capture its judgment policy. This is why, we consider, differences of the operator–autonomy interaction styles produced the different collaboration performances in the beginning of experiments as shown in Figure 9.

Based upon the above discussions, we can regard the direct access to Y_J as promoting the operator's understanding of the autonomy's and/or the total system's behaviors, enabling the two to share the judgments of the robot control. Therefore, MII style of human–robot interaction could effect those operations in an unsuccessful state where their well intent-sharing is significant for a recovery. From this point of view, our approach with the shared communicational modality is useful.

5 Conclusions

This paper presents a new collaboration style for a human operator and an autonomous robot in a teleoperation system. Our proposing model of human–robot interactions provides the *shared communicational modality* between the operator and the robot autonomy by making mutual constraints between their respective [PP,PA] (i.e., proximal for both perception and action) variables, to promote their mixed-initiative interactions. Using an actual teleoperation system into which our model was implemented, we analyzed and discussed the interactions performed by them. Our approach is useful as providing with the direct access to the significant property of their joint judgment for adequate revisions of their individual judgment policies and their adequate role-assignments.

References

1. Hirai, S.: Theory of Shared Autonomy. Journal of the Robotics Research in Japan, No. 11, Vol.6. (1993) 20–25 (in Japanese)
2. Vicente, K. and Rasmussen, J.: The Ecology of Human–Machine Systems II: Mediating "Direct Perception" in Complex Work Domain. Ecological Psychology, No. 2, Vol. 3. (1990) 207–249
3. Rasmussen, J.: Information Processing and Human–Machine Interaction: An Approach To Cognitive Engineering. North-Holland (1986)
4. Cooksey, R. W.: Judgment Analysis: Theory Methods and Applications. Academic Press (1996)
5. Kirlik, A.: The Ecological Expert: Acting to Create Information to Guide Action. Fourth Symposium on Human Interaction with Complex Systems, IEEE Computer Society (1998)
6. Allen, J. F.: Mixed-Initiative Interaction. IEEE Intelligent Systems, IEEE Computer Society (1999)
7. Horiguchi, Y., Sawaragi, T. and Akashi, G.: Naturalistic Human–Robot Collaboration Based upon Mixed-Initiative Interactions in Teleoperating Environment. Proceedings of the 2000 IEEE International Conference on Systems, Man, and Cybernetics (2000) 876–881

Web Personalization Techniques for E-commerce

Suwimol Sae-Tang[1] and Vatcharaporn Esichaikul[2]

[1] Telephone Organization of Thailand
Bangkok, Thailand
tung_ja@hotmail.com
[2] Asian Institute of Technology
Pathumthani, Thailand
vatchara@ait.ac.th

Abstract. With the advent of the Internet, there is a dramatic growth of data available on the World Wide Web. To reduce information overload and create customer loyalty, E-commerce businesses use Web Personalization, a significant tool that provides them with important competitive advantages. Despite the growing interest in personalized systems, it is difficult to implement such a system. This is because many business-critical issues must be considered before the appropriate personalization techniques can be identified. In this study, online businesses are classified into a number of categories. After that, personalization techniques that are used nowadays in E-commerce businesses are described. Finally, guidelines for selecting suitable personalization techniques for applications in each E-commerce business domain are proposed. The results of the study suggest that both customer-driven and business-driven personalization systems should be promoted on the site in order to increase customer satisfaction.

1   Introduction

As the World Wide Web becomes an increasingly important information source, Web surfers face the crucial challenge of how to search through a large stream of information to find what they need. Consequently, there is a demand for E-commerce sites to apply personalized recommendation systems, which can provide individual guidance to their customers.

Prior to the popular use of the Internet, terms like *relationship marketing* and *target marketing* were used in direct marketing to describe the importance of understanding the needs and interests of market segments. Understanding customers' requirements allows site owners to communicate to those market segments in a way that has an impact on individual customer (Allen, 2000). Unfortunately, the cost of traditional media is so expensive that even the most basic personalization cannot be performed. Even though the concept of personalization cannot work with the traditional media, it has come into reality with the arrival of the Web. This is why *Web Personalization* is very famous in E-commerce nowadays.

Web personalization is what merchants use to customize the sites and advertise their products. Personalization does its work by matching each viewer's interests based on his past behavior and by inferring opinions from other like-minded people

J. Liu et al. (Eds.): AMT 2001, LNCS 2252, pp. 36–44, 2001.

(Yu, 1999). There are many techniques that are used to provide personalized recommendations. Examples of these techniques are content-based filtering (Herlocker et al., 1999; Yu, 1999), collaborative filtering (Goldberg et al., 1992; Resnick et al., 1994; Shardanand and Maes, 1995), and rule-based technique (Dean, 1998; Allen, 2000).

Nowadays, personalization is being used at a growing number of Web sites, and interest in the employment of personalization is increasing at an even faster rate. Despite the growing interest in personalized systems, it is difficult to implement a recommendation system because many business-critical factors must be considered before the appropriate personalization techniques can be identified.

There is no single personalization technique that works well in every situation; therefore, selection of the appropriate techniques depends on the application that the site is trying to accomplish. In addition, two factors that complicate the selection of personalization techniques are the amount of available information and the nature of the products or services. Therefore, the purpose of this study is to propose guidelines for selecting a suitable personalization technique for each application in each E-commerce business domain. Using the appropriate techniques allows marketers to deliver customized contents to individual customer.

2   Online Business Classification

After exploring many of the world's largest Web sites, it was found that the sites could be primarily distinguished by business nature and workload pattern. In this case, workload pattern such as search traffic and transaction traffic will be considered. Based on the business nature and workload patterns, Web sites can generally be classified into five groups: publish/subscribe, online shopping, customer services, trading, and business-to-business. The detailed information for each business group is discussed as below.

2.1   Publish/Subscribe Group

This group of businesses provides visitors with information. Some examples include search engine sites, media sites such as newspapers and magazines, and event sites. Site contents of this group change frequently; as a result they have to make changes to page layouts. Most of the time, this business group deals with new or anonymous customers.

2.2   Online Shopping Group

The online shopping group allows its visitors to browse and buy the products they want. Examples are typical retail sites, where visitors buy books, clothes, and even cars. Site contents can be relatively static, such as a parts catalog, or dynamic, where items are frequently added or deleted. Search traffic is heavier than the publish/subscribe group, though the number of unique items sought is not as large.

Transaction traffic is moderate to high. Of the total transactions, typically between 1% and 5% are "buy" transactions.

2.3   Customer Services Group

This group of businesses provides services to their customers. For example, financial companies offer services by helping their customers to solve complex decision-making problems. In addition, the customer services group also includes sites that allow customers to perform services themselves. Samples of these sites are banking from home, tracking packages, and making travel arrangements. Search traffic is low volume, while transaction traffic is low to moderate.

2.4   Trading Group

The trading group allows customers to buy and sell products with each other, for example, at an auction site. Of all business groups, the trading group has the most volatile content, the highest transaction volumes with significant swing, the most complex transactions, and the greatest time sensitivity. Search traffic is moderate volume.

2.5   Business-to-Business Group

This group of businesses allows companies to buy from or sell to other businesses. Many businesses have implemented a Web site for their purchasing applications. Such purchasing activity may also have the characteristics of other groups, such as publish/subscribe group and customer services group. Transaction volume is low to moderate; however, the trend is on the increase. Transactions are typically complex because they have to connect with multiple suppliers and distributors.

3   Classification of Personalization Techniques

Even though it is possible to implement any or all personalization techniques in an application, some techniques require significant effort and may degrade system performance. As a result, it is better to apply only the suitable techniques for each application. In this section, recent personalization techniques are classified and then studied. This study classifies personalization systems into two main categories: customer-driven personalization and business-driven personalization systems (Luedi, 1997; Levin, 1999). Figure 1 displays a classification of personalization techniques.

3.1   Customer-Driven Systems

Customer-driven personalization systems allow customers to visit a site faster and more effectively. These techniques are normally operated under the customer's

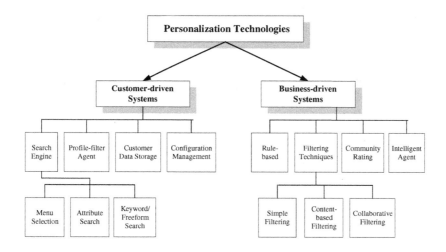

Fig. 1. Classification of Personalization Techniques

control; therefore, they provide contents that dynamically respond to customer preferences and requirements. Examples of customer-driven systems are as follows:

Search Engine. In this case, a search engine can be classified into three sub-categories:

Menu Selection. In the menu selection, customers must directly interact with the system in order to receive recommendations. Typically, customers choose from a set of predefined options on which to base their recommendations.

Attribute Search. Attribute search recommends products to customers based on syntactic properties of the products. Similarly, visitors can search for the needed information by using attributes of the content. Usually, attribute-based recommendations are manual because the customer must directly request recommendations by entering the desired syntactic properties of the products.

Keyword/Freeform Search. The keyword/freeform option requires the most interactions with the customer. Customers can use the freeform input of multiple items to request recommendation matches. While each application uses the keywords in a very different manner, it requires that the users know specifically what types of products they are interested in.

Profile-filter Agent. A profile-filter agent allows users to display their favorite news, stocks, and sports scores to update their interests. These systems filter information to present a subset of interests to a user, based on the profile that the user has previous defined. Though users can receive exactly what they want, they need to put in a lot of time and effort to get recommendations from the system. As a result, users may feel it is inconvenient to enter their requirements and interests.

Customer Data Storage Systems. These systems allow customers to set up a profile of interests on a site. In this case, a site allows customers to store information during a session, as in a shopping basket, or across visits, such as credit card numbers and shipping address.

Configuration Management Systems. Configuration management systems allow customers to design or assemble parts of their desired product by themselves. A well-known example is Dell's custom-configured computers.

3.2   Business-Driven System

Business-driven systems use an algorithm to automatically select customized content or product recommendations to deliver to their customers. These systems are often designed to learn user behavior over time. As a result, the longer and more often the systems are employed, the better the recommendations.

Rule-based Technique. This technique examines site activities and other data to find trends and patterns that will be set as business rules. Afterward, these rules are employed to suggest products or services in a personalized way to individual users. However, the performance of these systems is only as good as the rules that marketers define, and only as good as the customer data they have to work with. Therefore, it is very useful to do more sophisticated analysis on customer behavior and preferences to have a wealth of data about customers.

Filtering Techniques. There are three types of filtering techniques (IBM High-Volume Web site, 2000):

Simple Filtering. This technique classifies customers into categories based on their preferences or demographic data. The simple filtering systems recommend new products and services based on a customer's category.

Content-based Filtering. Content-based filtering recommends products to customers based on a set of products in which customers have expressed interest in the past. For instance, if a customer has placed a few products in his shopping basket, the personalized recommendation system may recommend complementary products to increase the order size. Content-based filtering systems can be automatic, if they are based on observations of customer behavior. However, they might require some manual effort if customers must explicitly type in several items in order to receive a recommendation.

Collaborative Filtering. Collaborative filtering generates recommendations by comparing a user profile against other users who have similar characteristics. Collaborative filtering systems are close to automatic because the recommendations themselves are generated automatically by the system. In this case, the system does have to learn over time from customer behavior. However, some systems are done explicitly by requesting customers to rate products. As a result, these systems move towards manual.

Community Rating. The sites usually recommend to visitors the highest-ranked books (or other product) in their topic of interest. In this case, the book ranking is based on the site's periodic surveys of its users.

Intelligent Agent. In these systems, the sites start by recommending a number of products or services to their customers. From time to time, they observe which products or services that customers often click on to read details. Eventually, the systems learn from these stops and show other similar selections; they present only information on the products or services that customers are really interested in.

4   Mapping of Personalization Techniques to Online Business Applications

After the site owners can determine which type of business they have, it is easier to identify the appropriate personalization techniques. Most effective recommendation systems blend different techniques. However, in this paper, only the main, most effective, and relatively simple technique is suggested for each application. Table 1 gives guidelines of personalization techniques for several key online applications.

Table 1. Guidelines of Personalization Techniques for Online Business Applications

Publish/Subscribe Sites	Personalization Technique
1. Demographic-based advertising	Simple filtering
2. Targeting ads and links based on what the visitor is browsing	Intelligent agent
3. Recommending classified ads — for example, notify the customer when there is a jeep for sale that is under $10,000 and less than 5 years old	Profile-filter agent
4. Searching classified database — for example, Jeeps under $10,000 that are less than 5 years old	Attribute search
5. Finding a specific article	Keyword/freeform search
6. Picking topics that customers want to receive news on	Menu selection

Online Shopping Sites	Personalization Technique
1. Promotion of cross-selling and up-selling products	Simple filtering
2. Selection of content or links based on the text that a visitor is browsing	Intelligent agent
3. Targeting ads	Simple filtering
4. Top N lists	Community rating
5. Targeted incentives, such as incentives to register	Simple filtering
6. Event reminders, such as spouse's birthday	Profile-filter agent
7. Searching for products based on attributes, such as price or features	Attribute search
8. Searching for a product by describing it in high-level terms such as "Sony" or "VCR"	Keyword/freeform search
9. Designing a product for their requirements	Configuration management
10. Setting rules for offering customers up-sell or cross-sell products when they buy a product	Rule-based
11. Selection from a finite list of title, format, length and genre options to define a search.	Menu selection
12. Recommending products to customers based on their history of purchasing	Content-based filtering
13. Shopping basket	Customer data storage
14. One-click ordering	Customer data storage
15 Recommending products based on preferences of people with similar taste	Collaborative filtering
Customer Service Sites	Personalization Technique
1. Targeting discussion groups	Simple filtering
2. Recommending Web sites, businesses, restaurants based on attribute matching	Profile-filter agent
3. Ranking news or weather based on user preferences	Profile-based filtering
4. Finding discussion groups postings based on keywords	Keyword/freeform search
5. Recommending Web sites, businesses, restaurants based on popularity rating	Community rating
Trading Sites	Personalization Technique
1. Finding a specific product	Keyword/freeform search

2.	Providing feedback profiles of other traders	Community rating
3.	Browsing for products based on predefined categories provided	Menu selection
4.	Keeping track of all bidding and selling activities with one click of the mouse	Customer data storage
5.	Getting recommendations about favorite subjects via e-mail	Profile-filter agent

Business-to-Business Sites		Personalization Technique
1.	Notifying employees of new documents in their area of interest	Profile-filter agent
2.	Recommending discussion groups based on employee's job	Simple filtering
3.	Targeting event reminders based on office location	Simple filtering
4.	Recommending documents based on the employee's stated knowledge profile and goals	Profile-filter agent
5.	Searching for documents using author and category	Attribute search
6.	Saving records of a company's supply purchases to the site	Customer data storage
7.	Searching for information on a particular topic based on keywords	Keyword/freeform search
8.	Allowing an employee to select among options, such as the look and feel of the user interface	Menu selection

5   Conclusion

Today, personalized recommendation systems are changing from innovations used by a few sites to serious business tools that are re-forming the world of E-commerce. Many of the largest commerce sites are already using recommendation systems to customize information and present only what is necessary to their customers. Although any personalization technique can be used to implement a recommendation system, it is better to use only the appropriate techniques.

From the study, both customer-driven and business-driven personalization systems should be promoted on the site. Even though customer-driven personalization allows a site to be more helpful and easier to use, it requires that users know precisely what they are looking for. Because these features require extra work on the part of customers, business sites should make these features optional and reward customers for participating on an ongoing basis.

On the other hand, business-driven systems are more valuable because they take the burden off the user. From a site's perspective, business-driven techniques are invaluable for cross-selling products. In addition, they also allow the sites to maintain one-to-one relationships with their customers. Even though business-driven recommendations can improve business results, they can be counter-productive if these techniques are poorly implemented.

References

1. Allen, C.: Personalization – Yesterday, Today and Tomorrow. Retrieved May 2000 from the World Wide Web:
   http://www.personalization.com/soapbox/columns/allen-column-1.asp
2. Dean, R.: Personalizing Your Web Site. Retrieved June 1998 from the World Wide Web:
   http://www.builder.com/Business/Personal/ss00b.html
3. Goldberg, D., Nichols, D., Oki, B. M., Terry, D.: Using Collaborative Filtering to Weave and Information Tapestry. Communications of the ACM 35 (1992) 61-70
4. Herlocker, J. L., Konstan, J. A., Borchers, A., Riedl, J.: An Algorithmic Framework for Performing Collaborative Filtering. GroupLens Research Project, Department of Computer Science and Engineering, University of Minnesota. Retrieved July 1999 from the World Wide Web: http://www.cs.umn.edu/Research/GroupLens/
5. IBM High-Volume Web Site: Web Site Personalization. Retrieved January 2000 from the World Wide Web:
   http://www-4.ibm.com/software/developer/library/personalization/index.html
6. Levin A.: Sorting through Personalization and Targeting. Fastwater Rapids: Volume 1.12. Retrieved January 1999 from the World Wide Web: http://www.fastwater.com/
7. Luedi, A. E.: Personalize or Perish. NetAcademy, The Mcminstitute University of St. Gallen, Switzerland. Retrieved July 1997 from the World Wide Web:
   http://www.netacademy.org/
8. Resnick, P., Iacovou, N., Suchak, M., Bergstrom, P., and Riedl, J.: GroupLens: An Open Architecture for Collaborative Filtering of Netnews. The Proceedings of ACM CSCW'94 Conference on Computer Supported Collaborative Work (1994) 175-186
9. Shardanand, U., and Maes, P.: Social Information Filtering: Algorithms for Automating "Word of Mouth". The Proceedings of ACM CHI' 95, Conference on Human Factors in Computing Systems (1995) 210-217
10. Yu, P. S.: Data Mining and Personalization Technologies. Database Systems for Advanced Applications. The Proceedings of the 6th International Conference (1999) 6-13

A Shopping Negotiation Agent That Adapts to User Preferences

Runhe Huang[1], Jianhua Ma[1], and Qun Jin[2]

[1] Faculty of Computer and Information Sciences, Hosei University, Tokyo 184-8584, Japan
{rhuang, jianhua}@k.hosei.ac.jp

[2] Dept. of Computer Software, The University of Aizu, Fukushima-ken 965-8580, Japan
jinqun@u-aizu.ac.jp

Abstract. This paper describes a shopping negotiation agent that can adapt user preferences and automatically negotiate with its counter party on behalf of a user it represents. The agent is built on a basis of the proposed negotiation model, the enhanced extended Bazaar model, which is a sequence of decision making model of negotiation with exploiting common knowledge, public information, and game theory. Since different users can have different preferences, it is important for the agent to have adaptation to different user preferences. This can be achieved by acquiring user preferences, tracing user's behavior on Web and mapping the behavior to a set of the preference parameters, creating the negotiation model class, and generating an instance negotiation model object with new/updated preference parameters.

1 Introduction

Online shopping is a hot topic that has been brought out with the rapid developments of the Internet and Web technologies. It is undeniable that daily life has become convenient with it. People do not drive to a store, do not travel to oversea, they can purchase the goods they want. People do not physically open a shop, build a store, they can sell goods. Forrester research, International Data Corp., and Nielsen Media Research have reported that the number of people buying, selling, and performing transactions on the Web are increasing at a phenomenal pace [1]. However, the potential of the Internet for transforming commerce is largely unrealized. E-purchases are still largely non-automated. The most current available online shopping systems are only limited to deliver to consumer orders of magnitude better ways to shop. Information about products and vendors is more easily accessible, and orders and payments are dealt with electronically. A human buyer is still responsible for collecting and interpreting information on merchants and products, making decisions about merchants and products, and ultimately entering purchase and payment information.

Software agent technologies [2] can be used to automate several of the most time-consuming stages of the buying process and adapt to user preferences as well. Some online shopping sites provide shopping services with so-called shopping agents or "bots". The first generation of agents is mainly designed for price comparison shopping such as Firefly [3], mySimon [4], etc. It behaves like a price comparison search engine and pops up a list of products with price as a result to its user. This of course saves people's time to visit a flooding of retail shops on Web sites. However,

J. Liu et al. (Eds.): AMT 2001, LNCS 2252, pp. 45–56, 2001.
© Springer-Verlag Berlin Heidelberg 2001

shopping is not just searching for a lower price product. There are something else that should be taken into considerations like quality, brand, service, and etc. Although the first generation of agents is still in practical use on many Web shopping sites, the second generation of agents that are designed for combinatorial value shopping such as Frictionless Commerce [5] is born. It overcomes the limitations of comparison shopping agents and holds on the promise of making shopping on the Internet better by finding not just lower prices but the best value for money that meets individual needs for quality, brand, service, and price. However, it is pity that neither price comparison shopping agent nor value shopping agent does automated negotiations on behalf of a user it represents. In traditional retail markets, prices and other aspects of a transaction are often fixed, leaving no room for negotiations. With widely use of the Internet, buyers no longer have physical space constraints and can get as much as information about goods from different shops via search engines or directly visit on-line shops, the traditional fixed price retail markets have to be changed to adapt to the Internet era since more and more stronger competition among on-line accessible shops. Negotiation thus becomes a key component of online purchasing. Like shopping in the real world, negotiation often occurs between two parties. Considering how to settle on the terms, negotiation varies in duration and complexity depending on the market [6]. It is common that the negotiation of price and other aspects of the deal are integral to the buying process. In general, users (such as buyers) are directly engaged in negotiation process with common knowledge, their experience, and certain learning or reasoning strategies. The human involved negotiations accrue trading costs that may be too high. Software agents with negotiation model built in can help buyers combat information overload and expedite specific stages of the online buying process. Replacing human, software agents can automatically find and prepare contracts on behalf of the real-world parties they represent. This automation saves human negotiation time, and agents are often better at finding deals in combinatorially and strategically complex settings [7], [8]. When different users have different preferences, automated agent-agent negotiation can rapidly find solutions that improve the utility for all parties [9] by adapting the negotiation model to different user preferences.

This paper describes a shopping negotiation agent that can adapt user preferences and automatically negotiate with its counter party on behalf of a user it represents. Integrated with the second generation of agents mentioned above, the shopping negotiation agent is going to be the third generation of shopping agents with which users make even better shopping on the Internet. This paper is mainly focused on briefly describing a hybrid negotiation model exploiting common knowledge, increasing experience, game theory and some learning strategies, and explaining how the proposed negotiation model based shopping negotiation agent adapts to user preferences.

This paper is organized as follows: next section gives a brief description of the proposed negotiation model – the enhanced extended Bazaar negotiation model and explains how the proposed negotiation model based shopping negotiation agent negotiates. Section 3 is focused on describing adaptation of the shopping negotiation agent to user preferences. Finally, conclusions are drawn and future work is addressed.

2   The Shopping Negotiation Agent

Negotiation itself is not a new issue. It has a wider meaning. It can be an international crisis negotiation or hostage crisis negotiation, it can be a meeting schedule negotiation, or it often means economic negotiation. In this context, negotiation is limited to the economic negotiation. Negotiations occur in our daily life and have different levels that are from simple to sophisticated, just as negotiation between two 3 years old boys would be different from negotiation between two 40 years old businessmen since one negotiates based on a simple model while another negotiates based on a much more sophisticated and complex model that uses experience, common knowledge, public information, and is of learning ability. The negotiation model for a shopping agent is supposed to reflect negotiations of real-world humans. It should be able to adapt to users' preferences and exploit experience, common knowledge, and incoming information from counter party, and public information in the process of decision making.

The enhanced extended Bazaar model combines the extended Bazaar model with "lose bounded" Nash bargaining solution [10] for finding initial strategies for probability distribution of hypotheses on each belief. The extended Bazaar model is an extension of the original Bazaar model proposed by Zeng and Sycara [11] and takes wholesalers into considerations in negotiations. The original Bazaar model is a sequential decision making model of negotiation that uses Bayesian beliefs to make initial beliefs about the opponent such as reservation price and these beliefs are updated depending on the opponent's actions during negotiation processes. However, both the original Bazaar model and the extended Bazaar model use the uniform probability distribution of hypotheses on each belief as the initial strategy. To improve the quality of negotiation process, the enhanced extended Bazaar model is proposed by using a better initial strategy that is a result of "lose bounded" Nash bargaining solution together with using common knowledge and public available information. Learning is beneficial in the sequential negotiation and becomes more efficient and effective with exploiting common knowledge and public information. Learning is one of the important abilities for shopping negotiation agents. They find better and better solutions of how to making an offer or counter-offer during continuously interactions with the other parties at each stage.

2.1   Description of the Negotiation Model

The enhanced extended Bazaar model uses a 10-tuple,

   <G, W, D, S, A, H, Ω, P, C, F>,

to model a negotiation process [12]. Where, G contains two elements - negotiation parties: a buyer and a seller, W contains an element - wholesaler, D is a set of issues (such as price, quality, maker, quantity, service, etc.) the negotiation is concerned with, S is a set of agreement descriptions on each issue, A is a set of all possible actions, H is a set of history sequences, Ω contains a set of relevant information entities that represent the buyer's knowledge about the negotiation environment (such as average wholesale price, average retail price, in stock or not, popular or not, etc.) and beliefs on the seller (such as reservation price, bankrupt sale, inventory disposal sale, etc.), P is a set of subjective probability distribution concerned with each non-terminal history defined over Ω, C is a set of implementation costs concerned with each non-terminal history, and E is an evaluation function of the buyer's action. An action in a negotiation process is one of the following three types: *agree* if the evaluation result equals 1, *quit* if the evaluation result equals 0, or *make an offer* that can outcome the ultimate utility (select one offer that has a maximum fitness).

In most situations people negotiate over a single issue. Although some negotiations are concerned with multiple issues, people still often negotiate each individual issue one after another at a time. Of course, it is possible to negotiate over multiple issues at a time by using a combinatorial utility function in which each issue is taken into consideration with a certain coefficient weight. To simplify explanation and make readers easy to understand the model, let us take the approach of negotiating over a single issue at a time to both single issue and multiple issues negotiations. Below we take am example of negotiation over a single issue: product price to show how a shopping negotiation agent on behalf of the buyer to negotiate product price with a seller based on the enhanced extended negotiation model.

2.2   How a Shopping Negotiation Agent Negotiates?

It is assumed that a seller and a buyer are willing to come to an agreement in the negotiation concerned with only the product price. The shopping negotiation agent on behalf of the buyer negotiates over the price with the seller. It is not difficult to envisage that in order to make a decision (an offer or a counter offer), the shopping negotiation agent should have certain knowledge about current market situation and/or his counter party. The knowledge can be common knowledge, public information and private data. Of course, with more knowledge, the agent can make a better decision. Ideally, if an agent has perfect and complete knowledge, it can make an optimal decision. It is however not often the case in real-world negotiations. For common knowledge, it can be pre-acquired and added into knowledge base for the agent. For public information, with Internet searching and filtering technologies, it can be also obtained beforehand or in real-time. While for private data, it is usually secure from other parties getting it. Therefore, necessary knowledge can only be learnt in the course of interactions with counter party during negotiations. With imperfect knowledge and incomplete information at beginning, an agent may use an initial strategy for his belief (the seller's estimated reservation price) and strategy is updated in each negotiation round towards a better one (more closer to the seller's real reservation price) until it is good enough to make a decision that both parties reach agreement and the buyer benefits from the deal (ultimate utility of the buyer). If the agent can get a belief on the seller's reservation price that is closer enough to the real one, the agent can make an offer or counter offer (product price) that the seller will agree and the deal is beneficial to the buyer. The following shows how the agent learns to know the seller's reservation price during interactions with the seller.

The seller's reservation price, RP_{seller} is one of the relevant knowledge or information entity of the buyer in Ω. RP_{seller} is the seller's selling threshold below which the seller will not sell the product. Similarly, the buyer also has a reservation price RP_{buyer} above which the buyer will not buy the product. The range between RP_{seller} and RP_{buyer} thus forms a zone of agreement, that is to say, an offer within the zone is likely to be acceptable to both. If the zone of agreement is known, the buyer can make an advantageous offer that can maximize his payoff or ultimate his utility and the seller can accept. However, the zone of agreement is unknown to either the seller or the buyer. At beginning, at time k=0, they can only guess or estimate the opponent's reservation price. If B_j, j=1, 2, …, b, are denoted as b initial hypotheses on the belief, RP_{seller}, with a uniform probability distribution $P_{k=0}(B_j)=1/b$. It is quite reasonable to do so when a trading agent has no knowledge about environment and other parties before a negotiation process starts. However, it is more effective to use "lose bounded" Nash bargaining solution of game theory to find a better solution. Instead of setting the probability of each hypothesis $P_{k=0}(B_j)=1/b$, for each j, $P_{k=0}(B_j)$ is calculated based on public available information related to RP_{seller} as follows:

- To collect public available information (such as a list of prices) to estimate the seller's reservation price RP'_{seller}.

$$RP'_{seller} = (\Sigma GP_i + \Sigma(WP_j + \Delta_{wp}))/(u+v) \tag{1}$$

Where, GP_i (j=1, 2, …, u) a list of prices on a product, WP_j (j=1, 2, …, v) is a list of wholesale prices, and Δ_{wp} is extra cost for retail sale on the seller side.

- To use the collected information or the estimated reservation price in Nash bargaining solution to find a solution $s=x$.

$$\max(RP_{buyer}-x)(x-RP'_{seller}), \quad x = (RP_{buyer} + RP'_{seller})/2 \tag{2}$$

- To calculate initial probability distribution using Nash bargaining solution x.

$$P'(B_j) = 1-|x-Bj|/x \tag{3}$$

In order to normalize the probability distribution,

$$P_{k=0}(B_j) = P'(B_j)/ \Sigma P'(B_j) \tag{4}$$

The calculation is based on the absolute difference between the solution and each hypothesis. The smaller the difference is, the higher probability the hypothesis is set with. The sum of all probabilities of all hypotheses should equal to 1.0.

At time k=1, when the seller gives an offer denoted as $h_k=pr(a^k_{seller})$, the buyer agent has to figure out his action as follows:

- to accept if $pr(a^k_{seller}) < RP_{buyer}-\beta_1$, $E_{[buyer,}$ $a^k_1=1$, a^k=quit, $\tag{5}$
- to quit if $(pr(a^k_{seller})-RP_{seller}<=C_1) \cap (pr(a^k_{seller})>RP_{buyer})$, $E_{[buyer,}$ $a^k_1=0$, a^k=quit, $\tag{6}$
- or to make a counter offer, otherwise.

In the case of making a further counter offer, it is necessary to calculate fitness F_{buyer} for all possible counter offer solutions s_j^k (j=1,2, …, N_p).

$$F_{buyer}(s_j^k=CP_{buyer}(j))=1-(CP_{buyer}(j)-RP_{seller})/(RP_{buyer}-RP_{seller}), \tag{7}$$
$$RP_{buyer}-C_1>CP_{buyer}(j)>RP_{seller}$$

s_{j0}^k is selected as the counter-offer if we have

$$F_{buyer}(s_{j0}^k)=\max_j\{F_{buyer}(s_j^k)\}, j_0 \in j \tag{8}$$

Where, $CP_{buyer}(j)$ is a possible counter-offer price made by the buyer, N_p is the number of all possible counter-offers of the buyer, β_1 is the buyer' profit coefficient, and C_1 is communication cost for one more round negotiation to the buyer. As a result,

$$s_{j0}^k=RP_{seller}*(1+\beta) \tag{9}$$

is the optimal counter offer for the buyer agent. Where, β is the buyer's type coefficient, $\beta<0$ means the buyer is risking, $\beta>0$ means the buyer is conservative, and $\beta=0$ means the buyer is neutral, that is the buyer is neither risking nor conservative. For different type of users, β will be set at different values. RP_{seller} in fact is unknown to the buyer agent, however the buyer's belief on RP_{seller} can be represented by a set of hypotheses, B_j, and RP_{seller} can be estimated by formula (10).

$$RP_{seller}=\Sigma_{j=1}^b P_{k=1}(B_j|h_{k=1})*B_j \tag{10}$$

Where, $P_{k=1}(B_j|h_{k=1})$ is also denoted as $P_{k=1}(B_j)$, the probability under the condition that the event, $h_{k=1}$, happens. It can be updated by Bayesian learning rule using prior probability distribution $P_{k=0}(B_j)$ and incoming event $h_{k=1}$ as follows.

$$P_{k=1}(B_j|h_{k=1})=P_{k=0}(B_j)* P_{k=1}(h_{k=1}|B_j)/(\sum_{j=1}^{b} P_{k=1}(h_{k=1}|B_j)* P_{k=0}(B_j)),$$
$$j=1, 2, ..., b \tag{11}$$

Where, $P_{k=1}(h_{k=1}|B_j)$ is the probability under the condition B_j and can be calculated using formula (12)

$$P_{k=1}(h_{k=1}|B_j)=1-(|(h_{k=1}/(1-\alpha)+WP_{k=1}+\Delta_{wp})/2-B_j|)/(h_{k=1}/(1-\alpha)+ WP_{k=1} + \Delta_{wp})/2),$$
$$j=1, 2 ,..., b \tag{12}$$

Where, $WP_{k=1}+\Delta_{wp}$ is the estimated seller's reservation price at time $k=1$ from information about the wholesale price. For different business, Δ_{wp} may be set a different value that is related to manpower cost, resource cost, and profit the seller wishes to make. To avoid $P_{k=1}(h_{k=1}|B_j)$ within a small value region, we scale it to the value region $[\gamma, 1.0]$ by using the following formula (13):

$$P_{k=1}(h_{k=1}|B_j) = 1-\gamma*(P_{max}- P_{k=1}(h_{k=1}|B_j))/(P_{max}-P_{min}), \ j = 1, 2, ..., b, \tag{13}$$
$$\text{Where, } P_{max}=\max_{j}(P_{k=1}(h_{k=1}|B_j)), \ P_{min}=\min_{j}(P_{k=1}(h_{k=1}|B_j)),$$

and γ is scaling coefficient within the region $[0.0, 1.0]$.

The above has demonstrated how the buyer makes a decision (a counter offer) at time $k=1$ after updating belief on RP_{seller}. In fact, at any time k, the process of updating belief and making decision is same when the seller has an offer or counter offer event. The above formulae are valid by replacing $k=0$ using $k-1$ instead and replacing $k=1$ using k instead. The negotiation process (offer and counter offer) continues until they reach an agreement or one of them quits from the negotiation process (they can not reach an agreement). The probability distribution is from initial no significant different distribution towards to a significant bias on a certain hypothesis. This demonstrates the proposed model based shopping agent is of learning ability through Bayesian rule updating during negotiations.

Negotiation over other issues such as quality, quantity, and maker follows similar approach and should take belief on the seller's reservation price as a basis of making a decision: offer or counter offer in the course of negotiations. Therefore, apart from evaluation function (formula (5), (6)), fitness function (formula (7)), and solution formula (9) that are different, other formulae should remain same.

2.3   Negotiation Model Classes

Based on a same negotiation model, negotiations over different issues such as quality, quantity, maker, and price, can be automatically conducted. To achieve this implementation, we take the object oriented design approach. It is a good idea to define the enhanced extended negotiation bazaar model as an abstract class, named as *Enhanced_Extended_Bazaar* as shown in Fig. 1. From this class, a number of subclasses can be derived, such as *Price_Negotiation*, *Quality_Negotiation*, *Quantity_Negotiation*, *Maker_Negotiation*, etc. These subclasses inherit all non user preference parameter variables (denoted as NP1, NP2, ..., NPm), user preference parameter variables (denoted as UP1, UP2, ..., UPn), and all non abstract methods, and implement abstarct methods defined in the superclass, such as *evaluation_agree()*, *evaluation_quit()*, *fitne_value()*, and *offer_solution()* as shown in Fig. 2.

```
public abstract class Enhanced_Extended_Bazaar
{
    NP1 np₁; NP2 np₂; ...; NPm npₘ;
    UP1 up₁; UP2 up₂; ...; UP1 upₙ ;
    public void Enhanced_Extended_Bazaar
            (NP1 np₁, NP2 np₂, ..., NPm npₘ, UP1 up₁, UP2 up₂, ..., UP1 upₙ ){
        this.np₁ = np₁; ......; this.npₘ = npₘ
          this.up₁ = up₁; ......; this.upₙ = upₙ
    }
    ......  // other constructors
    public void set_up1(UP1 up₁){
        this.up₁ = up₁;
    }
    ......  // other set methods set_up2, ...
    public void set_upn(UPn upₙ){
        this.upₙ = upₙ;
    }
    public double RP_fromPublicInfo(){
        ...... // formula (1)
    }
    public double Nash_bargainSolution(){
        ...... // formula (2)
    }
    public void init_probability_distribution(){
        ...... // formula (3) & (4)
    }
    public void update_probability_distribution(){
        ...... // formula (12), (11), (10) & (13)
    }
    abstract int evaluation_agree(){  }
    abstract int evaluation_quit(){  }
    abstract double fitness_value(){  }
    public double max_fitness(){
        ...... // formula (8)
    }
    abstract double offer_solution(){  }
    ...... // other methods
}
```

Fig. 1. Enhanced_Extended_Bazaar abstract class

Below gives only an example of defining the *Price_Negotiation* subclass. For each other subclass regarding a negotiation over a certain issue, like *Quality_Negotiation* subclass, *Quantity_Negotiation* subclass, and *Maker_Negotiation* subclass, their definitions are similar to the definition of *Price_Negotiation* subclass except specific implementations of the abstract methods are different in each other subclass. Different subclass is therefore used for negotiations over different issues.

```
public class Price_Negotiation extends Enhanced_Extended_Bazaar
{
    ......
    public void Price_Negotiation(NP1 np1, ..., NPm npm, UP1 up1, ..., UPn upn)
    {
        super(np1, ..., npm, up1, ..., upn);
        ......
    }
    ...... // other constructors
    abstract int evaluation_agree(){
        ...... // implement formula (5)
    }
    abstract int evaluation_quit(){
        ...... // implement formula (6)
    }
    abstract double fitness_value(){
        ...... // implementat formula (7)
    }
    abstract double offer_solution(){
        ...... // implement formula (9)
    }
    ...... // other methods
}
```

Fig. 2. Price_Negotiation class

3   Adaptation to User Preferences

It is natural that people unconsciously take their personal preferences into considerations when they do shopping, individuals have different preferences, and their preferences may change from time to time. Someone may prefer a certain brand of products and don't care about price while someone may be strict on looking for lower price. Someone likes to take a risk while someone is conservative. Someone likes to get bargaining by buying a quantity of products while someone would not like to do so. Someone likes red color in winter but light blue color in summer. How we can make the shopping negotiation agent works well for different users? Adaptation to user preferences is a critical point for the shopping negotiation agent.

3.1 Acquiring User Preferences

To achieve the adaptation of the shopping negotiation agent to user references, the first step is to acquire user preferences. As for shopping, user preference may be divided into two categories: general preferences and specific preferences. The former is of generality and is a category of preferences that all users are likely to specify explicitly or implicitly such as price, quality, quantity, maker and what issue to be negotiated. Fig. 3 shows an example of a user inputting his general preferences.

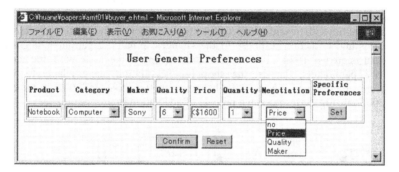

Fig. 3. An example of user general preference setting interface

The latter is a category of preferences that is specifically concerned with a certain type of products. Preference items vary with different kind of products. For computer related products like notebook PC, users may specify color, size, weight, CPU, and memory, while for automobile related products like car, users may specify, number of door, capacity, engine, interior, and other optional parts. Fig. 4 shows two examples of users setting specific preferences concerned two different kinds of products.

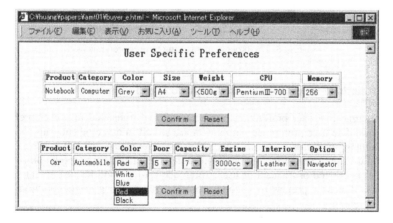

Fig. 4. Two examples of user specific preference setting interface

Of course a straightforward way of acquiring user preferences is to provide interfaces as shown in Fig. 3 and Fig. 4 for users to input their preferences interactively. An alternative approach is to employ an agent to automatically look up user's profile, trace user's shopping behavior on Web and find out user's personality so as to result user's preferences. This approach is more intelligent involved but requires Web technology, data mining techniques, and sophisticated mapping functions to map acquired information to user's preferences. For example, if a user is often to visit an online shop for a certain product with a fixed maker or brand, then his agent may interpret his behavior by a mapping function as he may like this product but would like to negotiate over price. The second step needs to translate the user preferences to the user preference parameters, up_1, up_2, ..., up_n, which are used in the shopping negotiation model as in Fig. 1 and Fig. 2. If the user preferences are allowed to update anytime, there are needs of an event listener to the changes of any user preferences and an action response to the changes. Finally, a particular negotiation object that is created from a negotiation model learns to negotiate with updated user preference parameters, that is, the shopping negotiation agent adapts to a new negotiation situation and tries to make better and better (counter) offers in the course of negotiations. Fig. 5 shows such a process of adaptation to user preferences.

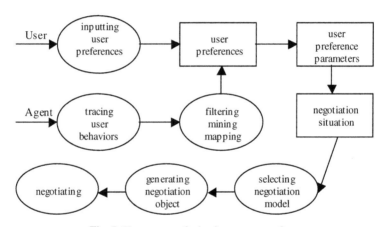

Fig. 5. The process of adapting to user preferences

3.2 Negotiation Model Object That Adapts to User Preferences

Let us assume that user preferences are acquired and translated into user preference parameters. The user preference parameters are stored in a vector $\{up_1, up_2, ..., up_n\}$. Each element in vector is an object of a user preference class (UP_1, UP_2, ...UP_n). Acquired user preferences can be passed to a shopping negotiation model object when the object is created or by a set of user preference setting methods, set_up1(), ..., and set_up$n$(). If a user prefers to negotiate product price, the price negotiation model object is created.

model_1 = **new** Price_Negotiation(..., up_1, up_2, ..., up_n);

The instance object, model_1, of the class, Enhanced_Extended_Bazaar, is thus generated by calling a constructor method and the acquired user preference parameters are passed to the object as the constructor method's arguments. When a changing user preference event is caught, the changed user preference value, for example, up_1, is reset to model_1 object by setting method.

model_1.set_up1(up_1);

Similarly, up_2, up_3, ..., and up_n can be reset to the model_1 in the same way when it is necessary.

model_1.set_up2(up_2);

......

model_1.set_upn(up_n);

For a different user, a different instance object with different user preferences can be generated. Users' preferences can be thus reflected in the generated instance model object and events of updating user preferences can be caught and get response from the negotiation object. Negotiation is going to adapt to an newly updated situation gradually.

It is necessary to point out that user preference parameters, up_1, up_2, ..., up_n, are not reified in this paper since they vary with different issues and different kinds of products. However, we can give an example below to see connection of a user preference to a user preference parameter in the negotiation model. If a user would like to negotiate product price, the price the user inputs, for example, <$1600, is interpreted as the user's (buyer) reservation price, RP_{buyer}, and passed to methods, *evaluation_agree()*, *evaluation_quit()*, and *fitne_value()* that calculate formulae (5), (6), and (7), respectively, in the *Price_Negotiation* model. When this preference changes, the formulae are calculated with different RP_{buyer} values. We can see how the shopping negotiation agent catches user preference change events and reflects the changes to the instance model object anytime. Although it takes a certain amount of time for the agent to adjust, it certainly can adapt to updated user preferences through Bayesian learning method and propose a better and better (counter) offer to reach agreement with the seller and maximize buyer's benefit.

4   Conclusions and Future Work

Negotiation is an important component of online shopping to buyers. Although there are a few commercial available online shopping systems that enable buyers to negotiate with sellers, negotiation has been for sure receiving increasing attention from researchers. In traditional retail markets, prices and other aspects of trading are fixed and leaving no room for negotiations, but this has to change due to strongr competition among a flooding of online shops. This paper describes a shopping negotiation agent that is built based on the enhanced extended Bazaar model and demonstrates how the agent negotiates with a seller on behalf of a buyer it represents. With Bayesian learning method, the agent learns to negotiate (making a better and better offer or counter offer) in the course of interactions with the seller.

Different users have different preferences, how to reflect such personal preferences in the negotiation model and how to make a negotiation agent adapts to a user's changing preferences are explained in this paper. Based on the oriented object design principle, different negotiation model classes derived from its super abstract class, *Enhanced_Extended_Bazaar*, are applied to negotiations over different issues. User preferences can be acquired by user's inputs and/or an agent to trace user shopping behaviors on Web. Acquired user preferences are translated to user preference parameters that are passed to the negotiation model object as auguments of the constructor method or via setting methods. The shopping negotiation agent can reflect individuals' preferences and adapt to changing negotiation situations. Our future work will be focused on

- developing an agent that can trace a user's shopping behaviors on Web, track the user's shopping history, and learn to know the user's preferences, and
- constructing a negotiation model that is derived from the enhanced extended Bazaar model class and can negotiate a combinatorial mutliple issues at a time.

Acknowledgements. This work has been partly supported by 2000-2002 Japanese Ministry of Education Grant-in-Aids for Scientific Research Contract No. 12558012.

References

1. Maes, P., Guttman, R.H., Moukas, A.G.: Agents that buy and sell. Communication of the ACM, 42(3): 81-92, 1999.
2. Russell, S., Norvig, P,: Artificial Intelligence, A Modern Approach. Petice-Hall, 1995.
3. Judge, P.C.: "Firefly: The Web Site that Has Mad Ave. buzzing", BusinessWeek online, http://www.businessweek.com/1996/41/b349690.htm,1996.
4. CNET Networks, http://www.mysimon.com/, 1998.
5. Frictionless Commerce Inc., http://www.frictionless.com/, 2001.
6. Oliveira, E., Rocha, A.P.:   Agents advances features for negotiation in electronic commerce and virtual organizations formation process. In C. Sierra and F. Dignum, editors, Book on European perspectives on AMEC. Springer-Verlag, June 2000.
7. Gerding, E.H., van Bragt, D.D.B., La Poutre, J.A.: Scientific Approaches and Techniques for Negotiation: A Game Theoretic and Artificial Intelligence Perspective.   ACM Computing Classification System: 1.2.11, J.4, 1.2.6., 1999.
8. Oliver, J.R.: A machine learning approach to automated negotiation and prospects for electronic commerce. Journal of Management Information Systems, 13(3): 83-112, 1996.
9. Gerding, E.H., van Bragt, D.D.B., La Poutre, J.A.: Multi-issue Negotiation Processes by Evolutionary Simulation. In Workshop on Complex Behavior in Economics, Aix-en-Provence, France, May 2000.
10. J.F. Nash,: The bargaining problem. Econometrica, 18:155-162, 1950.
11. Zeng, D., Sycara, K.: Bayesian learning in negotiation. International Journal of Human Computer Systems, 48:125-141, 1998.
12. Tao Huang, Runhe Huang, and Jianhua Ma, "Negotiation Modeling in E-trading", in the Proceedings of the Fourth International Conference on Human and Computer, September, 2001, Japan.

Combining Meta-level and Logic-Based Constructs in Web Personalization

Sofie Goderis [1], Gustavo Rossi [2], Andres Fortier [2], Juan Cappi [2], and
Daniel Schwabe [3]

[1] Programming Technology Lab, Vrije Universiteit Brussel
sgoderis@vub.ac.be
[2] LIFIA-Facultad de Informatica-UNLP, Argentina
{gustavo, andres, jcappi}@lifia.info.unlp.edu.ar
[3] Depto de Informatica, PUC-Rio, Brazil
schwabe@inf.puc-rio.br

Abstract. In this position paper we analyze the problem of Web Applications personalization from a design point of view. We focus on which design constructs are necessary to achieve modular and evolvable personalized Web Applications. We claim that personalization involves different concerns (e.g. rules, profiles, etc.) that should be clearly identified and decoupled; we show how to add personalized behaviors to existing applications in a non-intrusive way, by using reflective mechanisms found in most object-oriented languages.

We first introduce our approach to Web Applications modeling that separates conceptual from navigation and user interface design; we next introduce personalization patterns and briefly show how they can guide the designer towards his objective. We finally present our approach and some ongoing research directions related with the design of an object-oriented framework for Web Applications personalization.

1 Introduction

Designing personalized Web Applications implies dealing with different concerns such as building different interfaces according to user preferences or Web appliances, providing customized links; showing personalized information, adapting application's functionality, etc. To solve these problems we have to model the user, implement personalization policies and rules and integrate them into the application. Except from trivial read-only Web Applications (such as www.my.yahoo.com), the process of personalizing existing Web software is a good example of complex applications' evolution. This is due mainly to the very nature of Internet software in which the rate of change (of requirements, marketing decisions, etc) is quite fast.

Though user modeling and profile derivation has been already discussed in the literature [Perkowitz00], design aspects related with this problem have been seldom taken into account. The aim of this short paper is to present our conceptual framework for dealing with those design issues in a modular way, emphasizing concerns separation from requirement elicitation to application's implementation.

J. Liu et al. (Eds.): AMT 2001, LNCS 2252, pp. 57–64, 2001.

By clearly understanding and decoupling the design concerns involved in a personalized e-commerce application, we can keep the software manageable; we can also provide the basis for reusing designs and design experience. We have a better way to understand the kind of interactions appearing in a personalized application from an abstract point of view (independent of the specific aspects of the application), and to simplify them by following well-knwon design patterns. The structure of this paper is as follows: we first present our view of Web Applications design; then we introduce personalization patterns and show that all these patterns are finally mapped to objects' behaviors. We then explain our strategy for personalizing those behaviors using meta-level constructs. A discussion on possible implementations using a logic programming framework is finally discussed.

2 Our View of Web Applications Design and Personalization

We follow the OOHDM approach to Web Applications design [Schwabe98] The key concept in OOHDM is that Web Application models involve a Conceptual, a Navigational Model and an Interface Model [Schwabe98]. Those models are built using object-oriented primitives with a syntax close to UML [UML00]. The concern of the conceptual model is to represent domain objects, relationships and the intended applications' functionality. In the OOHDM approach, users do not navigate through conceptual objects, but through navigation objects (nodes) that are defined as views on conceptual objects. As we consider Web Applications as hypermedia applications, we define links connecting nodes, as views on conceptual relationships. Finally, the abstract interface model specifies the look and feel of navigation objects together with the interaction metaphor.

Using this approach as a conceptual framework to reason on personalization we have mined personalization patterns in existing Web Applications [Rossi01a]. Next we summarize those patterns using a simplified format describing the problem and the corresponding solution. For the sake of simplicity we ignore interface personalization.

2.1 Link Personalization

Problem:
Web Applications involve dealing with a large number of objects and the way in which we reach them may depend on many different factors. We want to provide different users (individuals or roles) with different linking topologies.

Solution:
Personalize links by calculating the end-point of the link with user-related information. When we personalize links, all users access the same information objects and although anchors may look similar (see for example the link to Recommendations in www.amazon.com), each individual has a different customized topology.

2.2 Structure Personalization

Problem:
Many applications involve not only dealing with thousands of objects but also with a great variety of subjects and services. We may want to circumscribe the navigation space to the aspects the user is interested in.

Solution:
Personalize (or let the user do it) the structure of the Web Application. Consider the information space as a set of aggregated objects (or modules) and select only those objects that the user may want to consume as for example in www.my.yahoo.com.

2.3 Content Personalization

Problem:
In some Web Applications we may want to provide each individual user with a slightly different content for a particular information item.

Solution:
Define personalized contents in nodes by letting node attributes vary according to the user; for example e-stores providing personalized prices for their products.

2.4 Behavior Personalization

Problem:
Web Applications combine hypertext navigation with other functionality (such as bidding, adding products to a shopping cart, etc). Suppose that we want to provide individualized responses to a particular operation.

Solution:
Personalize the application behavior by making this behavior dependent of the user who triggers it.

In Figure 1 we summarize the previous discussion showing how the OOHDM approach deals with personalization in an abstract way. Notice that the previously presented patterns are independent of the method you use to build Web Applications: they exist on their own.

Understanding previous patterns we can map the personalization requirements of our application to one of those patterns and then analyze how to deal with the design structures underlying those patterns. The aim of this paper is to analyze the process of building personalized applications focusing on those design aspects. In particular we want to show that correct design decisions impact positively on the applications' evolution, simplifying the process of obtaining personalized applications. A first approach for dealing with personalization in Web Applications can be found in [Rossi 01b].

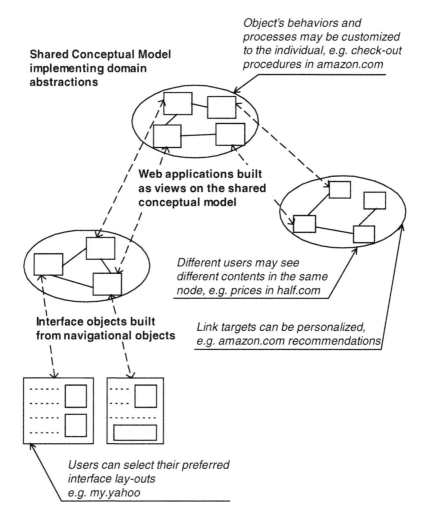

Fig. 1. Personalization in an OOHDM model.

3 Design Issues and Concerns Related with Personalization

It is easy to see that most (if not all) examples of personalization involve some kind of adaptable conceptual model. Therefore, understanding how to personalize a conceptual (application) model is essential for achieving personalized nodes, links and behaviors. The field of adaptive software is not new (See [Oreizy 99]) though we are mainly interested in those design constructs that can simplify the process of adding personalization features to a Web Application.

There are basically three concerns related with personalization: the user profile, the personalization rules and the application of those rules for a particular individual. Hard-coding personalization rules together with core application objects yields difficult to maintain software, because the pace of evolution of customization rules (and the associated user profiles) is faster than changes in the basic application model. Suppose for example that in an electronic store we have a Class Product with a method *price* to calculate its price. If we want to personalize the price such that we provide discounts to some customers (for example according to their buying history), we can modify the code of *price* such that it interacts with the user profile to get the information. However, each time we change the personalization rule we must change that method; the solution simply does not scale-up, since we keep tweaking the model's behavior to accommodate to the discount policies.

The same is true if we want to have different recommendation algorithms for different customers, or customized check-out procedure according to user preferences.

While variations in the domain model, such as adding new products or paying mechanisms can be solved by sub-classing and composing objects, changes related with personalization rules are more difficult to handle.

As we describe in the next section, the solution to this problem is not to decide which object in the domain model should be responsible for taking care of things like holding the algorithms or the policies, but to understand that software constructs related with personalization must be dealt in another way. We think that by building a robust design in the meta-level we can achieve the exact degree of decoupling between the application's domain model and the personalization-related constructs, obtaining a scalable architecture.

4 Our Approach

The key of our approach is the recognition that those concerns related with personalization, namely the user profile, the rules and the application of rules, must be decoupled from the Web Application model and further decoupled from each other. We next summarize our approach explaining the micro-architectural constructs we used for solving this problem:

4.1 Modifying the Base Application's Behavior

There are basically two approaches for solving this problem: using decorators [Gamma95] or intercepting behaviors with a meta-level approach. The latter solution clearly recognizes the fact that this problem should be treated as a separated aspect of the application and dealt with in an orthogonal way. We used an idea similar to method wrappers that "trap" the desired behavior and let us call the personalization code. The idea is that each time an object receives a message that should be personalized, we automatically "invoke" some functionality in the meta-level that "reasons" about the base application level and modifies the application's behavior.

For example we can solve the price problem by intercepting the message *price* and provide a way to trigger rules that provide the personalized behavior. Moreover, we can do this in an instance basis (i.e. only some products have a personalized price).

When considering the price problem, we know in advance that each time the message price is sent, the price might have to be personalized. We can thus statically determine what personalization rule is to be used. However, in some cases determining what personalization rule is to be used, cannot be decided until runtime. This dynamic determination occurs for instance when personalization is different for different types of users. Making the distinction between static and dynamic determination of personalization will improve our approach significantly.

4.2 Implementing Rules

Rules should be treated as first class citizens in personalized applications. As they tend to evolve quickly and may be usually combined to implement complex business strategies, we must have a flexible approach for rules design. We are now experiencing with the SOUL meta-programming framework [Wuyts01]. SOUL integrates Smalltalk and Prolog by letting designers write Prolog rules (in the meta-level) governing the behavior of the base level. Though originally conceived for synchronizing design and implementation, we have used SOUL to express personalization rules. Inheriting well-known Prolog features, rules are modular and easy to express. They can invoke base application's code and can be maintained efficiently, i.e. it is easy to add new rules or to modify existing ones as they are written in a natural way (*action* if *conditions*).For the price problem we use the following personalization rule:

```
Rule updatePrice(?ResultString) if
  isReceiver([Product],[#price],[?aProductObject]),
            currentCustomer(?ID),
            changePrice(?ID,[?aProductObject],
            ResultString).
```

These rules specify that if a certain Product object receives the message *price*, the personalization of this price, specified for the current customer, has to take place. The rule results in a piece of Smalltalk code, specifying how the price should be adapted, that will be executed by the Smalltalk base level.

4.3 Dealing with the User Profile

The user profile is an important component in every personalized application. Facts about the user can be specified using Prolog or they may just be "traditional" objects. In the first case, the user profile is stored at meta-level and consists of a set of facts, such as those that we see next.

```
Fact name(id408, John).
Fact age(id408, 28).
Fact boughtProducts(id408, <BookID20, BookID403, CDID230>).
```

Accessing this data is simply done by using the right predicates. For instance, `name(id408, ?UserName)` will provide us with the name of the particular user with identity id408.

Another possibility is to consider the user as an object on base level, but this will only influence the predicates used to access the profile (and not the personalization rules that use these predicates). For instance, accessing the user's name now requires the rule that we see below.

Rule `name(?User, ?Name)` **if** `equals(?Name, [?User getName]).`

Such that the name is retrieved from the user object at base-level (i.e. ?User). In our approach this is rather straightforward, because SOUL provides the necessary mechanisms to do so.

The rule-based system behind Prolog allows us to write inference rules to classify users according to the observed facts. In this way, we can associate algorithms to different types of users and write the code that assigns the correct algorithm to the current user as a set of logic predicates. These predicates may be executed each time we want to personalize an object's feature or with other strategies (once a day, each time we require it, etc). Keeping the user profile as a separate module allows us to specify different strategies to support its evolution (both in structure and contents). For example, while for some applications, new facts about the user are added as a consequence of an application's operation (buying a product for example), it may be the case that we want to record the products he visited; with our meta-level approach we can just intercept the corresponding behavior (displaying a product for customer c) and add a fact to our information base (prolog predicates) in a transparent way.

5 Discussion and Concluding Remarks

We have briefly outlined our approach for personalizing Web Application models. It is based in separating the main concerns behind personalization (rules, profiles, core model) and providing a design model for supporting this decoupling. Using a meta-level approach guarantees that we can seamlessly add personalized behaviors in a non-intrusive way, without affecting core application's functionality.

We are now studying how to provide generic meta-level classes and objects and templates for rules that can be used in different applications. The idea is to have abstract skeletons for personalization acting as application frameworks.

In this way, we will be able to personalize Web Applications by just composing the base functionality with objects taken from some of these classes thus simplifying the task of adding rules, generating user profiles and applying the rules to the chosen application's objects.

References

[Gamma95]   E. Gamma, R. Helm. R. Johnson, J. Vlissides: "Design Patterns. Elements of reusable object-oriented software", Addison Wesley 1995.

[Oreizy 99]   P. Oreizy, M. Gorlik, R. Taylor, D. Heimbigner, G. Johnson, N. Medvidovic, A. Quilici, d. Rosenblum, and A. Wolf: "An architecture-based approach to self-adaptive software". IEEE Intelligent Systems, pages 54-62, May 1999.

[Perkowitz00] M. Perkowitz, O. Etzioni: "Adaptive Web Sites" In Comm ACM, August 2000, p.p. 152-158.

[Rossi01a]   G. Rossi, D. Schwabe, J. Danculovic, L. Miaton: "Patterns for Personalized Web Applications", Proceedings of EuroPLoP 01, Germany, July 2001.

[Rossi01b]   G. Rossi, D. Schwabe, R. Guimaraes: "Designing Personalized Web Applications", Proceedings of the 10th International Conference on the WWW (WWW10), Hong Kong, 2001,Elsevier, p.p.

[Schwabe98]   D. Schwabe, G. Rossi: "An object-oriented approach to web-based application design". Theory and Practice of Object Systems (TAPOS), Special Issue on the Internet, v. 4#4, pp.207-225, October, 1998.

[Wuyts01]   Roel Wuyts: "A Logic Meta-Programming Approach to Support the Co-Evolution of Object-Oriented Design and Implementation" Phd Thesis. Programming Technology Lab, VUB, Brussels, 2001.

Web Personalisation – An Overview

San Murugesan and Annamalai Ramanathan

School of Computing and Information Technology
University of Western Sydney, Australia
s.murugesan@uws.edu.au

1 Introduction

The Web has become a universal interface in a diverse range of applications seamlessly interconnected through the Internet, intranets and extranets. The Web users, however, have vastly different needs and their skills and cognitive abilities are also vary widely. Thus, on the Web, one-size does not fit all its users. To realise the full potential of this versatile and ubiquitous medium, Web interface and Web applications have to be customised to suit an individual user or a group of users.

Web personalisation aims to tailor the Web to provide the users what they want and how they want it, rather than providing the same content, in the same style or format, to all its diverse range of users. Interest in Web personalization is rapidly increasing and the number of commercial organisations touting to provide software and services for personalization is mushrooming. Personalisation is seen as a major advancement in the evolution of Web and Web-based applications, and is being deployed in e-business and other Web applications.

Web personalisation emulates the 'corner store relationship' of a traditional small retail shop environment where the salesperson knows most of its customers and their individual needs, call them by name and advice their customers about products that they are interested in. This kind of personalisation enables to build customer loyalty and retain customers.

Is Web personalisation a hype or an opportunity? It is an opportunity and it transpires in different forms: personalised links, personalised content, or recommendation for a product or information or service. For example, amazon.com offers details about the books their customers are likely to be interested. Portals like Yahoo.com allow users to select content and structure to construct their own MyYahoo pages. Major objectives of Web personalisation are:
- To provide personalized Web interface/navigation
- To provide customized information content
- To provide the information content in a customized format
- To offer special deals to valued online customers
- To study user/customer online behaviour
- To provide a 'human face' to the Web

J. Liu et al. (Eds.): AMT 2001, LNCS 2252, pp. 65–76, 2001.
© Springer-Verlag Berlin Heidelberg 2001

Businesses and Web-based system developers are using personalisation service features as a way to make a Web site easier to use, increase sales, create a one-to-one experience, improve customer service, save customer time, increase customer loyalty, attract a broader audience, achieve cost savings, target advertising and build a community (Forrester [2]).

Personalisation is, however, not a silver bullet. Its goals and objectives must be defined clearly, and it must be designed to be useful and usable. Designing and developing a personalised Web-based system involves a good planning, and strategy for collecting and analysing data productively and economically. Hence personalisation should be considered during the design stage itself. Personalization of the Web for a given application(s) calls for a well-thought-out process; simply using a personalisation technology on ad hoc manner without clear goals and strategy and without addressing some the major issues in implementation is a recipe for failure. Successful Web personalization calls for identification of the goals of personalization, adoption of appropriate strategies and techniques, and subsequent evaluation of their effectiveness. These aspects are, however, often overlooked and not adequately addressed in academic and popular publications.

This paper provides an overview on Web personalisation. It provides an overview of some of technologies supporting personalization and their relative merits. Then it discusses the major issues and considerations in Web personalization.

2   Approaches, Techniques, and Methodology

Web personalisation can be done either offline (personalised newsletters, e-mail) or online (real-time recommendations), and at different levels of sophistication from simple personalised Web pages (that call you by name and greet you) to one-to-one marketing (tailoring the content, structure, promotions etc. all suit to the suite user's needs and demands). Personalisation is done based on information about the collected directly (Fill-in-forms) or indirectly (Click stream analysis, cookies etc.) and analysed using myriad of tools to predict the interest of the users.

Personalisation could be done either at the client-side using plugs-in with the user's Web browser or at the server/middleware in real-time.

2.1   Client-Side Personalisation

These tools work on users' browsers to personalise the interface, layout and sometimes contents of a Website. Adaptive user interfaces [27] is a tool that personalises the application interfaces to suite the user, such as allowing the user to reconfigure their desktop.

Intermediaries [6] personalise the information stream that flows between the client and the server. Maglio and Barrett [6] have developed WBI, a programmable hypertext transfer protocol proxy server designed for easy development and deployment of intermediary applications or plug-ins. For example, a WBI plug-in can do the extra work of indicating the hyperlink download times by means of traffic signal lights on your browser and another WBI plug-in can transcode a HTML to WML code.

2.2 Server-Side Personalisation

As mentioned earlier, the level of personalisation at the server side could range from shallow to deep personalisation. At a shallow level of Web personalisation, e-mails and hyperlinks could be personalised. Businesses send e-mails to their customers informing about the new product that may be of interest to them. In link personalisation, Web sites greet you with names and present special content with selected keywords. Through the keywords, the content of the Web pages is arranged differently for different users.

Deep level of personalisation offers more personalised offerings: users are reminded and or recommended of some tailored product/information/service that suit their needs.

Web personalisation involves three major tasks:
1. Explicit or implicit collection of users' data and their preferences and Web behaviour patterns.
2. Analysis of the users data using algorithms, artificial intelligence and/or collaboration methods to infer their needs and interests and preference
3. Recommendation and/or presentation of tailored information to the users

Figure 1 provides a snapshot of different methods and techniques of Web personalisation. Personalisation could be based on data from a single user or a group of users with similar interests, and the level of personalisation (shallow or deep). Thus, we have four categories of personalisation: Shallow-Single, Shallow-Group, Deep-Single, Deep-Group. The different personalisation methods and techniques that are suited for each category is shown in Figure 1 (It also indicates whether personalisation is could be done online or offline). As Web personalisation could be done in many ways using different techniques, appropriate choice of them for a given application is very important.

Luedi [14] presents appropriate personalisation techniques for selected categories/domains of interest such as corporate knowledge management, merchandising and retail etc. Table 1 shows appropriate personalisation for different categories of applications [15].

2.2.1 Data Collection
Data collection is the backbone of personalisation, because the recommendations and tailoring of Web content would be based on the collected data. It is also tougher task, since users have to be convinced to provide the required information about themselves and that their privacy would be protected (see W3C privacy guidelines P3P standards).

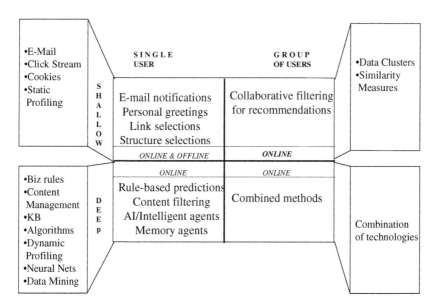

Fig. 1. Web Personalisation Technologies

For user profiling, data can be collected explicitly or implicitly. Web forms, interview, surveys, users' rating on certain commodities or services are explicit profiling where the users know what information they provide about themselves. Data collection using implicit methods includes cookies, click-stream analysis, Web site stay time, and the Web log data. Though the users are not aware of the data

Table 1. Web Site Categories and Suitable Techniques of personalisation (Adapted from [15])

Personalisation Technique	Applications				
	Publish/ Subscribe	Online Shopping	Self-service	Trading	B2B
Rule-Based Prediction		X	X	X	X
Simple Filtering	X	X	X	X	X
Content-based Filtering	X		X	X	X
Collaborative Filtering		X	X		X

collection, they should be properly told about what, how and why this information is obtained and used [see P3P guidelines].

User profiling can be classified into: static profiling and dynamic profiling [22]. The static profiling refers to analysis of the Web log data to infer and use the user's behaviour pattern to personalise Web sites. Off-the-shelf tools such as Personify [20] and Accure [21] analyses the log data and reports on users visit on a website. Dynamic profiling predicts the users next click (and or the next product users' likely to buy) based on clicks and associated rules.

In addition to information collected or inferred from the users, third-party data sources such as demographic data and opinion databases of people are also used.

2.2.2 Data Analysis and Usage

To analyse and infer the collected data, algorithmic techniques, rule-based filtering, content-based filtering, collaborative filtering and hybrid filtering techniques can be used. The suitability of this algorithms/methods to specific methods is highlighted with examples.

Algorithmic Techniques

User's recent actions trigger appropriate algorithms to predict the following actions. The algorithm is based on analysing users' actions over a period of time and building a confidence level for a sequence of actions. For example, if users go from 'a' to 'b' to 'e' always, then whenever a user is through 'a' and 'b' then 'e' is automatically shown up. If somebody breaks it (goes to 'd', after 'a' and 'b') then the confidence level for that sequence of actions is reduced. This concept is similar to 'observational Personalisation' (Mulvenna and others [9]). Incremental Probabilistic Action Model (IPAM, Davison and Hirsh [7]) is an example of this, where it learns to predict the actions of users interacting with Unix command-line shell.

The advantages of this approach are that users are wouldn't be asked to provide specific information about themselves. However, the prediction needs to be analysed over a period and certain level of confidence needs to be established. This works well for predicting simple actions of users and is not appropriate for deeper levels of personalisation such as tailoring the contents.

Rule-Based Filtering

Based on a domain-specific rule-base, the rule-based filtering comes up with recommendations corresponding to users' actions/selections. Typical rules are: "If A then B" or "If A and B then C not D". An example of a rule is "if customer bought a pair of shoes, then offer him/her a pair of shocks." Rules are constructed by analysing user behavior on the Web sites, common sense, demography and using third party knowledge bases. User's action triggers the rules that meets the their conditions. Broadvision [19] uses rule-based predictions using the past data on users' behaviour to provide information of interest to individual users.

The advantage of the rule-based methods is that they are explicit and can be controlled well, and one can find out which product can be offered to whom. However, rule engines do not handle dynamic data or it cannot be made flexible to fit into the future use. Thousands of business rules may be required for each domain and generation and maintenance of rules are labour intensive.

Content-Based Filtering

Content-based filtering offers tailored Web contents of Web. For example, if a user reads more of sports news and politics in an online newspaper, then in the next visit, he/she is offered with more of sports and politics news. It is done by grouping all the contents of a Web site into categories and then matching the users' interest against these categories.

Content-based predictions are the best when the content can be easily categorised and when the users' interest is easily matched against these categories. Newspapers, films and video are good examples for content-based predictions, because categorization of these is easy. However, content-based predictions are narrow focused and sometimes becomes difficult to group into content categories in a rapidly evolving area.

Amazon.com uses the content-based recommendations for suggesting more books for their users on the same subject. Yahoo allows users to create their own content and layout for home pages.

Collaborative Filtering

Collaborative filtering is similar to 'word of mouth' principle – asking your friend's opinion who has similar tastes like you. In Web personalisation, this is done by collecting users' preferences/ratings on selected categories of items and then group users according to their similarity for likeness of items. So, a group of likeminded people is formed. When one needs how he/she would like a new category, then this can be recommended from the ratings available from his/her group (assuming that sufficient members from the same group has rated this new item). Generally functions of similarity measures are used to group like-minded people in collaborative filtering. Different predictive algorithms [18, 23] have been developed.

The above principle can also be used in online buying. It could be like finding out what products the customer is searching for, what are the things already bought (in shopping cart) and what's the customer's dealings with the store etc to match similar cases (grouping with like shoppers) and suggest further items to this user using the behaviour of the group in the past. CDNow and DVD Express are using this technology.

Collaborative filtering works very well with commodity items such as books, films etc., which can be rated quantitatively and when many people are willing to do. Also, you need opinions of a lot of people to form effective solution for a single user. It requires a large customer base in order to give effective solutions, also such a large volume of users should be volunteering to share their opinion. People may not be good at consistent rating and may exhibit different ratings to the same thing at different times due to the environment and other factors. Also, Popular products are likely to be suggested, as it is likely to be represented more in the users' rating. A small set of population can lead to imperfect results and also this method may not work for users who are atypical and cannot be grouped with any likeminded groups.

Macromedia's Likeminds is an example for collaborative filtering. Macromedia uses its proprietary technology along with patented collaborative filtering. It uses a variety of user and product data to engage Web visitors with accurate product recommendations.

Hybrid Methods

More than one technique can be used for predicting users' Web bahaviour. Methods combining content based and group based predictions seem to perform better than when these algorithms work independently. In this hybrid approach, first decision is based on the collaborative filtering and then the content categorization is used to match the individual users interest. Thus the disadvantages of each method is overcome and predictions made on the basis of both the methods combined seem to work better than that of individual predictions, but at the cost of additional processing of data. Balabanovic [24] has shown how the hybrid approach can help in the Web-based predictions.

The ClixSmart (Smyth, B. and Cotter, P. [8]) content personalisation engine is an example of this type. It uses 3 components namely the profile manager (capture the behaviour and domain preferences of users), personalisation manager (collaborative filtering and content filtering is done here) and presentation manager (includes the HTML, XML and WML presentations). The combination method proves to be quiet effective than the results of the individual methods, as the authors suggest that ClixSmart has been very successful and attracted many customers without significant marketing or advertising.

MIHU [12] is prototype system that demonstrates online decision support for providing customer treatments in Web-based storefronts and information sites, using a combination of technologies. In this system, decisions are made based on a language that incorporates flowchart constructs, rules-based constructs, and a variety of specialized constructs to facilitate reasoning based on heuristics and partial information.

Intelligent Recommendation Analyser (IRA) of IBM T.J.Watson Research Centre [25] uses multiple recommendation methods and technologies to address the need of a different type of product/store requirements etc.

2.2.3 Recommendations and Presentation

Recommendation refers to the output of the data analysis and the mode of delivery to the users. Pednault [5] said, "true personalisation implies not only adapting content for the individual, but also how that content is communicated for maximum effect"

Information derived from the data analysis varies from opinions (like/dislike), products/commodities (books, video, music etc) recommendations, categories (drama, sports, humour etc) and services (enquiries, stock profiles, banking etc). These output is delivered through different modes which may be offline (e-mail) or online (real-time recommendations). Opinion, selected products, tailored services is delivered to the users on the Web in real-time. Also the output categories can be presented on the Web through a set of hyperlinks or through dynamically generated content.

3 Personalisation: Some Considerations

Where to personalize a product or service depends on the nature and marketing potential of the product, information or service, and ambition of the business and its financial potential.

It can be done at clients' side (eg. personalistion tools) or on the Server side (AI-Based personalization). When it is done on the client side, client become responsible for getting personalization from the server or it can modify the information it has received from the server, thus reducing the load of the server. However, server has to transfer the whole information to the client. When the personalization is done on the server, then client becomes passive and no plug-in applications are run on the client. However, scalability becomes an issue when the server is overloaded. The advantages/disadvantages, and scalability of personalizing at client-side and server-sides are fully discussed in [27].

3.1 Personalisation Coordinators

Personalisation Coordinators, as the name implies, coordinates and orchestrates between the variety of suppliers and a customer. They are generally third party services, which 1) help the customers to detail their suitable parameters of a product/service, 2) search their supplier-base to match the users-need and 3) co-ordinate between the customer and the supplier(s) to arrange for product order, delivery etc. Most of the times, the coordinators have nothing to do with the manufacturing of products. For example, Garden.com [29] coordinates the supply chain from its set of over 100 suppliers to deliver the garden products to the needs of individual users. As a first step, it helps the customers to decide what type of garden they want with their climate and land and then it helps them to select different garden products like plants and then with this in mind, it searches their supply-base to arrange order and delivery.

4 Enabling Technologies

Web personalisation is now entering mainstream arena owing to emergence of newer technologies that enrich the way of analysing data and help to predict better about the users' preferences. Technologies such as data mining, neural networks, natural language generation, intelligent agents and eXtensible Markup Language (XML) are enriching Web personalisation.

Data mining refers to analysing a huge volume of data to find out certain relationship among the data that wasn't explicit. Data mining is generally used to find out the relationship of data in huge databases for marketing and other research purposes. Now, Web usage mining and related technologies are gaining ground in Web personalisation. There are different techniques in data mining itself. Vu [25] described how the data mining techniques such as clustering, association, classification and similarity indexing could be used for personalisation. For more details on web usage mining and personalisation, see Spiliopoulou [10].

Neural net is basically a network of neurons arranged in different levels with different activation functions that is trained to arrive at a pre-decided result from a set of given inputs. Neural nets are finding its use in e-commerce as it can handle complicated algorithms and can be 'trained' to automatise certain decision. It is used in personalisation to generally predict the users visit. For example with a set of data of inputs (users' clicks) and outputs (next click), neural nets can be trained so that when such a combination occur on the real time, it can predict where the user will be targeting next.

Natural Language technologies and their utilities in the form of speech recognition, reaction to spoken and written words will become a major technological feature in personalisation. Milosavljevic[26] has explained how this technology can be used in e-commerce with the help of personalised electronic product catalogues.

5   Issues of Personalisation

5.1   Privacy Issues – Personalisation or Personal Intrusion?

Personalisation is all about collecting users' personal preferences and using this information to present tailored products/information/service. As personalisation mainly depends n collecting users' personal data, privacy plays a major role. The business should keep the personal details of the users confidentially and it should be used only for the purpose it has been collected. We briefly describe some of the privacy issues here.

On the one hand, organizations should be careful about what and how the data is collected from the users and how they are going to maintain this data within a department, between departments and organization. Also security of this information is important. On the other side, users are always not 'ready' to give their personal wishes unless they are convinced that their data will be used properly and they will be benefited from that. To convince the users, they should be clearly told about why the information about them is collected and how it will be used.

What is the users' reaction towards privacy issues? According to a survey by personalisation consortium [31], only a few consumers (15% of 4500 users) are unwilling to provide personal information to Web marketers in exchange for better services. Fifty one percent of respondents said they would share personal information in exchange for better service, while 33 percent had no opinion. Seventy three percent of the users are happy if their Web site remembers them and 62 percent of them, in fact said they dislike giving information that has already been provided.

To deal with the privacy issues, W3C has come up with 'Platform for Privacy Preferences Project' (P3P) standard. P3P is a standard architecture and grammar for the expression of users' preferences and Web site practices regarding the collection and exchange of user information. So companies have to adopt this standard, which makes them to deal explicitly what information is required from the user, what information is tracked and how the information will be used for personalisation. P3P states that privacy information should be presented in machine-readable form and hence browsers can read and compare the preferences with the users' choice.

LPWA [27] has tried an approach called 'Annonymizers' to deal with the privacy problems. In this project, the real identity of actual users are hide and only the data collected from them is used for personalisation.

5.2 Technological Issues

When the system is implanted with huge user base, then performance and scaling of the system become the real issues. Hence, depending on the size of the application, user base, number of users expected for the system, offline/on-line recommendation, and response rate, one has to decide on the technologies to be used with the system. For example, MyYahoo has million of pages, which required a custom-defined database to get users' preferences on real-time. Yahoo designed their own database, instead of going for industry database solutions. Performance and scaling is a major issue when the server is overloaded with many users and when real-time processing is attempted for each user. Content caching can be used to improve the performance of the system. What content can be cached to users can be decided by any predictive algorithms. Thus this reduces the workload of the server to some extent.

Knowledge representation becomes important when AI techniques are used in personalisation. Minsky [4] states "To make machines deal with common sense things, we must use multiple way to represent knowledge, acquire huge amounts of that knowledge and find commonsense ways to reason with it."

When the personalisation involves more than one application or when it requires communication between different applications, interoperability becomes an issue. XML and related technologies can solve this problem. See XML section in this paper.

Personalisation Interface should be made simple. Personalisation features should not make users to spend time on learning them. Also users don't want to spend lot of time on initial set-up. If personalisation features require complicated set up and time to learn, then it is against the principle of interface design [30].

6   Conclusion

Personalisation should be considered at the design stage itself and is no more a post-production process. It is not sufficient to think about the personalisation during the implementation stages. Several research papers in this area suggest different methodologies for including personalisation at the design stage. Object-Oriented Hypermedia Design Method (OOHDM [11]) is one such attempt.

Personlaisation and related technologies are improving. However, matching technologies is not sufficiently well developed to safely predict what will be interesting to users. Further, personalisation is time-dependent, means people may have different wishes at different times, so just basing on the past will not hold good in all the cases. For example, if someone is shopping for a friend, then the user may show different preferences in the new visit.

Web personalisation is assuming greater significance and relevance now as many different people use the Web for different purposes.

References

1. Wells, N. and Wolfers, J. Finance with a personalised touch, *Communication of the ACM,* Aug 2000, Vol.43, NO.8, pp: 31 – 34.
2. Hagen, H. and Souza, R. Smart Personalisation. *The Forrester Report (July 1999).*
3. Kramer, J. Noronha, S. and Vergo, J. A user-cantered design approach to Personalisation, *Communication of the ACM,* Aug 2000, Vol.43, NO.8, pp: 45 – 48.
4. Minsky, M. Commonsense-Based Interfaces, *Communication of the ACM,* Aug 2000, Vol.43, NO.8, pp: 67-73.
5. Pednault, E.P.D. Representation is everything, *Communication of the ACM,* Aug 2000, Vol.43, NO.8, pp: 80-83.
6. Maglio, P. and Barrett, R. Intermediaries personalise information streams, *Communication of the ACM,* Aug 2000, Vol.43, NO.8, pp: 96 – 101.
7. Davison, B.D. and Hirsh, H. Predicting sequences of user actions. *Predicting the Future: AI Approaches to Time-Series Problems.* Tech. Report WS-98-07, AAAI Press.
8. Smyth, B. and Cotter, P. A Personalised television listings service, *Communication of the ACM,* Aug 2000, Vol.43, NO.8, pp: 107 – 111.
9. Mulvenna, M.D., Anand, S.S. and Buchner, A.G. Personalisation on the Net using Web Mining, *Communication of the ACM,* Aug 2000, Vol.43, NO.8, pp: 123 – 125.
10. Spiliopoulou, M. Web usage mining for Web site evaluation, *Communication of the ACM,* Aug 2000, Vol.43, NO.8, pp: 127 – 134.
11. Rossi, G. Schwabe, D. and Guimaraes, R. Designing personalised Web applications, *WWW10, May 1-5, 2001, Hong Kong*, pp: 275 – 284.
12. Anupam, V. Hull, R. and Kumar, B. Personalizing E-commerce Applications with On-line Heuristic Decision Making. *WWW 10, May 1-5, 2001, Hong Kong*, pp: 296 – 307.
13. Steger, H. and Smith, M. Evaluating the sticky factors of E-Commerce sites, Rubric, 1999.
14. Luedi, A.F. Personalise or Perish, *Electronic Markets*, Vol.7 No. 3, pp: 22 25.
15. IBM high volume Web site team, Web site Personalisation, 2000, wsyiwyg://14/http://www7b.boulder…echarticles/hvws/personalise.html
16. NetPerceptions. NetPerceptions recommendation Engine. www.netperceptions.com, 1999
17. Macromedia. Likeminds. www.macromedia.com/, 1999.
18. Breese, J.S., Hackerman, D. and Kadie,C. Empirical analysis of predictive algorithms for collaborative filtering. In *Proceedings of the Fourteenth Conference on Uncertainty in Artificial Intelligence,* pp: 43 – 52, July 1998.
19. Broadvision Technologies. Broadvision. www.broadvision.com, 1999.
20. Personify. Personify technologies. www.personfiy.com, 1999.
21. Accrue. Accrue technologies. www.accrue.com, 1999.
22. VanderMeer, D., Dutta, K. and Datta, A. Enabling Scalable Online Personalisation on the Web, *EC'2000*, Oct 2000, Minneapolis, Minnesota.
23. Shardanand, U. and Maes, P. Social Information Filtering: Algorithms for Automating "Word of Mouth". *Proceedings of the Conference on Human factors in Computing Systems – CHI '95,* 1995
24. Balabanovic. M. and Shoham, Y. *Content-Based, Collaborative Recommendation. Communications of the ACM,* Vo. 40, No.3, 1997.
25. Yu, P.S. Data Mining and Personalisation Technologies, *IEEE,* 1999.

26. Milosavljevic, M. Electronic Commerce via Personalised Virtual Electronic Catalogues. CollECTeR'98, 1998, pp: 26 – 37.
27. Bowne. Open Sesame Technical White Paper, Bowne International Solutions, 1999.
28. Wind, Y. 2001. The Challenge of "Customereization" in Financial Services. *Communications of the ACM,* June 2001, Vol44, No.6, pp: 39 – 44.
29. http://www.garden.com
30. Nielsen, J. 1998, Personalisation is Over-Rated.
    http://www.useit.com/alertbox/98/1004.html
31. Personalisation Consortium. 2000, at www.personalization.org

Business-Oriented Web Personalization: A Decision-Making Approach

Carlos Alberto Odorico de Moraes Filho and Francilene Procpio Garcia

Computer Science Department - UFPB
carlin@dsc.ufpb.br, francilene@ieee.org

Abstract. This article brings an overview about personalization conducts and their impacts on the organization's businesses, presenting and organizing critical aspects to the development of full personalization patterns within e-Business systems. There are two key purposes of what we call full personalization: websites personalization - more usual and known and, the business process personalization - more strategic and less usual. A decision-making approach based on the application of the score method is recommended. A tool - Person_DSS, was then developed to support executives and technical staffs, providing a ranking of the key technologies. Results of a case study accomplished in a food distribution organization are also presented.

Introduction

In view of the information technology (IT) dissemination everywhere together with the growing use of the Internet, new ways has emerged to carry out business operations - usually named as e-Business.

The e-Business arrives modifying the main organization's beliefs, encouraging people to reflect on their businesses strategies, including factors such as: (1) reengineering of internal and external processes; (2) restructuring of the organization toward Internet; (3) finding how better to go with the targeted market expectations; and (4) finding how to address such targeted markets to obtain and guarantee a larger retention of customers and/or partners.

It is assumed e-Business as a new paradigm, performing own rules and needing a specific business model. This new model, Internet driven, comes with a new culture focusing on a trusted relationship with customers and partners, originating the fundaments of the full personalization.

Most of the publications treat personalization just as the changes covering the websites structures. In this article, this abstraction is extended to full personalization, which represents the combination of websites and business processes personalization.

Business process personalization is occupied with the customization and/or optimization done through the application of IT, influencing directly the business processes. This personalization pattern expects to reach the customers and partners, generating powerful impacts on the organization.

J. Liu et al. (Eds.): AMT 2001, LNCS 2252, pp. 77–82, 2001.

In the case of websites personalization, the main focus is on the several types of content filtering. These filtering methods always act in some way to offer better alternatives to the final users while surfing in the Internet. That increases the degree of the customer's fidelity to websites, besides to foster a potential growth in the sales.

By way of the full personalization, new business opportunities can emerge. The key entities inside of e-Business systems, in general oriented to reach at some point a full personalization, are presented in the Figure 1.

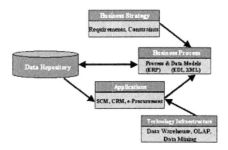

Fig. 1. Development model of e-Business systems.

The evolution of the e-Business

For the organizations, the effective use of new technologies is the key for the success in the Internet era. IT begins to be applied within the organization, starting from the usual task automation until the business models restructuring.

The main characteristics of e-Business systems are:

– Integrate the organization to reach more flexibility. The value chain components can be connected to share the same information;
– Supply a whole vision about the organization and its customers;
– Reduce operational costs;
– Integrate suppliers.

The evolution of IT applications in business environments (Figure 2) is characterized by initial phases, where individual productivity tools go on, up to the arrival at some point of total integration, where internal and external business processes breed new processes views.

Some stages of the systems evolution are arranged taking into consideration the degree of IT applications in the organizations. When the internal and external processes converge to some point, new processes arise supporting full personalization inside e-Business systems.

When the organization reaches a required level of integration and convergence, all the information on business processes is stored in a central repository - a Data Warehouse or a database, for instance.

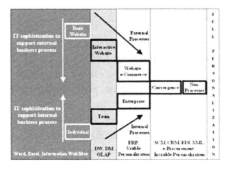

Fig. 2. How the systems evolve to reach at full personalization [1].

Personalization versus e-Business

Throughout the materialization of the Internet and e-Business systems, the customer became the key element of the business; a gratified customer buys and comes back again.

The benefits achieved by a personalized e-Business system can be extremely interesting. However, that is costly. Still a business process restructuring requires a larger adaptation to the new technologies in order to obtain advantages. In this way, it seems that for an organization to enter into the virtual world with a greater possibility of success, it may require:

- Evaluate if its business process is ready to be extended and/or integrated together with its partners' business process;
- Verify the value chain of the information generated by the organization;
- Verify the hardware and software infrastructure required to support the new applications;
- Verify the capacity of its staff to assimilate changes, and the will of the direction to implement these new technologies.

In summary, all organization that intends to implement full personalization in its systems should first rethink its business before try a larger integration with its partners and customers.

The Person_DSS System

Strategy of the Solution

The system intends to support decision-making process to achieve a progressive full personalization in the business context of the organization. The decision-making approach applies a quantitative technique - the scoring method.

The user of the tool, an individual or a group, evaluates and judges the questions according to their degrees of relevance for the organization's business context. The result of this evaluation presents a ranking of technologies that better support the full personalization.

System Functionalities

The internal operation of the tool is shown in the Figure 3. There are two components: one to outline technologies having in mind the basic elements of an e-Business system, and one to filter the current situation in the organization. These two components handle inputs, the analysis in the processing step, and all the reports.

The initial inputs are obtained by way of answers supplied by the decision-maker concerning to the current situation of the organization, including particularities of the market niche. The filter processing tries to find if the organization is able or interested in any business-oriented personalization pattern. Its function is to indicate if the decision-maker is ready to go on.

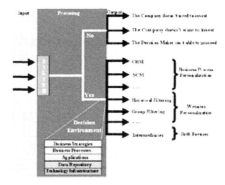

Fig. 3. Person_DSS tool - Internal operation.

Before the process to proceed, it is verified if the answers supplied by the decision-maker arrived at a minimum score of 50% of the feasible total. Otherwise, the system suggests three possible alternatives to decision-maker's thinking.

If the given answers exceed the necessary score (larger than 50%), the system will process others questions concerning to the five basic architectural components of a typical e-business system - business strategy, business process, applications, data repository and technology infrastructure (as illustrated in the Figure 1).

Just after the decision-maker gives any score to any pointed question, that score is added to the final sum of alternatives technologies. At the end of the processing phase, a ranking of the most important technologies to that organization is provided.

While elaborating the set of questions, as Table 1 illustrates, their corresponding weights, and the relationships with alternatives technologies, it was applied a set of suggestions and comments given by interviews done in a market survey. In addition, it was considered few published investigations about real cases of web personalization and suggestions of specialists and business-people.

In order to balance different opinions of decision-makers in the same organization, Person_DSS performs a comparison report among the evaluations. As result of this comparison report, it can be visualized if the decision-makers' opinions are addressing similar goals to organization based on personalization.

Question	Technologies	Weights
Business Strategy		
Does the company have a fidelity program?	CRM	10
Business Process		
Does the company have electronic data exchange?	EDI, SCM, XML	8
Applications		
Is there easy support for developed applications?	Intermediary Filtering rules	9
Data Repository		
Does the company have data replication?	Intermediary	10
Technology Infrastructure		
Does it support easy expansion?	Inference, Group filtering, OLAP, Data Mining	7

Fig. 4. Questions, Technologies and Weights

Person_DSS: A case study

Organization profile

To apply the Person_DSS tool in a real case, it was selected a food distribution organization - Distribuidora Internacional de Alimentos S.A. (International Food Dealer) - DIA. This organization operates in the northeast of Brazil, its headquarter is in Natal-RN, and other two branches are placed in the cities of Campina Grande-PB and Aracaju-SE.

Accomplished results

The major results obtained in the application of the tool Person_DSS to guide the organization on full personalization alternatives are demonstrated in the Figure 4.

Through the results obtained at the end of the evaluation, it is perceived that the organization needs to improve the electronic data interchange among the head quarter, the branches, and partners - note that EDI and XML got the highest percentage.

Ok key importance to DIA is also customer relationship and supply chain management. This shows that DIA is aware with the new world tendencies for such business sector. Its score for CRM was 80% and for SCM was 70%.

Other technologies are also suitable to foster DIA in the full personalization process of its systems, such as e-Procurement (62%), ERP (58%), Data Mining (52,5), and Data Warehouse (52%). The changes suggested may generate new investments and high risks, being recommended to measure some aspects to control ROI.

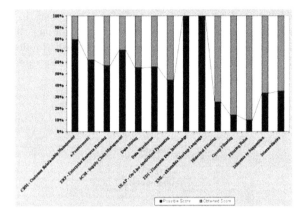

Fig. 5. Results of the evaluation done in the organization DIA.

Conclusion

It was verified along this article that to achieve a full personalization, in general, it is necessary some way of processes reengineering (internal and external). Other key factor investigated shows that to arrive at full personalization, the website may aggregate value to the business and, not only, support the sale process (e-Commerce).

To apply better IT solutions in the organizations, it should be considered multiple criteria such as technology, administrative, and financial factors, besides being necessary a global vision of the targeted market. It is known that these factors vary according to the personalization degree that each organization wants to reach. After to investigate all these relative factors, it was possible to arrive at a consistent decision support toll - the tool Person_DSS.

Acknowledgments

To whole functional body of the DIA organization, for the contribution and support. To National Science and Technology Commission (CNPq) for the scholarship supported during this research.

References

1. Ginige, A., Murugesan, S., Kazanis, P.: A Road Map for Sucessfully Transforming SMEs into e-Business. Cutter IT Journal, v. 14, n 5, (2001) 39-49

A Personalized Interface Agent with Feedback Evaluation

Weihua Li [1] and Xiaodong Fu [2]

[1] Guangdong University of Technology, Guangzhou, China
lw@gdut.edu.cn
[2] Guangdong Education Institute, Guangzhou, China

Abstract. This paper introduces a human-Web interface agent for Web information search and filtering. It presents the architecture of the personalized interface agent and its implement scheme. It discusses the problem of relevant feedback evaluation for updating the user interest profile. It proposes to use a decision tree to learn user information interests from sets of documents that users have classified. The decision tree is transformed into a Boolean query string that improves the agent's filtering ability.

1 Introduction

With the rapid development and extensive use of WWW, "information overload" arises on Internet. Vast amount of Emails, net-news, electronic commercial advertisements and query results returned by search engines are poured out to users. People have to sift out useful information from thousands pieces of data, like sift gold from sand. They hope to have automatic tools to do this work, which results in the research of information filtering software system.

Traditional software tools are not suitable for building information filtering system used on WWW. As the users' information interests are variable, it is difficult to model users' variable interest preferences by unchangeable software. As a matter of fact, however, these are exactly the kinds of problems that intelligent agent techniques were designed to attack! An agent is a self-contained program capable of controlling its own decision-making and acting, based on its perception of its environment, in pursuit of one or more objectives [1]. Let the filtering agent learn user's interest by the machine-learning technique. For example, it records that on a particular home page, the user always downloads new papers by a certain author. Once this is established, the agent can begin to do this itself, on behalf of the user.

This paper introduces a personalized human-Web interface agent that can search and filter information on the Web for users. The agent can request to some search engines, extract relevant information and return the filtered information according to the user's interests. It uses relevant feedback evaluation algorithms to update the user interest profile. The interface agent works on a WWW client and is built by Java language. The paper is organized as follows. In next section it describes the roles of hu-

J. Liu et al. (Eds.): AMT 2001, LNCS 2252, pp. 83–89, 2001.

man-Web interface agent. In section 3, it presents the implement scheme of the interface agent for Web information search and filtering. In section 4, it discusses the relevant feedback algorithm and shows how to update the user interest profile by evaluation. The last section will be the conclusions.

2 Human-Web Interface

Search engines and classified directories have become essential tools for locating information on the World Wide Web [2]. Automated search engines, while being the most comprehensive tools in terms of Web coverage, are particularly prone to inaccuracy. Manually maintained classified directories, although intuitive to use and largely accurate, cover just a small fraction o the information available. In general tools for information resource discovery on the World Wide Web suffer, to varying degrees, from being:
− incomplete - i.e. they do not cover all the information available; and
− inaccurate - they contain information that is out of date, incorrect or classified incorrectly and they provide users with poor quality, often irrelevant information.

If users need accurate and complete Web information, they need an approach to sift out useful information from thousands pieces of data returned by search engines. This results in one kind of human-Web interface software for information filtering.

Information filtering is a name used to describe a variety of processes involving the delivery of information to people who need it. The following features are the most commonly mentioned characteristics or features of the filtering system [3]:
− An information filtering system is an information system designed for unstructured or semistructured data.
− Information filtering systems deal primarily with textual information.
− Filtering system involve large amounts of data.
− Filtering applications typically involve streams of incoming data.
− Filtering is based on descriptions of individual or group information preferences.
− Filtering is often meant to imply the removal of data from an incoming stream.

One of the main problems in building a system for personalized information filtering is the construction of a profile of the user's information interests [4]. There are three subproblems involved. The first is finding a representation for the user profile that allows both power and flexibility. Second, it is important that user be able to communicate her desires and interests to the system so that an initial profile can be constructed. Finally, the system has to be responsive and change this initial profile as the interests of the user change over time.

Traditional software tools are not suitable for building changeable information filtering system. In order to overcome the above problems, this paper proposes to build a human-Web interface agent to facilitate user filtering the Web-available incoming information. Intelligent agency is a crucial tool in coping with the complexities of the information-rich problems imposed by the explosion of data residing on the current and future Internet. Intelligent agent-based systems, employing intelligent and autonomous problem-solving agents, can constantly sift the available sources of information on user behalf.

For the first subproblem, this interface agent uses the most widely known vector space model [5] to represent the user profile. The model treats texts and queries as vectors in a multidimensional space, the dimensions of which are the words used to represent the texts. Queries and texts are compared by the vectors, using, for examples, the cosine correlation similarity measure.

This representation is both power and flexibility. The query or text representation can be weighted to take account of their importance. The agent records the user's interests in the knowledge base, arranging them in a weighted vector. It compares the interest vector with the Web document vectors and reorders them according to the similarity values. The user may neglect the results at the end of the list.

For the second subproblem, the interface agent lets user input keywords, relevant words or irrelevant words. The agent observes what the user requests and records down into the initial profile.

For the third subproblem, the interface agent gives each interest a time weight. On one hand, if the user continually requests the same interest, its time weight will increase. On the other hand, if time elapse, the time weight will decrease. Therefore, the out-of-date interests will be deleted.

Agent-based information filtering system needs to dynamically extract information from unfamiliar documents. Some systems rely on a pre-specified description of certain fixed classes of Web documents. Agents rely on a combination of test queries and domain-specific knowledge to automatically learn descriptions of Web services. Intelligent agents can use the learned descriptions to enable automatic information extraction. For example, an agent can learn to extract information from unfamiliar resources by querying them with familiar objects and matching the output returned against knowledge about the query objects.

3   The Interface Agent Implement Scheme

Maes defines interface agents as: Computer programs that employ artificial intelligence techniques in order to provide assistance to a user dealing with a particular application. The metaphor is that of a personal assistant who is collaborating with the user in the same work environment [6].

The artificial intelligence techniques that our interface agent employs are knowledge base and machine learning approaches. The agent is given a minimum of background knowledge, and it learns appropriate "behavior" from the user. It can become gradually more helpful and competent. The learning approach also presents a satisfactory solution to the trust problem. If the agent gradually develops its abilities, the user is also given time to gradually build up a model of how the agent makes decisions, which is one of the prerequisites for a trust relationship. Furthermore, the particular learning approach adopted allows the agent to give "explanations" for its reasoning and behavior in a language the user is familiar with, namely in terms of past examples similar to the current situation.

The agent has a knowledge base to record the relative data and regulars. A user features table in the knowledge base records the interested and uninterested subjects of that user. Each subject will be given a weight value to indicate the degree that the user concerned. The agent has a reasoning machine to change the weight value and renew its knowledge base. The reasoning is based on user features table and user information table. There is a manage subsystem controlling the internal states of the agent.

The interface agent consists of observation, training and feedback mechanisms. The observation mechanism records what documents or Web service the user regularly visits. The training mechanism can train the agent by inputting subjects the user is interested. Both mechanisms can construct a user initial profile. The feedback mechanism receives direct feedback or indirect feedback from the user and rapidly collects the data the agent needs to learn. This mechanism can change the initial profile as the interests of the user change over time.

The agent has a graphics user interface to interact with a user. It posts the user's request to some popular automated search engines and gets results from them. It then extracts relevant information from the search results to form the vectors. The agent calculates the cosine correlation similarity of the result vectors and the user interest vector in the knowledge base. If the similarity is great than a threshold value, the relevant information will send to the user. Otherwise it will be deleted.

The system is built by Java Development Kits version 1.2 (JDK1.2). Java has excellent network properties and is suitable for Web programming. The knowledge base is built by relational database such as Microsoft Access. Java system uses JDBC API to access databases. SQL language is used to abstract knowledge and to reason. For example, the following three steps will recommend user's interested information to users:

- SELECT a Web document FROM visited set WHERE the order of the document¡Ü20;
- SELECT close related words FROM related words table WHERE subjects in Table 1;
- SELECT a Web site information (including URL subjects) FROM retrieve database, visited sites set WHERE (subjects in table 1) OR (subjects in table 2).

In order to update the user profile incrementally and continuously, the system uses relevant feedback to learn user interests. The next section will discuss this evaluation approach in details.

4   Relevant Feedback

There are several machine learning approaches that can be used to learn a user profile, such as Bayesian classifier, Nearest Neighbor, PEBLS, Decision Trees, TF-IDF, Neural Nets [7].

The interface agent uses a decision trees to learn user information interests from sets of message or other online documents that users have classified. The agent learns from sample documents that users submit while browsing, without surveying them as to their interest in a set of sample documents. This makes the agent significantly easier to use than other preference-learning agent. After the system gives filtering results, the user may tell the agent whether a document is relevant or irrelevant to him.

The agent uses the feedback sample sets to induce a decision tree, by ID3 algorithm. ID3 is a recursive algorithm proposed by Quinlan [8] to induce decision tree from samples. It is assumed that the sample sets are described by eigenvector <f1(u), f2(u),...,fk(u)>, in which fi(i=1,...,k) are Boolean variable. Thus the goal conception is a Boolean function of f1,..., fk. The decision tree of which is the induced result.

The ID3 algorithm is written by Java. The first step is collecting the sample set. The program uses FileInputString(String name) class to get the user feedbacks. The key codes are as follows:

```
FileInputString istream=new FileInputString("lwh.txt");
DataInputStream ds=new DataInputStream(istream);
While ((b=ds.readLine())!=null) {
   StringTokenizer st=new StringTokenizer(b, ",");
   ...
}
```

The second step is building the decision tree. The program uses static void Creattree(BintNode node, Res arr[], String zhen1[], String fu1[]) class to build the tree. The key codes are finding the root node:

```
if ((tp!=1.0)&&(tp!=0.0))
  A=tp*Math.log(tp)/Math.log(2)+(1-tp)*Math.log(1-
tp)/Math.log(2);
else if((tp1!=1.0)&&(tp1!=0.0))
  B=tp1*Math.log(tp1)/Math.log(2)+(1-tp1)*Math.log(1-
tp1)/Math.log(2);
  else B=0;
tt=tp2*A+(1-tp2)*B;
fin[bu3/2].value=-tt;
...
BintNode root=new BintNode();
creattree(root,fin,zhen1,fu1);
...
```

Once the agent has induced a decision tree, it transforms the tree into a Boolean query string. This transformation is quite straightforward. The key codes are as follows:

```
while (buffer1.parent!=null) {
  if (buffer1.parent.rchild==buffer1)
    tt=tt+"!"+buffer1.parent.value.trim()+"&&";
  else
    tt=tt+buffer1.parent.value.trim()+"&&";
  buffer1=buffer1.parent;
}
```

The agent uses this learned query strings to update the user profile. For example, if the profile has an interest record of "computer", now it will become "computer&&software&&!hardware".

The above ID3 algorithm needs extract semantically significant phrases from each document [9]. The interface agent avoids extracting from the whole document, because this processing is extremely costly. The agent checks the keywords that are presented in the TITLE, HEAD, URL, KEYWORDS, DESCRIPTION, and TEXT tags. The results indicate that this extraction tactic is useful in practice.

The experimental results show that the interface agent greatly facilitates users search and filtering the Web-available information.

5   Conclusion

Automated search engines scan millions of Web documents that contain keywords. They return many responses that are irrelevant, outdated, or unavailable, forcing the person to manually sift through the responses searching for useful information. This is the situation that filtering system demands: WWW documents are semistructured data and they are textual information. There are large amounts of returned documents and they come like a stream. Filtering these returned documents must accord with users' information preferences. Last, WWW documents are removed from the returned stream.

The potential of information filtering to help people sifting and visualize the contents of the Web is enormous. But the richness and diversity of information sources has brought problems. Intelligent agents are the suitable technological devices in Web document filtering. These kinds of agents pose some fairly big problem for the machine-learning community.

This research is funded by Guangdong Provincial Natural Science Foundation.

References

1. Jennings, N., Wooldridge, M.: Software agents. IEE REVIEW 1 (1996) 17-20.
2. Jenkins, C., Jackson, M., Burden, P., Wallis, J.: Searching the World Wide Web: an evaluation of available tools and methodologies. Information and Software Technology 39 (1998) 985-994.
3. Belkin, N.J., Croft, W.B.: Information Filtering and Information Retrieval: Two Sides of the Same Coin? Commun. ACM 12 (1992) 29-38.
4. Sheth, B., Maes, P.: Evolving agents for personalized information filtering. In: Proceedings of the Ninth IEEE Conference on AI for Applications. IEEE, New York (1993) 345-352.
5. Salton, G., McGill, M.J.: Introduction to Modern Information Retrieval. McGraw-Hill (1983).
6. Meas, P.: Social interface agents: Acquiring competence by learning from users and other agents. Software Agents-Papers from the 1994 Sping Symposium, AAAI Press (1994) 71-78.

7. Sycara, K.P.: Levels of Adaptivity in Systems of Coordinating Information Agents. In: Klusch, M., Weiß, G. (eds): Cooperative Information Agents II. Springer-Verlag, Berlin Heidelberg New York (1998) 172-189.
8. Quinlan, R.: Learning Efficient Classification Procedure and Their Application Chess And Game. In: Michalski, R.S., Carbonell, J.G., Mitchell, T.M. (eds): Machine Learning: An Artificial Intelligence Approach. Tioga Publishing, Palo Alto (1983).
9. Krulwich, B., Burkey, C.: The InfoFinder Agent: Learning User Interests through Heuristic Phrase Extraction. IEEE Expert 12 (1997) 22-27.

VHML – Directing a Talking Head

Andrew Marriott[1], Simon Beard[1], John Stallo[2], and Quoc Huynh[1]

[1] School of Computing, Curtin University of Technology,
Hayman Rd. Bentley, Western Australia.
{raytrace,beardsw,huynhqh}@cs.curtin.edu.au
http://www.vhml.org/

[2] Microsoft Corporation, One Microsoft Way
Redmond, WA 98052-6399, USA.
johnsta@microsoft.com

Abstract. The computer revolution in Active Media Technology has recently made it possible to have Talking Head interfaces to applications and information. Users may, with plain English queries, interact with a lifelike computer generated image that responds to them with computer generated speech using textual information coming from a knowledge base. This paper details the research being done at Curtin University in creating a Virtual Human Markup Language (VHML) that allows these interactive Talking Heads to be directed by text marked up in XML. This direction makes the interaction more effective. The language is designed to accommodate the various aspects of Human-Computer Interaction with regards to Facial Animation, Body Animation, Dialogue Manager interaction, Text to Speech production, Emotional Representation plus Hyper and Multi Media information. This paper also points to audio and visual examples of the use of the language as well as user evaluation of an interactive Talking Head that uses VHML. VHML is currently being used in several Talking Head applications as well as a Mentoring System. Finally we discuss planned future experiments using VHML for two Talking Head demonstrations / evaluations. The VHML development and implementation is part of a three-year European Union Fifth Framework project called InterFace.

1 Introduction

The Virtual Human Markup Language (VHML) uses / builds on existing (de facto) standards such as those specified by the W3C Voice Browser Activity, and adds new tags to accommodate functionality that is not catered for. The language is XML/XSL based and consists of the following sub-systems:

- •DMML   Dialogue Manager Markup Language
- •FAML   Facial Animation Markup Language
- •BAML   Body Animation Markup Language
- •SML   Speech Markup Language
- •EML   Emotion Markup Language
- •GML   Gesture Markup Language

J. Liu et al. (Eds.): AMT 2001, LNCS 2252, pp. 90–100, 2001.
© Springer-Verlag Berlin Heidelberg 2001

Although general in nature, the intent of VHML is to facilitate the realistic and natural interaction of a Talking Head/Talking Human (TH) with a user. One specific intended use can be found in the deliverables of the InterFace project (http://www.ist-interface.org/) and general applications can be found in Pandzic [1].

In 1999, the Facial Animation research group at Curtin University developed an FAQBot Talking Head [2] that provided spoken answers to natural language enquiries from users about Frequently Asked Questions. The enquiry was matched against the FAQBot's domain knowledge base to provide a vocal, textual and visual response. The FAQBot had a persona that modified the visual response dependent upon whether the TH was basically a happy, hesitant, sombre, etc type of person. The FAQBot was an instance of a generic MPEG-4 TH – other TH applications such as a Virtual SalesPerson, a Virtual Story Teller and a Virtual Lecturer were also created in 2000.

Figure 1, in the lower left-hand corner, shows the visible part of a TH application - an MPEG-4 compliant Facial Animation Engine (FAE) [3]. The invisible part is the Text to Speech Synthesis (TTS) system, the Artificial Intelligence (AI) system and the Personality system. The user types their question into the TH client and this sends it across the MPEG-4 network to the Dialogue Manager (the server). The server works out what was requested, gets the appropriate response, converts that into audio plus FAPs to control what the face does and then sends these back across the network to the client so that the TH speaks the response. With MPEG-4 technology, the interaction can take place across a very low bandwidth channel and hence is available to the home user.

The Artificial Intelligence sub-system is based upon research on Agents ([4] as well as at http://www.cs.bham.ac.uk/~amw/agents), Intelligent Tutoring Systems (Farrow [5], Inlärning [6] and the Tap Project [7]), Chatterbots and Natural Language Parsing [8].

This TH system has been seen to be acceptable as an HCI [2] with effective use of the system being detailed in Marriott [9] and an improved version using an early version of VHML in Marriott et al [10].

2   Extensible Markup Language (XML)

In figure 1, the information returned from the server Knowledge Base should be marked up in such a way that it is easily parsed, searched, categorized, etc and this implies a consistent markup language. Also the final rendering and delivery of the marked up text depends upon whether the output scene is text only, audio only, face or full body and could be in many forms:

- a straight textual interface for a very low bandwidth interface,
- an interactive Web based multi and hyper media display,
- a voice enabled system which lets the user hear the answer,
- a Talking Head system with complex facial gestures and voice which shows the personality or emotion of the Talking Head,
- an entire synthetic human figure with body language.

The information markup should stay the same but the way in which it is displayed should change dependent upon the form of output - textual, vocal, Talking Head, Body Language. XML and XSL provides this technology.

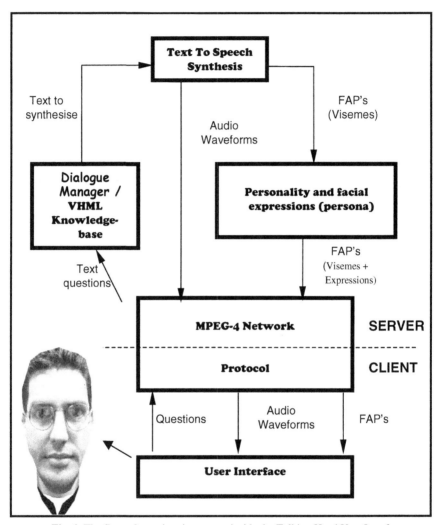

Fig. 1. The flow of questions/responses inside the Talking Head User Interface

XML is the Extensible Markup Language [11]. It is a simplified dialect of the Standard Generalized Markup Language (SGML) that is relatively easy to learn, use and implement, and at the same time retains much of the power of SGML. It is important to note that XML is not a markup language in itself, but rather it is a *meta-language* - a language for describing other languages. Therefore, XML allows a user to specify the tag set and grammar of their own custom markup language.

Using XML is easy. The text of figure 2 may be the Knowledge Base response to the user enquiry "What are you?" and has been marked up with a VHML sublanguage – DMML. It would become plain text after the substitution of the XML atomic tags. (This is not the normal way in which XML does substitution of string values that are constant but the values shown are not necessarily constant).

```
<first_name/>, <welcome/>. I am <mentorName/>.
I was developed by <mentorMaster/>.
<mentorDescription/>
<mentorPurpose/>
You can find out more about me from <mentorHomeURL/>.
```

Fig. 2. Segment of XML marked up text showing the use of atomic tags

In a normal interactive session, the Talking Head client will (hopefully) know the name of the user. This name may be used to set a Dialogue Manager variable that can be used later in conversation. In this example, `<first_name/>` is the stored name of the user who is making the enquiry, `<welcome/>` is a language dependant greeting that has been set dependant upon the user's home country or domain name, `<mentorName/>` is the name of the Dialogue Manager, etc. So the final plain text may become something like:

Freda, Guten Tag. I am Mentor. I was developed by Andrew Marriott. ….

Some of the DMML atomic tags are set dynamically for each user, some are set dynamically once per user session and some are semi-hard coded into the system.

The text in figure 3 contains VHML markup tags that could be used to add emotional, facial and speech effects to the response. These tags and their effect would need to be suppressed for a text only display but would add emotion to a voice and/or facial rendering. It is also necessary to cater for varied functionality in the voice producer. That is, is it *possible* to use the emotion tags to affect the voice with this specific TTS system? Some tags may not be enforceable on some TTS systems.

```
<sad>
 You <emph>said</emph> to me once <pause length="short"/>
 that pathos left you unmoved, but that beauty,
 <emph affect="b" level="moderate">mere</emph> beauty,
 could fill your eyes with tears.
</sad>
```

Fig. 3. Text marked up with complex XML tags to specify emotion

Notice that the `<mentorHomeURL/>` in figure 2 would probably become a URL and hence the pure text may contain "http://www....". Therefore, in the "rendering" :

1. A web based display may turn that into a link
2. A vocal display may have to change the text into something like "You can find out more about me *from the link www.blah*".
3. A Talking Head may say the above and also open up a new browser window.
4. A Virtual Human may point to the link, etc.

XSL is a stylesheet language designed to be used with XML data and documents to help in the different "renderings". Unlike HTML, which defines the rendering or display behaviour for each of its elements, XML says absolutely nothing about how the data is to be displayed. XSL allows the author to apply formatting operations to XML elements. XSL is a language in which the author can indicate that the *<emph>* element should be ignored or should be rendered (by the Face and/or the TTS).

Finally, severely marked up information (figure 4) containing complex vocal, facial gesture and perhaps body language tags must also be displayed realistically on a display that can effect all the required marked up functionality. We can convert this marked up text into the appropriate format by using the XML document plus XSL.

```
<vhml>
<p><neutral>
 The bartender <l_roll intensity="5"
 duration="1500"/>takes out his six-shooter and
 <smile intensity="5" duration="2000"/>
 <emph level="moderate">shoots</emph> the dog in the
 <emph>leg</emph>,
 and the dog runs out the saloon, <emph level="moderate"
 affect="b"> <hu intensity="7" duration="1800"/><r_roll
 intensity="5" duration="1800"/>howling</emph> in pain.
</neutral></p>
<p><neutral>
 Three <emph>years</emph> later, the <nod intensity="4"
 duration="1000"/> wee dog appears <emph target="e">
 again</emph>, wearing boots, jeans, <l_roll
 intensity="4" duration="1000"/><pause length="short"/>
 chaps, a Stetson,<r_roll intensity="5"
 duration="1000"/><nod intensity="5" duration="1000"/>
 gun belt, and <emph level="moderate">
 guns</emph>. He ambles <rate speed="-30%"> slowly
 <l_roll intensity="5" duration="2000"/><nod
 intensity="5" duration="2000"/> </rate> into the
 saloon, goes up to the <hd intensity="6"
 duration="2950"/>bar, leans <emph level="strong">
 over</emph> it, and says to the  bartender,
</neutral></p>
<p><neutral><speaker gender="male" name="us1">
 'I'm here to <l_roll intensity="5" duration="1000"/>
 <emph affect="b" level="moderate">git</emph> the man
 that <smile 4 intensity="1000"/> shot muh <emph
 level="moderate">paw</emph>.' </speaker>
</neutral> </p>
</vhml>
```

Fig. 4. Complex VHML tagged text

3   VHML Structure

Detail of the design and implementation of the VHML rendering onto a Talking Head can be found in Marriott [10]. A preliminary document specifying the structure of VHML can be found in VHML [12].

VHML uses sub-languages to facilitate the direction of a Virtual Human interacting with a user via a Web page or stand alone application. For example, a Virtual Human that has to give some bad news to the user - "I'm sorry Dave, I can't find that file you want." – may speak in a sad way, with a sorry face and with a bowed body stance. In a similar way, a different message may be delivered with a happy voice, a smiley face and with a lively body. VHML tags such as `<smile>`, `<anger>`, `<surprised>` (figure 5) have been specified to produce the required vocal, facial and emotional actions.

---

smile

Description:

   The `smile` element, as the name suggest animates the expression of a smile in the Talking Head animation.

   The mouth is widened and the corners pulled back towards the ears. The larger the `intensity` value for the `smile` element, the greater the intensity of the smile. However a value too large, produces a rather "cheesy" looking grin and can look disconcerting or phony. This however can be used to the animator's advantage, if a mischievous grin or masking smile is required.

   The `smile` element is generally used to start sentences and is used quite often when accentuating positive or cheerful words in the spoken text .

Attributes: Default EML Attributes.
               duration must have a value.

Properties: none (Atomic element).

Example:

   `<smile duration="5000"/>` Potatoes must be almost as good as chocolate to eat!

Fig. 5. Example VHML tag definition

4   Examples and Evaluation

Audio examples of VHML marked up text can be found in JRPIT [13], movies of a Talking Head using VHML in JRPIT [14] and experiment evaluation details in JRPIT [15].

Table 1 shows the results of user classification of these 2 Talking Head experiments with / without speech markup. A similar experiment was done with speech and facial markup.

Table 1: Participant responses when asked to choose the Talking Head that was more understandable/expressive/natural/interesting.

Demonstration	Understandable	Expressive	Natural	Interesting
TH 1	2.2%	4.4%	15.6%	2.2%
TH 2 (early VHML)	82.2%	86.7%	71.1%	84.4%
Neither	15.6%	8.9%	13.3%	13.3%

Both experiments indicate that a TH with markup is perceived to be *more interesting, understandable, natural/human like,* and *expressive.* Therefore a student using a VHML Virtual Lecturer is likely to remember and understand more, a customer of a VHML Virtual SalesPerson is likely to return to the e-store building up "goodwill".

5   Current Applications

In early stages of use of VHML are the
- MetaFace system (http://www.metaface.computing.edu.au) and the
- **Mentor System** (http://www.mentor.computing.edu.au/).

Both are Dialogue Managers that respond to user requests and hence there is a need for a consistent domain knowledge base so that it may be shared between systems.

With the **Mentor System,** (figure 6) users may query the system in English about various aspects of their study. It will greet the user in a non-deterministic fashion occasionally using various parts of the user's full name It will respond to various requests with varying phrasing such as "what is the weather", "what is the time", etc. Occasionally, in response to a weather update request, it will data mine a weather Web site to report accurate meteorological information, etc. A recent experiment indicated that the system correctly recognised over 75% of user requests. The system is not merely reactive but also offers timely unsolicited advice about assignments, study deadlines and time-tabling issues. Core to this is the central **Mentor** Dialogue Manager and Knowledge Base Manager - a Java based mini operating system in its own right

The rendering of the response can be via plain text, a Web page or Talking Head and hence the Knowledge Base is being marked up in VHML with an XSL-like transform engine as the last stage of the output processing before it is sent to the "display".

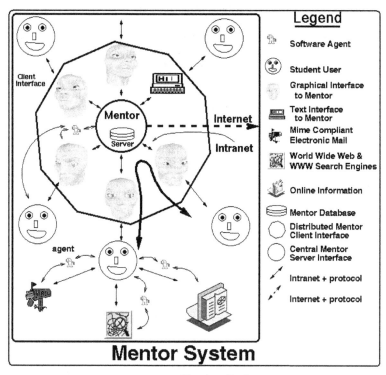

Fig. 6. The *Mentor System*

6 Future Research

In order to further test and improve VHML, the Facial Animation research group at Curtin is working towards a Talking Head Demonstration that will:

- be Web based for PC's running Windows/Linux with Netscape or IE. The demonstration will also run stand alone,
- use heads (plural) - that is, we will show the Talking Head as various models, in various levels of realism. This will be 2 ½ D-> 3D photorealistic. The heads will have an integrated personality,
- be interactive. That is, users will interact with the Talking Head since it will connect to one of our Dialogue Managers - Mentor or MetaFace,
- use VHML. All responses delivered will be marked up in VHML - EML, SML, FAML, GML.

The demonstration will consist of two experiments:

1. A detective story - this will demonstrate the emotional capability of the Talking Head and demonstrate the power of VHML. The story will be

interactive in that the listener can solve the mystery through a question-answer mechanism.

2. An information provider for enquiries about Talking Head Technology (see Figure 7). The system will demonstrate the Dialogue Manager functionality of the Talking Head and, through VHML, its believability as a humane interface to information. The demonstration will also test the suitability of different head types to convey information and how well different personalities convey information.

The demonstration will be concluded by an evaluation of the users of the Talking Head via online questionnaire or similar. The questionnaire will be used to test the effectiveness of VHML in making a "better" Talking Head interface.

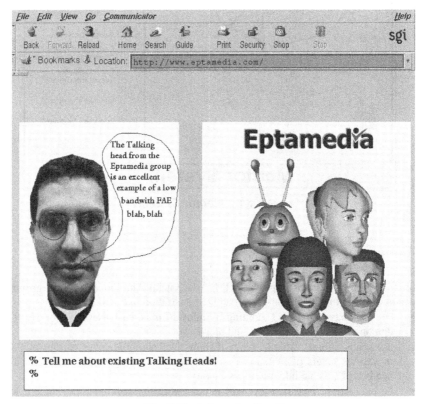

Fig. 7. The Information Provider

As part of the preparation for the demonstration, the group will perform an inspection / verification of the implemented VHML tags, develop new tags and formulate a long-term strategy for VHML evolution as an international standard.

A format (in XML) plus a Dialogue Management Tool (DMT) will also be needed for the production of dialogues. That is, some stimulus from the user, typically a question, produces some output from the DialogueManager with some weighting or confidence level (Figure 8). The DialogueManager may also move into a different state having provided that response:

User : Can you tell me about Talking Heads?   [STIMULUS]
DM : Yes, *<smile>*what would you like to know?*</smile>* [RESPONSE]
(DM now moves into state concerned with knowledge about Talking Heads)

Fig. 8. User Dialogue plus State Change

Dialogue Managers such as MetaFace and the **Mentor System** will use this format for common stimulus-response data and dynamically convert it into their own internal knowledge base format.

7 Conclusion

It can be seen that the TH **with** primitive VHML-like tags is perceived by users as being more human-like. In terms of TH applications, this may mean that a Virtual Lecturer or Virtual Distance Education Tutor with appropriate persona and tags is seen as being erudite and approachable, a Virtual SalesPerson in a Web page is seen as trustworthy and helpful, etc. Scenarios that use full VHML functionality will hopefully be seen as even more humane, more believable.

In general, the use of VHML as a means of directing the TH side of an interface to information and applications is seen as acceptable and useful. Further work needs to be done in creating more tags and fitting these to the appropriate TH persona- a phony smile will always be seen as a bad thing in a face regardless of whether the face is real or not.

This low-level development of the TH tags must be accompanied by research into high-level tag classes that embody an overall feel to a body of text. Currently, the marking up of text is manually intensive, tedious and prone to error. As can be seen in figure 4, it is difficult to see the text for the tags! Current research is investigating the automatic marking up of text for a given subject / context / type of presenter. A long-term goal is for THs that can remember how certain text / words were marked up in the past and use this knowledge to transparently process minimally tagged text in a similar manner – ie. the THs learn from experience.

The TH project forms a small part of a European Union 5th Framework Project whose objective is to define new models and implement advanced tools for audio-video analysis, synthesis and representation. The human machine interface will have a face and voice, a body and gestures and will use all its artificial senses to "understand" high level messages coming from the user and will use all its virtual actuators to provide back acoustic-visual responses.

One deliverable of the project is a Web site that will disseminate the results of the project via a full-body Virtual Presenter who will give an interactive overview on many topics such as advances in MPEG-4 / MPEG-7 standardisation, international research on face and body animation, and speech synthesis. Therefore, it is necessary that the knowledge base is marked up with tags that reflect a full-body presentation.

In conclusion, what is innovative and important is the possibility of directing the way in which a Virtual Human interacts with users so as to appear to be more human, humane and believable.

Could a Talking Head present this paper at a conference and hold your attention?
Would you retain the same amount of information?
Would you sit back and relax?
A VHML compliant Talking Head may one-day be able to do that.

References

1. Pandzic, I.S., *Life on the Web.* Journal of Software Focus, 2001. **To be published.**
2. Beard, S., *et al. FAQBot.* in *Pan Sydney Area Workshop on Visual Information Processing.* 1999. Sydney: University of Sydney.
3. Lavagetto, F. and R. Pockaj, *The Facial Animation Engine: towards a high-level interface for the design of MPEG-4 compliant animated faces.* IEEE Trans. on Circuits and Systems for Video Technology, 1999. **9**(2).
4. CACM, *Special Edition on Intelligent Agents.* Communications of the ACM, 1994. **37**(7).
5. Farrow, S., *Student Modelling for Intelligent Tutoring Systems.* 1995. **http://cedude.ce.gatech.edu/Students/S.Farrow/modelling/references/home.html**.
6. Inlärning, *IT, ITS and AI References.*, . 1995, Kollegiet för Inlärning, Kognition och. Online at http://www.cs.curtin.edu.au/~raytrace/phdpapers/restored_papers/its.html.
7. Project, T., *TAP: A Software Architecture for an Inquiry Dialogue-based Tutoring System.* 1995. **http://jupiter.sas.ntu.ac.sg:8000/research/tap.html**.
8. Marriott, A., R. Pockaj, and C. Parker, *The Face of E-commerce*, in *Internet Commerce and Software Agents – Cases, Technologies and Opportunities*, S. Rahman and R. Bignall, Editors. 2001a, Idea Group Publishing.
9. Marriott, A., *A Java based Mentor System*, in *Java in the Computer Science Curriculum (to be published)*, T. Greening, Editor. 2001c, LNCS, Springer.
10. Marriott, A., *et al., The Face of the Future.* Journal of Research and Practice in Information Technology, 2001b. **32**(3/4): p. 231-245.
11. W3C, *Extensible Markup Language (XML) 1.0. Accessed April 1997. Online at http://www.w3.org/XML/*, . 1997, W3C.
12. VHML, *Virtual Human Markup Language. Online at http://www.vhml.org/*, . 2001.
13. JRPIT, *Audio examples of VHML. Online at http://www.interface.computing.edu.au/papers/jrpit-hci/audio*, . 2001a.
14. JRPIT, *Video examples of VHML. Online at http://www.interface.computing.edu.au/papers/jrpit-hci/video/*, . 2001c.
15. JRPIT, *Experiment details for VHML. Online at http://www.interface.computing.edu.au/papers/jrpit-hci/html/ and http://www.interface.computing.edu.au/papers/jrpit-hci/word-docs/*, . 2001b.

Believable and Interactive Talking Heads for Websites: MetaFace and MPEG-4

Simon Beard[1], Donald Reid[1], and Russell Shepherdson[2]

[1] Curtin University of Technology, Perth, Western Australia
{beardsw, donald}@cs.curtin.edu.au
http://www.interface.computing.edu.au
[2] Singapore Engineering Software Pte Ltd, Singapore
shepherdsonrussell@ses.st.com.sg

Abstract. The MetaFace[1] system is being developed to provide a well-defined metaphor and metaphor-enabling framework for websites. This will be achieved through the use of a talking head, complete with facial animation, speech synthesis and artificial intelligence (an anthropomorphic metaphor). Of paramount importance to talking head technology, such as MetaFace, is the concept of believability. By creating a believable character, users are likely to spend more time using software because of motivational properties. Motivation can affect how long a user interacts with a website and thus is a very important aspect of e-commerce (and not just for online purchases). The MPEG-4 standard is a key technology of MetaFace and similar systems because it includes specifications for facial animation and is highly efficient when communicating this data over the Internet. This paper discusses the technical aspects of MEPG-4 facial animation, how MPEG-4 can affect believability, and how to overcome any inhibitive aspects.

1 Introduction

Humans perceive that *"media = real life"* [1] when interacting with computer systems, and anthropomorphic interfaces (interfaces based on human interaction) are designed to capitalize on this effect. Some anthropomorphic interfaces (pedagogical agents) try to address user learning. There is some research to suggest that these agents have potential to assist the learning process [2]. Other research shows less of a learning impact and more of an influence upon users' perceptions of complexity [3], [4]. Motivation perhaps exceeds the pedagogical benefits from these types of agent [5], and research has shown that pedagogical agents can achieve user motivation through believability [4], [2]. Motivation is important because it allows users to maintain their attention span for much longer as well as generate an interest in the material being presented. The MetaFace framework hopes to use this to increase the popularity and success of websites.

---

[1] MetaFace is being developed at Curtin University of Technology and forms part of a three-year European Union Fifth Framework project called InterFace.

J. Liu et al. (Eds.): AMT 2001, LNCS 2252, pp. 101–112, 2001.

Johnson, Rickel & Lester [5], assert that there are four rules that users must address when constructing a believable agent character. Firstly, the agent must show that it is always alive, and secondly, it must control its visual impact so as not to distract the user. The agent must exhibit complex behaviour so it is not easily predictable and boring, and lastly, it must display natural and unobtrusive behaviour. Bates [6] shows that there are parallels between animated films and animated agents with respect to how they must sustain believability, especially with respect to expression.

Many applications are being developed today for talking heads [5], [7], [8]. The MetaFace system aims to provide a metaphor that allows users to perceive the Internet as an easy to use resource of information. It has a client/server architecture and is capable of finding information on behalf of a user, presenting the information in a web browser and interacting with the user by means of speech and facial animation and utilizing a believable facade. A user can interact with an animated face, by using the keyboard to input natural language. Interaction can also occur inside the web browser via Java, HTML and any other web technologies.

Apart from just being a believable character, MetaFace requires a high level of interactivity to achieve the goals for which it is being constructed. This can only be achieved in an Internet situation if efficient communication is used. MPEG-4 deals with many types of communication including facial animation, and can utilize an Internet connection as slow as 1kbs for a talking head [9]. As a result, it needs to be known how MPEG-4 will affect the construction of a believable talking head.

A post "*dot com crash*" press release by Jupiter Communications Incorporated predicts that in 2006, US online consumers will spend in excess of $130 billion through on-line channels [10], and $632 billion through off-line channels, based on web interaction in 2005 [11]. The long-term importance of projects like MetaFace will emerge from the need for businesses to establish an online presence (even if they are not trying to sell products online). Motivation and thus believability will play a large part of website interaction for anthropomorphic interfaces.

2   MPEG-4 Facial Animation

Several facial animation systems have been developed in the past few years, but most suffer from the same limitation. Each of them uses a proprietary architecture and syntax for animating a synthetic face. This makes it hard to use these systems outside the application area for which they were constructed. The ISO/IEC international standard defined in 1998 [12] tries to overcome all the divisions in the world of facial animation by defining a standard way to deal with virtual faces.

The facial animation component of MPEG-4 uses three inter-working concepts that make it possible to standardize virtual faces and their animation: feature points, the neutral face, and normalization of values.

A "*feature point*" describes a key point of the face (i.e. the corners of the lips, the tip of the nose, and so on). The feature points are used both to define the appearance of the face and to animate it. Facial Animation Parameters (FAP's) are transported over a network connection in order to move the feature points for a face (see Fig. 1).

The second concept to describe is the *"neutral face"*. The neutral face represents the starting position of a synthetic face: the mouth is closed and the gaze is directed perpendicular to the screen plane, the eyes are open and the eyelids are tangent to the iris. All FAP's describe animation with respect to the neutral face, and the neutral face is also used to normalize the FAP values.

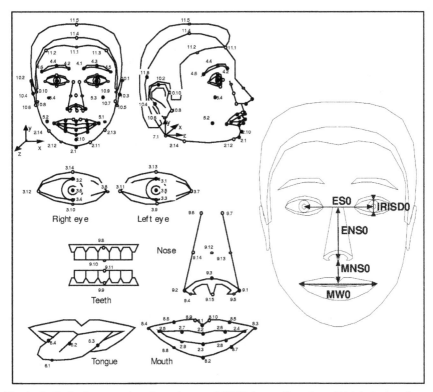

Fig. 1. (Left) the feature points the make up a MPEG-4 compliant face. (Right) the location of Facial Animation Parameter Units (FAPU). Illustrations taken from [12].

"Normalisation of FAP values" is the last concept that is needed by MPEG-4 to standardise virtual faces. By normalising FAP values the defined feature points can be used on and extracted from any synthetic or real face. Normalisation is achieved through use of Facial Animation Parameter Units (FAPU). A FAPU (see Fig. 1) is the distance between some key facial points (i.e. the distance between the tip of the nose and the middle of the mouth, the distance between the eyes, etc.). In total six FAPU have been defined for the MPEG-4 standard. The value of a FAP is expressed in terms of fractions of one of the FAPU. In this way, the movement described by a FAP is adapted to the actual size and shape of a model. This means that any MPEG-4 compliant face - human or caricature - can be animated by any MPEG-4 player.

The 68 FAP's defined by MPEG-4 are divided into two groups: hi-level and low-level. Of importance to speech systems are the two hi-level FAP's: viseme and expression. A viseme is defined as the visual equivalent of a phoneme, and is the mouth posture when pronouncing a phoneme. Expressions can be sad, happy, angry, etc. Through the use of visemes, expression, and low-level animation MPEG-4 has the potential needed for believable talking heads.

3   MPEG-4 and Believability

To date, Curtin has focused exclusively on three-dimensional facial animation [13], [14]. Since the attention of this paper is on believability, not realism, a two-dimensional face from the MetaFace system will be used to illustrate this discussion. The style for this two-dimensional animation was influenced by the popular television comedy series *"South Park"* [15]. South Park is known for its believable characters despite its rudimentary animation techniques, and these characters are in fact animated in a parameterized way, similar to that of MPEG-4 [16]. It is a popular theory that anthropomorphic interfaces need not be realistic human characters, but instead it is the visual qualities that count [17].

In order to assess how MPEG-4 facial animation can affect believability, it is important to define the factors that can potentially empower or inhibit believability. Believability is affected by visual qualities and computational properties [5]. Since it deals with the representation and communication of facial animation, MPEG-4 affects only visual qualities. Computational properties are a problem for the developer. Therefore rules one and two for believable agents [5] (Discussed Sect. 1) are not directly affected by MPEG-4 and are for the developer to implement. Rules three and four (the need for complex behaviour patterns and natural unobtrusive behaviour), however, can be potentially inhibited or empowered by MPEG-4.

A character has to be capable of *"complexity"* in model and animation before it can have complex behaviour patterns. There must be means by which a character may be manipulated in complex ways. In order to have natural and unobtrusive behaviour, there must be means for the character to appear *"natural"*.

Following is a discussion in the areas of low-level, expression, and viseme FAP's, and how each affects believability for facial animation, through *"complexity"* of model and manipulation, and the potential *"naturalness"* of the character.

3.1   Low-Level FAP's

The parameters for low-level animation are values (positive and negative) that describe a uni or bi-directional movement of a feature point, using a FAPU as a unit measurement. To further illustrate, say that *"FAP 33"* (the middle left eyebrow control point, currently at the neutral position) was set to a positive value, the head model, in response, would arch the middle of the left eyebrow to a position above the neutral position (illustrated by Fig. 2).

The simplicity of MPEG-4 control makes construction of a face easy. As an example, by defining three control points for an eyebrow, each can be moved separately by different FAP's, and moving each control point affects a drawing primitive. This can be easily extended to allow for an eyebrow more complicated that a three point drawing primitive (see Fig. 2). The actual interaction of points can be far more complex than the example shown. This arbitrary complexity of feature point animation means that simple drawing primitives don't limit MPEG-4 faces.

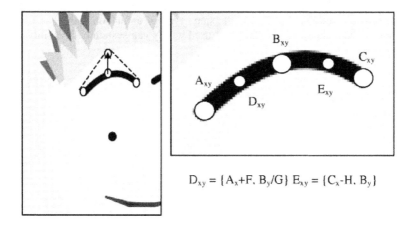

$$D_{xy} = \{ A_x+F, B_y/G \} \ E_{xy} = \{ C_x-H, B_y \}$$

Fig. 2. (Left) FAP 33 is given a positive value. (Right) complex drawing primitives.

MPEG-4 faces don't even need to implement all feature points defined by the MPEG-4 standard. FAP's can be easily ignored. FAP's can also be linked to other facial features not defined by MPEG-4. For example, a fish model could be used with MPEG-4 facial animation by linking the anatomy of the fish to the anatomy of a face. Fins can move instead of eyebrows, gills can open and close instead of eyes blinking etc. This again demonstrates the arbitrary complexity of MPEG-4 facial animation

The freedom to create arbitrarily complex models [18] contributes towards empowering the believability of the facial animation. The ability to also animate in an arbitrarily complex manner furthers the cause. This means that MPEG-4 facial animation can range from the two-dimensional head, to complex three-dimensional movement, to the extraordinary.

There is a chance of obtrusive behaviour, which inhibits believability, if facial control points are moved in an unnatural way by the server responsible for sending FAP's (e.g. the face may be moved in a physically impossible way). This is the classic consumer/producer software engineering problem, and is present in all aspects of MPEG-4 facial animation. The responsibility for correct facial animation lies with the source of the FAP's, and isn't a concern of MPEG-4.

A problem associated with using two-dimensional faces with MPEG-4 (a three dimensional standard) is in resolving FAP movement incorporating the Z-axis, during either rotation or planar movement. This is not a MPEG-4 problem, but because developers may want to use a two-dimensional character, it is worth exploring the ramifications for believability.

There are two different solutions to the Z-axis problem in two-dimensional MPEG-4 animation, namely resolving Z movement as XY movement or using drawing states. Resolving XY movement can be accomplished in only some cases. For example, animating eyeball rotation can be accomplished as a pupil and iris translation from the center of the eye. Using states is a more robust solution, but often produces poorer results. States are used in cases such as head rotation, where there may be two or more overlay drawings depending upon the value of the low level FAP. For example, a head may be turned side on when "*head yaw*" reaches 90°, or front on when "*head yaw*" is near 0° (see Fig. 3). This is the same type of animation technique used by South Park. The technique is crude, but if used wisely can sustain believability in the character.

Fig. 3. Two drawing states for head rotation.

3.2 Expression FAP's

As part of the MPEG-4 facial animation standard, particular attention is paid to the high-level animation of expression and visemes. Through the use of minimal parameters and efficient communication MPEG-4 is able achieve quite complex animation.

Table 1. MPEG-4 expressions [12]

Expression select	Expression name	Textual description
0	Na	Na *(Neutral Face)*
1	Joy	The eyebrows are relaxed. The mouth is open and the mouth corners pulled back toward the ears.
2	Sadness	The inner eyebrows are bent upward. The eyes are slightly closed. The mouth is relaxed.
3	Anger	The inner eyebrows are pulled downward and together. The eyes are wide open. The lips are pressed against each other or opened to expose the teeth.
4	Fear	The eyebrows are raised and pulled together. The inner eyebrows are bent upward. The eyes are tense and alert.
5	Disgust	The eyebrows and eyelids are relaxed. The upper lip is raised and curled, often asymmetrically.
6	Surprise	The eyebrows are raised. The upper eyelids are wide open, the lower relaxed. The jaw is opened.

Six different expressions (Table 1) are defined by the MPEG-4 standard. There is evidence to suggest that there exist six universal categories of facial expression that are recognized across cultures [20], [21], [22]. These expressions are the same as defined for the MPEG-4 standard. The use of cross-cultural expressions empowers the use of believability for MPEG-4 facial animation, through the naturalness of the selection of expressions available.

The important parameters for an MPEG-4 expression are *expression 1*, *intensity 1*, *expression 2*, *intensity 2*. Intensities are within the integer range 0 to 63, and the final expression can be expressed thus:

Final expression = expr 1 x (intensity 1 / 63) + expr 2 x (intensity 2 / 63) .   (1)

Few concise explanations of human facial expression properties exist. The guidance given by the MPEG-4 standard is too loosely defined for believable talking heads. For a better understanding on how to create an expressional face, the reference material by Faigin [23], a renowned realist artist, was studied and compared with the MPEG-4 expression standardization.

Both the MPEG-4 standard and work by Faigin clearly state what is required for each expression. Following is a table that shows the differences between each.

Table 2. Comparison of Faigin and MPEG-4 specifications

Joy	Faigin and MPEG-4 guidelines are very alike for this expression, with the exception of Faigin adding that the mouth should be wider, and lips thinned and against the skull
Sadness	For this expression Faigin specifies additional information not present in MPEG-4. Eyes appear narrower because of the downward pressure by the oblique above-the-lid fold.
Anger	Faigin again identifies and additional property for the expression, namely the narrowing of the eyes because of downward pressure on the upper eyelid.
Fear	The two specifications for this expression are similar, the only difference being that Faigin specifies a slight dropping of the mouth, where as, MPEG-4 makes no such mention.
Disgust	Both specifications are very similar for this expression.
Surprise	Again both specifications are very similar.

As a summary, both disgust and fear were very similarly specified in each of the references. The only difference being that with disgust, according to Faigin, the eyes may be narrowed if desired. The major differences in the rest of the expressions revolve mainly about the effect of the eyelid and brow on the perceived shape of the eyes. As seen in Fig. 4, anger and sadness rely heavily on this effect. The eyes seem to be especially important for judgements of fear, sadness, and surprise, but less important than the mouth during judgements happiness, anger and disgust [24]. The eyes are partially closed during sadness, disgust, and contempt in an apparent attempt to reduce contact with objects in the visual field. Partial closure also occurs during happiness, as a spreading reaction from the lower face [24]. Neither MPEG-4 or Faigin discuss the use of pupil dilation with respect to conveying expression. Hess [25] suggests that pupil size reflects a person's attitude toward objects and people. An increase in pupil size may accompany a positive attitude, wheras pupil constriction occurs during negative reactions.

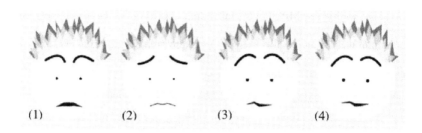

Fig. 4. The use of brow and pupil dilation is essential to the perception of anger (1) and sadness (2). Eye closure can be an important aspect of disgust as (3) and (4) illustrate.

From this comparison of MPEG-4 expressions, we can see that the guidelines for MPEG-4 can inhibit the naturalness of expression thus inhibit believability in the talking heads. Bates [6] shows that expression, its obvious and natural appearance, is a key aspect of believable characters. Therefore when constructing believable characters using the MPEG-4 facial animation standard it is advisable to research other specifications for expressions, and also implement some extra facial features not specifically defined by MPEG-4, such as a brow for altering the perceived shape of the eyes and pupil dilation (see Fig. 4). These additions are still in keeping with the standard. MPEG-4 allows proprietary facial animation engines to interpret FAP's however they choose, as long as they adhere to the communication standard.

The face has the capacity to show more than one expression at a given instant. These are called affect blends [26]. MPEG-4 allows for these affect blends and thus empowers believability by providing naturalness for a virtual face. Blending different expressions is a simple exercise of taking the in-between positions of facial features (defined by control points) for two expressions, and drawing the resulting face.

According to the MPEG-4 specification, the expression should only have an effect on other FAP's that are currently allowed to be interpreted. The current expression can be set to a new neutral position without altering mouth closure, eye opening, gaze direction, and head orientation, before FAP's are applied. Blending low-level animation with expressions is achieved through specifing all animation as the displacement of control points away from their neutral face positions. In this way when an expression is used it becomes the new neutral face temporarily and the control points are just starting from a new location. The use of the neutral position makes the blending of low-level FAP's and expressions a simple exercise, the results are very natural, and can be quite complex.

The MPEG-4 specifications for blending expressions empowers believability for virtual faces. The use of neutral positions and the rules for not altering mouth closure, eye opening, gaze direction, and head orientation during the use of an expression for a neutral position, makes expressions for a talking head unobtrusive. A problem with MPEG-4 believability, however, is that there is still the outstanding problem of the perceived shape of the eyes in sadness, anger, and potentially disgust. MPEG-4 seeks to stop obtrusive behaviour by not altering eye closure for a neutral face, but it can have a dramatic effect on the naturalness of the expression (see Fig. 5).

3.3 Viseme FAP's

The important viseme parameters are *viseme 1*, *viseme 2* and *blend*. Blend is in the range 0 to 63 and defines the blending of the two visemes, in a way similar to blending different expressions. The final viseme is given by the following equation:

$$\text{Final viseme} = \text{viseme } 1 \times (\text{blend} / 63) + \text{viseme } 2 \times (1 - \text{blend} / 63) \ . \tag{2}$$

In real life our visemes change when talking with an expression (a person can smile while they are talking). This makes the blending of expression and viseme paramount to the believability of a talking head since the face is all that is seen of the character. Furthermore, when people speak, there is almost always emotional information communicated along with audible words. This emotional information is conveyed not only through qualities of the voice, but through multiple communiction channels including emotional visible facial expressions [27]. In order to blend visemes and expressions, visemes have to be specified as displacements of control points relative to the mouth on the neutral face. If the neutral position is set to the current expression then visemes are simply animated as displacements relative to new neutral position (similar to low-level and expression blending). The current expression can be set to the new neutral position without altering mouth closure, eye opening, gaze direction, and head orientation, before FAP's are applied. By adhering to this specification the facial animation problem of talking without fully shutting the mouth can be overcome. For example, the facial properties for joy, make it such that the corners of the mouth may be moved for the new neutral face, but the mouth has to stay shut when following the MPEG-4 specification.

The MPEG-4 viseme table caters for fourteen different phonemes. Different facial animation reference materials suggest that the number of important visemes is between seven and eighteen [28], [27]. Some TTS (Text To Speech) systems (used to add speech to talking heads) also have the added problem of generating more phonemes than the given phoneme to viseme translations. This makes it mandatory to carry out research and categorize the best mapping from phonemes to visemes and how exactly each viseme should look, before integrating all technologies.

The fourteen visemes specified by the MPEG-4 standard are on par with guides given by other facial animation references. Although TTS systems may exhibit more phonemes than there are visemes, it is an easy job to translate many phonemes to one viseme. MPEG-4 does not define the visual equivalent of phonemes, but it is a simple matter of research to construct purpose built sets. This stated, it is easy to see that MPEG-4 visemes do empower believability in facial animation, through their naturalness and the complexity of blending with expressions.

4   Preliminary Results

To assess the believability of talking heads being developed at Curtin, preliminary testing was conducted to gauge the effectiveness of the text to speech synthesis system using a Speech Markup Language (SML) and the facial scripting system using a Facial Animation Markup Language (FAML) for a three dimensional head.

Two storyteller demonstrations were constructed for gathering data. The first storytelling demonstration used emotive speech and coordinated facial gestures and expressions. The second demonstration consisted of the same storyteller with no emotive markup for the speech and only fundamental gestures and expressions (the neutral face with eye blinking and slight head movement). Participants were asked four basic questions to assess the believability for each demonstration:

1. *"Which talking head do you think portrayed the best 'story teller' character?"*
2. *"Which talking head do you think was more natural / human-like?"*
3. *"Which talking head do you think was more expressive?"*
4. *"Which talking head do you find more interesting?"*

Similar demonstrations can be found at the Curtin InterFace website [29].

Table 3. Preliminary results assessing believability

	Best story teller	More natural	More expressive	More interesting
With markup	89%	69%	86%	83%
Without markup	9%	14%	6%	9%
Neither	3%	17%	9%	9%

From this table it can be seen that believability is certainly within the realm of MPEG-4. The fact that a clear majority of people regarded the expressional talking head as the best storyteller shows believability for that application. The indicators such as interest/motivation naturalness and expressiveness also support this conclusion.

5 Conclusion

It has been shown that low-level FAP's for the MPEG-4 standard do in fact empower believability of the facial animation. This is achieved by having arbitrarily complex models and animation. The only problem occurs for two-dimensional faces that must resolve movement incorporating the Z-axis, but this can be overcome with expertise.

There is evidence to suggest that there exist six universal categories of facial expression that are recognised across cultures. These expressions are the same as defined for the MPEG-4 standard. The use of cross-cultural expressions empowers the use of believability for MPEG-4 facial animation, through the naturalness of the selection of expressions available.

From a comparison of MPEG-4 expressions with views expressed by artists and psychologists we can see that the guidelines for MPEG-4 can inhibit the naturalness of expression. When constructing believable characters using the MPEG-4 facial animation standard it is advisable to research other specifications for expressions, and also implement some extra facial features not specifically defined by MPEG-4, such as a brow for altering the perceived shape of the eyes.

The MPEG-4 specification for blending expressions, visemes, and low-level animation empowers believability for virtual faces. The use of neutral positions and the rules for not altering mouth closure, eye opening, gaze direction, and head orientation during the use of an expression for a neutral position makes expressions for a talking head unobtrusive. There is still the outstanding problem, however, of the perceived shape of the eyes in sadness, anger, and potentially disgust. MPEG-4 seeks to stop obtrusive behaviour by not altering eye closure for a neutral position, but it can have a dramatic effect on the naturalness of the expression.

MPEG-4 visemes have been shown to empower believability in facial animation, through their naturalness and complexity of blending with expression.

Initial results have shown that using the MPEG-4 infrastructure it is possible to construct believable facial animation for interactive characters. MPEG-4 has enough flexibility for facial animation systems to achieve what developers perceive as important, whether that is realism, believability, interactivity, or any similar concept. The MetaFace system shows that MPEG-4 can be used in two-dimensional, believable, and interactive talking heads, which further illustrates the flexibility of the standard. There are certain areas of MPEG-4 that inhibit the use of believability, but for every inhibition there is a logical solution, as outlined in this paper. Add to this conclusion all of the ways that MPEG-4 empowers believability and it can be seen that this standard is definitely the way to achieve believability in interactive talking heads for the Internet.

References

1. Reeves, B., Nass, C.: The Media Equation. Cambridge University Press, Cambridge (1996)
2. Lester, J., C., Converse, S., A., Kahler, S., E., Barlow, S., T., Stone, B., A., Bhogal, R., S.: The Persona Effect: Affective Impact of Animated Pedagogical Agents. In: Pemberton, S. (ed.): CHI'97 Human Factors in Computing Systems. ACM, Atlanta (1997) 359-366
3. van Mulken, S., André, E., Müller, J.: The Persona Effect: How Substantial Is It?. In: Johnson, H., Nigay, L., Roast, C. (eds.): People and Computers XIII, proceedings of HCI'98. Springer (1998) 53-66
4. Lester, J., C., Zettlemoyer, L., S., Grégoire, J., P.: Explanatory Lifelike Avatars: Performing User-Centered Tasks in 3D Learning Environments. In: Third International Conference on Autonomous Agents. ACM, Seattle (1999) 24-31
5. Johnson, W., L., Rickel, J., W., Lester, J., C.: Animated Pedagogical Agents: Face-to-Face Interaction in Interactive Learning Environments. The International Journal of Artificial Intelligence in Education (2000)
6. Bates, J.: The Role of Emotion in Believable Agents. Vol. 37. No. 7. Communications of the ACM (1994) 122-125
7. Marriott, A., Pockaj, R., Parker, C.:A Virtual Salesperson. In: S. Rahman, R. Bignall (eds.): Internet Commerce and Software Agents: Cases, Technologies and Opportunities. Idea Group Publishing, Melbourne (2000)
8. Kiwilogic: Kiwilogic's CEO is "Powered by LifeFX"?. Available: http://www.kiwilogic.com/htm/news/press_0003.htm (2001)
9. Battista, S., Casalino, F., Lande, C.: MPEG-4: A Multimedia Standard for the Third Millennium, Part 1. Vol. 6. No. 4. IEEE Multimedia (1999) 74-83
10. Jupiter Communications Inc.: Reports Of The Death Of Online Retail Are Greatly Exaggerated, Says Jupiter Media Metrix. Available: http://www.jup.com/company/pressrelease.jsp?doc=pr010522 (2001)

11. Jupiter Communications Inc.: Online Retailers Missing Greatest Opportunity: Web-Influenced Spending to Exceed $630 Billion in 2005. Available: http://www.jup.com/company/pressrelease.jsp?doc=pr000518 (2000)
12. ISO/IEC: Text for ISO/IEC FDIS 14496-2 Visual. Available: http://www.cselt.it/mpeg/working_documents.htm (1998)
13. Beard, S., Marriott, A., Pockaj, R.: A Humane Interface. In: OZCHI 2000: Interfacing Reality in the New Millennium. Sydney (2000) 168-175
14. Marriott, A., Beard, S., Haddad, H., Pockaj, R., Stallo, J., Huynh, Q., Tschirren, B.: Face of the Future. Journal of Research and Practice in Technology, Vol. 32. No. 3 (2001) 231-245
15. Comedy Central: South Park. Available: http://www.comedycentral.com/tv_shows/southpark/ (2001)
16. Stough, E.: Eric Stough. Assistant, Issue 5. Alias Wavefront (1998) 30-31
17. Pandzic, I.: Life on the Web. Software Focus, (to be published) John Wiley and Sons Ltd. (2001)
18. Garaventa, P., Pockaj, R., Bonamico, C., Lavagetto, F.: A Mesh Simplification Algorithm Applied To Mpeg-4 Compliant 3D Facial Models. In: The International Conference on Augmented Virtual Environments and Three-Dimensional Imaging. Mykonos (2001) 173-176
19. Pockaj, R.: Face Models. Available: http://www.dsp.com.dist.unige.it/~pok/RESEARCH/MPEG/models.htm (2000)
20. Ekman, P.: The argument and evidence about universals in facial expressions of emotion. Handbook of Social Psychophysiology, John Wiley and Sons Ltd. (1989)
21. Ekman, P., Oster, H.: Cross-cultural Studies and the Issue of Universality. Emotion in the Human Face. 2nd edn. Cambridge University Press, London (1982)
22. Ekman, P., Friesen, W.: Unmasking the Face: A Guide to Recognising Emotions for Facial Clues. Prentice-Hall Inc., Englewood Cliffs, New Jersey (1975)
23. Faigin, G.: The Artist's Complete Guide to Facial Expression. Watson-Guptill, New York (1990)
24. Collier, G.: Emotional Expression. Lawrence Erlbaum Associates Inc., New Jersey (1985)
25. Hess, E.: The Tell-Tale Eye. Van Nostrand Reinhold Company, New York (1975)
26. Ekman, P., Friesen, W., Ellsworth, P.: Research Foundations. Emotion in the Human Face. 2nd edn. Cambridge University Press, London (1982)
27. Parke, F., Waters, K.: Computer Facial Animation. A K Peters, Wellesley, Massachusetts (1996)
28. Ratner, P.: 3-D Human Modeling and Animation. John Wiley and Sons Ltd., Brisbane (1998)
29. Curtin InterFace: Movie examples from Improved Facial Animation Subsystem. Available: http://www.interface.computing.edu.au/papers/jrpit-hci/movies/ (2001)

Building Multi-modal Personal Sales Agents as Interfaces to E-commerce Applications

Yasmine Arafa and Abe Mamdani

Dept. of Electronic and Electrical Engineering
Imperial College of Science, Technology & Medicine
Exhibition Road, London SW7 2BT
+44 (0) 207 5946319
{y.Arafa@ic.ac.uk}

Abstract. The research presented explores a new paradigm for human-computer interaction with electronic retailing applications. A paradigm that deploys face-to-face interaction with intelligent, visual, lifelike, multi-modal conversational agents, which take on the role of electronic sales assistants. This paper discusses the motivations for enriching current e-commerce application interfaces with multi-modal interface agents and discusses the technical development issues they raise, as realised in the MAPPA (EU project EP28831) system architecture design and development.

The paper addresses three distinct components of an overall framework for developing lifelike, multi-modal agents for real-time and dynamic applications: *Knowledge Representation and Manipulation*, *Grounded Affect Models*, and the convergence of both into support for multimedia visualisation of lifelike, social behaviour. The research presents a novel specification for such a medium and a functional agent-based system scenario (e-commerce) that is implemented with it. Setting forth a framework for building multi-modal interface agents and yielding a conversational form of human-machine interaction, which may have potential for shaping tomorrows interface to the world of e-commerce.

Keywords. Electronic Personal Sales Assistants, Multi-modal Interface Agents, Conversational Lifelike Characters, Affective Computing, Multi-Agent Systems.

1 Introduction

Electronic commerce has recently shown enormous potential benefits of lower trade costs, wider reach and reasonably reliable and faster infrastructure for electronic markets. As transactions between companies or vendors and their customers become more digitally self-serviced and since customer services are becoming a primary value-added function in every business, human involvement and personalisation becomes a key issue. Prompting us to deploy new paradigms that can provision for even more personalised interactions that complement current e-commerce functionality and services. Paradigms providing personalised services that reach the individual with different information profiles and levels of expertise, and that can provide more intelligent, socially intuitive interaction. For these reasons we use the

J. Liu et al. (Eds.): AMT 2001, LNCS 2252, pp. 113–133, 2001.

metaphor of a Personal Agent working on behalf of the customer in an electronic-based marketing environment.

The shift towards highly personalised interfaces in which communication between user and computer is mediated by an agent metaphor is currently one of the major steps in the evolution of the user interface technology. We extend this metaphor to provide an animated human-like embodiment of the Electronic Personal Sales Assistant (e-PSA) endowed with a distinct and predefined personality adequate to individuals' cultural and social communication protocols and needs. Anthropomorphizing the Personal Sales Assistant represents an important aspect of current interface-agent research aiming towards highly personalised services. The motivation for this type of personalisation is that an animated figure (eliciting human-like communication capabilities) may add an expressive dimension to the PSA's communicative features that can further add to the effectiveness and personalisation of the interface and the application on the whole.

The ability to visually express *Affective* behaviour is essential for creating believable interactive PSA characters regardless of the domain they are deployed in. In order to simulate affective expressions in an interactive environment the agents not only require an adaptive model for generating behavioural responses but also further require a multimedia model to manifest their behaviour through animated facial or bodily graphical expressions and gestures. There has been much research underway regarding such visual expressions and indeed have produced many sophisticated algorithms that are capable of producing reasonably effective representations of affective states and personality traits. However, such work generally does not focus on modelling in a dynamic real-time environment where behaviour is both goal driven as well as data driven. Our work concentrates on linking multimedia animated expression and motion generation with the processes responsible for producing affective expressive behaviour given the dynamic nature of real-time systems.

In order to make progress in building such systems, a principled method of modality integration, and a general architecture to support it is needed. Such a framework should provide real-time capabilities and sufficient flexibility to enable rapid integration within different architectures and applications. A multi-agent system is being developed which facilitates the interoperation of semi-autonomous knowledge-based intelligent software. The advantages of such architectural frameworks are modularity, distribution and asynchrony required for real-time systems like e-commerce. We further need to define new models and implement advanced tools to facilitate the mapping of agent behaviour to audio-video synthesis and representation mechanisms in order to provide essential technologies for the implementation of large-scale virtual and augmented environments. To realise this goal, the research activities are governed by a set of scientific and technological objectives that are clustered in three main areas of work:

1) The development of technology to support multi-users functionality, advanced interactive media representation, delivery of content, agents and behaviour and interfaces;
2) The integration of technology in a common agent platform;
3) The development of real-time applications based on the specified platform in order to demonstrate the integrated technology.

For such multimedia applications to compete in the electronic marketplace and supply client-centred information, the underlying service domains should adhere to an open service infrastructure. This means that successful management of content production and delivery of interactive multimedia requires suitable authoring tools if an effective method for distributed content handling in a given service domain is to be provided. This paper presents an overview of the content-based representation methodology used for describing multimedia content, referred to as *Assets* and describes a conceptual overview of a multimedia content-based representation model to support the integration of multimedia lifelike visualisation, and an intelligent agent architecture, which can enable open distributed information and service delivery. We provide a framework for the content-based meta-data (so called *Assets*) authoring process.

To set the scene, this paper first sets forth the motivations behind embodied anthropomorphic e-PSAs, describes the key capabilities they offer, and discusses the technical issues they raise based on our design and development experience on the EU MAPPA project (EP28831). The paper further sets forth the key functionality that lifelike agents will need to succeed at face-to-face communication. Finally, the implemented architecture is briefly described at the end of the paper.

2   Online Trading Applications

Although the number of vendors holding electronic sites that provide and facilitate online trading have rapidly increased in the past few years, research results have shown that their acceptance and economic success has, as yet, not reached their full potential nor their projected peak [22]. With focus on consumer-machine interaction, there are a number of common factors that may have partially or wholly contributed to this ineffectiveness and may very well affect any future success:

1) deficiencies and complexity of usability and navigation;
2) deficiencies in personalisation and delivery of individualised services;
3) deficiencies and lack of consideration for the social aspects of the interaction design and implementation;
4) lack of consideration and accommodation for customers' mental dispositions and states.

How often has one abandoned a site before reaching checkout? How often has one lost interest in an interaction due to the complexity of navigation and the volume of information presented? How many times have vendors lost a sale because a customer had to navigate out of checkout to find information and never returned? Recent research also provides evidence that individual social tendencies, personalities and affective states have major impact on an interaction and on overall performance [12]. Specific influences include the following:

1) anxiety, caused by the complexity of an interaction, influences the attention span and concentration focus [8];
2) mental state and mood influences memory and recall by biasing recall of information in accordance with current affective state [6];
3) both the above collectively influence and delay decision making [13].

Affect[1] and customers' mental states play a major role in any social interaction process and hence have significant effect upon customers' behaviour using e-commerce applications. One of the roles played by Affect is to detect and identify possible problems in human interactions, which can prompt the need for an adaptive reaction. We believe that one important precondition to the success of e-commerce applications are the construction of appropriate user interfaces that accommodate and sense social behaviour. In spite of the importance of the consumer interface most studies primarily focus on the technical issues of their implementation and have neglected the full effects of social behaviour.

Current lack of accommodation for individualised social behaviour, tendencies and mental states in most human-computer applications can lead to adverse efficiency results which, moreover, could result in failure to meet the anticipated objectives. Probably e-commerce will not achieve it's full potential until it is able to "win customer acceptance" and breakdown the intrinsic complexities of usability-barriers and the information cost structure. We address and leverage these issues by deploying anthropomorphic Electronic Personal Sales Assistants capable of sensing and responding appropriately to individualised social behaviour as discussed in the following section.

3 E-personal Sales Assistants

Anthropomorphic e-PSAs are lifelike animated characters endowed with the ability to communicate through multiple modalities, which includes written dialogue, spoken language, and facial and body gestures and expressions. Acting as personal sales assistant, these characters can connect with search engines to find the right product for each customer. They are given the ability to effortlessly answer customers' questions, at any point in a sales cycle; and also give advice and recommendation. They cannot only establish a business-to-customer relationship, they can continue to develop it by providing and maintaining accurate customer profiles, monitoring customer preferences, and shopping patterns and habits. These assistants offer several advantages: personalised information delivery; collaborative marketing and sales, relevant reliable market and customer data. Given the added ability to sense and accommodate Affect they are better able to relate to difficult situations and adapt the interface accordingly.

e-Commerce customer interfaces have, so far, primarily treated the software application as a physical means to get to and achieve the required services. To be used effectively the customer must first learn and master its functionality. Face-to-face interaction with an anthropomorphic e-PSA allows the user to disassociate the interface from the complexity of the underlying application. Research by Reeves and Nass in The Media Equation [23] has indicated that human interactions with computers are intrinsically social in nature. These results suggest that interface

---

[1] Affective computing is "computing that relates to, arises from or deliberately influences emotions" [21].

metaphors that leverage this social tendency and that are specifically designed to accommodate social rules of interaction and engagement may ultimately be more successful.

Communicative e-PSA agents are autonomous Interface Agents that employ intelligence and adaptive reasoning methods to provide active, autonomous and collaborative services to integrators of a virtual environment [16, 27]. Interface agents differ from customary interfaces in that they are expected to change behaviour and actions autonomously according to users' actions and the surrounding system environment as an interaction progresses. The communicative agent metaphor aims towards providing effective highly personalised services. Personifying this metaphor with a context generated lifelike character is a visual dimension to providing personalised services. The motivation for this type of personalisation is that an animated figure, eliciting quasi-human capabilities, may add an expressive dimension to the agent's communicative features, which can add to the effectiveness and personalisation of the interface and the virtual interactive experience on the whole. Furthermore, there is strong evidence that Affect has major influence on learning and recall [5], reasoning and decision-making [10], both collectively effecting system usability and efficiency. In e-commerce it may influence loyalty and the buying behaviour [3].

Particularly important capabilities of an agent that must interact with the human user is Believability, in terms of how the agents behaves and expresses itself and that these expressions are appropriate to the context of the interaction [5]. Affect has been proven to be important in enhancing the expressive or visual believability of an agent [5]. For the agent to effectively achieve believable lifelike behaviour it must have the appropriate knowledge to handle and reason about affect so as to produce the believable response.

3.1 The Role of an E-PSA

Their role is to act as mediators between the human and the computer cyberspace and to be capable of personalising an interface by monitoring and sensing individuals' capabilities, interests, and preferences [11, 16]. As such, e-PSA functionality is realised on two levels: the service level and the interface level. The e-PSA is, hence, considered a service agent that must communicate and negotiate with other agents in a multi-agent system to determine which and how services are to be provided. As all software agents are distinguishably characterised by the services they provide, the e-PSA is principally characterised as a user-oriented agent. It is expected to facilitate and provide mechanisms that enhance an application's efficiency and usability from both interface and functionality perspectives. The e-PSA may take on different functional roles like Sales or Advertiser agents in e-commerce [28]; Helper or Personal Assistant agents in different application domains [2, 17], Presenters [1]; as Pedagogical or Training agents [15, 20] or many more.

3.2 Visual Characters with Affect

There are many modalities in which an e-PSA character may express its behaviour. e-PSA mediation and behaviour can be expressed visually through animated figures or talking heads, verbally through speech and voice intonation or textually through natural language phrases. We are currently concerned with visually expressing behaviour through animated graphical characters, focusing on enabling a character-based technology rather than maintaining domain specific services and functionality.

For e-PSAs to convincingly show appropriate and believable behaviour they must first understand and reason about affect, relate to context at hand, and converge both through the generation of behavioural changes based on emerging emotions. We use affect primarily for its influential implications on behaviour, and specifically because it allows the implementation of a social channel of interaction that is fundamental to the effectiveness and believability of a conversation. For this channel to be truly affective, the e-PSA character must not only facilitate the channel, but also must appropriately respond to cues from the user and the system environment and further, be able to produce affective responses that reinforces the intended message rather than confuse the situation [5].

3.3   Real-Time E-PSA Characters in Multi-agent Environments

Being in a Multi-Agent System (MAS) environment, the e-PSA requirements differ from that of synthetic characters in drama applications. Their embodiment needs to be driven by real-time data and goals both from other service agents, as well as from the user, rather than from pre-defined action scripts. In an MAS, agents interact with each other through the surrounding world, where there are mechanisms for sharing knowledge of activities and common knowledge base that constructs the agent communication language. Since the e-PSA is an autonomous agent which performs some task(s) on behalf of an entity, communicates asynchronously with other entities in the world and responds asynchronously to events in the world. The synchronous nature of the agents implies that they respond to events, which occur, as they happen rather than requiring a global synchronisation signal. We characterise these systems as real-time, on one hand, because the data is not pre-canned and on the other hand, because emotional stimuli and responses are immediate and the emotional output can be used as emotional input to close the autonomous agents' loop.

4   Design Issues

A good interface should be deigned to be as simple and as natural as possible so that it requires minimal efforts on the user's side. The aim here is to realise a natural and friendly interface resembling common face-to-face communication in real-time. The visual character of the e-PSA should be designed and developed to facilitate multi-modal presentation by an animated figure capable of affective behaviour, gesturing, greeting, pointing and explaining.

Being a conversational character the design must allow for mixed-initiative interaction in which control is passed between both the customer and the agent.

Basically, there are three modals of interaction between the customer, the ePSA and the service agents within a multi-agent system:

- *e-PSA-to-Customer initiative:* Where the e-PSA will inform the customer of current activities and feedback, or may request input from the customer.
- *Customer-to-ePSA: initiative* Where the customer initiates an input query or request to its e-PSA agent, who, co-ordinates with the appropriate service agents in the system to provide the required response.
- *Agent-to-Agent:* Where service agents including the e-PSA interact together to achieve a goal and provide a required service.

As a software agent the requirements for developing an e-PSA are:

- general agent components as in a multi-agent system;
- social and mental model upon which agent affective and social behaviour are determined;
- visual framework for providing an interface, interaction, information delivery, and character manifestation;
- separation of the visual requirements and the reasoning requirements into individual components;
- an interface between the visual framework and the service agents within a multi-agent system.

We can summarise the basic component structure of the e-PSA agent in figure 1. The e-PSA has a well-defined and distinctive role to play in the MAS application. This role generally defines the overall constraints that bound the services the agent may provide. It defines a set of rules that governs the agents behaviour in the MAS trying to accomplish a set of given tasks to reach the desired goal. The behaviour is influenced by changes and the contextual state of the immediate surrounding environment. In turn changes in the environment and the resulting behaviour may also affect the task plans and accomplishment. Which, also, may consequently affect the overall role of the agents. This is why we represent the components as intertwined circles. We add an Affect model to deal with the social tendencies of the interaction and accordingly, the model further affects all other components of the agent structure.

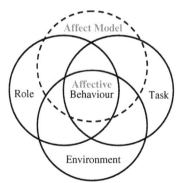

Fig. 1. Agent Structure

The agent architecture is the basic system design for structuring processes and knowledge needed for an agent to undertake everyday tasks in the real world.

Being in real-time introduces an added set of challenges for face-to-face interaction. Namely, the nature of the interaction requires:

1) the interpretation and handling of multiple data types (text, speech, gestures);
2) synchronisation and analysis of multiple input mediums;
3) handling redundant, unclear and missing data;
4) temporal and contextual constraints;
5) the requirement for seemlessness; and
6) selection, generation and synchronisation of appropriate response modal output.

In order for these agents to accomplish given tasks in the real world environment, they must make decisions and execute actions in real-time as well as handle uncertainties. These uncertainties arise from various reasons: knowledge about the environment is partial and approximate, environmental changes are dynamic and can only partially be predicted. Traditional deliberative approaches to planning are not fully capable of adequately handling with uncertain environments. We use a reactive approach by defining a set of local behaviours that are independent of action generating entities. This approach better handle uncertainty by not entirely relying on reasoning about the environment and predicting how changes may correspond to the plans set out. Hence, the goal-directed behaviour of the agent is not explicitly planned; alternatively they emerge from changes to the local behaviours.

The design consideration of an effective e-PSA agent should include the following features and capabilities:

- Mixed initiative interaction
- Conversational model
- Mental and Affective model
- Specific and defined role
- Perception of
  1) world and the surrounding environment (including the media content making up the interface) and
  2) individual customers' profiles
- Reasoning engine
- Adaptive capabilities
- Learning mechanisms.

The implementation considerations of the e-PSA animated figure should include:

- Platform independency as the character will most definitely be deployed over various operating systems and media players.
- Simplicity to break the complexity of usability barriers.
- Synchronisation and control of social and adaptive behaviour.
- Synchronisation and control of interactive presentation.

5 Framework

Our approach addresses three distinct components of an overall framework for supporting affect-based multi-modal behaviour in Interface Agents: *Knowledge Representation and Manipulation, Grounded Affect Models* and the convergence of both into support for multimedia visualisation of lifelike behaviour. The research presents a novel specification for such a medium and a functional agent-based system scenario (e-commerce) that could be implemented with it. The objective of the proposed scenario will demonstrate: firstly, that the methodology supports the requirements of life-like characters, and secondly, that the agent-based interaction implemented is a useful way of supporting the tasks described in the scenarios The developed modules collectively define a framework for creating and implementing interface agents with life-like qualities.

5.1 Knowledge Representation & Manipulation

The research attempts to show that there is a fundamental need for a technical support for the semantic manipulation of data content required for the creation of affective life-like interface agents in a multi-agent environment. Supporting the argument, that if the current revolution in user interfaces is about "rich design", the next will be about "rich behaviour" [23]. This need is identified by examining trends in the human-computer interaction and software agent literature, as well as, advances in computational psychology theory. In our opinion the crucial advance in the upcoming generation of "natural interfaces" will be the degree to which content is understood and acted on by an interface agent, and not just presented to the user.

Multimedia is an appropriate technology for providing information services, in terms of information visualisation and user inter-action. In the presented framework the information services are provided by agents, which simplifies the addition of new services dynamically. Multimedia provides rich interaction models for users and is required for ease of access, ease of comprehension, and engagement of interest. However, multimedia service provision tends towards a tightly coupled system. This means that changes to the system require re-compilation, if, for example new services are to be included. The architecture also does not support a rich user context model for reasoning in general ways about the types of related services that may interest the user.

The development conducted so far has produced an approach to enabling the multimedia Interface Agent behaviour, in which components are converged by using a meta-level annotation language. This meta-data is an abstract description of any components required for interface agent functionality. These components may be visual in nature, but they can also be abstract, high-level components that represent tasks, actions, behaviours, traits, and goals. These components can, further, expose their semantics to the various affect engines defined. Thus, domain-specific components of an interface can be augmented with contextually generated (dynamic) components, based on these rule references. The component's structure, for the most part, refers to its connections to other components on the input and output side and its association to a schematic or a functional subsystem. Functional knowledge about a component is its intended use in the system and its contribution to the higher-level functions of the system. Knowledge of component behaviour concerns its states. Together, the structural, functional and behaviour knowledge determines how the appropriate behaviour of contextual action.

Understanding the Environment: Knowledge Abstraction

For lifelike interface agents, like the Personal Sales Assistant, to be effective they must exhibit some form of intelligence in the sense that they are intuitive, proactive and responsive to user preferences and requirements as well as to the world as a whole. To be capable of this the PSA must have a semantic and contextual understanding of the information being exchanged. This requires a theoretical framework for representing knowledge and belief of agents interacting with other agents. This includes frameworks for representing media objects in the environment, multi-modal features, data, uncertain knowledge about the surrounding environment evolving with experience and time, awareness of the implication of time constraints, and context-based behaviour. For this purpose we define so called *Assets* [7], which are annotations (meta-level descriptions) of objects being manipulated between the visual framework (PSA) and the backend system (service agents). This provides an understanding of the content being handled and hence a better awareness of the environment and an abstract way of handling multimedia. These abstractions hold physical and conceptual meaning and also include expected initial emotional indicators. We are also examining criteria and ways in which these indicators may vary according to the context of agent conversational acts. With an aim of using this as a base for building agent's social and adaptive behaviour. These *Assets* and the Asset Description Language offer:

- a structured way of co-ordinating multimedia content and domain data for agents without agents having understand the raw content (raw multimedia);
- an automated process for returning information, and changes regarding the state of the environment to agents in a language the agents can understand;
- a content language in its own right as it holds rich information. The template in which the *Assets* are defined provides an expected co-ordination of information. The Asset description language allows this process to be automated. Everything in the structure is explicit so an agent can select the aspects, which are important to it. An agent could use the structure to communicate and share information with other agents through an action, a domain and a task model.

Content Language

Specifying a content language allows the introduction of a mechanism and means for maintaining social feedback into the behaviour model (audio-visual multimedia and/or internal behaviour), allowing affect-based actions to directly affect the social structure in the course of an interaction. We also facilitate for a reciprocal feedback loop to social structure, in which one agent's friendly attitude, for example, results in another agent adjusting their belief about social distance, and hence changing the second agent's future conversational strategies. This social feedback should result in interpretable and interesting changes in the way two agents treat one another over the course of a social interaction. In a practical application, this may prove useful as one criterion for promoting trust between agents in a multi-agent environment competing in an electronic commerce setting. Agents may convey these social findings to the human user, which, in turn, may also promote the user's trust in dealing with a particular sales agent.

The content language provides the specific more context-oriented information. We use meta-level representation to convey more specific semantics of data being exchanged. By including meta-representation of the data in the content part of the communication act, an added dimension provided to agent comprehension of the actual meaning within the content exchanged. The Assets not only serve as data that agents manipulate but also serve as a basis for defining a social framework. Since any information can contain vast amounts of embedded knowledge, Asset descriptions can therefore have potential to convey associated and inferred perception. Adding social attributes that can collectively serve as choices that influence interface agent perception about the underlying semantics of the content and attributes to it's behavioural and personality traits, provides an improvisational basis that serves as a key aspect in determining an interface agent's character.

These Asset descriptions essentially ground five important aspects of information sharing between agents and entities [18]. The aspects defined to allow the sharing of content across a distributed system and facilitate scalable service provision and communicating affect are as follows:

- **Affect model**: defines emotional and personality attributes;
- **Domain model**: defines the intended use of content, in terms of the services it is intended for;
- **Task model**: defines the tasks the Asset may perform;
- **Action model**: supports the understanding of what should happen when the Asset is interacted with. The actions are defined with a scripting language. They are dynamic and are replaceable depending on the interaction. The actions specify the type of return information about the current event that the agent is interested in,
- **Media content**: defines properties, types and values to be understood by a presentation system if content renderable.

The affect model includes indicators to affect-based responses expected when a defined Asset is being handled in a normal or non-context sensitive way. These indicators are associated, using a set of selection rules, with a predefined intended behaviour. This planned behaviour is then modified to incorporate context-sensitive variables to select the appropriate affect-based behaviour. The resulting behaviour is then mapped to a visual (animated) representation. Variations of animated expression (or intonation) can be realised by altering and adjusting the intensity of the behaviour according to the immediate situation.

Meta-data Representation

Meta-data descriptions are important for permitting data and knowledge exchange between programmes. Assets are system entities that are made up of services, data or renderable screen objects. These Assets are intended for the exchange of knowledge during agent communication as well as to facilitate for content reuse. The Asset descriptions provide a semantic view of the content being handled giving the agents insight knowledge of the conversational acts and thus allowing agents to reason about and react accordingly in a more intelligent manner. Multimedia content is viewed in terms of service-provisioned descriptions that provide visual meaning for the presentation system as well as augmented attributes instantiated when used within a particular application domain. The contextual semantic, visualisation entities, as well as the relationships among objects are what explicitly model the Assets. The Assets are abstracted encapsulations of this information providing a means by which an agent can interpret the underlying semantics of the object being used and by a presentation system to understand the mechanisms and services required for rendering the multimedia objects.

The underlying conceptual model of these Assets is that they are object abstractions that provide content-based data, which, translates into knowledge about the multimedia content. The Asset abstractions are described as meta-data templates that encapsulate semantic annotations of the Media Content, Domain (service provided), Tasks and Action models. The meta-data template is defined by a meta-data language. The syntax of which is expressed in BNF (terms, expressions etc.), that determine the grammar that defines the meta-data structure. The structure is the ontological level between the meta-data template and the meta-data language and is necessary if the language definitions need to be changed (this is common in computationally reflective systems). This is the level at which Asset descriptions and service descriptions have a common model. The actual structure for an Asset template takes the following set of terms: header, content (composite or atomic), domain, script and task. Each term is specialised by a set of phrases, which are applicable within a service model. The syntax has to be refined using delimiters. The description language-base includes a terminology and a set of basic atomic properties that are defined as contextual implications giving the described objects their functional semantics.

The multimedia data model addresses the aspects related to data presentation, manipulation and content-based retrieval. It provides a set of requirements based on which the Asset manager can function. The Asset model is to contain many Asset descriptions, which will allow the selection of Assets for potentially any purpose. The purpose of this model is to dynamically generate objects for a Presentation System to render or for use with other applications that require objects of similar characteristics. The importance of the flexibility of the model is to not only to facilitate Asset reuse within one application but moreover to allow other applications to also reuse these dynamically generated Assets. The base Asset model consists of:

- Object Description, providing an annotated view of raw data;
- Visual Description, aiding a presentation service in describing the temporal and spatial relationships among different Assets for renderable objects;
- Content Semantics, a semantic view of the stored objects;
- Service Descriptions, instantiated to an application domain;
- Initial Affect Indicators that an Asset will convey in a non-context sensitive environment. These may change drastically according to the past and immediate states of the agent within an MAS and the state of the environment itself.

These initial indicators alone cannot determine behavioural reactions. The impact would depend on past experiences, the current mental state and the environment. So the actual influence of such indicators will be determined by these variable factors that are governed by the context in which the content is being conveyed. Nevertheless, these indicators serve as the innate knowledge an agent may start with, and based on which may influence its behaviour.

Asset Description Model and Structure

The Assets are intended for the exchange of knowledge during agent communication as well as to facilitate for content reuse. The contextual semantic, visualisation entities, as well as the relationships among objects are what explicitly model the Assets. The Assets are abstracted encapsulations of this information, providing a means by which an agent can interpret the underlying semantics of the object being used and by a presentation system to understand the mechanisms and services required for rendering the multimedia objects. Hence, Assets can be objects of multimedia, services, affective feedback or any other type of data.

Object type specifies the multimedia type, service,
Content-based describes the object content which will contribute to its functional semantics,
Non-content-based (includes conceptual & physical properties)
Conceptual properties include:
  provisional indicators: indicators to an expected emotion the content may convey
  domain subset of the ontology
  tasks denoting actions or functional roles
  script *s*to represent a sequence of instructions
Physical properties, attributes that aid in the physical representation of visual objects

Asset Description Structure

Semantic Information

The semantic concept of information is in regards closer to the notion of the meaning that may be conveyed by a message, object or content being handled. It is applicable to internal state as well as external communications. This includes concepts of mental states and processes such as understanding, believing, perceiving and many more.

All semantic information processing depends ultimately on (internal) syntactic capabilities as it also depends on syntax processing. Agents, not necessarily interface agents, need representational forms whose syntactic manipulation is semantically useful. A working system always has a physical level of syntactical description. Descriptions on higher-levels may be emergent in that the concepts needed to describe them cannot be defined in terms of the lower-level physical descriptions. The semantic information included in the meta-data descriptions used in the prototype described for Assets includes one that conveys indicators about the mental behaviour exhibited in the current state of the interface agent. These indicators influence the personality traits exhibited by the lifelike character depending on past experiences and the immediate environment.

5.2 Grounding Affect Models

To address grounding affect in agent architectures we extend the common, typically (cognitive), agent architecture that is currently designed to have a head-body form. Taking a human analogy, the architecture is extended to include a heart module yielding an encapsulated agent shell architecture of head-heart-body. This means a more reflective reasoning, the Head part, based on explicit intensions such as Beliefs, Desires and Intentions as in the classical BDI-architecture developed in AI. The Body part indicates a more reflexive (or learned) behaviour and the Heart maintains and manipulates the affect models of emotion and personality.

Efforts such as those by Elliott [11], Velazquez [26], Reilly [24], and Sloman [25], have been fundamental in defining the computational theories to provide agents with affective behaviour but do little in creating a formal method for building them. Affect models for agents will only be widely applicable when there is an organised way to map design models to the effected behaviour representations in real-time applications. An extended BDI agent architecture, BDI&A (Belief, Desires, Intentions and Affect) that grounds the affective behaviour of the agents servers to integrate existing theories of affect with real-time agent behaviour and action and provides a formal method for building such agents.

In this paper we will not detail on the affect model any further as we concentrate on mapping contextual agent behaviour into multimedia visualisation.

5.3 Visualisation Support

Animated lifelike character representations of interface agents will only be widely deployed when there are real-time mechanisms to contextually map character and affect models to effected believable personifications. To approach this we utilise the design elements of an architecture for including personality and emotional responsiveness in an interface agent: semantic abstraction and annotation of the knowledge being manipulated; consequently, mapping the resulting semantic understanding into appropriate initial planned behaviour; and translating this behaviour into context-sensitive character traits by varying the planned response using variable emotion indicators; then finally representing this in a selected modality(ies). Currently, there are several commercial and proprietary agent animation tools available (e.g. MS Agent, Jack, PPP Persona, …), as well as, several emotion engines or mechanisms (Affective Reasoner, S&P,…) that are available to generate and govern believable behaviour of animated agents. However, there is no common mechanism or API to link the underlying engines with the animated representations.

A Character Mark-up Language (CML) is proposed to bridge the gap between the available underlying emotion engines and agent animation tools. CML provides a map between these tools using *Assets* by automating the movement of information from XML Schema structure definitions into the appropriate relational parameters required to generate the required animated behaviour. This would allow developers to use CML as a glue-like mechanism to tie the various visual and underlying behaviour generation tools together seamlessly, regardless of the platform that they run on and the language they are developed with.

Visual Behaviour Definition

The Character Mark-up Language defines the syntactic, semantic and pragmatic character presentation attributes using structured text. CML is based on the definition XML Schema structures. The character mark-up-based language extends the descriptions for facial expressions used in the FACS system. FACS (Facial Action Coding System) defines a set of all the facial movements performed by in a human face [8]. Although FACS is not an SGML-based language in nature, we use their notion of Action Units to define not only facial expressions but also body and hand gestures and movements.

The CML defines a script like that used for a play. It describes the actions and sequence of actions that will take place in the Presentation System. The script is a collection of commands that tell the objects in the world what to do and how to perform actions. At this stage the script defined is sequential, we are currently working on further extensions to include synchronisation of actions being performed. The language is used to create and manipulate objects that are held in memory and referenced by unique output-ontology objects. The structure of the language begins with a command keyword, which is usually followed by one or more arguments and tags. An argument to a command usually qualifies a command, i.e. specifies what form of action the command is to take, while a tag is used to denote the position of other necessary information. A character expression mark-up module will add emotion-based mark-up resulting from emotional behaviour generation rules to the CML descriptions.

Animated character behaviour is expressed through the interpretation of XML Schema structures. These structure definitions are stored in a Schema Document Type Definition (DTD) file using XSDL (XML Schema Definition Language). At run-time character behaviour is generated by specifying XML tag/text streams which are then interpreted by the rendering system based on the rules defined in the definition file.

The language contains low-level tags defining specific character gesture representations defining movements, intensities and explicit expressions. There are also high-level tags that can define commonly used combinations of these low-level tags.

CML is used to dynamically define, at runtime, the mapping of the generated agent behaviour to the required multimedia animation and/or the audio channels required and is encapsulated in the *Asset* structure defined in the previous section. Once *Assets* have been created they are passed on to the appropriate agents to handle, manipulate and render at the presentation system.

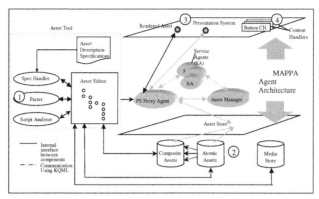

Fig. 2. General Architecture using Assets

5.4   General Framework

Figure 2 following, shows a simplified overview of the distributed architecture in MAPPA (not all the agents and components used in the MAPPA system are defined in this figure) and the Asset Tool. The Asset Tool is an authoring mechanism to generate the required *Assets*. The intention is to delineate how *Assets* fit into an overall agent architecture manifesting the relationship between an Asset Manager, as described in [2], and the *Asset* authoring tool. The Asset Manager acts as a fully-fledged agent in the dynamic system, where as the Asset Tool provides the components necessary for a static development system.

The components which remain the same between dynamic mode (service integration) and multimedia development (static mode) are: (1) The parser and content specification from the Asset tool, (2) the two databases which contain the Asset descriptions, (3) the presentation system which manages layout of visual objects and content handlers, and (4) the content handlers which are actually used to render the description to the screen. During dynamic mode agents are introduced and the proxy agent (termed the presentation mediator) parses the Asset description to the required format. In development (or static) mode the presentation parser of the Asset description is used with the Asset Tool and a direct connection is made to the presentation system. In dynamic mode these components are managed and accessed at an agent level which means a rich communication layer, dynamic bindings of actions to multimedia content objects and domain model management.

6   E-PSA Mappa Implementation

In a real-time multi-agent environment the e-PSA inhabits a world, which is dynamic and unpredictable. To be autonomous, it must be able to perceive its environment and decide its actions to reach the goals defined by its behavioural models. To visually represent the behaviour, the relevant actions and behaviour must be transformed into visual motional actions. The design of a visual affect-based e-PSA requires components to endow them with perception, behaviour processing and generation, action selection, and behaviour interpretation into believable graphical representation. Taking a human analogy, the design of these components are grouped into the following modules, and are delineated in *figure 3*:

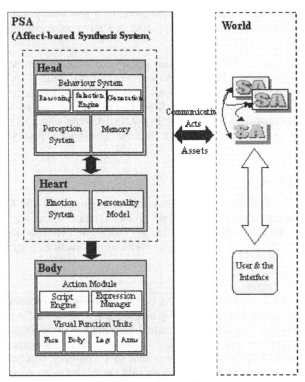

Fig. 3. Agent System Overview
(SA=Service Agent)

- **Head**, which deals with perception, continuous memory, reasoning, and behaviour selection and generation;
- **Heart**, which maintains and manipulates the affect models of emotion and personality; and the
- **Body**, which deals with behaviour action execution and visual representation.

Head – Perception

The perception system provides the state of the world to the behavioural and emotional modules through agent communication and content sharing. The behaviour system uses this information, along with information of past experiences and memory to select the appropriate behavioural response. The resulting behaviour is fed into the action module to generate the appropriate script for animated visual representation.

Heart – Emotion Engine

We use emotion to describe short-term variations in internal mental states, describing focused meaning pertaining to specific incidences or situations. The emotional model is based on description of emotions by Ortony et. al. [19]. Emotions are viewed as brief short termed, and focused with respect to a particular matter. We assume that a char-acter need not exhibit all the attributes of the emotion or personality definition to be a successful affect model. It needs to incorporate at least some basic features of affect.

We use personality to characterise long term patterns of emotion, and behaviour associated with the synthetic character. Person-ality is the general behaviour character-istics that do not arise from and are not pertaining to any particular matter. We model the broad qualities that include individually distinctive, and consistently enduring yet subject to influence and change. Psychologists have characterised five basic dimensions of personality, so known as, the Five-Factor model [9] of independent traits.

Body – Visual Action Module

This module handles and channels the audio-visual embodiment of the Interface Agent. For the visual character representations of the interface agent we use the Character Mark-up Language (CML) as specified in *section 5* to define the syntactic, semantic and pragmatic character presentation attributes using structured text.

The MAPPA Picture

The system snapshot below shows the MAPPA e-PSA, assisting and recommending wine products. The Presentation System display method, many "products" are shown in a single display window. This area serves as an on-screen metaphor for a *shelf* of products, as might be encountered in any shop or store. It is an alternative to the "catalogue pages" approach familiar to all those that shop "on-line" regularly. This approach largely overcomes two familiar problems with the catalogue approach. First, the customer may browse a large number of products quickly in a single page. This avoids the familiar problem of navigating many pages to locate a particular item. Second, the contents of the "shelf" may be quickly configured to display particular products of interest to the customer.

The user may *riffle* through the products by running the mouse pointer over them. As each product is touched by the pointer it raises slightly and a brief product description immediately appears above it, emulating a shelf product. *James*, the ePSA, may be called to provide further information by clicking on a product image. The RSVP effect, which is both distinctive and visually effective, is not easily envisaged from the still image of wine bottles. The effect has garnered unanimous interest whenever demonstrated informally or presented under controlled test conditions [4].

The ePSA, which is based on Microsoft's Agent technology, is animated over the top of the display. The Agent's utterances are generated in a variety of ways, some scripted within the control program, some derived from an extensive product informa-

Fig. 4. MAPPA Presentation System

James[1] provides individualised recommendations.

tion database, and can be generated by a JESS based expert system Agent, which has access to both general product (wine) knowledge, and user preferences collected during the current and from previous sessions.

7   Summary and Conclusions

We have addressed the issue of adding value to electronic commerce by introducing Affect adaptive anthropomorphic electronic personal sales assistant agents. We propose to leverage some of the shortcomings of current e-commerce potentials by identifying with the customer to "win his/her acceptance". We argue that e-commerce applications will only reach their full potential when there is more widespread focus on considerations for individualised social behaviour and tendencies while designing and implementing their customer interface.

Developing such interfaces will require research in many disciplines. The study stimulates novel research with highly multi-disciplinary approaches and users, involving areas of psychology, knowledge representation and manipulation, visualisation and, moreover, the integration of all three. The major challenges in building real-time e-PSAs are getting them to intuitively interact with the customer and the surrounding environment, as well as, planning, recognising and visualising their behaviour through context sensitive character traits. We presented an agent-base approach to implement the e-PSA and briefly presented its architecture delineating the salient components required to effectuate its proposed and desired features.

Finally, by introducing virtual sales assistants we also introduce many open issues among which are the following few: Will these sales characters bring forth both the good and bad qualities of human sales assistants? Can we always trust their advice and recommendations? Do their visual characters make them more trustworthy? Will they really work on behalf of the customer or will their main concern be the financial gains of the vendor? If e-PSAs are to be our own personal assistant, who will provide its services? The vendor or a third part or both? If e-PSAs are produced by the vendor then we can question their intentions; yet if they are produced by a third part then can we trust the accuracy of the information? With that said, we still believe that e-PSA agents can be very helpful both for interaction and engagement with the customer, for the enhancement of the adaptability of the system providing personalised services and possibly, ultimately, improving sales. Further out-of-the-lab evaluation will help to answer these questions.

Acknowledgments. The work on MAPPA is supported by a grant from the European Commission ESPRIT projects funding, under grant number EP28831. Special acknowledgement goes to Mark Witkowski for designing and developing the MAPPA store interface shown in *figure 4* and to Patricia Charlton.

References

[1]   André, E, Rist, T., & Müller ,J. Integrating Reactive & Scripted Behaviour in a LifeLike Presentation .Agent. In: 2nd Int. Conf. on Autonomous Agents '98, pp. 261-268, 1998.

[2]   Arafa, Y., Charlton, P., & Mamdani, E. Engineering Personal Service Assistants with Lifelike Qualities, EBAA'99 WS at AA'99, 1999.

[3]   Arafa, Y., Dionisi, G., Mamdani, A., Martin, S., Pitt, J., & Witkowski, M. Towards Building Loyalty in e-Commmerce Applications, AA'00 WS on Agents in the Industry, 2000.

[4]   Arafa, Y., Fehin, P., Pitt,J. &Witkowski, M. Indicators to the Effect of Agent Techno on Consumer Loyalty, AISB 2001.

[5]   Bates, J. The Role of Emotion in Believable Agents. In Communication of the ACM.Vol. 37, No.7, pp122-125,1994.

[6]   Bower, G.H., & Cohen P.R. Emotional Influences in Memory & Thinking: Data & Theory. Clack. & Fiske Eds, Affect & Cognition, pp 291-233: Lawrence Erlbaum Association Publishers, 1982.

[7]   Charlton, P., Mamdani, A., Olsson, O., Pitt, J., Somers, F., Waern, A. Using an Asset Model for integration of Agents and Multimedia to Provide an Open Service Architecture, Multimedia Applications, Services and Techniques, Lecture Notes in Comp. Science, (ECMAST '97), pp 635-650, 1997.

[8]   Damasio, Antonio R. Descartes' Error: Emotion, Reason, and the Human Brain. NY: Avon Books, 1994.

[9]   Digman, J. M., 1990. Personality Structure: Emergence of the Five-Factor Model. Annual Review of Psychology 41:417-440.

[10]   Ekman, P. & Rosenberg, E. L. What the Face Reveals: Basic & Applied Studies of Spontaneous Expression Using Facial Action Coding System. Oxford University Press, 1997.

[11] Elliott, C. (1993) Using the Affective Reasoner to Support Social Simulation, IJCAI'93, p194-200

[12] Hudlicka, E. & Billingsley, J. Affect-Adaptive User Interface, LEA, Proceedings of HCI'99 International, 1999.

[13] Lang, P. The Emotion Probe: Studies of Motivation and Attention , American Psychologist 50 (5):372-385 1995.

[14] Lashkari, Y., Metral, M. & Maes, P. Collaborative Interface Agents. Proc.12th conf. AAAI, pp444-449. AAAI Press, 1994

[15] Lester, J., et al, Deitic & Emotive Communication in Animated Pedagogical Agents,1st Int. WS on Embodied Conversational Chars, 1998.

[16] Maes, P. Agents that Reduce the Work Overload. Communications of ACM 37(7):31-40, 1994.

[17] Mauldin, M. VERBOTS:Putting a face on NL, invited presentation at Autonomous Agents'99, ACM Press, 1999.

[18] Mc Guigan, R., Delorme, P., Grimson, J., Charlton, P., Arafa, Y. 1998. The Reuse of Multimedia Objects by Software Kimsac, OOIS'98.

[19] Ortony, A., Clore, G. L., & Collins A. The cognitive Structure of Emotions. Cambridge University Press. 1990.

[20] Paiva, A. & Machado, I. Vincent an Autonomous Pedagogical Agent for on-the-job Training, in the Intelligent Tutoring Systems, Ed. V. Shute, Pub. Springer-Verlag, 1998

[21] Picard, R. Affective Computing. The MIT Press, 1997.

[22] Pin, R. New FollowUp.Net Service Determines Why Shopping Carts are Abandoned, 1999.http://www.followup.net/press.

[23] Reeves, B. & Nass, C. The Media Equation. CSLI Publications, Cambridge University Press, 1996.

[24] Reilly, W.S., & Bates, J. Emotions as Part of a Broad Agent Arch., Working notes WS on Arch. Underlying Motivation & Emotion, 1993.

[25] Sloman, A. (1987) "Motives, mechanisms and emotions", Cognition and Emotion, 1:217-234

[26] Velásquez, J. A Computational Framework for Emotion-based Control. Proc. SAB'98 WS on Grounding Emotions in Adaptive Sys, 1998.

[27] Wooldridge, M. & Jennings, N. Intelligent Agents: Theory & Practice. Knowledge Eng. Review10(2):115-152. 1995.

[28] Yamamoto, G. & Nakamura, Y. Agent-based Electronic Mall: e-Marketplace: Proc. of AA'99 demonstrations, 1999.

Feature vs. Model Based Vocal Tract Length Normalization for a Speech Recognition-Based Interactive Toy

Chun Keung Chau, Chak Shun Lai, and Bertram Emil Shi

Consumer Media Center/Human Language Technology Center
Department of Electrical and Electronic Engineering
Hong Kong University of Science and Technology, Clear Water Bay, Kowloon,
HONG KONG
{eechau, eebert}@ee.ust.hk

Abstract. We describe an architecture for speech recognition based interactive toys and discuss the strategies we have adopted to deal with the requirements for the speech recognizer imposed by this application. In particular, we focus on the fact that speech recognizers used in interactive toys must deal with users whose age ranges from children to adults. The large variations in vocal tract length between children and adults can significantly degrade the performance of speech recognizers. We compare two approaches to vocal tract length normalization: feature-based VTLN and model-based VTLN. We describe why intuitively, one might expect that due to the coarser frequency information used by the model-based approach, that feature-based VTLN would outperform model-based VTLN. However, our results indicate that there is very little difference in performance between the two schemes.

1 Introduction

Speech recognition technology enables us to build interactive systems which respond to users spoken input. We are developing an interactive toy which enables users to influence the flow and outcome of stories being told by the toy. Stories written for the toy contain choice points, at which the user can choose from multiple possible branches. Different choices will lead the user down different paths, resulting in different story outcomes. At each choice point, the toy uses speech recognition to identify the particular branch the user wishes to follow.

Our interactive toy consists of three parts: the story telling engine, the authoring environment, and the speech recognition system.

The story telling engine is responsible for telling multi-path story and the speech recognition system is responsible for recognizing the keywords from users and telling the result to the story telling engine to decide the flow of the story. When the story is told and once a branching point is reached, the story telling engine will send a list of keywords, to the speech recognition system. Then speech recognition system will

J. Liu et al. (Eds.): AMT 2001, LNCS 2252, pp. 134–143, 2001.
© Springer-Verlag Berlin Heidelberg 2001

record the speech of the users, spot the keywords from the speech and return the recognition results to the story telling engine. The story telling engine will then dynamically synthesize the story content by following the branch of the story flow corresponding to the speech recognition results.

The authoring environment provides authors with a graphical user interface for structuring their content to represent a desired flow for content delivery by the interactive toy. It also provides a platform for manipulating the materials. The branches of story flow and the expected users' responses are decided by authors at this stage. The expected users' responses are treated as keywords. The output of this environment is a database which contains the text of the story, multi media content, as well as the branching structure. This database is all that is required by the story telling engine to tell the given story. Stories can be shared and distributed over Internet in this format.

The speech recognition system takes the list of expected keywords from the story telling engine and determines which of the keywords was spoken by the user. Although the number of keywords at any point in time is limited, for maximum flexibility, we must be able to handle a large number of possibilities. Therefore, we use phone base HMM model. To form a keyword, we can concatenate the phone base models. Thus, the number of models is minimized.

To enable users to interact more naturally with the toy, the speech recognizer must be able to handle input which contains other words in addition to one of the expected keywords. In addition, it must also be able to recognizer when the utterance contains none of the expected keywords.

1.1 Requirements on the Speech Recognizer

A robust speech recognizer is essential because the interaction between human and machine using speech recognition technology is a key of our system. Therefore, we focus on two areas to deal with the changing environment.

Keyword spotting enables users to speak commands or requests without concern to the exact syntax of the request, as long as their utterance contains one or more of the keywords which the system has been designed to detect. A filler model is used to do the keyword spotting in order to extract the main theme of the speech. As users respond to the speech recognizer with a whole sentence with natural way, we need a method to extract the keyword. Thus, filler model is a method to achieve the goal. Keyword spotting techniques are important to the interactive toy project because during playing, users will not know exactly what keywords they allowed to speak. Therefore, we need to extract the keywords from users' speech.. In order to implement keyword spotting, a filler model [10], [11], [12], [13] and [14] usually used to absorb the non-keyword part of the utterance. A filler model can be trained by any speech data. Data contained keyword speech can also used for training filler model. and the structure of filler model can be single state with multiple Gaussian mixtures [10].

The second area, which is the focus of this paper, is dealing with the fact that the recognizer must deal with a wide range of users, from children to adults. Variations in the vocal tract length can significantly degrade the performance of speech recognizers.

The length of the vocal tract can vary by as much as 25% between speakers and the effect of this is to cause differences in the short-term spectrum of the same sound uttered by different speakers [1]. This variation can degrade the performance of speech recognizers. For example, models trained on adult data typically do not perform well with children [4]. In the remainder of this paper we discuss our approach to compensating for this problem.

2   Vocal Tract Length Normalization

One possible solution to compensate for the mismatch is to do vocal tract length normalization (VTLN). Previous work has shown that VTLN can be performed either on the incoming speech during the computation of MFCC features[1][2][3] or on the models[6][7]. Further improvements can be gained by applying VTLN both in training and during recognition[5]. Feature based approaches have the advantage of higher frequency resolution, as they operate directly upon the FFT-derived spectrum of the incoming speech. Model based approaches, on the other hand, transform Gausian means by shifting the Mel scaled filterbank outputs, and thus have much coarser frequency resolution. Thus, we might expect their performance to lag that of feature-based approaches. However, they have the advantage that they can be applied only once, rather than to each incoming frame of speech. In addition, no changes or additions to an existing MFCC front end need be made.

In this paper, we compare the performance of these two approaches. Interestingly, our results show little difference in the performance of the two approaches. In addition, we observe that applying VTLN during training has the potential to improve performance of model based approaches, which is consistent with work using a feature based approach[5].

The procedures of feature and model warping are described. Then, we present our experimental results comparing the performance on the two schemes in improving the speech recognition performance of adult models presented with children's speech in the TIDIGITS task.

2.1   Theory

The vocal tract is commonly modeled as a tube with varying cross section, which is excited either at one end or at a point along the tube [2] and [9]. Acoustic theory tells us that the transfer function of energy from the excitation source to the output can be described in terms of the resonances of the tube. Such resonances are called formants for speech, and they represent the frequencies that pass the most acoustic energy from source to output. The vocal tract length has a large effect on the formant frequencies. When the vocal tract length gets longer, the positions of formants shifts down and the shape of power spectrum will be compressed accordingly. Conversely, shortening the vocal tract shifts the formants upwards. This variation is a source of mismatch between the input utterance and the model during recognition.

Vocal tract length normalization seeks to remove this mismatch. The feature-based approach to VTLN modifies features extracted from the speech waveform, so that they better match the model. The model based approach modifies the model to better match incoming features. The features used in this work were standard MFCC features, computed as shown in Figure 1.

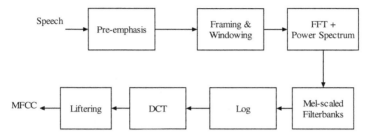

Fig. 1. Block Diagram of MFCC Feature Extractor

3   Feature-Based VTLN

The feature-based approach studied here was based on resampling the FFT derived spectrum. Frequencies f were mapped to new frequencies $G(f)$ according to the equation below [1]:

$$G(f) = \begin{cases} \alpha f, & 0 \leq f < f_0 \\ \dfrac{f_{\max} - \alpha f_0}{f_{\max} - f_0}(f - f_0) + \alpha f_0, & f_0 \leq f < f_{\max} \end{cases} \tag{1}$$

where α is the warping factor, $f_{\max}$ denotes the maximum signal bandwidth, and f_0 denotes the frequency at the band-edge.

Resampling is performed by computing a new spectrum, where the spectral amplitude at a particular frequency bin, f, is equal to the spectral amplitude at the frequency $G^{-1}(f)$ in the original spectrum. If $G^{-1}(f)$ does not coincide with an exact bin frequency, linear interpolation is used to estimate the spectral amplitude from the two nearest bins. For example, if the input frequency spectrum is more wideband than the average case due to a shorter vocal tract length, α smaller than 1 will compress the input FFT spectrum.

4 Model-Based VTLN

In the model-based approach, we transform MFCC means according to a transformation, which is parameterized by the warping factor so that the model better matches the incoming speech.

4.1 Transforming the Static Coefficients

The first step in transforming the means of the static coefficients is to compute the filterbank outputs corresponding to the static means by inverting the log and DCT operations shown in Figure 1. Any high order MFCC coefficients discarded during feature extraction are replaced by zero-padding. From these filterbank outputs, the transformation tries to predict the filterbank outputs which would result if the incoming speech were frequency warped as follows. For each filterbank i,

1. Let f be the center frequency corresponding to that filterbank, and compute the frequency which would warp to the filterbank center via equation (1), $f_{warp} = G^{-1}(f)$.

2. Let $\underline{f_{warp}}$ be the largest filterbank center frequency smaller than f_{warp} and $\overline{f_{warp}}$ be the smallest filterbank center frequency larger than f_{warp} and let $\underline{b_{warp}}$ and $\overline{b_{warp}}$ be the corresponding outputs derived from the MFCC means.

3. Use linear interpolation to calculate the new filterbank output, b_{new}:

$$b_{new} = \underline{b_{warp}} \frac{\overline{f_{warp}} - f_{warp}}{\overline{f_{warp}} - \underline{f_{warp}}} + \overline{b_{warp}} \frac{f_{warp} - \underline{f_{warp}}}{\overline{f_{warp}} - \underline{f_{warp}}} \tag{2}$$

The new MFCC means are then obtained by applying the log and DCT operations to this new set of filterbank outputs.

Note that the in this case, if the incoming speech is more wideband than the average, corresponding to a shorter vocal tract length, a value of α larger than one will shift the model to match the model to the incoming speech. Thus, the warping factor used in the model-based transformation is the inverse of that used in the feature-based transformation. In the following, we will reference all results to the warping factor used in the model based transformation, with the understanding that this warping factor is inverted to apply the feature-based VTLN.

4.2 Transforming the Delta and Acceleration Coefficients

The delta coefficients can be transformed in a similar manner. Note that the static MFCC mean (m) is obtained from binned spectrum (b) by the equation

$$m = C \ln b \tag{3}$$

where C denotes the matrix used to compute the DCT. Differentiating both side of this equation with respect to time, we obtain the relationship between the delta MFCC coefficients and the delta filterbank outputs,

$$\Delta m = \frac{C\Delta b}{b} \tag{4}$$

Reorganize the terms, the equation becomes:

$$\Delta b = bC^{-1}\Delta m \tag{5}$$

where C^{-1} is the invert DCT. The warping process applied to the delta filterbank outputs is the same as that applied to the static filterbank outputs. The new delta MFCC coefficients are obtained by applying equation (4).

Similarly, for the acceleration coefficients, we differentiate equation (3) twice to obtain

$$\Delta^2 m = C\left[\frac{\Delta^2 b}{b} - \left(\frac{\Delta b}{b}\right)^2\right] \tag{6}$$

Reorganize the terms, the equation becomes:

$$\Delta^2 b = \left[\Delta^2 m C^{-1} + \left(\frac{\Delta b}{b}\right)^2\right]b \tag{7}$$

This equation enables us to obtain the acceleration coefficients for the filterbank output, which are similarly warped and transformed back to the MFCC domain to obtain the new model parameters.

Note that the frequency information used in the model-based approach is much coarser than that used in the feature based approach. In the feature based approach, the entire FFT spectrum (e.g. 256 points) is resampled. In the model-based approach, on the filterbank outputs are resampled (e.g. 26 points). Thus, intuitively, we might expect that the performance of the feature-based approach to be better than that of the model based approach. Surprisingly, our experimental results indicate that there is little difference in performance.

5   Experimental Results

5.1   Database & Model Configuration

To evaluate the model warping method, we built 2 sets of connected digit model from the TI-digits database: an unnormalized model (UM) and a normalized model (NM).

All 25 men and 25 women in the training set were used in training. The UM were obtained by training on unwarped data.

To train the NM, we grouped the training data according to gender. Then, for each gender we applied the model warping described in the previous section to the MFCC features of the training data with a set of warping factors, from 0.88 to 1.12 with the step size 0.04. We tested the warped training data using the unnormalized model and chose the warping factor that gave the highest accuracy for each gender as a gender-dependent warping factor, and used the corresponding set of warped training data to train the normalized models.

The 11 digit models used were 9 state left-to-right HMM models with a single mixture component. The silence model trained had 3 states, 4 mixtures and loop back path.

The adult models were tested on the children's testing set of the TI-digits corpus (both boys and girls), in order to evaluate the effectiveness of the feature and model-based VTLN algorithms.

In these experiments, we are interested in comparing the capability of the two approaches in compensating for the difference in vocal tract length between the adults used in training and the children used in testing. Because the warping factor used strongly affects the performance of a VTLN algorithm, rather than trying to identify a particular warping factor, which might favor the feature or the model based approach, we present our results as a graph of accuracy versus warping factor. In particular, each point represents the accuracy resulting from choosing the same warping factor for all the data or models.

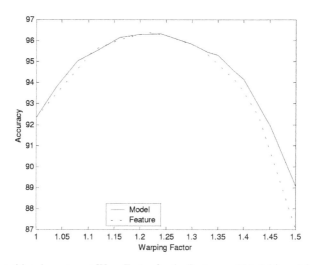

Fig. 2. Recognition Accuracy vs Warp Factor for the Feature and Model-based Approaches

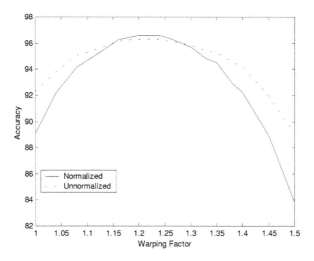

Fig. 3. Recognition Accuracy vs. Warp Factor for Model Warping using Normalized and Unnormalized Models

Figure 2, compares the word accuracy as a function of warping factor for the model and feature-based approaches when tested with the unnormalized models. The performance of the two approaches is nearly identical. Note that the optimal global warping factor is about 1.25, which is consistent with data [8], indicating that the third formant in children is approximately 1.25 times that of adults.

Figure 3 compares the performance of the model based approach on the normalized and unnormalized models. The performance using the normalized models is clearly much more dependent upon accurate estimation of the proper warping factor, than the unnormalized models. However, the accuracy is higher if the correct warping factor is used.

Table 1: The best performance (word accuracy) obtained on the test set

VTLN used	Unnormalized Model	Normalized Model
None	92.34%	89.10%
Model-based	96.33%	96.59%
Feature-based	96.37%	96.62%

Table 1 shows that the performance of the model and the feature based approaches is approximately the same, if the best warping factor is used. There is a slight reduction in the error rate, about 7%, with the use of the normalized models. This is consistent with results reported in [5] using a feature based approach. Thus, it appears that applying VTLN during training can improve the performance of both feature and model-based VTLN.

6 Summary

This paper has described our architecture for speech recognition based interactive toys. This application requires speech recognizers to respond to input which may contain extra words and to users with a wide range of ages. We have described our approaches to addresing these issues, with particular attention to the latter. In particular, we investigated the use of feature and model-based approaches to VTLN. Our results indicate that despite the coarser frequency resolution used in the transformation, the model-based approach achieves performance which is essentially identical with that obtained using a feature-based approach. Our results also indicate that the performance of the model-based approach can be improved by reducing the variability of input utterances by applying VTLN to the training data. Best performance of the feature based and model based approach occurred at the same warping factor.

Acknowledgements. This research was supported by the Hong Kong Government Industry Department under the Innovation and Technology Fund Grant AF/264/97 and by the Hong Kong Research Grants Council under grant number RGC CA97/98.EG02.

References

1. Lee, L. and Rose R.,"A frequency warping approach to speaker normalization", *IEEE Transactions on Speech & Audio Processing*, vol. 6, no. 1, pp. 49-60, Jan. 1998.
2. Eide, E. and Gish, H., "A parametric approach to vocal tract length normalization", *Proc. IEEE Intl. Conf. on Acoustics, Speech and Signal Processing*, Atlanta, GA, USA, vol. 1, pp. 346-348, 1996.
3. Wegmann, S., McAllaster, D., Orloff, J. and Peskin, B., "Speaker normalization on conversational telephone speech", *Proc. IEEE Intl. Conf. on Acoustics, Speech and Signal Processing*, Atlanta, GA, USA, vol. 1, pp. 339-341, 1996.
4. Wilpon, J.G. and Jacobsen, C.N., "A study of speech recognition for children and the elderly", *Proc. IEEE Intl. Conf. on Acoustics, Speech and Signal Processing*, Atlanta, GA, USA, vol. 1, pp. 349 –352, 1996.
5. Welling, L., Haeb-Umbach, R., Zubert, X. and Haberland, N., "A study on speaker normalization using vocal tract normalization and speaker adaptive training", *Proc. IEEE Intl. Conf. on Acoustics, Speech and Signal Processing*, Seattle, WA, USA, vol. 2, pp. 797-800, 1998.
6. Claes, T., Dologlou, I., ten Bosch, L. and van Compernolle, D., "A novel feature transformation for vocal tract length normalization in automatic speech recognition", *Speech and Audio Processing, IEEE Transactions*, vol. 6, no. 6, pp. 549-557, Nov. 1998.
7. Cox, S., "Speaker normalization in the MFCC domain", *Proc. 6th International Conference on Spoken Language Processing*, Bejiing 2000.

8. Appleton and Perera, eds., *The Development and Practice of Electronic Music*, Prentice-Hall, p.42, 1975.
9. Rabiner, L. R., *Fundamentals of Speech Recognition*, Prentice-Hall, Inc., 1993.
10. Wilpon, J.G. and Jacobsen, C.N., "A study of speech recognition for children and the elderly", *Proc. IEEE Intl. Conf. on Acoustics, Speech and Signal Processing*, Atlanta, GA, USA, vol. 1, pp. 349-352, 1996.
11. Rose R. C., "Discriminant wordspotting techniques for rejecting non-vocabulary utterances in unconstrained speech", *Proc. IEEE Intl. Conf. on Acoustics, Speech and Signal Processing*, San Francisco, CA, USA, vol. 2, pp. 105-108, 1992.
12. Knill K. M., Young S. J., "Fast Implementation Methods for Viterbi-Based Word-Spotting", *Proc. IEEE Intl. Conf. on Acoustics, Speech and Signal Processing*, Atlanta, GA, USA, vol. 1, pp. 522 –525, 1996.
13. Rose R. C., "Keyword Detection in Conversational Speech Utterances Using Hidden Markov Model Based Continuous Speech Recognition", *Computer Speech and Language*, vol. 9, no. 4, pp. 309-333, 1995.
14. Lai, C.S. and Shi, B. E., "A One-Pass Strategy for Keyword Spotting and Verification", *Proc. IEEE Intl. Conf. on Acoustics, Speech and Signal Processing*, Salt Lake City, Utah, vol. 1, pp. 377-380, 2001.

A Genetic Algorithm Based Approach to the Synthesis of Three Dimensional Morphing Sequences

Stephen Wang-Cheung Lam and Kelvin Yuen-Hin Ho

Department of Computing, The Hong Kong Polytechnic University,
Hung Hom, Kowloon, Hong Kong, People's Republic of China.
cswclam@comp.polyu.edu.hk

Abstract. Morphing process continuously transforms one object to another. The morphing sequence is the ultimate product of a morphing algorithm. In general, the morphing algorithms proposed in the literature aim at providing a unique or just a small amount of possible morphing sequences with benefits such as better shape deformation characteristics or works minimization. This may limit the possibility of creating variations in morphing sequence and therefore hinder artists' creativity. On the contrary, in this paper, we propose a new morphing algorithm, which aims at generating a huge amount of possible morphing sequences. The key concept underlying this work is the application of an evolutionary-like algorithm to the morphing issue. Each intermediate object in the morphing sequence is taken as an offspring of the source and target objects. A software tool is developed based on this concept. It was demonstrated that this tool could generate a variety of three dimensional morphing sequences.

1 Introduction

Morphing has proven to be a powerful tool for generating various kinds of visual effects in film and television. As stated in [1], a three-dimensional metamorphosis or *morphing* of graphical objects includes the interpolation of their shapes as well as an interpolation of their attributes which are color, textures, and normal fields and so on. Morphing gives the animator the ability to "fill" the gap between key-framed objects by creating the intermediate objects. In order words, it allows designers to blend existing shapes in order to create new shapes. Since the problem is difficult and the quality of a morphing sequence is subjective, there exists a lot of approaches dealing with various types of objects, relying on different techniques. Previously published morphing techniques [2][3] deal mainly with the morphing between two polygonal-based models. In general, these algorithms displace the vertices, edges and faces of the first model over time to coincide in position with the corresponding vertices, edges and faces of the second model. As stated in [1], three dimensional morphing techniques can broadly be classified into two approaches based on the representation scheme of the three-dimensional objects. They are volume based [4][5][6] and boundary representation [3][7][8][9] based approaches.

As stated in [10], *evolutionary algorithms* mimic the process of natural evolution, which is the driving process for the emergence of complex and well-adapted organic structures. A single individual of a population is affected by other

J. Liu et al. (Eds.): AMT 2001, LNCS 2252, pp. 144–152, 2001.
© Springer-Verlag Berlin Heidelberg 2001

individuals of the population (e.g. by food competition, predators, and mating), as well as by the environment (e.g. by food supply and climate). The better an individual performs under these conditions the greater is the chance for the individual to live for a longer time. While these individuals are alive, they generate offspring, which in turn inherit the genetic information of their parents. This process of evolution leads to a penetration of the population with the genetic information of individuals of above average fitness. The non-deterministic nature of reproduction leads to a permanent production of novel genetic information and therefore to the creation of differing offspring [11]. Readers who are interested in the fundamental theory of evolutionary algorithms can find more details in [12]. Many examples of evolutionary programming applications in engineering can be found in [13]. Evolutionary algorithms have already found some applications in computer graphics. For example, in [14], evolutionary algorithm is applied to generate various amazing strange objects. In [15], it has been used in synthesizing neural systems as well as morphologies of virtual creatures so as to simulate motions like swimming, walking and jumping. It has also found to be useful in the generation of transfer functions [16]. Recently, in [17], it has been applied to the problem of mesh optimization of 3D facial images.

As pointed out in [1], given two shapes, there is an infinity of *transformations* that can take one shape into the other. Although it seems impossible to define an optimal morphing sequence between any two shapes, intuitive solutions clearly exist. By just looking at a particular sequence, we can tell whether it is pleasant or not. However, many of these criteria are purely subjective aesthetic criteria, and they depend on the context in which the transformation is performed. Therefore, the ability for the user to control the metamorphosis is an important feature of a morphing tool. Usually, the control is provided through allowing the user to specify some corresponding feature elements [5] or corresponding anchor points [4] of two shapes. User controls supported by other algorithms can be found in [1].

In animation or film production, creating morphing sequence becomes an essential activity. To stimulate creativity, it is desirable for the artists or designers to choose a morphing sequence from a set of them or create a specific morphing sequence based on some basic elements. In order to support that, in this paper, we propose a new method in generating morphing sequences. We first model the source and target objects using the shape feature generation process model (SFGP model) [18]. As a result, a set of cell division rates are generated to represent these two objects. Subsequently, the intermediate objects are interpolated between the source and target objects by intercrossing them. The intercross process is in fact a division rate combination process. Since there are many possibilities in this combination process, it is possible for us to obtain a lot of different morphing sequences. Note that in this application the usual optimization function of evolutionary algorithm has not been utilized. Rather, the intercross process is the main focus of this research.

The remainder of this paper is structured as follows. In section 2, we present a brief review of the rule based shape representation system stated in [18]. In section 3, we describe our evolutionary algorithm based morphing algorithm. In section 4, we show a morphing sequence generated by our algorithm. Finally, in section 5, we summarize our contributions and suggest some topics for future research works.

2 Review on Rule-Based Shape Representation System

As stated in [18], the shape of a living organism (*phenotype*) is represented by genetic information (*genotype*) [19]. A genotype is encoded as a set of developmental rules and after executing that set of rules, a particular phenotype is developed. In the *Shape Feature Generation Process* model proposed in [18], there are two key components. They are a set of *shape feature generation rules* and a *cell division model*. When the SFGP proceeds, shape generation starts with the primary shape (i.e. sphere) and rules are applied to the cells on the sphere according to their positions and local conditions. After a long period of growth, the final shape is generated.

2.1 Cell Division Model

In this section, we explain the methodology called *cell division*, which is the basis of the SFGP model. As mentioned above, the cell division model is inspired from the early development of a living creature. In nature, development of an organism starts with a single cell (i.e. the fertilized egg). The egg goes through a cleavage process to form a multi-cellular structure. The cell division process simply divides the egg into a population of smaller cells progressively to form the early embryo [20]. The cell subdivision process carries out on the embryo continuously until the organism is fully developed. In [18], a sphere is used to represent the embryo. Also, the set of rules of division for a point, or a cell in biological point of view, on the sphere is specified. The shape feature generation process is taken as a series of cell division. At the beginning, there are just a small number of cells distributed on the surface of a sphere. According to the cell division rules, they divide into two or more cells and spread over the sphere. Consequently, after a certain period of growth, we can measure cell density in different regions of the sphere surface. Through equating the density of cells to the distance from the center of the sphere to the surface of the shape, the cell division model can generate fairly complicated shapes. Clearly the more points (cells) that are defined, the higher will be the precision of the representation.

2.2 Shape Representation Using Rules

The set of rules that govern the series of cell division is processed by a *classifier system*. A classifier system (CS) is a kind of rule-based system based on genetic algorithm [21], with general mechanisms for processing rules in parallel, for adaptive generation of new rules, and for testing the effectiveness of existing rules [18]. CS provides a framework in which a population of cell division rules encoded as bit strings and they evolve on the basis of intermittently given stimuli and reinforcement from its environment. Explicitly, the cell division rules in the classifier system stated in [18] form a population of individuals, which evolve over time. For each rule, <condition> is the criteria of local density around the cells, and <action> contains the information recording the direction and distance of movement of the daughter cell after a cell division. After a number of cell divisions, the distribution of the density of cells is measured. Through relating the density information of each point of the sphere surface to distance from the center of the sphere to the surface of the object, the sphere is constructed as a star-like shaped object. Finally, a shape fitness function can be measured and it can be acted as a penalty function for controlling the shape development process.

2.3 Shape Combination

A combined set of rules is obtained by exchanging parts of the set of rules using *crossover*. The crossover operation cuts the part of the set of rules, which may hold the required features of the shape and exchanges it for the same part of the set of rules of the other shape. Therefore, after exchanging rules, the features of shapes are preserved in most cases. In our system, we employ the basic mechanism of shape representation and combination stated in [18]. However, we do not use any optimization scheme in evolving the division rules. In fact, the cell division rate will not be changed after the initial set up. In other words, we just create a simple *division rate base* for the corresponding object and not a classifier system. Details of our morphing algorithm will be shown in the next section.

3   Evolutionary Algorithm Based Morphing Sequence Generation

The aim of this section is to illustrate how a morphing sequence can be generated by a evolutionary algorithm. We classify objects into two categories: (a) *simple objects* and (b) *complicated objects*. Simple objects are those star-like 3D objects that can be constructed by a cell division process carried out on just one sphere. On the contrary, complicated objects, because of their complicated shapes, cannot be easily constructed based on a single sphere. For those objects, we need to model them using multiple spheres.

3.1 Simple Objects

Let S_A and S_B be the two surfaces of two objects $\mathcal{A}$ and $\mathcal{B}$ respectively. Our aim is to create an intermediate object **M**, which is formed by combining subsets of the division rate sets of objects $\mathcal{A}$ and $\mathcal{B}$. The following procedure shows the details of our algorithm.

1. Load two objects $\mathcal{A}$ and $\mathcal{B}$ and represent each of them with a sphere. Each sphere is centered inside the corresponding object. For this simple object case, the center is at (50,50,50) and radius 1. The surface of the sphere is divided evenly into regions by latitudes and longitudes. In our experiments, we create 2048 regions evenly on the surface of the sphere. A cell c_i is allocated to the center of each region R_i.
2. For a cell c_i on the sphere, we measure the distance d_i between the center o of the sphere and a point p on the surface of the object in the direction of oc_i.
3. Set the number of cells in R_i to d_i.
4. In general, there are two parameters, which control the cell division. One is the division rate D_i and another is division size n. The division rate D_i represents the inverse of the time elapsed for each split in region R_i while division size

represents the number of cells generated from one cell by each division. Hence, we have,

$$N = n^{(T/D_i)} \tag{3.1.1}$$

where N is the total number of cells after T units of time. We then calculate the division rate by the following formula.

$$D_i = \frac{T \cdot \log n}{\log N} \tag{3.1.2}$$

In our experiments, we set n to 2 and T to 5. Hence, with step 3, we obtain the following formula.

$$D_i = \frac{5 \log 2}{\log d_i} \tag{3.1.3}$$

5. As mentioned before, based on the *shape feature generation process* (SFGP), we first generate two sets of division rates that represent a source and a target object respectively. Using these two sets of division rates, the intermediate objects can be obtained by mixing the corresponding sets of division rates of the source and target objects. Since there are many possible combinations, theoretically, it is possible to obtain a lot of different morphing sequences and this is exactly the ultimate purpose of this paper. In general, we have

$$D(t) = D_S(t) \cup D_T(t) \tag{3.1.4}$$

where $\mathbf{D}(t)$ represents the division rate set of an intermediate object at time a≤*t*≤b. $\mathbf{D}_S(t)$ and $\mathbf{D}_T(t)$ represents the subsets of division rates from the source and target objects constituting $\mathbf{D}(t)$.

We have suggested some morphing sequence generation approaches, which will be described in section 3.3. As shown in steps 3 and 4, unlike the SFGP method stated in [18], we don't use any optimization method in creating our cell division process. The division rate is simply set to model the shape of the underlying object. In our scheme, each cell divides into two cells. At a consequence, after a time period, the cell division produces a distribution of cell density at the surface of the sphere. Also, we restrict the generated cells within their source regions and we calculate the density of cell within each region. Though equating the density of cells to the distance to the surface of the object from the center of the sphere, the cell division process can generate any star-like object. The more regions the sphere-surface are composed of, the better will be the shape representation. Since the cells in the sphere are evenly allocated on the sphere, we can easily construct a triangular mesh for the sphere based on the neighborhood relationship of the cells. At a consequence, all the objects in the morphing sequence can be rendered based on their corresponding triangular meshes. Since each cell c_i on the sphere can only be associated with a distance d_i only, this algorithm is restricted to the type of star-like object.

3.2 Complicated Objects

A complicated object is an object that cannot be represented simply by the SFGP of a single sphere. They are non-star shaped objects. For such a complicated object, we may imagine that it is composed of a number of simple objects. In other words, a complicated object is represented by a set of spheres. Intuitively, we assign one sphere for each constituting simple object and the previous algorithm is then applied to these simple objects individually. Of course, the same number of spheres is allocated for the source and target object. The user is required to define the locations of the spheres in both objects and to associate each sphere of the source object to the corresponding sphere of the target object. The intermediate objects in the resulting morphing sequence will then be constructed by the union of the intercross of the corresponding pairs of spheres.

3.3 Some Division Rates Combination Approaches

In this section, we explain the following division rate set combination approaches for generating the intermediate objects:

Left-to-right: In this approach, the sets of division rates of the source and target objects are sorted according to the corresponding physical positions of regions represented by them. In this case, we sort the division rates from the left side to the right side of the object.

Right-to-left: This approach is basically the same as the previous one except the division rates are sorted from right to left.

Inclined: In this approach, the division rate is sorted according to a specific direction and the morphing process is carried out along that direction. We first set a three-dimensional coordinate system using three orthogonal axes with its center coincide the center of the object. The direction is specified by stating the angle of rotation about the x and y axes.

Random: In this approach, we do not sort the division rates. Here, we represent the division rate sets as $S=\{D_{S1},..,D_{Sn}\}$ and $T=\{D_{T1},...,D_{Tn}\}$. The division rates of an intermediate object X_j is constructed by randomly replacing an arbitrary D_{Si} with D_{Ti} where j equals to the amount of replaced division rates. The whole morphing sequence is represented by the sequence $X=[X_0,X_1,...,X_n]$.

Linear Interpolation: Similar to the random approach, here, we do not sort the division rates. The division rates of the intermediate objects are constructed by linearly interpolating the corresponding division rates of the source and the target objects.

4 Experiments

Because of space limitation, in this paper, we can only illustrate the effectiveness of our algorithm using one pair of three-dimensional objects. They are two mice using multiple spheres and linear interpolation approach. This experiment is run on a Pentium III 500MHz microprocessor with 256M RAM based PC system and all the objects used in performing experiments are scaled to fit a 100×100×100 unit cube. After setting the locations 8 corresponding spheres of the source and target objects, the computation time used to create the morphing sequence is about eighteen minutes; figure 1 shows the experimental results.

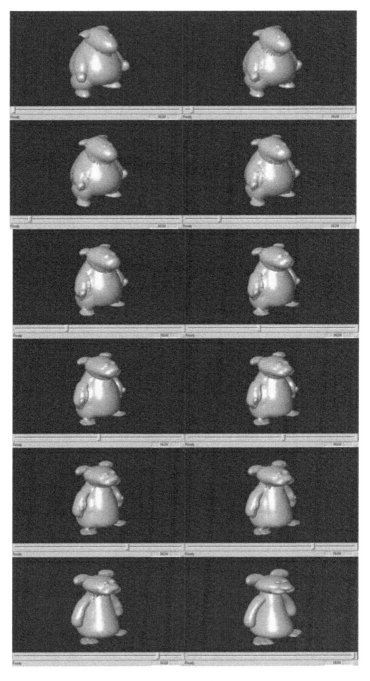

Fig. 1. This figure shows the morphing results using multiple spheres and linear interpolation approach on two mice.

5 Conclusions

In this paper, based on the *shape feature generation process* (SFGP) model, we first generate two sets of division rates that represent a source and a target object respectively. We find it difficult to compare our algorithm to the existing ones as few of them focus on creating many possible morphing sequences. However, recently, a user intensive morphing system is reported in [22]. The user of that system can draw key correspondences on the surfaces of the input models, and to specify the paths that the corresponding features will follow during the morph. Potentially, with this level of user involvement, that system can create many possible morphing sequences. Compared with that system, our algorithm provides coarser level of interactions, which is the specification of sphere sizes and locations only. However, given this simple specification, our algorithm can still produce many different possible morphing sequences. Besides, employing the method stated in [22], the user-specification time for creating each morphing sequence is around four hours. Comparing to the computation time recorded in the experiment section, our algorithm can be taken as a quick solution to this issue.

References

[1] Lazarus F and Verroust A. Three-dimensional Metamorphosis: a Survey. *The Visual Computer* 1998; Vol. 14, No. 8/9, 373-389.

[2] Kaul A and Rossignac J. Solid-Interpolating Deformations: Construction and Animations of PIPs. In *Proceedings of EUROGRAPHICS '91*, September 1991, 493-505.

[3] Kent JR, Carlson WE and Parent RE. Shape Transformation for Polyhedral Objects. In *Proceedings of SIGGRAPH'92*, 1992, 47-54.

[4] Cohen-Or D, Levin D and Solomovici A. Three-Dimensional Distance Field Metamorphosis. *ACM Transactions on Graphics* 1998; Vol. 17, No. 2, 116-141.

[5] Lerios A, Garfinkle CD and Levoy M. Feature based Volume Metamorphosis. In *Proceedings of SIGGRAPH'95*, 1995, 449-464.

[6] Rossignac J and Kaul A. AGRELS and BIBs: Metamorphosis as a Bezier Curve in the Space of Polyhedra. In *Proceedings of Eurographics'94*, 1994, 179-184.

[7] Beier T and Neely S. Feature-based Image Metamorphosis. In *Proceedings of SIGGRAPH'92*, 1992, 35-42.

[8] Lee, SY, Chwa KY and Shin SY. Image Metamorphosis Using Snakes and Free-Form Deformations. In *Proceedings of SIGGRAPH'95*, 1995, 439-448.

[9] Lazarus F and Verroust A. Metamorphosis of Cylinder-like Objects. *International Journal of Visualization and Computer Animation* 1997; 8:131-146.

[10] Back T, Hammel U and Schwefel H P. Evolutionary Computation: Comments on the History and Current State. *IEEE Transactions on Evolutionary Computation* 1997; Vol. 1, No. 1, 3-17.

[11] Fogel DB. Evolutionary Computation: Toward a New Philosophy of Machine Intelligence. *Piscataway, NJ: IEEE Press*, 1995.

[12] Michalewicz Z, Genetic Algorithms + Data Structures = Evolution Programs. *Springer-Verlag*, 1994.

[13] Dasgupta D and Michalewicz Z (edited). Evolutionary Algorithms in Engineering Applications. *Springer-Verlag*, 1997.

[14] Todd S and Latham W. Evolutionary Art and Computers. *Academic Press*, 1992.

[15] Sims, K. Evolving Virtual Creatures, *In Proceedings of SIGGRAPH'94*, 1994, 15-22.

[16] He T, Hong L, Kaufman A and Pfister H. Generation of transfer functions with stochastic search techniques. In *Proceedings of the conference on Visualization '96* , 1996, 227-234.

[17] Fujiwara Y and Sawai H. Evolutionary Computation Applied to Mesh Optimization of a 3D Facial Image, *IEEE Transactions on Evolutionary Computation* 1999; Vol. 3, No. 2, 113-123.

[18] Taura T, Nagasaka I and Yamagishi A. Application of Evolutionary Programming to Shape Design, *Computer-Aided Design* 1998; Vol. 30, No. 1, 29-35.

[19] Smith, JM. Evolutionary Genetics. *Oxford University Press*, 1989.

[20] Wolpert L. The Triumph of the Embryo. *Oxford University Press*, 1991.

[21] Holland, JH. Adaptation in Natural and Artificial Systems. *MIT Press*, 1992.

[22] Gregory A, State, A, Lin MC, Manocha D and Livingston MA. Interactive Surface Decomposition for Polyhedral Morphing, *The Visual Computer* 1999; 15:453-470.

A COMPARATIVE STUDY OF ANT-BASED OPTIMIZATION FOR DYNAMIC ROUTING

Kwang Mong Sim[1] and Weng Hong Sun[2]

[1]Department of Information Engineering, Chinese University of Hong Kong,
Shatin, NT, Hong Kong. Email: kmsim@ie.cuhk.edu.hk
[2]Business Information System, Faculty of Business Administration,
University of Macau. Email: fbawhs@umac.mo

Abstract. An ANT is a mobile agent that is capable of solving various kinds of routing and congestion problems in computer networking by continuously modifying routing tables in respond to congestion. In a distributed problem solving paradigm, a society of ANTs (each contributing some information) collaborate to solve a larger problem. In recent years, Ant-based algorithms were used to solve classical routing problems such as: Travelling Salesman Problem, Vehicle Routing Problem, Quadratic Assignment Problem, connection-oriented/ connectionless routing, sequential ordering, graph coloring and shortest common supersequence. By introducing the general idea of Ant-based algorithms with a focus on Ant Colony Optimization (ACO) and their mathematical models, this paper brings together a collection of ACO algorithms discussed their features, strength and weaknesses.

1. Introduction

With the growing importance of telecommunications and the Internet, more complex networked systems are being designed and developed. As networked systems become more complex so are the underlying software and the control rules. The challenges of dealing with the vast complexity of networking tasks such as load balancing, routing and congestion control accentuate the need for more sophisticated (and perhaps more intelligent) tools to solve these problems.

Drawing upon some of the cutting edge technology in the field of autonomous agents, several agent-based paradigms ([18][29][31][34]) were devised to solve control and allocation problems in telecommunications and networking. For example, agents can adopt a model that focuses on providing Quality of Service or Load Balancing [29][30][32] to minimize congestion and implement sophisticated control and signaling techniques in network systems. Similarly, with the use of agents, heterogeneous network system, such as the Internet, can achieve co-ordination, flexibility and integration. One of the major agent problem-solving paradigms in routing problems is ANT algorithms [5][29][33]. ANT algorithms were inspired by the study of biological ant colonies. The key characteristic of ANT algorithms is the concept of *stigmergy*[28], a form of indirect communication used by biological ants[1] to coordinate their activities such as foraging or nest building. This indirect communication is achieved by individually altering the common environment that can also be percieved by other ants. In particular, this paper focuses on the model of ant's *foraging behavior*[14], where stigmergic communication is accomplished by layering *pheromone*[14], a chemical substance that an ant deposits to induce changes in the environment. These changes are sensed by other ants, which implicitly serve as a signal to influence their behaviors. This indirect coordination enables a colony

---

[1] This also reflects in other social insects.

J. Liu et al. (Eds.): AMT 2001, LNCS 2252, pp. 153–164, 2001.
© Springer-Verlag Berlin Heidelberg 2001

of ants to solve larger problems. To model the problem solving paradigm of a colony of biological ants, a society of artificial ants (ANTs) are model as a society of mobile agents. In ANT algorithms, an ANT is a simple mobile agent that is capable of solving various kinds of routing problems by simulating the laying of pheromone in biological ants. In ANT algorithms, the laying of pheromone is simulated by recording in a counter the number of ANTs that pass a node. The decision of an ANT is influent by a function of pheromone concentration and other heuristic values that is different from a biological ant. This is because an ANT is modeled as a mobile agent, which has other capabilities [18] such as look ahead functions, local optimization [21] and backtracking that can be enriched to solve complex problems. Through the use of a society of ANTs, an Ant Colony Optimization (ACO) provides a framework for solving optimization problems. The ACO algorithm [19] is a particular class of ANT algorithms. Within this framework, ANT's structures and procedures are formulated to find the solution of (constrained) shortest path/minimum costs problems on graphs. This paper discusses the approaches of ACO and their applications for routing problems such as the constructions and updates of routing tables within a network to facilitate the selection of optimal route for each node. By analogy, routing tables correspond to pheromone tables that can be manipulated by a colony of ANTs distributed over a network. For instance, an ACO algorithm was proposed [23] to solve simple routing problems (e.g., finding the shortest path). Subsequently, it was formulated as a framework augmented with mathematical models and additional data structure (memory) for daemon control, to deal with more sophisticated combinatorial optimization problems such as the Asymmetric Traveling Salesman Problem, Graph Coloring and Vehicle Routing Problem. To date, there have been several research [18][13][33][34] that applied or enhanced [9] ACO algorithms for different optimization problems.

In Section 2, the method of how ANT can be used to solve routing problems in a network is shown. In Section 3, the mathematical model of Ant Colony Optimization, which includes ANTs' decision model and required adjustments of applying ACO in a distributed network is presented. Furthermore, the Simple ACO algorithm and subsequent enhancements such as ACO with meta-heuristics are discussed. In Section 4, recent approaches to address the issue of *stagnation* in ACO algorithm will be summarized and compared.

2.   Ant-based algorithms

In this section, the problem solving technique of a colony of biological ants for finding the shortest path to a food source is discussed (section 2.1). Analogies are drawn between the problem solving of ants and network routing problems (section 2.2).

2.1 Problem-solving Paradigm of (biological) ant

Suppose that there are 4 ants and 2 routes leading to the food source: R_1 and R_2 (figure 1) such that $R_1 > R_2$. Along the 2 routes, there are 4 nodes: N_1, N_2, N_3 and N_4 (food source). Initially, all ants (A_1, A_2, A_3 and A_4) are at the decision point N_1 and they have to select between R_1 and R_2 to reach N_4.

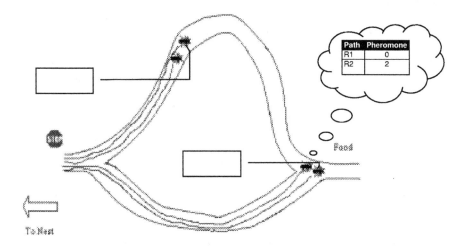

Figure 1. Biological ant's foraging behavior.

1. At N_1, all ants have no knowledge about the location of *food* (N_4). Hence, they randomly select from $\{R_1, R_2\}$. Suppose that A_1 and A_2 choose R_1 and A_3 and A_4 choose R_2.

2. As A_1 and A_2 move along R_1 and A_3 and A_4 move along R_2, they leave a certain amount of pheromone along their paths τ_{R1} and τ_{R2} respectively.

3. Since $R_2 < R_1$, A_3 and A_4 reach N_4 before A_1 and A_2. When A_3 and A_4 pass R_2 to reach N_4, $\tau_{R2} = 2$, but A_1 and A_2 have yet to reach N_4 and $\tau_{R1} = 0$. To return to N_1 from N_4, A_3 and A_4 have to choose between R_1 and R_2. At N_4, A_3 and A_4 detect that $\tau_{R2} > \tau_{R1}$, hence they select R_2.

4. As A_3 and A_4 pass R_2 for the second time to reach N_1, τ_{R2} is incremented to 4. The increase in τ_{R2} further consolidates R_2 as the shorter path. When A_1 and A_2 reach N_4, $\tau_{R2} = 4$ and $\tau_{R1} = 2$. Hence, A_1 and A_2 select R_2 to N_1.

In this example, any ant at N_2 (respectively N_1) will be able to determine the shorter path once A_3 and A_4 reach N_2 (respectively N_1). In comparison to networking routing techniques such as distance vector or link state routing, the approach of ants seems to converge to a solution more rapidly[33].

2.2 ANTs and Dynamic Routing

By modeling an ant colony as a society of mobile agents the biological ant's problem-solving paradigm can be adopted to solve routing problems in a network. In the above example, the infrastructure of ants' foraging in the network (with R_1 and R_2) corresponds to packets' travelling along a packet switching network. The length of R_1 and R_2 in figure 1 corresponds to their costs whereas the biological ants correspond to mobile agent (ANTs) moving back and forth to collect and update routing information. As shown in step 2 (section 2.1), the pheromone can be considered as a routing preference, similar to a routing entry of the routing table inside a router in Distance Vector Routing or Link State Routing. This routing preference can be determined either by only pheromone or by a function of pheromone (with other heuristic values). Furthermore, pheromone manipulation is carried out by mobile agents (ANTs), either biased or un-biased[2]. This paradigm has several advantages over traditional routing algorithms.

In comparison to Distance Vector/Link State routing, this problem-solving paradigm can reach its *convergence*[33] within a short period of time without transmitting a lot of routing entries (low overhead[5]). In a network, the concerntration of pheromone can be modeled by using a counter to record the number of ANTs that pass through a node. The main component of this algorithm is the use of this indicator to replace distance or number of hops to indicate route's preference. Since the exchange of pheromone is implicit without directly transmitting routing entries, routing overhead is considerably reduced[5]. Moreover, ANTs' pheromone laying can also reflects network configuration or topology changes, which makes this algorithm more adaptive and decentralized. The comparison between traditional routing algorithms and ANT algorithms is summarized in Table 1:

Table 1: ANT algorithms vs traditional routing algorithms		
	Routing Algorithms	**ANT algorithms**
Building routing preference	By Transmission time / delay	By Pheromone laid
Routing information exchange	Separate routing entries transmission	Can be piggybacked in data packets
Adaptive to topology changes	Slow	Fast
Routing overhead	High	Low
Routing control	Centralized / static	Decentralized / adaptive

A particular class of ANT algorithms is the Ant Colony Optimization (ACO) algorithm, which defines the structure of an ANT within a mathematical model and other procedures capable of solving routing problems. In sections 3 and 4, the evolution of ACO algorithms, and various approaches to enhanced ACO are discussed.

3.   Evolution of Ant Colony Optimization algorithm

The ACO algorithm was formulated to solve routing problems[19]. A colony of ANT is specified with: (1) the notion of their manipulation to pheromone table in the common environment and (2) their decision making policy on route selections. (1) refers to the issue of how many ANTs are able to deposit pheromone (in the pheromone table) and how much they are depositing, which can vary from different implementations of ACO. (2) refers to the mathematical model of their decision tables. ANTs' decision table is a probabilistic model that involves the computation of a function of pheromone and other heuristic values. In addition to ANTs' structure, there are many other procedures and approaches involved in different implementations of the ACO algorithm. In sections 3.1 and 3.2, the evolution of ACO algorithms is presented.

3.1 Simple Ant Colony Optimization

---

[2] It is discussed in section 4.3.

Early Ant Colony Optimization (ACO) algorithms were formulated using graph theory to solve the Traveling Salesman Problem (TSP) as follows. Let $G = (N, E)$ be a connected graph with $|N|$ nodes and $|E|$ edges. For each edge (i, j) of G, there is an associated pheromone value τ_{ij} (routing preference parameter). A colony of ANTs is defined as a set of mobile software agents that can traverse across edges to assess and manipulate pheromone value. However, each ANT has access limited to local pheromone value (pheromone of adjacent edges). An ANT increases the same amount of pheromone ($\Delta\tau_{ji}$) to each visited edge as it travels along a path. To construct the decision table of an ANT's, the probability P_{ij} to choose an edge (i, j) is computed as follows [4][5]:

$$P_{ijk}(t) = \frac{\varpi\tau_{ij}(t) + (1-\varpi)\eta_{ij}}{\varpi + (1-\varpi)(|N_i|-1)} \qquad (1)$$

where $j\in N_i$ (Neighbor set of i) and $0 \le \varpi \le 1$ is a weighting parameter representing the relative weights of pheromone and η_{ij} is a heuristic value. η_{ij} is determined by an edge's distance (q_{ij}) as follows:

$$\eta_{ij} = 1 - \frac{q_{ij}}{\sum_{l\in N_i} q_{il}} \qquad (2)$$

In this model, an ANT's decision preference is determined by the adjustment of ω that controls the relative weights between pheromone (τ) and the heuristic value (η). However, this weighting parameter ω was later replaced by two separate parameters, α and β. α and β were taken as exponents of the two major probability factors (distance and pheromone) [23][25] from (1) into an ANT's decision table. This is to increase the power of parameter to ANT's decision. In [23][25] η_{ij} refers to *visibility* rather than heuristic value calculated by distance as interpreted in [4],[5]. Thus, the probability P_{ij} for choosing an edge (i, j) is given as follows:

$$p_{ij}(t) = \frac{[\tau_{ij}(t)]^\alpha \cdot [\eta_{ij}]^\beta}{\sum [\tau_{ij}(t)]^\alpha \cdot [\eta_{ij}]^\beta} \qquad (3)$$

In addition to TSP [5][23][25], this simple ACO algorithm was also applied to solve problems such as load balancing problems [29][30][31][32]. The simple ACO algorithm were modified and enhanced with meta-heuristic to solve other and more sophisticated problems such as the Graph Coloring and Asymmetric Travelling Salesman Problems.

3.2 Ant Colony Optimization (ACO) meta-heuristic

ACO augmented with meta-heuristic was proposed by Dorigo et al [19] and the framework is given as follows:

Let $C = \{c_1, c_2, ..., c_{Nc}\}$ be a finite set of components N_c and $L = \{l_{cicj} | (c_i, c_j) \in C \times C\}$ be the power set of possible connections/transitions on the Cartesian product $C \times C$. A connection cost function $J_{cicj} \equiv J(l_{cicj}, t)$, computed by some time measure t or others, is defined for each l_{cicj}, where $l_{cicj} \in L$. Hence, $|L| \le N_c^2$. Let $\Omega \equiv \Omega(C, L, t)$ be a finite set of contraints assigned over the elements of C and L that is calculated by a function of t. The states of the problem are defined in terms of sequences $s = <c_i,$ $c_j, ..., c_k, ...>$ over the elements of C (or, equivalently, of L). Let S be the set of all possible sequences and $S`$ be all the sub-sequences that are feasible with respect to the constraints $\Omega(C, L, t)$, and $S` \subseteq S$. For any s, where $s \in S`$, $s$ defines one of the problem's feasible states within $S`$ and $|s|$ = the length of s. Moreover, $s_1 \in N_{s2}$ (the neighbor state set of s_2) if (i) $s_1, s_2 \in S$; (ii) the state s_2 can be reached from s_1 in one logical step, that is, $s_1 = <c_1, c_2 ...c_k>$ and $s_2 = <s_1, c_j>$.

A solution $\Psi \in S`$ satisfies all the problems' requirements. Ψ is multi-dimensional if it is defined in terms of multiple distinct sequences over the elements of C. A cost $J_\Psi(L, t)$ is associated with each Ψ and $J_\Psi(L, t) = (J_\Psi(l_{cicj}, t))$, for all $l_{cicj} \in L$. The solution to the optimization problem for a graph $G = (C, L)$, can be defined as feasible paths on G and the ACO algorithm can be applied to find the minimum cost path feasible to the constraints Ω. Note that neither the pheromone calculation nor ANTs' probabilistic decision changes in this model. However, a memory structure is added for the ANT that can be used to build and compare feasible solutions and retrace the path backward[19]. As a result, it seems that this model can find the most cost effective feasible solution [19] (under constraints Ω). Finally, a *daemon* procedure is also available to simalteanously adjust all ANTs' decision to favor pheromone or visibility (or heuristic information). Thus, pheromone laying is now classified as online (by ANTs) and offline (by daemon action).

Dorigo et al [19] suggest that this new model can solve problems of:

♦ NP-hard combinatorial problems [26] which dimension of the full state space graph is exponential in the dimension of the problem representation

♦ Shortest path problems in a dynamic graph that its properties change over time (such as costs or topologies).

♦ Those problems in which the computational architecture is distributed as in the case of parallel and network processing

The ACO meta-heuristics has been adopted in many applications[8][19] with procedures augmented to address different kinds of problems. For example, the amount of additional pheromone is no longer a constant among different ants[3]. Most of these implementations let the 'best' ant[4] deposits more pheromone than regular ants to reduce the time to convergence[33]. However, these implementations differ slightly in parallelism or pheromone depositing mechanism while the main philosophy were kept unchanged.

In [5], the ACO algorithm was empirically compared to many traditional routing algorithms and obtained favorable results. Nevertheless, two issues arise from the attempt to implement the ACO algorithm: *stagnation* and *adaptiveness*. Stagnation occurs when a network reaches its convergence (or equilibrium state); an optimal path P_o is chosen by all ANTs and this recursively increases an ANT's preference for P_o. This may lead to: 1) congestion of P_o, 2) dramatically reducing the probability of selecting other paths. (1) and (2) are undesirable for a dynamic network since: i) P_o may become non-optimal if it is congested; ii) P_o may be disconnected due to network failure; iii) other non-optimal paths may become optimal due to changes in

---

[3] Privileged Pheromone Laying is discussed in Section 4.3.
[4] The best ant is usually referred to the ant who has the shortest travel time.

network topology; iv) new or better paths may be discovered. Adaptiveness refers to the degree of sensitivity of network dynamics (topology changes or link failures). For optimality, the objectives of these approaches are to prevent stagnation and to promote adaptiveness.

4. Approaches to Mitigate Stagnation

The approaches to reduce stagnation fall into 3 categories: pheromone control (section 4.1), ANTs' decision control (section 4.2) and Privileged Pheromone Laying(section 4.3).

4.1 Pheromone control:

Pheromone control includes mechanisms to reduce past experience and encourage the exploration of previous non-optimal paths or new paths.

Aging and Evaporation: In addition to an ANT's structure, a procedure of evaporation is needed to reduce the effect of past experience. Evaporation prevents pheromone values in optimal paths from being excessively high so that all ANTs neglect non-optimal paths. In each iteration, the pheromone values in all paths are discounted by a factor p such that: $\tau_{ij} \leftarrow \tau_{ij} \times (1-p)$. Additionally, past experience can also be reduced by adjusting the amount of pheromone laid for each ANT by its age (aging [29][30]). Both methods include recency as a factor of routing preference so that if a favorable path is not chosen recently, its preference will be gradually eliminated. This effect is obvious for the procedure of evaporation but not for aging.

For aging, an ANT is depositing less pheromone as it moves from node to node. This is equivalent to applying *privileged pheromone laying*[5] on old ANTs. This is based on the rationale that old ANTs have not been successfully in locating optimal paths since they stayed too long in the network to reach its destination. However, this aging mechanism induces bias on ANTs that need to travel a longer route.

Aging and Evaporation make existing pheromone value less significant than the latest pheromone update. On the contrary, this encourages discoveries of new paths as well as trial runs on non-optimal paths and help to resolve stagnation.

Limiting and Smoothing Pheromone: Stuzle and Hoos [33] proposes a policy to limit the amount of pheromone in all paths. By setting an upper and lower bound, the preference gap between optimal and non-optimal paths becomes smaller. This eliminates the situation of having a dominant path which prevents stagnations.

Another similar approach is *pheromone smoothing*[33], which also discourages dominant path. Pheromone smoothing is analogous to evaporation that is also reduces existing pheromone. However, evaporation takes a constant discount rate to all paths whereas smoothing decrease more pheromone on the best paths. Hence, its effect of avoiding dominant path is higher than evaporation and aging.

Although these four techniques significantly resolves stagnation problems and promote adaptiveness, it is not preferred (except for aging) in a static network. This is due to the effect that these techniques are encouraging trial runs on paths with unknown optimal level. In a static network (or a network reaches equilibrium) where optimal paths are unchanged, these techniques only direct ANTs to non-optimal

---

[5] Privileged Pheromone Laying is described in Section 4.3

paths which in turn degrade overall performance. Thus, it seems prudent to apply these approaches on rare occasions rather than on a frequent basis. Researchers have to set the best trade-off between stability and adaptivity. Nevertheless, in the case of aging, this phenomenon is not explicit and there is no direct observable difference of applying aging in a dynamic or static network.

4.2 ANTs' decision control:

By directly controlling ANTs' decisions, all ANTs or a subset of ANTs can be directed to unexplored paths. This is accomplished by adjusting the ANTs' preference to favor factors[6] (e.g., visibility, priority or others) other than pheromone (either by adjusting α, β, or by daemon) as they move. Thus, after certain adjustments, all ANTs will occasionally take paths that contain less pheromone to incorporate network dynamics. In some models[30], instead of affecting all ANTs decision, a set of 'dumb' ANTs or Random Walk ANTs (which always choose their routes at random), is initiated to significantly increase non optimal paths' preferences.

Different value set of α and β: In (3), section 3.1, the probability of a given ANT to choose a certain path is a function of the pheromone and a heuristic value. The values of α and β can be adjusted as their respective weights to this probability. By using different value sets of α and β, the behavior of the ACO algorithm's search process can be altered. If $\alpha > \beta$, ANTs favor paths with more pheromone whereas a high β directs ANT to favor paths with higher heuristic values. The values of α and β are adjusted to different extent for different network status.

When the pheromone value does not reflect paths' optimality, a lower α is preferred. This applies to the initial stage of a network or there are sudden changes (link failure or new paths) in the network. However, at the equilibrium state of the network (or convergence), a high α is preferred. Recent research [33] proposes that if different value set of α and β can be changed dynamically depending on network states, performance will be significantly increased.

Besides stagnation and adapitiveness, other approaches can be categorized as Privileged Pheromone Laying (only selected ANTs can lay pheromone) which can achieve faster convergence.

4.3 Privileged Pheromone Laying:

One of the early improvements of the ACO algorithm focuses on privileged pheromone laying among a subset of ANTs. Experiments [5][24][25] show that by permitting the best ANTs to deposit more pheromone significantly reduces the time of convergence for a network. Two issues are considered for this mechanism: (1) assessment of ANTs' solution quality, (2) the methods of laying extra pheromone which in turn, depend on the number of ANTs to be selected.

To assess ANTs' solution quality, the simplest measure is to compare the total trip time [24][25]. Stuzle and Hoos [33], however, use FDC (fitness-landscape) analysis to evaluate how close a given ANTs' trip time is to the optimal time. The analogy of this function can be compared to a mountain wanderer searching for a smooth walk in the landscape. The FDC function depicts the distribution of paths on a given

---

[6] Different strategies are being developed among different implementations and they will be described at a later section.

landscape and evaluates the fitness of a solution to the optimal solution. It was found [33] that using FDC analysis, more accurate results were obtained.

The second issue concerns the methods of laying extra pheromone. If priority is to be given to the best ANTs, then no pheromone can be laid before ANTs' solution are assessed. Thus, it is necessary to use a *backward ANT*[24][25], which walks all the way back to lay pheromone after the solution quality has been evaluated. This, however, creates a problem of doubling the network traffic. Hence, the number of backward ANTs should be minimized. Due to the above reason, some research [33] allow only the best ANT to deposit pheromone or allow a set of best ANTs [2] to deposit pheromone to reduce this overhead. Nevertheless, it seems inconsistent to the idea of ant colony if only one ANT is permitted to deposit pheromone.

Nevertheless, if only one ANT is allowed to deposit pheromone, the general idea of a colony of ant to solve a problem does not persist.

Another alternative is the use of aging (section 4.1), which reverses the mechanism of privileged pheromone laying. Aging works in a way that old ANTs deposit less pheromone with the argument that solutions of old ANTs are less likely to be optimal. Aging produces similar effect as privileged pheromone laying but avoid the problem of overloading the network traffic. However, the effectiveness of aging on choosing the best ant is not as obvious.

In summary, comparison of the features, strength and weaknesses of the various approaches to mitigate stagnation are tabluated in table 2 in Appendix 1.

5. Conclusion

This paper has introduced the problem solving paradigm of ant colonies and drew analogies to solving problems in network routings. The simple ACO and ACO meta-heuristics were reviewed. The issue of stagnation associated with ACO meta-heuristic was studied. Approaches to mitigate the problem of stagnation have been reviewed and compared.

6. Reference

[1] B. Bullnheimer, R. F. Hartl and C. Strauss, *An improved ant system algorithm for the vehicle routing problem*, Annals of Operations Research , 89, 1999

[2] B. Bullnheimer, R.F. Hartl, and C. Strauss, *A new rank-based version of the ant system: a computational study*, Technical Report POM-03/97, Institute of Management Science, University of Vienna, 1997.

[3] Di Caro, G. & Dorigo, M., *Mobile Agents for Adaptive Routing*, Proceeding 31st Hawaii International Conference Systems Scicneces (HICSS-31), Kohala Coast, Hawaii, p. 74-83, Jan 1998.

[4] Di Caro, G., & Dorigo, M., *Two ant colony algorithms for best-effort routing in datagram networks*, Proceedings of the Tenth IASTED International Conference on Parallel and Distributed Computing and Systems (PDCS'98), p. 541-546.

[5] Di Caro, M. Dorigo, *AntNet: Distributed Stigmergetic Control for Communications*, Journal of Artificial Intelligence Research 9, p. 317-365, 1998

[6] E. Bonabeau, F. Henaux, S. Guerin, D. Snyers, P. Kuntz, G. Theraulaz, *Routing*

in telecommunications networks with 'smart' ant-like agents, Intelligent Agents for Telecommunications Applications '98.

[7]   E. D. Weinberger, Correlated and uncorrelated fitness landscapes and how to tell the difference, Biological Cybernetics, 63, p. 325-336, 1990

[8]   F. Kruger, D. Merkle and M. Midendorf, *Studies on a parallel ant system for the BSP model*, BSP model, Unpublished manuscript.

[9]   H. M. Botee and Eric Bonabeau, *Evolving Ant Colony Optimization*, Advance Complex Systems, 1, p.149-159, 1998

[10]   I. A. Wagner, M. Lindenbaum, A. M. Bruckstein, *Efficient Graph Search by a Smell-Oriented Vertex Process*, Annuals of Mathematics and Artificial Intelligence, 24, p. 211-223, 1998

[11]   I. A. Wagner, M. Lindenbaum, A. M. Bruckstein, *Smell as a Computational Resource - A Lesson We Can Learn from the Ant*, Proceeding ISTCS'96, p. 219-230, http://www.cs.technion.ac.il/~wagner

[12]   I. A. Wagner, M. Lindenbaum, A. M. Brucksten, *Cooperative Covering by Ant-Robots using Evaporating Traces*, Technical report CIS-9610, Center for Intelligent Systems, Technion, Haifa, April 1996

[13]   I. A. Wagner, M. Linderbaum, A. M. Bruckstein, *ANTS: Agents, Networks, Trees, and Subgraphs*, IBM Haifa Research Lab, Future Generation Computer Systems Journal, North Holland (Editors: Dorigo, Di Caro and Stutzel), vol.16, no 8, p. 915-926, June 2000

[14]   J. L. Deneubourg, S. Aron, S. Goss and J. -M. Pasteels, *The self-organizing exploratory pattern of the argentine ant*, Journal of Insert Behavior, 3: 159-168, 1990

[15]   L. M. Gambardella and M. Dorigo. HAS-SOP, *An hybrid ant system for the sequential ordering problem*, Technical Report 11-97, IDSIA, Lugano, CH, 1997.

[16]   M. A. Gibney & N. R. Jennings, *Market Based Multi-Agent Systems for ATM Network Management*, Proceedings 4th Communication Networks Symposium, Manchester, UK. 1997.

[17]   M. Bolondi and M. Bondanza, *Parallelizzazione di un algoritmo per la risoluzione del problema del commesso viaggiatore*, Master's thesis, Dipartimento di Elettronica e Informazione, Politecnico di Milano, Italy, 1993.

[18]   M. Dorigo, G. D. Caro, L. M. Gambardella, *Ant Algorithms for Discrete Optimization*, Artificial Life, 5, 2, p. 137-172, 1999

[19]   M. Dorigo, G. Di Caro, *The Ant Colony Optimization MetaHeuristic*, in Corne D., Dorigo M. and Glover F., New Ideas in Optimization, McGraw-Hill, May, 1999. ISBN: 0077095065

[20]   M. Dorigo, L. M. Gambardella, *Ant Colonies for the Traveling Salesman Problem*, BioSystems, 43:73-81, 1997

[21]   M. Dorigo, L. M. Gambardella, *Ant colony system: A cooperative learning approach to the travelling salesman problem.* IEEE Transactions on Evolutionary Computation, 1(1997) p.53-66

[22]   M. Dorigo, *Optimization, Learning and Natural Algorithms* (in Italian), PhD thesis, Dipartimento di Elettronica e Informazione, Politecnico di Milano, IT, 1992

[23]   M. Dorigo, V Maniezzo, and A. Colorni, *Positive feedback as a search strategy*, Technical Report 91-016, Dipartimento di Elettronica, Politecnico di Milano, IT,

1991

[24] M. Dorigo, V. Maniezzo & A. Colorni, *The Ant System: A Autocatalytic Optimizing Process*, Technical Report No. 91-061 Revised, Politecnico di Milano Italy, 1991

[25] M. Dorigo, V. Maniezzo & A. Colorni, *The Ant System: Optimization by a Colony of Cooperating Agents*, IEEE Transactions on Systems, Man, and Cybernetics-Part B, 26 (I):29-41, 1996

[26] M. R. Garey and D. S. Johnson, *Computers and Intractability*, W.H. Freeman and Company, 1979

[27] P. F. Stadler, *Towards a theory of landscapes*, Technical Report SFI-95-03-030, Santa Fe Institute, USA, 1995

[28] P.P. Grasse, La reconstruction du nid et les coordinations interindividuelles chez *bellicositermes natalensis et cubitermes* sp. La theorie de la stigmergie: essai d'interpretation du comportement des termites constructeurs, Insectes Sociaux 6, p. 41-81, 1959

[29] R. Schoonderwoerd, O. Holland, J. Bruten and L. Rothkrantz, *Ant-based load balancing in Telecommunications Networks*, Adaptive Behavior, vol.5, no.2, 1996.

[30] Ruud Schoonderwoerd, Owen Holland, Janet Bruten, and Leon Rothkrantz, *Ants for Load Balancing in Telecommunication Networks*, Technical Report HPL-96-35, HewlettPackard Laboratories Bristol, 1996.

[31] S. Appleby, S. Steward, *Mobile software agents for control in telecommunications Networks*, in BT Technology Journal Vol. 12, No.2, 1994

[32] Schoonderwoerd, R., Holland, O., Bruten, J. *Ant-like agents for load balancing in telecommunications networks*, Proceedings of the First International Conference on Autonomous Agents, p. 209-216, ACM Press.

[33] Thomas Stuzle and Holger H. Hoos, *MAX-MIN Ant System*, Future Generation Computer Systems Journal, 16(8):889-914, 2000

[34] V. Maniezzo, A. Carbonaro, *Ant Colony Optimization: An Overview*, III Metaheuristic International Conference, Angra dos Reis, Brazil

Appendix One

Table 2: Comparison of Approaches

	Description	Strength	Weakness
Pheromone control			
Reduce past experience			
Aging	old ants deposit less pheromone	no particular	bias on ANTs traveling long distance
Evaporation	all existing pheromone decreases by an evoparation rate	no particular	no particular
Encouraging exploration			
Pheromone smoothing	shortern pheromone gaps between the optimal and non-optimal paths	encourages exploration	not favored to static network
Limit to pheromone	set a max and min limit for pheromone	encourages exploration	no particular
ANTs' decision control			
Random walk ANT	ants choose their paths randomly	no particular	not favored to static network; consume extra bandwidth
Adjust alpha and beta	adjust ANTs' routing preferenece to pheromone or other heuristic values	no particular	n/a
Others: Privileged Pheromone laying	best ANTs deposit more pheromone		backward ant doubles data traffic
Assessment of ANT's solution quality			
ANT's total trip time	use the total trip time to evaluate ANTs' solution quality	easy to implement	not accurate
Fitness Landscape function	use the FDC analysis to evaluate how close an ANTs' solution to optimal	more accurate	no particular
Methods of laying extra pheromone			
one ANT deposits pheromone	only one ant is allowed to deposit pheromone in each iteration	consume less bandwidth	less accurate; longer time to converge
subset of ANTs deposits pheromone	only a subset of pheromone is allowed to deposit pheromone in an iteration	more accurate	consume more bandwith
Aging (related to ANT's solution quality conceptually)	old ANTs deposit less pheromone	do not need to assess solution quality; no backward ant	unwarranted bias on ANTs traveling long distance

What Kind of Cooperation Is Required by Situated Agents?

The Principle of Situated Cooperation*

Angélica Muñoz-Meléndez and Alexis Drogoul

Laboratoire d'Informatique de Paris 6
Université Pierre et Marie Curie
Case 169-4, place Jussieu, 75252 Paris Cedex 05
Angelica.Munoz,Alexis.Drogoul@lip6.fr

Abstract. The notion of *cooperation* in computer science has a strong rational connotation. A cooperative system is composed of cognitive individuals which have explicit knowledge about their users and other individuals of the group, have propositional attitudes, and are capable of negotiating agreements and making contracts. We are concerned with the design of cooperative robots; and the traditional conception of cooperation is not easily applicable to Robotics not only because of the limitations of Robotics but also because the traditional concept of cooperation does not explain its own pre-requisites and hypotheses. This paper outlines the concept of *situated cooperation* in the context of situated agents, particularly robots.

Keywords: multi-agent systems, collective robotics, situated cooperation.

1 Introduction

In computer science, the term cooperation is mostly used in the domains of Multi-Agent Systems (MAS) and Distributed Artificial Intelligence (DAI) and has a strong rational connotation. Individuals with a high cognitive level form a system. They have explicit knowledge about their users and other individuals of the group and are able to "watch" them. They have propositional attitudes known as beliefs, desires and intentions. Individuals are also capable of negotiating agreements and making contracts [15]. This approach has been successfully implemented in enterprise modeling [2], electronic commerce [13], the development of internet agents [4] and personal assistants [5], among others applications.

This notion of cooperation is not easily applied to the design of situated individuals, for example robots, due to technological constraints in Robotics that do not allow the implementation of high-level cognitive individuals. Cooperation in Robotics is concerned with the design of groups of robots that are able to execute collectively simple tasks, such as foraging and handling objects. Robots neither negotiate, nor deliberate when

---

* The research described in this paper is supported by a grant of the *Laboratoire d'Informatique de Paris 6*, under the inter-themes collaboration contracts 1999. The first author is supported by CONACYT/SFERE, contract number 70359.

acting together. Instead, they use local perception and low-level communication. This approach has been successfully implemented in the collective transportation of objects and *box-pushing* applications [9].

We are concerned with the design and implementation of multi-robot systems. Our research is focused on the identification of those conditions that allow the emergence of cooperation, *i.e.* how, beyond simple principles, a robot actually becomes cooperative, rather than how cooperative robots are engineered. We suggest that the notion of cooperation should be redefined in the context of collective robotics and we propose the concept of situated cooperation.

This paper is organized as follows: section two introduces the concept of situated cooperation. Section three describes several applications of the principle of situated cooperation: a multi-agent system of self-assembly pieces, and a group of robots that are able to rescue partners with a flat-battery. Section four discusses related and future work.

2   The Principle of Situated Cooperation

Cooperation is traditionally associated with the idea of a *benefit* resulting from the mutual interactions of the members of a group [1]. This gain is obtained by measuring and comparing the performance of different groups with or without various skills such as mutual recognition or communication. This notion of benefit is very abstract and does not help to understand and design cooperative robots.

The kind of behavior we are interested in is also known as *solidarity* and is similar to the notion of *altruism* in biology. Ethologists have observed, for instance, how a sick or injured dolphin is helped by its partners to stay on the surface of the water, in order to allow it to breathe. This is, by the way, the same kind of behavior that is displayed when dolphins save human beings [7].

We are interested in reproducing cooperative behavior with our robots and in understanding the mechanisms above and beyond this behavior. We argue that a kind of cooperation, related to the *needs* and *tendencies* of a robot, may be achieved with non-cognitive but situated individuals.

Situated robots have simple communication and perception capabilities and are able to do simple tasks (*e.g.* wander, avoid to obstacles and navigate). They are situated because they are directly *connected* to the environment and deal with it by themselves.

2.1   Hypothesis

We propose the principle of situated cooperation as a general design guideline for building cooperative individuals, particularly robots.

> **Situated cooperation** is the result of individual and collective actions towards the maintenance of the members of the group within a *viability zone* using available resources of the environment.
>
> The **viability zone** is the state where an individual can survive and its operation is preserved [10]. This zone is defined by the **essential variables** of the individuals of the group. These essential variables represent values that are necessary for the existence of an individual (*e.g.* the energy supply for a mobile robot).

Individuals that use the principle of situated cooperation try to do their tasks and continue to operate by themselves whenever possible. For that, they try to use all available resources of the environnment to stay within or return to the viability zone. These resources may be internal to the robot or external, in the form of partners resources. Partners can contribute their resources to an individual in trouble in order to keep it within its viability zone.

In order to cooperate, individuals have to have information about available resources and about the priority of their tasks. Individuals ask for external resources from the cheapest one to the most expensive one. Partners contribute according to their own state and the task they are doing when a request for help is received. This kind of knowledge, which can be prefixed by the designer or acquired by robots, is used by a lot of situated systems and must not be confused with cognitive knowledge.

Thus, situated cooperation is a bottom-up process that takes into account the resources and the availability of robots. Two applications of this principle are described below.

3 Implementations

3.1 A Self-Assembly Multi-agent System

We have designed a self-assembly multi-agent system, a kind of puzzle whose pieces are agents able to gather together into a shape present in the environment. The form that the agents will shape is predefined, but neither the form nor its location is known by agents.

This experiment has been programmed using Starlogo©[1]. The user of our system can define agents or groups of agents that are able to wander into the environment. The shape of the puzzle is also indicated by the user and represents the viability zone of the agents. Agents are randomly placed and their goal is to reach and stay within the viability zone (vz). When agents reach the vz, they try to distribute themselves within it, avoiding collisions. Each of the groups has a *leader* that proposes a movement for its group to execute. Figure 1 illustrates our puzzle.

Agents use the principle of situated cooperation to help their group to succeed. Even if some agents reach the viability zone, the continue to wander until all the agents of the group have reached it. The behavior of our agents is summarized in algorithm 1.

```
Algorithm 1. Search for the viability zone and assemble pieces
Start
  if agent is leader then propose a movement, choose among:
    1. if agents of the group in vz and no collisions, do not move
    2  if agents of the group in vz and collisions, look for a
       free place in vz
    3. if not all agents in vz, then execute random movement
  else
    follow and propagate the proposed movement
End
```

---

[1] Starlogo is a programming environment of decentralized systems, developed at the *Massachusets Institute of Technology*, available at:
http://el.www.media.mit.edu/groups/el/Projects/starlogo/

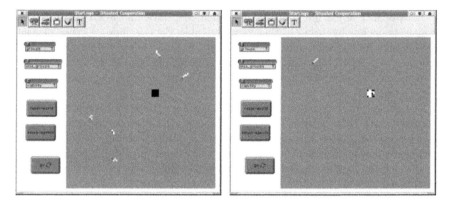

Fig. 1. Two states of our self-assembly system with five groups of five agents. The leaders are the squares of different colors situated at one extremity of each group. The agents started from the initial state (left) and four groups have succeeded in reaching the viability zone indicated by the big square (right).

We have compared the performance of cooperative and non-cooperative agents to the assembling of a puzzle. Cooperative agents act in groups, and non-cooperative agents act alone. The zone that agents have to search for and assemble in - always squares - has been randomly located and corresponds to the total area occupied by the agents. We have experimented a fixed number of iterations - 1000 iterations for each agent - and compared the percentage of the viability zone that was occupied by agents at the end of the experiments. Populations of the same size were tested on exactly the same puzzle. In all cases, cooperative individuals filled a bigger area of the viability zone than did the non-cooperative individuals. The results are shown in figure 2.

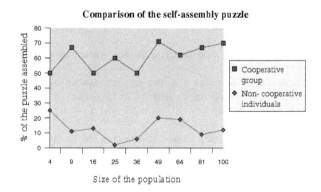

Fig. 2. Performance of two kinds of agents, cooperative and non-cooperative, in the assembling of a puzzle

3.2   The Rescue of Mobile Robots

We have also used the principle of situated cooperation in the design of the MICRobES[2] robots [3]. The principle was useful when defining the behavior of self-vigilant robots able to rescue a robot with flat battery. In this case, robots cooperate to keep partners within a viability zone that is not a physical area, as in the puzzle application, but a zone determined by the energy supply of a robot. When a robot is no longer able to ensure its supply by itself, it sends a call for help, and partners may perform actions to help it.

We are conducting these experiments with eight MICRobES robots: they are Pioneer 2-DX mobile robots from ActivMedia©, provided with bumpers, sonars, video-camera and radio-modems. We are experimenting with several forms of communication and coordination, and studying their effects on cooperation. More details can be found in [11,12].

4   Final Considerations and Future Work

Research on collective handling of objects and box-pushing is closely related to our work, in particular the implementation of the rescue of a robot. Interesting algorithms and collaborative strategies have been reported by Stillwell [14], Mataric [9], Kube [8] and Yamada [16]. They show how groups of non-cognitive robots are able to coordinate their movements in order to push an object collectively.

The notion of situated cooperation is also used by Garbis [6] in a study of rescue training. This work discusses the difference between the cooperation that can be pre-planned and can relay on plans, and the situated cooperation required in dynamic systems, in order to deal with emergencies. Even though this is research in the field of communication studies, it concerns questions that are relevant to our work.

In this paper we have described general design guidelines to implement cooperative situated individuals. We have introduced the notion of situated cooperation, a principle that allows behavior in the form of solidarity, taking into account the resources and availability of individuals in a group. We have argued that situated cooperation is a phenomenon that emerges in a bottom-up process from the interactions among low cognitive level individuals in a group. This principle may be useful to design self-vigilant, self-adapting situated individuals.

The experiments described are in progress and future work will focus on ways of making our robots self-sufficient in terms of energy supply. The implementation of reinforcement mechanisms will be considered, in the near future, in order to enable the robots to identify, by themselves, the priority of tasks and the availability of resources.

References

1. Axelrod R. The Evolution of Cooperation. Basic Books (1984)
2. Chaib-draa B. Industrial Applications of Distributed AI. In: *Readings in Agents*, Huhns M.N., Singh M.P. (eds). Morgan Kauffmann, USA (1998) 31-35

---

[2] MICRobES is an acronym in French for Implementation of Robot Collectivities in a Social Environment.

3. Drogoul A., Picault S. MICRobES : vers des collectivités des robots socialement situés. In: *Actes des 7èmes Journées Francophones sur l'Intelligence Artificielle Distribuée et les Systèmes Multi-Agents*, Gleizes M.P., Marcenac (eds). Hermès, Paris (1999) 265-277
4. Durfee E.H., Kiskis D.L., Birmingham W.P. The Agent Architecture of the University of Michigan Digital Library. In: *Readings in Agents*, Huhns M.N., Singh M.P. (eds) Morgan Kauffmann, USA (1998) 98-108
5. Etzioni O., Weld D. A Softbot-Based Interface to the Internet. In: *Communications of ACM*, July'94. ACM Press. (1994)
6. Garbis C., Waern Y. Team coordination and communication in a rescue command staff. The role of public representations. Public artefacts in rescue training. In: *Le Travail Humain*, Special Issue on Human-Machine Cooperation. 62(3) (1999) 273-291
7. Goldberg J. Les sociétés animales. Delachaux et niestlé, Lausanne-Paris (1998)
8. Kube C.R., Bonabeau E.: Cooperative transport by ants and robots. Dans: *Robotics and Autonomous Systems*. Elsevier Science (2000) 85-101
9. Mataric M., Nilsson M., Simsarian K.T. Cooperative Multi-Robot Box-Pushing. In: *Proceeding IROS-95*. Pittsburgh, PA (1995) 556-561
10. Meyer J.A., Guillot A. Simulation of Adaptive Behavior in animats: Review and Prospect. In: *From animals to animats. Proceedings of the First Conference on Simulation of Adaptive Behavior*. Meyer J.A., Wilson S.W. (eds). MIT Press, USA. (1991) 2-14
11. Muñoz A., Drogoul A. Towards the Design of Self-Vigilant Robots using a Principle of Situated Cooperation. In: *Proceedings of the RoboCup Rescue Workshop*. ICMAS 2000. Boston, Mass. USA (2000)
12. Muñoz A.: Cooperation in Collective Robotics. In: *Proceedings of ACAI'01, Student Sessions*. ACAI'01 Prague Cz. (2001) 64-71
13. Sanholm T., Lesser V. Issues in Automated Negotiation and Electronic Commerce: Extending the Contract Net Framework. In: *Readings in Agents*, Huhns M.N., Singh M.P. (eds). Morgan Kauffmann, USA (1998) 66-73
14. Stillwell D.J., Bay J.S. Toward the Development of a Material Transport System using Swarms of Ant-like Robots. In: *Proceedings of the 1993 IEEE International Conference on Robotics and Automation, Vol. 1*. IEEE Computer Society Press, USA (1993) 766-771
15. Sycara K. Multiagent Systems. In: *AI Magazine*. Summer 1998. AAAI Press, USA (1998)
16. Yamada S., Saito J. Adaptive Action Selection without Explicit Communication for Multi-robot Box-pushing. In: *1999 IEEE/RSJ International Conference on Intelligent Robots and Systems* (1999)

A Fault-Tolerant Scheme of Multi-agent System for Worker Agents

YunHee Kang[1], HoSang Ham[2], and ChongSun Hwang[3]

[1] Department of Computer and Communication Engineering, Cheonan University,
115, Anseo-dong,
Cheonan 330-180, Choongnam, Republic of Korea
yhkang@infocom.cheonan.ac.kr
[2] Electronics and Telecommunications Research Institute
161, Gajeong-dong,
Yusong-Gu, Daejon, 305-350, Republic of Korea
hsham@etri.re.kr
[3] Department of Computer Science and Engineering, Korea University
5-1, Anam-dong, Seongbuk-ku,
Seoul, 136-701, Republic of Korea
hwang@disys.korea.ac.kr

Abstract. The paper introduces a fault-tolerant scheme of MAS (Multi-Agent System) for worker agents using the checkpointing and rollback recovery mechanism. To discuss the fault-tolerance of working agents in MAS, we consider the extended MAS model based on task delegation and observation which can be independent of node failures. In the proposed MAS, to preserve global consistency, the facilitators maintain a task plan in a stable storage by using checkpoints taken when either completing a task plan or receiving a response of a subtask within the task plan. In this paper, we present a fault-tolerant scheme which takes over blocked worker agent problem of MAS by using communication-induced checkpointing.

1 Introduction

In any wide-area distributed system such as Internet, fault tolerance is crucial from real-world application. MAS(Multi-Agent System) is a distributed system that some agents need services to solve a goal and others provide services on node [1][2][7].

MAS consists of a group of agents that can take specific roles within an organizational structure [7]. MAS focuses on the collaborative resolution of global problems by a set of distributed entities. Agents attempt to satisfy their own local goals as well as the collaborative global goals. In MAS, the middle agent manages the capability and the preference which held by the set of agents in a working environment, and typically receives the advertisements from other agents having a specific capability. These advertisements contain agent's information such as location, capability, etc.

MASs are prone to failures in any traditional distributed system. Agents become suddenly unavailable due to *node* or *communication link* failures. To tolerate the failure of working agents in MAS, we consider the fault-tolerance of MAS model based on task

J. Liu et al. (Eds.): AMT 2001, LNCS 2252, pp. 171–181, 2001.

delegation and observation which can be independent of an arbitrary number of node failures.

This paper proposes a novel approach to fault-tolerance of worker agent's execution in MAS. The MAS has its roots in the multi-broker architecture [5]. We apply a fault-tolerant scheme of MAS for worker agents using the checkpointing and rollback recovery mechanism to preserve reliable computing in MAS.

The proposed scheme provides availability of facilitators and consistency of agents. We observe some case of agents failure and show that the proposed MAS is well-formed and recoverable. The algorithm for checkpointing of facilitators guarantees global consistence of agents in failure-free. The algorithm for rollback-recovery preserves the recovery of faulty agent by coordination between faulty agent and facilitator.

The rest of the paper is organized as follows: Section 2 describes an extended MAS model. Section 3 describes system model. Section 4 describes a fault-tolerant scheme and observations. We conclude in section 5 with some future directions.

1.1   Related Works

In MAS, each agent must be able to locate the other agents who might have capabilities, which are necessary for the execution of tasks, either locally or via coalition formation. The agent requesting the information to the facilitator receives information about the agent having the capability of corresponding to the task.

Middle agents are used to accept and respond routing request from an agent to locate services, to register capability [1][3][4]. Different systems define their own middle agents differently based on interaction types. For example, facilitators in Genesereth's federated systems [1], SRI's Open Agent Architecture [3], and matchmakers and brokers in RETSINA [4].

The facilitator manages the capability and the preference held by the set of agents in MAS and typically receives the advertisements from other agents having a specific capability. When a matching agent receives this advertisement, it records the name of the advertiser and the associated capability. Other agents may ask the facilitator to find an agent with a specific capability.

There are few works to discuss fault handling in MAS in a viewpoint of distributed system [5][6]. In distributed AI, it assumes that agents execute under the fault-free condition. However, as MAS scales up, its failure probability may also be higher. Espcially, if the long running MAS applications are executed on the systems, the failure probability becomes significant. In MAS, the multiple brokers are proposed to be used as middle agent for fault-tolerant mechanism [5]. In the MAS based on multiple brokers, the middle agents act as the facilitators for enhancement of availability [4]. In large MASs with multiple middle agents, those middle agents take the location service by *the proxy of naming service* for each other or function as resource facilitators by *the proxy of resource management service* for each other.

Three classes of algorithms have been proposed in the literature to determine consistent global checkpoints: independent, coordinated, and communication-induced [8][11][12]. In communication-induced checkpointing, the coordination is done in a lazy fashion by piggybacking control information on application messages [11].

Without system-wide coordination, each agent is forced to take checkpoints based on some MAS application messages it receives from other agents. Sufficient information is piggybacked on each agent so that the receiver can examine the information prior to processing the message. If processing the message would violate the specified constraint, the receiver is forced to take a checkpoint before the processing. No special coordination messages are exchanged. A facilitator, the supervisor of worker agents, takes a checkpoint by saving those state on stable storage of the facilitator when it has received the messages from worker agents having tasks.

We propose the MAS based on multiple facilitators interact with agents and other facilitators. In the MAS, the facilitator maintains current state of the task plan in a stable storage by using checkpoints with piggybacking control information such as task status, sequence number taken when either completing a task plan or receiving a response of a subtask within the task plan.

2 The Extended MAS Model

MAS provides clean separation between individual agents and their interactions in overall systems [10]. The separation is natural for the design of multi-agent architecture.

In the proposed MAS, we consider an observation of agents to tolerate failures. At critical points in the reliable execution of agents, it is important to detect the non-deterministic state of the agent set composed of facilitators and agents in MAS. The facilitator defines the task and the constraint on it. In order to execute a task, the facilitator has to set actions, fulfill the constraint and return the result. The actions are done by the workers at any host.

The MAS model has two main advantages in aspects of fault-tolerance and concurrent execution.

1. Fault tolerance - If one worker fails to return within a given deadline, the supervisor can start another one or redefine the subtasks and then start a new one.
2. Concurrent execution - There can be many workers working for one supervisor and each of these workers operates independently. This speeds up collection results of the subtasks and so speeds up the whole process.

The paper focuses on interactions between agents and facilitators, and techniques for the fault tolerant system design of MAS and development process is beyond the scope of this paper.

3 System Model

We consider MAS, denoted by S, consisting of n ($n \geq 0$) agents which is interacted by message passing via facilitators. Each pair of agents is connected by a two-way reliable channel whose transmission delay is unpredictable but finite. Agents are registered into facilitators consisting of m facilitators, $F=\{f_1, f_2, f_3, \ldots, f_m\}$, which coordinate the group of agents.

In MAS, communication from components of S is said to satisfy First-In-First-Out(FIFO) delivery if for all messages m and m'.

$$send_i(m) \rightarrow send_i(m') \Rightarrow deliver_j(m) \rightarrow deliver_j(m')$$

Agent execution is a *sequence of task state intervals*, each started by a nondeterministic event. Execution during each state interval is deterministic, such that if an agent starts from the same state and is subjected to the same non-determinant events of the same locations within the execution, it will always yield the same output [9].

Agents are autonomous in the sense that they do not share memory, do not share a common clock value, and do not have access to private information of other agents such as clock drift, clock granularity, clock precision, and speed. We assume, finally, agents follow a fail-stop behavior. Agents can be inactive in a finite bound time due to a failure.

An agent produces a sequence of events and the hth event in agent p is denoted as $e_{p,h}$; each event moves the task from one state to another. We assume events are produced by the execution of internal, send or receive statements. It can be modeled as a partial order of event $= (\widehat{E}, \rightarrow)$, where $\widehat{E}$ is the set of all events and $\rightarrow$ is the *happened-before* relation defined as follows:

Definition 1. *An event $e_{p,h}$ proceeds an event $e_{q,k}$ denoted $e_{p,h} \rightarrow e_{q,k}$ iff :*

- *$p=q$ and $k=h+1$, or*
- *$e_{p,h}=send(m)$ and $e_{q,k}=receive(m)$, or*
- *$\exists e_{r,z} : (e_{p,h} \rightarrow e_{r,z}) \wedge (e_{r,z} \rightarrow e_{q,k})$*

A checkpoint C dumps the current task state onto the stable storage in a facilitator. A checkpoint of agent p is denoted as $C_{p,sn}$ where sn is called the *index*, or *sequence number*, of a checkpoint. Each agent takes checkpoints either at its own pace or induced by some communication pattern.

4   Checkpointing and Rollback Recovery Mechanism

In this section, we describe a hybrid recovery scheme composed of *a coordination based recovery scheme* and *a facilitator based recovery scheme*. The coordination based recovery scheme enables each agent to participate in the execution of task to recover a failure worker agent by forcing the agent to piggyback only an additional n-size vector, where n is number of agents. The facilitator based recovery scheme allows the facilitator to remove the failure worker agent when it detects the timeout delay beyond a given deadline caused by node crash.

4.1   Assumption

Let G represent a goal and *TEG(Task Execution Graph)* internally represent the goal. Let $TEG_{i,sn}^{f_k}$ represents the ith task-plan with sn constructed by a facilitator f_k. TEG is composed of actions represented by ordering relationships described in definition 2.

In Fig. 1(a)(b), the arcs represents a parallel execution of subtask B and C.

Definition 2. *The three ordering relationships of actions:*

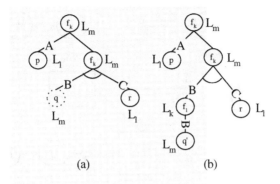

(a)   (b)

Fig. 1. Task Plan : Dotted circle represent fault worker agent

- $A \prec B$ denoting that action A must be performed before action B.
- $A \parallel B$ denoting that action A must be performed parallel B.
- $A \bullet B$ denoting that action A and B must be performed without order but only one finished either A or B.

In Fig. 1(a), an agent p executes a subtask A in in L_l. In parallel, a subtask B and C in execute in L_m and L_l. Each node maintains the place that is context for worker agent.

$$TEG_i = \{<A, p, L_l> , <B, q, L_m>, <C, r, L_l> \}$$

In Fig. 1(b) f_k delegate the task B from q to q' via f_l. In Fig. 1(a)(b), the task execution is represented with $TEG_{i,sn}^{f_k}$ in f_k and proceeded in a bottom-up manner.

4.2   Failure Model

In MAS model, we consider two types of failures; one is the fault of a task agent which plays a role of such worker agents as s, p, q and r, and the other is unavailable information agents such as R_s, R_p, R_q and R_r.

As shown in Fig. 2, a facilitator f_k delegates a task of a goal G from agent s and sends into one or more worker agents. To delegate a task, a facilitator f_k decomposes a task into subtasks, scatters the subtask to the worker agents such as p, q and r and finally integrates the result of subtasks which are assigned to worker agents. In the proposed MAS, it is necessary to negotiate between agents and facilitators such as f_k, f_l and f_m to achieve the goal assigned by a worker agent [7]. As is shown in Fig. 2, a facilitator exploits the interaction with agents and other facilitators to achieve a goal.

As shown by Fig. 3, there are two types of communication, one from s to f_k, the other from f_k to task agents such as p, q and r. The request is denoted by G, where $G=\{T_A, T_B, T_C\}$, where T_A, T_B and T_C mean subtasks decomposed by f_k.

The agent group AG_i, where $AG_i = \{p, q, r, s\}$, is a set of a request agent and worker agents which have subtasks corresponding to a task i derived on G. The facilitator manages the group of agents AG_i in order to preserve consistency of the agents. The facilitator also need to keep several checkpoints on stable storage. There is no direct communication between worker agents, and so we don't consider communication

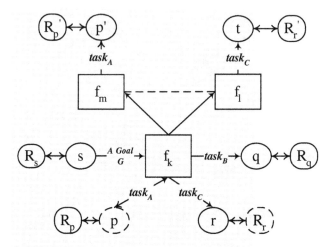

Fig. 2. The MAS model : dotted circle and round box represent failure agent

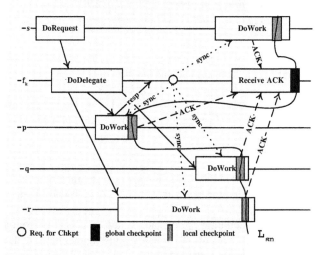

Fig. 3. The coordination between agents and facilitator in MAS model

between worker agent and information agent such as p to R_p, q to R_q and r to R_r and vice versa. The information agents are out of scope in the system model in $\mathcal{S}$.

In the context of this paper, a local checkpoint of agents is a saved copy of an earlier state of the tasks. A global checkpoint of the system is a set of local checkpoints, one for each task. A global checkpoint is consistent if the set of the local checkpoints forms a consistent global state.

We denote C_{sn} with a global checkpoint formed by checkpoints with sequence number sn and use the term consistent global checkpoint C_{sn} and recovery line L_{sn} interchangeably in Fig. 3.

The messages between the facilitator and the agents in AG_i are ordered in failure free: Agents communicate only with a facilitator, and the facilitator send the messages and route them to the appropriate places.

A set of task states, which consists of task in S, is *a global consistent state* if any pair of state is mutually consistent [9].

4.3   Communication Induced Checkpointing for MAS

In this paper, we apply the checkpointing mechanism based on communication-induced checkpointing as follows: each task agent is forced to take checkpoints based on some application messages. Sufficient information is piggybacked on each agent so that the receiver can examine the information prior to processing the message.

We assume that the system ensures the situation that there is no missing or orphan message in the concerned checkpointing interval, then the set of all the checkpoints taken by worker agents. Our observation means that the sending as well as receiving of any message have to be recorded in the same checkpoint of the sender and the receiver accordingly.

The facilitator maintains the checkpoints into not volatile memory but stable store to preserve. On the other hand the worker agents such as s, p, q and r, keep up the state of partial result of task onto main memory until a task is completed. In Fig. 4, the algorithm for checkpointing covers the worker failure by using communication-induced checkpointing.

4.4   Rollback Scheme

In failure-free, each facilitator f_k maintains $TEG_{i,sn}^{f_k}$ the same with a task plan TEG of an agent p on stable storage. An agent p has $TEG_{i,sn}^{p}$ the same with $TEG_{i,sn}^{f_k}$ assigned by f_k. When $TEG_{i,sn}^{p}$ is received, p takes a checkpoint including $TEG_{i,sn}^{p}$ on stable storage in order to synchronize TEG in f_k. An agent p always has the same sn value that f_k one.

In recovery time, the sequence number sn of an agent p is not the same with the number of sn of f_k. At step 4 of recovery algorithm, an agent p requests the result which is stored in stable storage by f_k until the sn of p is the same with that of f_k.

Let us assume that each work agent p has a variable sn_p which represents the sequence number of the last checkpoint. Each time a basic checkpoint $C_{p,sn}$ is taken by an agent p to start an explicit coordination with a facilitator f_k. In the first time, the faulty agent p requests the task in TEG which which is on the stable storage of a facilitator f_k, until sn of f_k is equal to sn of p.

In the algorithm of Fig. 5, recovering agent p rolls back to its checkpoint based on sn in its stable storage of f_k. In step 1) of the recovery algorithm, p restore the state from before a failure which is restored upon recovery and knows that a task plan $TEG_{i,sn}^{f_k}$ is completed. In step 2), 3), the agent p sequentially receives t holding a partial result of a subtask from a provider agent based on sn. And it compares its sn and the sn of a facilitator f_k. It then installs its checkpointed state from f_k. and resumes execution until its sn is the same with the sn of a facilitator f_k. In the final step of the recovery algorithm, the sn_i is set to sn_k of a facilitator f_k.

Data Structure at worker agents such as p, q and r.

  sn : sequence number

  T : task assigned by facilitator

Data Structure at facilitator f_k

  $TEG(TaskExecutionGraph)$: It is a graph represented with node and edge
    which is generated from a goal G,

  $TEV(TaskExecutionVector)$: It is a unit task vector having pointer
    to preserve a set of agents information related with TEG

  $TATable$: It is a task vector having pointer to the TEV.

  sn_k : It is a sequence number of f_k

/* The initial values are sn_k=0, $TEG=\perp$, $TATable=\perp$ and $TEV = \perp$ */

Whenever facilitator f_k **receives a goal** G **with a message** $m_{REQ(G)}$ **from agent** s

Procedure $Do\_Deleagtion$(message $m_{REQ(G)}$, sn sn_k) {
    construct TEG and TEV and Link $TATable$ entry to TEV.
        send T in TEG with sn_k to task agents and message to request agent
    for all $p \in TEV$ **do**
        receive ACK from p in TEV of G from related agents with G
    take a checkpoint of $TEG_{sn_k}^{f_k}$
    increase sn_k /* $sn_k \leftarrow sn_k + 1$ */
}

Whenever facilitator f_k **receives a message** $m_{RESP(G)}$ **from agent** p

Procedure $Do\_UpdateTEG$ (message $m_{RESP(G)}$, sn sn_k) {
    update TEG and TEV based on $m_{RESP(T)}$.
    multicast sn to the agents in TEV of G
    for all $p \in TEV$ **do**
        receive ACK from p
    take a checkpoint sn
    increase sn_k /* $sn_k \leftarrow sn_k + 1$ */
}

Action of any worker agent p **at completing task** T **for each task** $\in TEG_k$ **managed by facilitator** f_k **do**

Procedure Do_Work(task T) {
    receive T with $m_{req}(T)$ from f_k
    execute T interact with R_p autonomously
    increase sn
    send $m_{resp(t)}$ to f_k with sn
}

Action of any worker agent p **at receiving** sn **with** $m_{sync(sn)}$

Procedure Do_Sync(task T) {
    increase sn
    if ($m_{sn} > sn$) **then**
        $sn \leftarrow m_{sn}$
    take a checkpoint sn
    send ACK to f_k
}

Fig. 4. Algorithm of Checkpointing based on coordination

Data Structure at faulty worker agents such as p, q and r.
> sn : sequence number
> T: task assigned by worker agent

Whenever failure agent p restarts based on local checkpoint number sn
Procedure $Do\_Recovery$(message m) {
>   1. restore sn from stable storage of agent
>   2. request sn from a facilitator f_k
>   3. receive T with m_{sn} from f_k
>   /*start recovery based on a facilitator information*/
>   4. **if** $(sn < m_{sn})$
>   replay T corresponding m_{sn}
>   5. update sn /* $sn \leftarrow m_{sn}$ */
}

Fig. 5. Algorithm of Rollback-Recovery based on sn

4.5 Global Consistency

We propose a checkpointing and rollback recovery scheme based on communication-induced checkpoint to tolerate faulty worker agents. The advantages of the scheme is that the result of task is maintained by the facilitator only and the group of workers just hold the overall status of the task by piggybacked control mechanism related with the task.

In any time, worker agents are to be failure state, then those take over a failure state based on biggybacked information. From the viewpoints of communication, it improves the number of message to preserve the consistency and enhances the autonomous property of agents. Each agent takes a local checkpoint when one receives the request of checkpointing for synchronization with other agents.

Whenever failures occur, the facilitator do not consider the worker's status of task. In recovery time, the autonomous worker takes over the failures based on *active restart* by interaction with facilitator, then it takes rollback recovery to preserve global consistency in S.

The additional information required for such checkpoint synchronization is appended at the end of the piggybacked synchronization message. we observe that any global checkpoint taken in the system is consistent and hence the system has to rollback on to the last saved state in case of a failure.

> **Theorem 1 :** The group of agents, AG_i, related with task i is *consistent* iff
> : each agent in AG_i has the same number of sn on stable storage of the
> facilitator f_k.
> **Proof** : The sequence of events related to execution of agents can be con-
> sistent with the causal order. Causal order ensures the guarantee of causally
> ordered message delivery to the group of agents. Let m_{Chk_p} represent the
> piggypack message with a request for checkpoint related with an agent p
> and m_{ACK_p} represent the reply message after checkpointing by p. If two
> message m for m_{Chk_p} and m' for m_{ACK_p} are received and sent by p, then

m must be delivered everywhere before m'. m' causally depends on m(m happens before m').

- $k = h + 1$,
- $\forall p : e_{f,h} = send_{f_k}(m_{Chk_p})$ and $e_{f_k,k} = receive_{f_k}(m_{ACK_p})$,
- $\exists e_{r,z} : (e_{f_k,h} \to e_{r,z}) \wedge (e_{r,z} \to e_{f_k,k}) \Rightarrow |AG_i| = |m_{ACK_p}|$

This causal order delivery does not constrain the delivery order of two concurrent multicast messages; concurrent messages may be delivered in different orders at different destinations. But all agents respond with determinant information which piggybacks task-specific knowledge sn. We can use the multicast to preserve the total order of m_{ACK_p} and m_{Chk_p}. On the other hand, if two message m for m_{resp_p} and m' for m_{ACK_p} are received and sent by f_k, then m must be delivered in the node f_k before m'. m' causally depends on m.

Theorem 2 : The changed task plan is preserved with the *consistent* state of the group of agents AG_i.

Proof : Any long failure is derived to change the task plan related with task i in order to isolate the faulty agents. If the facilitator finds a faulty agent p, then p is excluded from AG_i, and reconstructs a task plan $TEG_{i,sn}^{f_k}$. On the other hand, if the faulty agents are in AG_i, the faulty agents are recovered from the last checkpoint based on local sn with interaction with facilitator f_k. In both cases, we can observe that the faulty agent can be either replaced by other worker agent or restart from the last checkpoint. Then system is globally consistent with its sound state.

In [5], a program running on a host can crash, and a host itself can crash thereby crashing all programs running on that host. We observe the algorithm 1-2 to maintain the global consistency in failure free and recovery.

Observation 1 : The facilitator f_k manages the $PROF_k$ in which the agents with capabilities and preferences are registered. The facilitator constructs a task plan by considering the situation of MAS by periodic communication between facilitators. The facilitator determines the worker of the subtask based on $PROF_k$ information. The facilitator f_k considers the interaction with other facilitators to determine the appropriate agent if there is no proper agent in $PROG_k$.

Observation 2 : A consistent state of the agent and the facilitator is preserved iff : when the sn value is increased in the execution, completion of the delegated subtask and the transmission of the result are maintained; when the altered sn value is multicasted to the group of agents related to the TEG; The sound agent updates its sn value to the sn value transmitted from the facilitator. Otherwise, the faulty agent will update its sn value to the sn value transmitted from the facilitator.

Observation 3 : The facilitator f_k maintains optimal agents in AG_i after looking up its $PROF_k$. The facilitator preserves the consistency of the agents in AG_i which are the components of $TEG_{i,sn}^{f_k}$. If an agent is a member of AG_i, its sn is preserved by piggybacked information via facilitator. The agent increases the sn by receiving the synchronization message m_{sync} from the facilitator.

5 Conclusion and Future Works

In this paper, we have introduced a scheme for fault-tolerance of agent execution in MAS. The fault-tolerant scheme improves the blocking avoidance of MAS which is based on an alternative in worker pool and recovery scheme of agents based on checkpointing. We designed *TEG(Task Execution Graph)* internally represent the goal. The TEG with sn is used to preserve consistency of worker agents in a MAS. We apply the sn of a checkpoint to preserve consistence of states for task execution between agent and facilitator.

In order to assess feasibility and applicability, we have developed a prototypical instance of our MAS model for agent services. This prototype, which we have termed *ANTS*, implements the major features and components of MAS model, in addition to some experimental agents. To facilitate the construction of agents we have also implemented the main primitives included in the design of TEG.

References

1. M. Genesereth: An agent based framework for interoperability, In: J. M. Bradshaw (eds.): Software Agents. AAAI Press. (1997) 317–345.
2. M.R. Genesereth and S.P. Katchpel: Software agents, Communications of the ACM. **37** No. 7, (Jul. 1994) 1029–1036.
3. D. Martin, A. Cheyer, and D. Moran: Building Distributed Software Systems with the Open Agent Architecture. Applied Artificial Intelligence. **37** No.12, (1999) 92–128.
4. Hao-Chi Wong and Katia Sycara: A Taxonomy of Middle-agents for the Internet. Proceedings of the Fourth International Conference on Multi-Agent Systems(ICMAS'2000). (2000)
5. S. Kumar, P. R. Cohen, and H. J. Levesque: The Adaptive Agent Architecture: Achieving Fault-Tolerance Using Persistent Broker Teams. Proceedings of the International Conference on Multi-Agent Systems(ICMAS2000). Boston,MA USA. (2000)
6. Johansen, D., Marzullo, K., Schneider, F.B., Jacobsen, K., Zagorodnov, D.: NAP: practical fault-tolerance for itinerant computations. Distributed Computing Systems. (1999) 180–189
7. H.V.D. Parunak.: Characterizing multi-agent negotiation. In International Workshop on Multi-Agent Systems(IWMAS-98). (1998)
8. O. Babaoglu and K. Mazullo: Consistent Global States of Distributed Systems: Fundamental Concepts and Mechanisms. University of Bologna, Italy (1993)
9. K.M. Chandy and L. Lamport: Distributed Snapshots: Determining Global State of Distributed Systems. ACM Transaction on Computer Systems. **3**, No.1 (1985) 63–75
10. K. Decker and K. Sycara and M. Williamson: Matchmaking and brokering. In Proc. of the Second International Conference on Multi-agents Systems (ICMAS-96), (1996)
11. R.Baldoni, J.H.Helary, A. Mostefaoui, and M.Raynal: A Communication-Induced Checkpointing Protocal that Ensures Rollback-Dependency Trackability. Proc. IEEE Int'l Symp.Fault Tolerant Computing. (1997) 68–77
12. R.Koo and S.Toueg : Checkpointing and rollback-recovery for distributed systems. IEEE Transaction on Software Engineering. **13** (1987) 558–565

Decentralized Control of Multi-agent Systems Based on Modal Logics and Extended Higher Order Petri Nets

Osamu Katai, Kentaro Toda, and Hiroshi Kawakami

Dept. of Systems Science, Graduate School of Informatics, Kyoto University, Sakyo-ku, Kyoto
606-8501, JAPAN
katai@i.kyoto-u.ac.jp, toda@sys.i.kyoto-u.ac.jp, kawakami@i.kyoto-u.ac.jp

Abstract. We introduce the notions of decentralized system structure of multi-agent systems, their behavioral and structural correctness, and centralized and decentralized control for attaining correct behavior, and also that of decentralized controllability which are then examined based on modal logical analysis of system behavior and Petri net representation of system structures.

1 Introduction

To cope with recent need for constructing sophisticated distributed and decentralized systems such as multi-agent systems [1,2,3], we will develop a general theory for the analysis and design of control systems for discrete event systems in such a way that the control is carried out in a decentralized manner. Here, "being decentralized" means that each subsystem (hereafter, we will call it "agent") has its own individual goal (hereafter, we will call it "task") which may be in conflict with other goals and also has its own territory over which it can control.

Thus the definition of "decentralized controllability" in this context and also the derivation of control rules (that is, the sequence of control actions) in a decentralized manner become very complex and have to be studied in detail.

In this research, we first introduce a Petri net representation of system structure [4] and then introduce a way of task representation by the use of modal logic [5]. More precisely, we employ a combination of two kinds of modal logics, i.e., "temporal logic" [6, 7] and "deontic logic" [8,9,10]. The temporal logic part represent the dynamical aspect of tasks and the deontic logic part represents the control structure such as "permission" or "obligation" for these agents. The potential "conflict" among these tasks is elucidated by translating their logical representations into their extended Petri net representations of tasks. These net representations are derived by a systematic analysis of logical representations of tasks, thus deriving their higher order Petri net representations.

Over these extended higher order Petri net representations together with the net representation of the original system to be controlled, we can analyze its controllability and the derivation of "legal" control action sequences. For this purpose, we introduce general definition of "decentralized controllability" of discrete event systems, and the systematic analysis of modal logical task representations yielding more concrete criterion for judging this notion of controllability.

J. Liu et al. (Eds.): AMT 2001, LNCS 2252, pp. 182–190, 2001.

2   Decentralized System Structure

In this paper, decentralized nature of systems is characterized as follows:

(a) Each agent has its own territory.
(b) Each control task is given to one of these agents.
(c) Each task can only control transitions that are in the territory of the agent to whom the task is given.
(d) Agents can interact each other.

This decentralized structure can be analyzed by introducing a higher order network representation of the system and two kinds of modal logic, that is, "temporal logic" and "deontic logic".

2.1   Modeling by Petri Net

The multi-agent system structure and the event-driven aspect of system dynamics can be represented by Petri net representation. Regarding each place as standing for a proposition, we only use 1-bounded Petri nets. Namely, each place has at mose one token. Each place corresponds to a proposition standing for a local state of the system. At each state, the propositions being the case are represented by the places having a token in them. Transitions represent changes of truth values of propositions.

2.2   Introduction of Temporal Logic

When we construct a model using Petri net, we regard the system as a discrete state system. In this case, the system dynamics is represented as a state transition sequence which is generated by moving tokens via firing of transitions step by step.

"Temporal Logic" is a kind of modal logics. In this framework, the dynamics of a system is represented as propositions such as "proposition A is true at the next time instant" by which we can treat the dynamics in a unified manner.

There are several different kinds of temporal logics in relation to treating time. In this paper, we will confine to the cases where the elapse of time can be treated discretely. Also, we will employ two kinds of temporal logics, i.e., branching and non-branching (linear) time logics.

When we regard a state transition sequence as "non-branching" one, "linear" temporal modalities concerning future events related to propositions, say A and B, can be represented by introducing the following (linear) *temporal operators*:

$\mathcal{T}$A: A is true *at next time instant.*
$\mathcal{G}$A: A is true *at any time in the future.*
$\mathcal{F}$A: A is true *at some time in the future.*
A$\mathcal{U}$B: A is true *until B will be true.*

It should also be mentioned that there are other temporal operators about past tense(temporal modalities), i.e., $\mathcal{Y}$, $\mathcal{H}$, $\mathcal{P}$, $\mathcal{S}$, that are the converse of $\mathcal{T}$, $\mathcal{G}$, $\mathcal{F}$, $\mathcal{U}$, respectively.

2.3   Introduction of Deontic Logic

Temporal logics only mention about when propositions become true. To represent a constraint ("norm") that a proposition should be the case (true), i.e., the way how the system "should" behave, we introduce another kind of modal logic, "Deontic Logic".

In this framework, we introduce the following *deontic operators*:

$\mathcal{O}_v A$: v thinks it *obligatory* (compulsory, necessary) to bring about that A or equivalently it is obligatory for v that p is the case.

$\mathcal{P}_v A$: v thinks it *permitted* (admitted, allowed) for him to bring about that A or it is *permissible* (admissible, allowable) for v that A is the case.

$\mathcal{I}_v A$:   it is *indifferent* (detached, disinterested) for v whether A is the case or not.

$\mathcal{F}_v A$: v thinks it *forbidden (prohibited)* to bring about that A or it is forbidden for v that A is the case.

It should be noted that the deontic operators apply not only to the fundamental statements, but also task (normative) statements involving deontic operators such as the above. Hence, for instance, $\mathcal{O}_v \mathcal{P}_{v'} A$ represents that it is obligatory for agent v that A should be permitted for agent v', i.e., v should regard that A should be permitted for v'. These statements can represent constraints on interactions among agents where some agents give an order to other agents.

Using deontic logic and temporal logic, control tasks of statements are represented as "nested" propositions as follows:

$\mathcal{O}_v \mathcal{F} A$:   It is obligatory for agent v that A will be the case in the future.

$\mathcal{P}_v \mathcal{G} A$:   It is permitted for agent v that A will be true forever.

2.4   Task Structure and Its Network Representation

To analyze systems and to design control sequences, nested structures of control tasks represented by modal logics must be examined in detail. Thus we will introduce an "extended Petri net" representations of control tasks by analyzing them. To do this, we will consider the relations between the deontic logical representation and the temporal logical representation. For example, a norm expressed by a deontic operator on a temporal operator is translated into an expression of reverse order of operators by the use of valid formulae such as

$$(\mathcal{O}_v A)\mathcal{U}B \supset \mathcal{O}_v(A\mathcal{U}B)$$

Namely, $\mathcal{O}_v(A\mathcal{U}B)$ can be translated into $(\mathcal{O}_v A)\mathcal{U}B$, a sufficient condition, yielding an extended Petri net representation of task $\mathcal{O}_v(A\mathcal{U}B)$ as showin in Fig1.

To illustrate the way how our approach works, we will use a simple example on the control of a "decentralized production line" shown in Fig.2. It consists of four agents: Agent1 - Agent4. Each task associated with each agent is activated through firing of the corresponding transition in its territory, e.g., in this case we have six tasks represented in a temporal deontic logical form. These associated tasks are then translated into an "extended Petri net" form. For example, a modal logical systematic analysis on the third task:

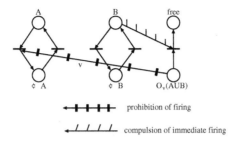

prohibition of firing

compulsion of immediate firing

Fig. 1. Extended Petri net representation of $A\mathcal{U}B$

"$\mathcal{O}_2(((\neg P_3)\mathcal{U}(\neg P_4 \wedge P_5))\mathcal{S}(\neg P_7))\mathcal{U}(P_7 \wedge \neg \mathcal{Y}P_7))$": after the completion of the production by Agent 4, Agent 2 should not start the production of material B until the material is stored only in stock P_5;

derives its extended higher order Petri net representation shown in Fig.3 [11]. It consists of module nets reflecting its subtasks, and they are joined with linkage relations prescribing concurrent (simultaneous) firing of linked transitions. It should be noted that the transitive closure of these linkage relations associates the task in analysis with the object system which is shown in the bottom part of Fig.3.

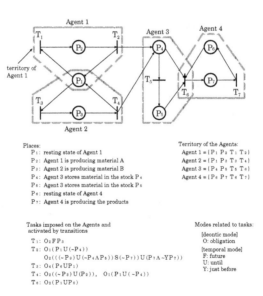

Places:
  P_1: resting state of Agent 1
  P_2: Agent 1 is producing material A
  P_3: Agent 2 is producing material B
  P_4: Agent 3 stores material in the stock P_4
  P_5: Agent 3 stores material in the stock P_5
  P_6: resting state of Agent 4
  P_7: Agent 4 is producing the products

Territory of the Agents:
  Agent 1 = {P_1 P_2 T_1 T_2}
  Agent 2 = {P_1 P_3 T_3 T_4}
  Agent 3 = {P_4 P_5 T_5 T_6}
  Agent 4 = {P_6 P_7 T_6 T_7}

Tasks imposed on the Agents and activated by transitions
  T_1: $\mathcal{O}_2\mathrm{F}P_3$
  T_2: $\mathcal{O}_1(P_1\mathrm{U}(\neg P_4))$
     $\mathcal{O}_2(((\neg P_3)\mathrm{U}(\neg P_4 \wedge P_5))\mathrm{S}(\neg P_7))\mathrm{U}(P_7 \wedge \neg \mathrm{Y}P_7))$
  T_3: $\mathcal{O}_4(P_6\mathrm{U}P_1)$
  T_4: $\mathcal{O}_2((\neg P_3)\mathrm{U}(P_2))$, $\mathcal{O}_1(P_1\mathrm{U}(\neg P_4))$
  T_5: $\mathcal{O}_2(P_1\mathrm{U}P_6)$

Modes related to tasks:
  [deontic mode]
  O: obligation
  [temporal mode]
  F: future
  U: until
  Y: just before

Fig. 2. Petri net representation of a decentralized multi-agent system involving modal logical representation of individual tasks

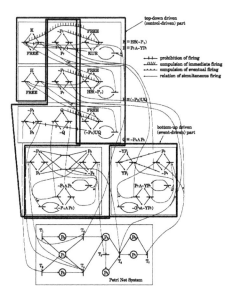

Fig. 3. Hierarchical extended Petri net representation of the system with an associated task and subtasks

3   Correctness of System and Its Behavior

3.1   A Sequence of State Transition

The system as a whole including the associated tasks to the agents can be represented by an extended higher order Petri net. Hence, so a state of the system can be "defined" as a "marking" over this extended net, i.e., the current distribution of tokens on the places. Thus, we can analyze the system behavior by tracking the change of the marking, which yield the state transition diagram. This diagram provides us with the basis of behavioral analysis and treating decentralized control of the system.

3.2   Behavioral Correctness

To control a system, we defined system correctness. A system can be regarded to behavior correctly if it satisfies the following conditions:

Def. 1. *(correctness of state transition sequence)*
A sequence of state transition (state transition sequence) is correct iff the following cases do not occur along with this sequence (of infinite length):

(1) For an arbitrary proposition A, A does not occur just after the state where task $\mathcal{O}_v \mathcal{T} A$ ($\mathcal{O}_v \mathcal{G} A$, $\mathcal{O}_v(A \mathcal{U} B)$) is given to an agent v.
(2) A never happens to be the case after the state (until B is the case) where task $\mathcal{O}_v \mathcal{F} A (\mathcal{O}_v(A \mathcal{U} B))$ is given to v.

3.3   System Correctness and Its Characterization

We have two kinds of system correctness as follows:

Def. 2. *(strong correctness of system)*
A system is strongly correct iff any state transition sequence generated by the system (system behavior) is correct. (Namely, there is no need to control the system.)

In terms of modal logical expressions, the above is characterized as:

$$\mathcal{G}_b(\mathcal{O}_v\mathcal{F}A \supset \mathcal{F}_lA)$$
$$\mathcal{G}_b((\mathcal{O}_v\neg(A\mathcal{U}B)) \supset A\mathcal{U}_lB)$$

where subscript **l** and **b** stand for types of temporal modalities, i.e., **l** is for "linear (non-branching)" and **b** for "branching" temporal modalities, more precisely,

$$\mathcal{G}_b : \text{necessarily persistent}$$
$$\mathcal{G}_l : \text{possibly persistent}$$
$$\mathcal{F}_b : \text{possibly eventual}$$
$$\mathcal{F}_l : \text{necessarily eventual}$$

We have practically more important and weaker notion of system correctness as follows:

Def. 3. *(weak correctness - centralized controllability)*
A system is called weakly correct iff we can extend an arbitrary generated state transition sequence so that it is correct by appropriately executing the firing of permitted (legal) transitions.

This can be characterized as

$$\mathcal{G}_b(\mathcal{O}_v\mathcal{F}A \supset \mathcal{F}_bA)$$
$$\mathcal{G}_b((\mathcal{O}_v\neg(A\mathcal{U}B)) \supset \neg(A\mathcal{U}_bB)).$$

4   Derivation of Control Rules – The Centralized Controllability

4.1   Method of System Correction

From the above results, we will have two ways for making an arbitrary system to behave correctly:

(i) to make the system strongly correct,
(ii) first to make the system weakly correct and then to control it so that its behavior (generated state transition sequence) becomes correct.

In the first approach, there is no more need to control it, i.e., any state transition sequence yielded from it is surely correct. In the latter approach, weak correctness itself is merely a precondition on controllability and there still remains need for supplementary control on permitted transitions. In other words, weak correctness guarantees the possibility of this supplementary control. In this paper we will pursue the latter approach which seems to be of practical importance than the former one.

4.2   System Correction in Terms of State Transition Diagram

Before describing system correction rules, we will characterize weak correctness in terms of the state transition diagram.

A system is weakly correct iff the following hold:

(a) for an arbitrary terminal state of its state transition diagram, there is no task associated with it of the form of $\mathcal{O}_v\mathcal{T}A$, and if $\mathcal{O}_v\mathcal{T}A$ is present there, then A is also present on that state, and if $\mathcal{O}_v(\neg(A\mathcal{U}B))$ is present there, then both $\neg A$ and $\neg B$ are also there;

(b) for every terminal "strong component" of its state transition diagram, the following hold;

   (b.1) if $\mathcal{O}_v\mathcal{F}A$ is present in a state at the component, there is a (possiblly another) state on which A holds;

   (b.2) if $\mathcal{O}_v(\neg(A\mathcal{U}B))$ is present in a state s, then there is a state s' on which $\neg A$ holds and there is a path joining s and s' along which B never holds.

For characterizing weak correctness, we introduce into the state transition diagram the notion of "condensation" of directed graph by decomposing it into "strong components" that are defined as being bidirectionally connected maximal subgraphs [12].

By this result, It can be readily seen that the follwing modifications on state transition diagrams are necessary for making systems to be weakly correct:

(ii.1) remove the terminal states from the diagram at which either a task of the form

$$\mathcal{O}_v\mathcal{T}A \text{ is present, or}$$

$$\mathcal{O}_v\mathcal{F}A \text{ and } \neg A \text{ are present, or}$$

$$\mathcal{O}_v(\neg(A\mathcal{U}B)) \text{ is present and at least one of } \neg A \text{ or } \neg B \text{ is absent}$$

(ii.2) remove the terminal strong components which include

$$\mathcal{O}_v\mathcal{F}A \text{ and } \neg A, \text{ or}$$

$$\mathcal{O}_v(\neg(A\mathcal{U}B)) \text{ is present and } \neg A, \text{ or}$$

$$\mathcal{O}_v(\neg(A\mathcal{U}B)) \text{ at a state } s \text{ and } \neg A \text{ at a state s' such that any path}$$

from s to s' includes a state at which B does not hold.

The above operations on state transition diagrams need to be applied repeatedly. Removal of terminal states or strong components will yield different terminal states and strong components. The operations proceeds until there is no need for the operations. If we still have remaining states in the diagram, the system is modified to be weakly correct.

4.3   Derivation of Control Rules – Centralized Control

The above modifications on transition diagrams can be translated into control actions on the extended Petri net systems. The removal of terminal "states" becomes

(ii.1') prohibit the firing of transitions just before (leading to) the removed states.

The removal of terminal (strong) "components" are also translated into the following:

(ii.2') prohibit the firing of transitions just before (leading to) the removed components.

5   Decentralized Control

5.1   Decentralized Controllability

In the above control operations, we have to consider the "decentralized" nature of systems, i.e., each agent has its own territory over which it can control. Namely, we should set the following:

Condition. *(system decentralization)*
Each prohibition of firing of a transition in operations (ii.1') or (ii.2') must be caused by a task which is given to an agent whose territory includes this transition.

In an extended Petri net representation, a control arc (prohibition of firing, compulsion of firing) must be linked to a transition in the territory of an agent whom the task yielding the control arc is derived as shown in Fig. 4. It also should be mentioned that there may be inter-agent relations which transfer obligations (tasks) among agents. If agent v can make another agent v' obey to v's norm, v can control transitions which is in v''s territory. Namely, the above relation from agent v to v' and v's norm $\mathcal{O}_v A$ yield v''s norm $\mathcal{O}_{v'} A$ saying that it is obligatory for v' that A is the case. That is to say, we have "valid" influence (transfer of norm) from v to v'. Therefore, agent v can control transitions in the territory of agent v'. If v'' cannot be controlled by v, then the influence from v to v'' is "invalid" as shown in Fig. 4. Moreover, if two valid influences collide with each other at a transition, where one influence prohibits its firing while the other influence compels its firing, then we have a "conflict" between the two tasks.

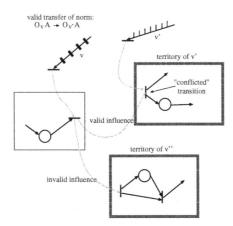

Fig. 4. Transfer of norms via relations of synchronous firing

Anyway, all the prohibition operations along with the course of deriving weakly correct system should be subject to this "extended" condition. It should also be noted that there may be various ways of deriving weakly correct systems, and only a portions of them may satisfy the above condition. Hence, it is not easy to verify the following property of an arbitrarily given decentralized system.

Def. 4. *(decentralized controllability)*
A system is calld "decentralizedly controllable" iff there exists a sequence of operations (ii.1') and (ii.2') in which all the prohibition of transition firing are in accordance with the above condition on system decentralization.

5.2   Complementary Control

As mentioned in Section 3, we need supplementary control actions over weakly correct systems for making their behavior correct. More precisely, by referring to conditions (b.1) and (b.2) in Section 4.2, we need the following operations:

(b.1') if we arrive at a state where a task of the form $\mathcal{O}_v\mathcal{F}A$ is present, then we must eventually (surely in the future) arrive at a state where A is realized.

(b.2') if we come to a state where $\mathcal{O}_v(\neg(A\mathcal{U}B))$ is present, then we must eventually arrive at a state where $\neg A$ holds by going through states at which B is not the case.

6   Conclusions

We have introduced the notions of decentralized system structure of multi-agent systems, their behavioral and structural correctness, and centralized and decentralized control for attaining correct behavior, and also that of decentralized controllability. The basic framework we adopted was modal logical analysis of system behavior and Petri net representation of system structures.

Due to the limitation of space, we could not show in detail the way of analyzing task interactions among agents. This can be done by examining the hierarchical linkage relations among tasks (subtasks) in Fig.3. Also, we could not include the actural ways of deriving control actions.

References

1. M. P. Singh(1994): Multiagent Systems, Springer-Verlag
2. T. Ishida(1997): Real-Time Search for Learning Autonomous Agents, Kluwer Academic Publishers
3. G. Weiss(ed.)(2000): Multiagent Systems, The MIT Press
4. J. L. Peterson(1981): Petri Net Theory and the Modeling of Systems, Prentce Hall
5. G. H. Hughes and M. J. Cresswell(1971): An Introduction of Modal Logic, Methuen
6. A. N. Prior(1968): Papers on Time and Tense, Oxford Univ. Press
7. N. Rescher and A. Urquhart(1971): Temporal Logic, Springer-Verlag
8. G. H. von Wright(1951): An Essay in Modal Logic, North-Holland Pub. Co., Amsterdam
9. L. F. Goble(1974): Gentzen Systems for Modal Logic, Notre Dame J. of Formal Logic, Vol.15, No.3, pp.455-461
10. R. Hilpinen(ed.)(1981): Deontic Logic: Introductory and Systematic Readings, Synthese Library, Vol. 33, D. Reidel
11. O. Katai(1981): Completeness and Expressive Power of Nexttime Temporal Logical System by Semantic Tableau Method, Rapport de Recherche INRIA, No.109
12. F. Harary et al.(1965): Structural Models; An Introduction to the Theory of Directed Graphs, J. Wiley

An Improved Foreground Extraction Approach

Erdan Gu, Duanqing Xu, and Chun Chen

Computer Science and Engineering Department, ZheJiang Univ., HangZhou, P.R.China,
310027
ged@cs.zju.edu.cn

Abstract. This paper describes an approach to expose the salient visual information from raw sensory data stream. At first, a general framework of media
application is introduced. Then, based on the implementation of an approach
proposed by MIT technical report, several improved techniques with respect to
the existing drawbacks in the original extraction method are applied to establish
our new framework. Finally, the result of our experiment system and its future
work are given.

1 Introduction

Multimedia that extends the domain of traditional computer data remains an opaque
data type, which may be captured, stored, retrieved, and presented but can not be
searched, manipulated, or analyzed. In order to make decisions based on the content of
a video stream [1], a video application requires a computational means of examining
the media data and exposing information of potential interest.

This paper focuses on one important part among video application: extracting foreground from a static scene. First, one relevant approach proposed in MIT technical
report [2] is discussed. And its implementation flow is illustrated as Fig.1.

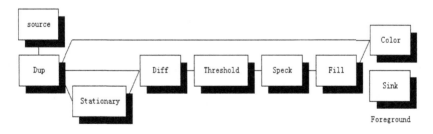

Fig.1 MIT implementation flow chart

An image payload, originating from the source module is firstly passed to a module
called VsDup, which makes three copies of the payload and passes them to a VsColor

J. Liu et al. (Eds.): AMT 2001, LNCS 2252, pp. 191–198, 2001.

module, VsDiff module, and VsStationary module. The VsStationary calculates best estimate of the background and sends the resulting output to the second input of the VsDiff module. The VsDiff module waits for an image payload to appear at each of its input ports and then outputs an image computed by taking the difference [3] between the two input images. The difference image is passed to VsThreshold module, which computes a binary map image by contrasting the magnitude of the difference and a specified threshold. In this case, the output map payload is passed down the pipe, first to the VsSpeck module which removes spurious data points and then to the VsFill module which fills in missing regions. The VsColor module combines the binary image payload with an original copy of the image. Finally the combined payload is passed to a sink module, which displays the resulting images and terminates the processing pipeline.

2   Our Proposed Improvement

The entire filter process mentioned above takes a stream of color images as input and produces a stream of output images where the pixels that are not part of the foreground have been masked or removed.

In VsDiff module, when the color of object, for instance, human skin, approximates to the color of background especially with intensive brightness, the foreground to be extracted may separate into several segments by subtracting background image from source image, which also reflects on the deformities in the output of VsThreshhold module. Consequently VsSpeck module that originally attempts to improve the segmentation removes the relatively small segments and results in the corresponding deformities of body in foreground. Against the deformity issue, we introduce a preprocessing technique based on block method. Moreover, the threshold [4] parameter specifics the cutoff for determining whether a pixel is considered to be in the foreground or the background. Too low a threshold will cause spurious pixels to appear in the foreground while too high a threshold can cause portions of foreground to blend into the background. To reduce the former, the output is first passed through a VsSpeck. However, spurious noise may include a dense cluster of spurious point, while VsSpeck module only works on a sparse region. So a more efficient speck-removal algorithm combined with one pass 4-connected component [5] is suggested alternatively in our framework. It only scans each frame once to complete the filter process instead of that two-scan used in VsSpeck module. In addition, to alleviate the consequence in case of high threshold, the output is passed through VsMaskFill, which uses the assumption of spatial coherence in the image plane to fill in. Though it works well on interior gaps of body and incurs low computational cost, it does not correctly handle shapes with particular concavities, and was not designed for multiple objects. To do a credible job on filling missing segments, an algorithm called CombineFill [6] is applied into. Rely on the data structure in one pass 4-connected component algorithm above, the combinefill algorithm is easy to carry out. Finally, a boundary tracking algorithm by dynamic programming [7][8] is suggested to achieve exact boundary. The entire scheme flow graph is described as Fig.2.

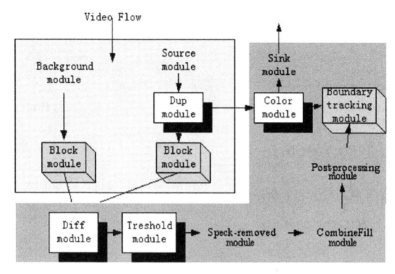

Fig. 2.

As Fig.2 shows, the introduction of block-based methods and the refinement of arbitrary boundary are the two main parts in the above processing. Thus, in the following sections, these two key techniques would be discussed in detail.

3 Introduction of Block-Based Method

Preceding the subtraction in Diff module, a block-based method, where 8*8-pixel blocks are used to reproduce image, is introduced to weaken the effect of illumination. Bypassing the predicament where the sole color information is inadequate to embody image context, block of pixels contain more information or features besides color and brightness than singular pixel to reduce ambiguity greatly. Many such features, often referred to as textures, have been proposed here.

Texture [9] is defined as an attribute representing the spatial arrangement of the gray levels of the pixels in a region. The block texture feature is quantified to indicate the variance of pixel gray-level in the block. The block texture feature is formulated as follows:

$$T = \sum_{i=1}^{8} \sum_{j=2}^{8} f |I(i, j) - I(i, j-1)| + \sum_{i=1}^{8} \sum_{i=2}^{8} f |I(i, j) - I(i-1, j)|$$

Here, I(i,j) represents Illustration in HSI. The transfer function between RGB and HSI color space is employed below:

$$I(i, j) = \frac{1}{\sqrt{3}}(R(i, j) + G(i, j) + B(i, j))$$

$$f(x) = \begin{cases} 0 & x < t_m \\ 1 & x \geq t_m \end{cases}$$

is the predetermined threshold.

The block color feature is defined as $C = \sum_{i=1} \sum_{j=1} H(i, j)$, H(i,j) is the Hue in HSI.

$$\begin{cases} x = \frac{1}{\sqrt{6}}[2R(i, j) - G(i, j) - B(i, j)] \\ y = \frac{1}{\sqrt{2}}(G(i, j) - B(i, j)) \\ H(i, j) = ang(x, y) \end{cases}$$

H(i,j) specifics the position of point (x, y) in polar coordinates.

In the following threshold module the function shown as Equa. (1) is defined for

$$P(x, y) = \begin{cases} 0 & (T_{xy} \leq T_m) \cap (C_{xy} \leq C_m) \\ 1 & (T_{xy} \geq T_m) \cup (c_{xy} \geq C_m) \end{cases} \tag{1}$$

capturing the integral region of foreground. As we could see, the block will be kept in the output of threshold module as the magnitude of difference of either the texture feature or the color in the corresponding blocks between current frame and background frame is greater than the specified threshold. Here, Tm and Cm respectively denote the magnitude of threshold of texture feature and that of color feature. The output of Threshold module passing through filters, Speck-removed module and CombineFill module, the arbitrary shapes of foreground is appeared. In this process, the filter algorithm of blocks instead of a single pixel is performed to speed up the time-consuming CombineFill algorithm by 64 times.

4 Boundary Tracking by Dynamic Programming

To refine coarse object edge, a dynamic programming scheme is employed to track the exact boundaries of the foreground objects. The area where the actual boundaries are located can be picked out from the arbitrary foreground region with continuous boundary, as Fig 3. Boundary points are always at the vector direction or opposite of the corresponding pixel points on continuous boundary, as Fig 4.

The range scales of the tracking domain is defined by $Width_1$ and $Width_2$ with commonly assuming $Width_1 = 2 \times Width_2$, that $Width_1$ denotes the search range at vector direction of the pixel point, does $Width_2$ at its opposite direction. In virtue of block-based method, the arbitrary foreground region contains almost all of the objects, thus the vector direction of pixel point on the continuous boundary is the primary search direction. After applying the method described above on each pixel point of continuous boundary, the domain for tracking is acquired.

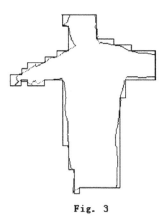

Fig. 3

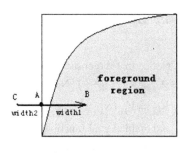

Fig. 4

4.1 Path Cost Calculation

In principle, boundary tracking is any algorithm which attempts to find or label abrupt changes in pixel value. Thus, the boundary points are distinguished by the features that boundary points have great difference with their neighborhood points in color or brightness. Denote by i the ith point in the line segment for tracking, then the kind of difference can be expressed as:

$$t_i \big|_{1 \le i \le width\,1 + width\,2} = \big|[(r_i - r_{i-1}) + (g_i - g_{i-1}) + (b_i - b_{i-1})]\big|/3$$

And Equa.(2) is given to make the cost of each point in the whole line segment comparable.

$$T_{max} = \max_{1 \le i \le width1+width2}(t_i)$$
$$C_i = t_i / T_{max} \times 100\% \tag{2}$$

Less the Ci, more possible the actual boundaries point.

For the continuity of foreground boundary, the category function below is utilized to calculate path cost of each line segment, in which Di,j is the distance between the ith point in current line segment and the jth point in next line segment:

$$D_{i,j} = \sqrt{(x_i - x_j)^2 + (y_i - y_j)^2}$$

Let Wi,j be the path cost from point i to point j:

It suggests that the cost Wi,j is determined as 200 by referring to the distance Di,j = 5. In conclusion, the cost of the whole path V can be constructed by the formulation below:

$$V = \sum_{i=1}^{n} C_{x_i} + \sum_{i=2}^{n} W_{x_i, x_{i-1}}$$

Here Xi figures the point selected from the ith line segment.

4.2 Dynamic Programming Model for Foreground Boundary Tracking

Notice that the cost function is $v_k(x_k, u_k) = C_{x_k} + W_{x_k + x_{k+1}}$ with the relation $X_{k+1} = U_k(X_k)$. Now define the goal function

$$V_{kn} = V_{kn}(x_k, x_{k+1}, x_{k+2}, \dots, X_n) = V_{kn}(x_k, u_k, u_{k+1}, \dots, u_{n-1}) = V_{kn}(x_k, p_{kn}(x_k))$$

and optimal goal function

$$f_k(x_k) = \underset{(u_1, \dots, u_{n-1})}{opt} V_{kn}(x_k, u_k, u_{k+1}, \dots, u_{n-1}) = \underset{p_{kn}(x_k) \in P_{kn}(x_k)}{opt} V_{kn}(x_k, p_{kn}(x_k))$$

Therefore the specific model is

$$\begin{cases} f_k(x_k) = \min_{u_k(x_k)} \{V_k(x_k, u_k) + f_{k+1}[T_k(x_k, u_k)]\} \\ v_k(x_k, u_k) = C_{x_k} + D_{x_k, u_k(x_k)} \\ k = n-1, n-2, \dots, 0 \\ f_n(x_n) = 0 \end{cases}$$

K denotes stage, for k=0,1....n-1, and X_k corresponds to state; Each stage K has a number of states associated with it, and the aggregate of these states is represented by $X_k = \{1, 2, \dots, i, \dots, Width_1 + Width_2\}$. Let $D_k(X_k)$ be the aggregate of the states for decision in stage K, then the decision at one stage K transforms into a state K+1 is expressed by

$$X_{k+1} = T(X_{k+1}, U_{k+1}); \ P_{0n}(X_0) = \{U_0(X_0), U_1(X_1), \dots, U_{n-1}(X_{n-1})\},$$

shows the decision sequence starting from state X0, where K-N sub-sequence can be obtained by $P_{kn}(X_k) = \{U_k(X_k), \dots, U_{n-1}(X_{n-1})\}$. The optimal decision marked by $P_{0n}*(X_0)$ is the decision with lowest path cost in decision sequence. The algorithm flow of whole dynamic programming is illustrated as following.

After tracking out the exact boundary of the foreground objects, the seed filling algorithm [10] is needed to fill the internal region and produce the final mask of the foreground objects.

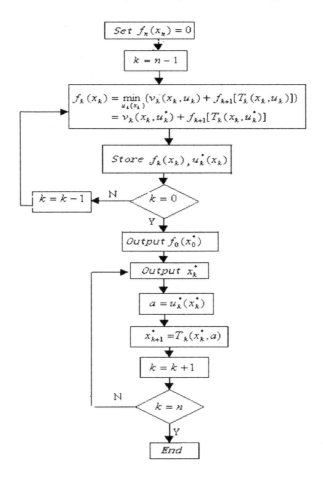

5   Experimental Result and Conclusion

The proposed improvement based on MIT approach was implemented into our new experiment system. Here, a comparison is illustrated by a series of image as the following: origin frame(as Fig. 5), result of MIT approach(as Fig. 6), result of arbitrary foreground(as Fig. 7), final result after boundary tracking(as Fig. 8). Obviously, our improved approach is superior to that of MIT approach. Meanwhile, Fig.9 and Fig.10 show one practical application on background replacement.

A major concern of future research will focus on the development of more sophisticated event recognition system through improvements in interpreting image [11]. Finally, we hope that our work is not only useful to researchers in the field of pattern recognition, but also worthwhile in the broader applications such as information retrieval system.

Fig. 5   Fig. 6   Fig. 7   Fig. 8

Fig. 9   Fig. 10

References

1. John R.Smith and Shih-Fu Chang. Visualseek: A Fully Automated Content-Based Image Query System, ACM Multimedia'96, 1996.
2. William F.Stasior, An Interactive Approach To The Identification And Extraction Of Visual Events, Technique Report, MIT/LCS/TR-742, Feb.1998.
3. C[harles W. Therrien. Decision Estimation and Classi_cation. John Wiley and Sons, New York, 1989.
4. Sahoo P.K., A survey of thresholding techniques, CVGIP, 1988, 41(2): 233~260.
5. Zhang Y.J., Segmentation evalution and comparison: a study of several algorithms, SPIE, 1993, 2094: 801~812.
6. M.J.Black,Combining intensity and motion for incremental segmentation and tracking over long image sequences, ECCV'92, 1992, 485-493.
7. Dreyfus S.E. and Law, A.M., The Art of Dynamic Programming, Academic Press, New York, 1977.
8. Zhang Z.F., and Li J.D., Dynamic Programming and Application, 1990, in Chinese.
9. IEEE Standard 610.4-1990, IEEE Standard Glossary of Image Processing and Pattern Recognition Terminology, IEEE Press, New York, 1990.
10. Kennneth R. CastleMan, Digtial Image Processing 1/e., Perceptive Scientific Instruments, Inc., 1997,
11. C.Wren, etc, PFinder:Real-Time Tracking of the Human Body, IEEE Transaction on Pattern Analysis and Machine Intelligence, 1997: 780-785.

Object Detection Simulating Visual Attention

Xingshan Li and Chunwei Yuan

Department of Biomedical Engineering
Southeast University
Nanjing, P.R.China 210096
{lixslixs,cwy}@seu.edu.cn

Abstract. It will be efficient for object detection to select only a subset of available sensory information before further detailed processing. In this paper, object detection is approached through simulating visual attention, which is modeled by a learned saliency map. The efficiency of the proposed method is verified in the eye detection problem.

1 Introduction

Selecting only a subset of the available sensory information before further detailed processing is crucial for efficient perception.[1] In the visual modality, this selection is frequently implemented by suppressing information outside a spatially circumscribed region of the visual field, the so-called "focus of attention."(FOA) In primates, the identification of behaviorally relevant objects and the analysis of their spatial relationships involve either rapid, saccadic eye movements or so-called "covert"(i.e., without eye movements) shifts of visual attention. While attention can be controlled in a voluntary manner, it is also attracted in a "bottom-up," automatic and unconscious manner to conspicuous, or "salient," visual locations. Focal attention is often thought as a gating mechanism, which selectively allows a certain spatial location and certain types of visual features to reach higher visual processes.[2]

Artificial system may employ this mechanism either. Koch and Ullman introduced the idea of a saliency map to accomplish preattentive selection.[3] Saliency map is an explicit two-dimensional map that encodes the saliency of objects in the visual environment. Competition among sites in this map gives rise to a single winning location that corresponds to the most salient object. If this location is subsequently inhibited, the FOA is shifted to the next most salient location, which constitutes the next target, endowing the search process with internal dynamics.
Object detecting simulating visual attention has been attempt by many researchers [2,4,5]. In these approaches, the object detection is divided into two stages: 'where stage' and 'what stage'. The 'where stage' seeks where salient objects are, and the 'what stage' identifies what the object is. Due to the bottom-up approach and exploring only the salient sites, these methods share the virtue of computing efficiency [2,4]. In these works, the most important and challenging is the constructing saliency map from features[2].

J. Liu et al. (Eds.): AMT 2001, LNCS 2252, pp. 199–204, 2001.
© Springer-Verlag Berlin Heidelberg 2001

In this paper, a method of constructing saliency map based on learning method is proposed. The saliency map is seen as nonlinear combination of features, and the nonlinear function is approached through a feed forward artificial neutral network (ANN) whose weight is learned through examples. The effect of the proposed method is verified in the eye detection problem.

2   The Learned Saliency Map

A central yet not thoroughly studied problem, both in biological and artificial systems related to attention, is that of combining multi-scale feature maps, from different visual modalities with unrelated dynamic ranges(such as color and motion), into a unique saliency map. There are three combination strategies have been employed: (1) Simple summation after scaling to a fixed dynamic range; (2)linear combination with weights learned, for each image database, by supervised additive training; (3) non-linear combination of features. [5] Because the relation between saliency and feature is very complex, linear combination cannot reflect this kind of complex relation. So nonlinear combination should be used to deprive the saliency in complex problems such as object detection. The nonlinear combination may be written as:

$$\text{Saliency} = f(\text{Features}) \qquad (1)$$

Where f is the task related complex nonlinear function. *Features* is a vector of image features.

To approach the object detection problem, the most salient sites in saliency map should correspond to the locations of the object to be detected. Therefore, the function f should contain information of the object to be detected. One way of introducing knowledge of interested object into f is learning through examples. Jeffrey Huang[4] deprive the saliency map using a consensus between navigation routines encoded as a finite-state automata exploring the facial landscape and evolved using genetic algorithms. In their approach, the position of the chin is assumed to be known. This is not necessarily true in some cases. And the FSA is based on the routine from chin to eyes, so the FSA in their work depend on far more features than that of eyes. These two points limits the robust of the Huang's method.

A learned method to approach nonlinear function f is proposed in this paper. Different to the Huang's method, the saliency value of one site depends only on the features of a limited surrounding area instead of the whole image.

It is well known that a suitable ANN may approach any function, and can discover underlying statistical regularities of the training example. So, in our approach, a feed forward artificial neural network (ANN) is employed to express the nonlinear function f.

To detect an object in an image, spatial information should be considered. For a site o in the feature map, the site and the surrounding sites form a Neighboring Site Group(NSG) of o, which contains 3*5 sites. When calculating the saliency value of one site, all features of the NSG are used. The tutor is manually defined to be high value at the locations of interested objects, and low value at others. After trained for several epochs, the ANN may be used to approach the nonlinear function f. In our approach, the Backpropagation(BP) training method is used.

The output of the ANN, which makes up the saliency map of the image, is expected to reach relatively high value at the location of interested objects, and relatively small value at others.

3   Implementation of Eye Detection

Eye detection is an essential task for automated facial recognition system. To design an automated face recognition(AFR) system, one needs to address several related problems: 1)detection of a pattern as a face(in the crowd). 2) detection of facial landmarks, 3)identification of the faces, and 4)analysis of facial expression. Locating the eyes serves, first of all, as an important role in face normalization and thus facilitates further localization of facial landmarks.[6]

There are two major approaches for automated eye location. The first approach, the holistic one, conceptually related to template matching, attempts to locate the eyes using global representations. The second approach for eye detection, the abstractive one, extracts(and measures) discrete local features, while standard pattern recognition techniques are then employed to locate the eyes using these measurements.[4] The method in this paper draws from both the holistic and abstractive eye location approaches.

The eye detection process that being used in this paper simulates the visual attention process of primitives. The task is divided into two stages: 'where stage' and 'what stage'. The 'where stage' seeks where salient objects based on the learned saliency map, and the 'what stage' identifies what the object is. Only the first stage is considered in this paper to verify the effect of the learned saliency map.

The process is introduced as following, which is also shown in figure.1.

1)   Feature Maps: The input consists of detected face images whose resolution are 200*180 using 8 bit gray levels. Three feature maps corresponding to mean, standard deviation (std), and entropy are then computed over 6*6 non overlapping windows, and then compressed to yield three 34* 30 feature maps.

2)   The Trained Saliency Map: After the feature extracting process, the images are transformed into three feature maps of 34*30 sites.

To deprive a saliency map, for each site, the features of the NSG are used. Facial images of different individual with different expression are selected as the training data set. For every training image, the eye locations are manually extracted, sampled to the size of 34*30 , which is known as the eye mask. The eye mask is then filtered with an 3*3 average filter, which will makes the center of the eye has the most high value. The processed eye mask acts as the tutor to train the ANN. After trained, the ANN may be used to construct the saliency map of an image. The features of each site's NSG are fed to the trained ANN, the output of the ANN is the saliency value of that site.

3)   Transfer of Focus of Attention(FOA): The FOA is an area of interested that will be future processed. The FOA, whose size is 5*9 in this paper, is located to the location of the most salient site in saliency map. Then eye identifying methods (which will be explained in next segment) are used to detect if an eye present in an

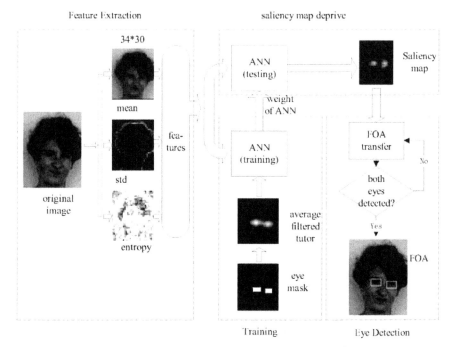

Fig. 1. The process of eye detection based on learned saliency map

FOA. After one FOA being processed, the attention will be transferred to the next salient FOA. The process stops when both eyes have been detected.

4)   Eye identification: When focus on one FOA, traditional methods such as model matching or other methods may be used to detect if an eye appear in the FOA. This stage is beyond the range of this paper. For the purpose of verifying the effect of the learned saliency map, a manual eye identifying method is employed in this paper.

4   Experiments and Results

The experiment material comes from the Vision Group of Essex University Face Database. [7] The test set contains face images of 18 male and female subjects, with image resolution 200*180 pixels (portrait format). A sequence of 20 images per individual was taken, using a fixed camera. During the sequence the subject moves his/her head and makes grimaces which get more extreme towards the end of the sequence.

The images are divided into two groups. In the first group with 10 individual, two images of each individual are randomly selected as training samples, and all the other images act as testing images, which build up the first test set. In the second group with 8 individuals, all images act as testing images, which build up the second test set.

Table.1 is a statistical result of the numbers of transfer of focus before both of the two eye locations have been focused. Comparing the two results with different testing data set, we may find that they make no obvious different. This shows that this method is robust to facial image of different individuals.

In the following stage for eye detection, it needs only to explore the FOAs. The average number of FOAs before both eyes detected is fairly small, say, in this experiment, only 2.3438 in the second test set. The site number in a FOA is 35, so average 82 sites needs to be explored instead of the whole image, whose site number is 1020.

Table 1. The statistical result of the experiments. The first test set contains 180 images of 10 individuals, whose images (not included in this test set) have been used as training data set. The second test contain 160 images of 8 individuals, whose images have never been used in training data set. With the mean, std and maximum is the statistical value of transfer of FOA before both eye have been detected, which correspond to average, standard deviation and maximum respectively.

data set	mean	std	maximum
first test set	2.1800	0.5282	7
second test set	2.3438	0.7443	6

5 Conclusion

By simulating primitive's visual attention, a saliency map based object detection method is employed in the eye detection problem. The information of the interested object may be represented in the nonlinear function f, which may be approach by a feed forward aritfical neural network whose weights are learned through training samples. Experiments show that the learned saliency map may be efficiently used in the eye detection problem.

Though only be tested in the eye detection problem, it is believed that the saliency map based object detection method may be used in other object detection problems.

Acknowledgments. This work is financially supported by NSFC (No. 69831010). And thanks to the Vision Group of Essex University for providing Face Database.

References

1. J.K. Tsotsos, S.M. Culhane, W.Y.K. Wai, Y.H. Lai. N. Davis, and F. Nuflo, "Modelling Visual Attention via Selective Tuning," Artificial Intelligence, vol.78, no.1-2,pp.507-545, Oct. 1995
2. Laurent Itti, Christof Koch, and Ernst Niebur, "A Model of Saliency-based Visual Attention for Rapid Scene Analysis", IEEE trans. PAMI, vol.20. no.11, pp1254-1259, Nov. 1998

3. C.Koch and S. Ullman, "shifts in Selective Visual Attention: Towards the Underlying Neural Circuitry," Human Neurobiology, vol. 4, pp.219-227,1985
4. Jeffrey Huang and Harry Wechsler, "Visual Routines for Eye Location Using Learning and Evolution", IEEE trans. Evolutionary Computation, vol. 4 no.1, pp73-82, April 2000
5. Laurent Itti and Chritof Koch, "Target Detection Using Saliency-based Attention", Proc. RTO/SCI-12 Workshop on Search and Target Acquisition (NATO Unclassified), Utrecht, The Netherlands, RTO-MP-45 AC/323(SCI)TP/19, pp. 3.1-3.10, June 1999
6. A. Samal and P.Iyengar, "Automatic recognition and analysis of human faces and facial expressions: A survey," Pattern Recognit., vol. 25, pp65-77,1992
7. Vision Group of Essex University Face Database, available at website http://cswww.essex.ac.uk/allfaces/index.htm

Fast Face Detection Using Neural Networks and Image Decomposition

Hazem M. El-Bakry

Faculty of Computer Science & Information Systems
Mansoura University – Egypt
hazemelbakry@hotmail.com

Abstract. In this paper, A new approach to reduce the computation time taken by fast neural nets for the searching process is presented. The principle of divide and conquer strategy is applied through image decomposition. Each image is divided into small in size sub-images and then each one is tested separately using a fast neural network. Compared to conventional and fast neural networks, experimental results show that a speed up ratio is achieved when applying this technique to locate human faces in automatically in cluttered scenes. Furthermore, faster face detection is obtained by using parallel processing techniques to test the resulted sub-images at the same time using the same number of fast neural networks. Moreover, the problem of sub-image centering and normalization in the Fourier space is solved.

1 Introduction

The human face is a complex pattern. Finding human faces automatically in a scene is a difficult yet significant problem. It is the first step in fully automatic human face recognition system. Face detection is the fundamental step before the face recognition or identification procedure. Its reliability and time response have a major influence on the performance and usability of the whole face recognition system. Foe web indexation applications, the processing time must be kept as low as possible as the number of images on the web increases continuously [1]. Among other techniques [2], neural networks are efficient face detectors [1,3,4].

The main objective of this paper is to reduce the detection time using neural networks. Compared to conventional neural networks, fast neural networks based on cross correlation between the input image and the weights of neural networks in frequency domain have shown a significant reduction in the number of computation steps required to detect an object (face/iris) in the image under test [3,6]. In section 2, fast neural nets for face detection are described. A faster searching algorithm for face detection that reduces the number of the required computation steps through image decomposition is presented in section 3. Accelerating the new approach using parallel processing techniques is introduced in section 4.

J. Liu et al. (Eds.): AMT 2001, LNCS 2252, pp. 205–215, 2001.

2 Fast Neural Nets for Human Face Detection

In this section, a fast algorithm for face detection based on two dimensional cross correlations that take place between the tested image and the sliding window (20x20 pixels) is described. Such window is represented by the neural net weights situated between the input unit and the hidden layer. The convolution theorem in mathematical analysis says that a convolution of f with h is identical to the result of the following steps: let $\mathbf{F}$ and $\mathbf{H}$ be the results of the Fourier transformation of f and h in the frequency domain. Multiply $\mathbf{F}$ and $\mathbf{H}$ in the frequency domain point by point and then transform this product into spatial domain via the inverse Fourier transform [6]. As a result of this, these cross correlations can be represented by a product in frequency domain. So, by using cross correlation in frequency domain, speed up in an order of magnitude can be achieved during the detection process.

In the detection phase, a sub image $\mathbf{I}$ of size mxn (sliding window) is extracted from the tested image which has a size $\mathbf{PxT}$ and fed to the neural network. Let $\mathbf{X_i}$ be the vector of weights between the input sub image and the hidden layer. This vector has a size of mxn and can be represented as mxn matrix. The output of hidden neurons $\mathbf{h(i)}$ can be calculated as follows:

$$h_i = g\left(\sum_{j=1}^{m} \sum_{k=1}^{n} X_i(j,k)I(j,k) + b_i \right) \qquad (1)$$

where g is the activation function and $\mathbf{b(i)}$ is the bias of each hidden neuron $\mathbf{(i)}$. Equ. 1 represents the output of each hidden neuron for a particular sub-image $\mathbf{I}$. It can be obtained to the whole image $\mathbf{Z}$ as follows:

$$h_i(u,v) = g\left(\sum_{j=-m/2}^{m/2} \sum_{k=-n/2}^{n/2} X_i(j,k)\ Z(u+j,v+k) + b_i \right) \qquad (2)$$

Equ.2 represents a cross correlation operation. Given any two functions $\mathbf{f}$ and $\mathbf{d}$, their cross correlation can be obtained by:

$$f(x,y) \otimes d(x,y) = \left(\sum_{m=-\infty}^{\infty} \sum_{n=-\infty}^{\infty} f(m,n)d(x+m,y+n) \right) \qquad (3)$$

Therefore, equ. 2 may be written as follows:

$$h_i = g\left(X_i \otimes Z + b_i \right) \qquad (4)$$

where h_i is the output of the hidden neuron **(i)** and h_i **(u,v)** is the activity of the hidden unit **(i)** when the sliding window is located at position **(u,v)** and **(u,v)** $\in$ **[P-m+1,T-n+1]**.

Now, the above given cross correlation can be expressed in terms of Fourier Transform:

$$Z \otimes X_i = F^{-1}\left(F(Z) \bullet F^*\left(X_i\right)\right) \tag{5}$$

Hence, by evaluating this cross correlation, a speed up ratio can be obtained compared to conventional neural networks. Also, the final output of the neural network can be evaluated as follows:

$$O(u,v) = g\left(\sum_{i=1}^{q} w_0(i)\, h_i(u,v) + b_0\right) \tag{6}$$

O(u,v) is the output of the neural network when the sliding window located at the position **(u,v)** in the input image **Z**.

For a tested image of NxN pixels, the 2D FFT requires $O(N^2 \log_2 N^2)$ computation steps. For the weight matrix X_i, the 2D FFT can be computed off line since these are constant parameters of the network independent of the tested image. The 2D FFT of the tested image must be computed. As a result, q backward and one forward transforms have to be computed. Therefore, for a tested image, the total number of the 2DFFT to compute is $(q+1)N^2 \log_2 N^2$. Moreover, the input image and the weights should be multiplied in the frequency domain. Therefore, computation steps of (qN^2) should be added. Finally, a total of $O((q+1)N^2 \log_2 N^2 + qN^2)$ computation steps must be evaluated for fast the neural algorithm.

Using sliding window of size nxn, for the same image of NxN pixels, $O((N-n+1)^2 n^2 q)$ computation steps are required when using traditional neural networks for the face detection process. The theoretical speed up factor η can be evaluated as follows:

$$\eta = O\left(\frac{q(2n^2 - 1)(N - n + 1)^2}{(q+1)N^2 \log_2 N^2 + qN^2}\right) \tag{7}$$

In our case, for N=500, n=20, q=30, a speed up factor of 37.8626 may be achieved. The speed up factor introduced in [7] for object detection which is given by:

$$\eta = O\left(\frac{qn^2}{(q+1)\log_2 N}\right) \tag{8}$$

is not correct since the number of computation steps required for the 2D FFT is $O(N^2\log_2 N^2)$ and not $O(N^2\log^2 N)$. Also, this is not a typing error as the curve in Fig. 2 in [7] realizes equ.8. Moreover, the speed up ratio presented in [7] not only contains an error but is also not precise. This is because for fast neural nets, the term (qN^2) must be added. Such term has a great effect on the speed up ratio. Furthermore, for conventional neural nets, the number of operations is $(q(2n^2 -1)(N-n+1)^2)$ and not (qN^2n^2).

2.1 Sub-image Normalization in Frequency Domain

In [1], the authors stated that image normalization to avoid weak or strong illumination can not be done in frequency space. This is because the image normalization is local and not easily computed in the Fourier space of the whole image. Here a simple method for normalization of sub-images in frequency domain is presented. Local image normalization can be obtained by normalizing the weights as follows:

Let $\overline{X}_{rc}$ be the zero-mean centered sub-image located at (r,c) in the input image ψ:

$$\overline{X}_{rc} = X_{rc} - \overline{x}_{rc} \tag{9}$$

where $\overline{x}_{rc}$ is the mean value of the sub image located at (r,c). We are interested in computing the cross correlation between the sub-image $\overline{X}_{rc}$ and the weights W_i that is:

$$\overline{X}_{rc} \otimes W_i = X_{rc} \otimes W_i - \overline{x}_{rc} \otimes W_i \tag{10}$$

where:

$$\overline{x}_{rc} = \frac{X_{rc}}{n^2} \tag{11}$$

Combining 10 and 11, we get the following expression:

$$\overline{X}_{rc} \otimes W_i = X_{rc} \otimes W_i - \frac{X_{rc}}{n^2} \otimes W_i \tag{12}$$

which is the same as:

$$\overline{X}_{rc} \otimes W_i = X_{rc} \otimes W_i - X_{rc} \otimes \frac{W_i}{n^2} \tag{13}$$

The centered zero mean weights are given by:

$$\overline{W}i = W_i - \frac{W_i}{n^2} \tag{14}$$

Also, equ. 13 can be written as:

$$\overline{X}_{rc} \otimes W_i = X_{rc} \otimes \left(W_i - \frac{W_i}{n^2} \right) \tag{15}$$

So, we may conclude that:

$$\overline{X}_{rc} \otimes W_i = X_{rc} \otimes \overline{W}_i \tag{16}$$

which means that cross-correlating a normalized image with the weight matrix is equal to the cross-correlation of the non – normalized image with the normalized weight matrix.

Normalization of sub-images in the spatial domain (in case of using traditional neural nets) requires $(N-n+1)^2 n^2$ computation steps. On the other hand, normalization of sub-images in frequency domain through normalizing the weights of the neural nets requires $2n^2$ operations. So, this proves also that, local image normalization in frequency domain is faster than that in the spatial one.

2.2 Image Testing at Multi Resolutions

Images are tested for the presence of a face (object) at different scales by building a pyramid of the input image which generates a set of images at different resolutions. The face detector is then applied at each resolution and this process takes much more time as the number of processing steps will be increased. In [7], the author stated that the Fourier transforms of the new scales do not need to be computed. This is due to a property of the Fourier transform. If f(x,y) is the original and g(x,y) is the sub-sampled by a factor of 2 in each direction image then:

$$g(x, y) = FT(2x, 2y) \tag{17}$$

$$F(u, v) = FT(f(x, y)) \tag{18}$$

$$FT(g(x, y)) = G(u, v) = \frac{1}{4} F(\frac{u}{2}, \frac{v}{2}) \tag{19}$$

This implies that we do not need to recompute the Fourier transform of images, as it can be directly obtained from the original Fourier transform. Then, the author claimed that the processing needs $O((q+2)N^2 \log^2 N)$ additional number of computation steps. Thus the speed up ratio will be:

$$\eta = O\left(\frac{qn^2}{(q+2)\log^2 N}\right) \tag{20}$$

Of course this is not correct, because the inverse of the Fourier transform is required to be computed at each neuron in the hidden layer (for the result of dot product between the Fourier transform of input image and the weights of the neuron, the inverse of the Fourier transform must be computed). So, the total number of computation steps needed for fast neural networks is $O((2q+1)N^2\log N^2 + 2qN^2)$ and not $O((q+2)N^2\log^2 N)$ as stated in [7]. Thus, the speed up ratio becomes:

$$\eta = \left(\frac{q(2n^2 - 1)(N - n + 1)^2}{(2q+1)N^2\log_2 N^2 + 2qN^2}\right) \tag{21}$$

3   A New Faster Algorithm for Human Face Detection Based on Image Decomposition

In this section, a new faster algorithm for face detection is presented. The number of computation steps required for fast neural nets with different image sizes is listed in table 1. From this table, we may notice that as the image size is increased, the number

Table 1. The number of computation steps required by fast neural networks (FNN) for images of sizes (25x25 - 1050x1050 pixels).

Image size	No. of computation steps in case of using FNN	Image size	No. of computation steps in case of using FNN
25x25	198699	550x550	179807163
50x50	949798	600x600	216787233
100x100	4419191	650x650	257448831
150x150	10759202	700x700	301827794
200x200	20156763	750x750	349957294
250x250	32742414	800x800	401868214
300x300	48616808	850x850	457589436
350x350	67861948	900x900	517148091
400x400	90547053	950x950	580569757
450x450	116732022	1000x1000	647878626
500x500	146469656	1050x1050	689330147

Table 2. The speed up ratio in case of using FNN and FNN after image decomposition into sub-images (25x25 pixels) for images of different sizes.

Image size	Speed up ratio in case of using (FNN)	Speed up ratio in case of using FNN after image decomposition
50x50	24.25264625	28.9825265
100x100	35.58726025	49.46609
150x150	38.23215	57.505628
200x200	38.95864075	61.75171375
250x250	39.0643085	64.37163475
300x300	38.9308755	66.1488105
350x350	38.698766	67.4328035
400x400	38.42770525	68.403988
450x450	38.14445975	69.16403675
500x500	37.8626125	69.77527175

of computation steps required by fast neural networks is much increased. For example, the number of computation steps required for an image of size (50x50 pixels) is much less than that needed for an image of size (100x100 pixels). Also, the number of computation steps required for an image of size (500x500 pixels) is much less than that needed for an image of size (1000x1000 pixels). As a result of this, for example, If an image of size (100x100 pixels) is decomposed into 4 sub-images of size (50x50 pixels) and each sub-image is tested separately, then a speed up factor for face detection can be achieved. The number of computation steps required by fast neural networks to test an image after decomposition may be calculated as follows:

1.   Assume that the size of the image under test is (NxN pixels).

2.   Such image is decomposed into α (LxL pixels) sub-images. So, α can be computed as:

$$\alpha = (N/L)^2 \tag{22}$$

3.   Assume that, number of computation steps required for testing one (LxL pixels) sub-image is β. So, the total number of computation steps (T) required for testing these sub-images resulted after the decomposition process is:

$$T = \alpha \beta \tag{23}$$

To detect a face of size 20x20 pixels in an image of any size by using fast neural networks after image decomposition into sub-images, the optimal size of these sub-images must be computed. From table 1, we may conclude that, the most suitable size for the sub-image which requires the smallest number of computation steps is 25x25 pixels. A comparison between the speed up ratio for fast neural networks and fast neural networks after image decomposition with different sizes of the tested images is

Table 3. The number of computation steps required for conventional, FNN and FNN after image decomposition into sub-images (25x25 pixels) for images of different sizes.

Image size	No. of computation steps in case of using conventional neural nets	No. of computation steps in case of using FNN	No. of computation steps in case of using FNN after image decomposition
50x50	11532000	949798	794798
100x100	78732000	4419191	3179191
150x150	205932000	10759202	7153179
200x200	393132000	20156763	12716763
250x250	640332000	32742414	19869942
300x300	947532000	48616808	28612717
350x350	1314732000	67861948	38945087
400x400	1741932000	90547053	50867053
450x450	2229132000	116732022	64378614
500x500	2776332000	146469656	79479770

Table 4. A comparison between the speed up ratio in case of using FNN and FNN after image decomposition into sub-images (5x5 pixels) for images of different sizes.

Image size	Speed up ratio in case of using FNN	Speed up ratio in case of using FNN after image decomposition
50x50	1.7592	3.1212
100x100	1.6373	3.3985
150x150	1.6054	3.4936
200x200	1.4904	3.5416
250x250	1.4437	3.5706
300x300	1.4065	3.5899
350x350	1.3759	3.6038
400x400	1.3499	3.6142
450x450	1.3276	3.6224
500x500	1.3081	3.6286

Table 5. A comparison between the speed up ratio in case of using FNN and FNN after image decomposition into sub-images (10x10 pixels) for images of different sizes.

Image size	Speed up ratio in case of using FNN	Speed up ratio in case of using FNN after image decomposition
50x50	5.6757	7.7400
100x100	5.9761	9.5323
150x150	5.8778	10.1712
200x200	5.7479	10.4984
250x250	5.6273	10.6972
300x300	5.5208	10.8308
350x350	5.4273	10.9267
400x400	5.3449	10.9989
450x450	5.2715	11.0552
500x500	5.2058	11.1004

listed in table 2 (n=20, q=30). A comparison between the number of computation steps required by conventional, fast neural networks and fast neural networks after image decomposition with different sizes of the tested images is listed in table 3 (n=20, q=30).

Table 6. A comparison between the speed up ratio in case of using FNN and FNN after image decomposition into sub-images (20x5 pixels) for images of different sizes.

Image size	Speed up ratio in case of using FNN	Speed up ratio in case of using FNN after image decomposition
100x100	5.6116	16.0457
200x200	5.5896	18.3011
300x300	5.4227	19.0703
400x400	5.2748	19.4582
500x500	5.1517	19.6920
600x600	5.0485	19.8483
700x700	4.9605	19.9601
800x800	4.8844	20.0441
900x900	4.8176	20.1095
1000x1000	4.7583	20.1619

In [4], the input window is broken into smaller pieces, of four 10x10 pixel regions, sixteen 5x5 regions, and six overlapping 20x5 pixel regions. Each of these regions will have complete connections to a hidden unit. In particular, the horizontal strips allow the hidden units to detect such features as mouths or pairs eyes, the nose, or corners of the mouth. As shown in tables 4,5, and 6, by using fast modular neural nets after image decomposition in regions of 5x5, 10x10, or 20x5, a faster speed up ratio can be obtained over conventional neural networks. So, the proposed new technique is faster than the system presented in [4] for face detection.

4   Simulation of the Fast Face Detection Process (after Image Decomposition) Using Parallel Processing Techniques

In the previous section, a new algorithm for face detection based on decomposing the image under test to many sub-images has been presented. Then, for each sub-image, a fast neural network has been used to detect the presence/absence of human faces.

Here, to further reduce the running time as well as increase the speed up ratio of the detection process, a parallel processing technique is used. Each sub-image is tested using a fast neural network simulated on a single processor or a separated node in a clustered system.

The number of operations (ω) performed by each processor / node (sub-images tested by one processor/node) =

$$\omega = \frac{\text{The total number of sub}-\text{images}}{\text{Number of Processors / nodes}} \qquad (24)$$

$$\omega = \frac{\alpha}{\text{Pr}} \qquad (25)$$

where Pr is the Number of Processors or nodes.

The total number of computation steps (γ) required to test an image by using this approach can be calculated as:

$$\gamma = \omega\beta \qquad (26)$$

As shown in table 4, using a symmetric multiprocessing system with 16 parallel processors or 16 nodes in either a massively parallel processing system or a clustered system, the number of computation steps is reduced as well as the speed up ratio (with respect to conventional neural networks) for human face detection is increased. Also, simulation results for 64 parallel processors are listed in table 5.

Table 7. The number of computation steps and the speed up ratio in case of using FNN after image decomposition into sub-images (25x25 pixels) for images of different sizes using 16 parallel processors or 16 nodes.

Image size	No. of computation steps	Speed up ratio
50x50	198699.42	115.9297065
100x100	198699.42	791.45744
150x150	596098.26	690.067536
200x200	794797.68	988.025822
250x250	1390895.94	715.2404305
300x300	1788294.78	1058.37937
350x350	2583092.46	1016.6791605
400x400	3179190.72	1094.463808
450x450	4172687.82	1067.10385075
500x500	9934971.00	1116.404348

5 Conclusion

A faster neural network approach has been introduced to identify frontal views of human faces. Such approach has decomposed the image under test into many small in size sub-images. A simple algorithm for fast face detection based on cross correlations in frequency domain between the sub-images and the weights of the neural net is presented in order to speed up the execution time. Moreover, simulation results have shown that, using a parallel processing technique, large values of speed

Table 8. The number of computation steps and the speed up ratio in case of using FNN after image decomposition into sub-images (25x25 pixels) for images of different sizes using 64 parallel processors or 64 nodes.

Image size	No. of computation steps	Speed up ratio
50x50	198699.42	115.9297065
100x100	198699.42	791.45744
150x150	198699.42	2070.20800125
200x200	198699.42	3952.105685
250x250	397398.84	3218.58792975
300x300	596098.26	3175.1393085
350x350	794797.68	3304.2081705
400x400	794797.68	4377.85625073
450x450	1192196.52	3734.863178
500x500	1390895.94	3987.158614

up ratio may be achieved. Furthermore, the problem of sub-image centering and normalization in the Fourier space has been solved. The proposed approach may be applied to detect the presence/absence of any other object in an image.

References

[1]   R. Feraud, O. Bernier, J. E. Viallet, and M. Collobert, " A Fast and Accurate Face Detector for Indexation of Face Images," Fourth IEEE International Conference on Automatic Face and Gesture Recognition, Grenoble, France, 28-30 March, 2000.

[2]   H. Schneiderman and T. Kanade, "Probabilistic modeling of local appearance and spatial relationships for object recognition, " In IEEE Conference on Computer Vision and Pattern Recognition (CVPR), pp. 45-51, SantaBarbara, CA, 1998.

[3]   H. M. El-Bakry, M. A. Abo-Elsoud, M. S. Kamel, "Fast Modular Neural Networks for Human Face Detection, " Proc. of IJCNN International Joint Conference on Neural Networks 2000, Como, Italy, Vol. III, pp. 320-323, 24-28 July, 2000.

[4]   H. A. Rowley, S. Baluja, and T. Kanade, " Neural Network - Based Face Detection," IEEE Trans. on Pattern Analysis and Machine Intelligence, Vol. 20, No. 1, pp. 23-38, 1998.

[5]   R. Klette, and Zamperon, "Handbook of image processing operators, " John Wiley & Sons ltd, 1996.

[6]   H. M. El-Bakry, "Fast Iris Detection using Cooperative Modular Neural Nets, " Proc. of the 6th International Conference on Soft Computing, Iizuka, Fukuoka, Japan, pp.638-643, 1-4 Oct., 2000.

[7]   S. Ben-Yacoub, "Fast Object Detection using MLP and FFT, " IDIAP-RR 11, IDIAP, 1997.

Modeling of Facial Expressions Using NURBS Curves[*]

Ding Huang[1], Wei Lin[2], and Hong Yan[1]

[1]School of Electrical and Information Engineering, University of Sydney,
NSW 2006, Australia
{hding, yan}@ee.usyd.edu.au
Department of Electronic Engineering, City University of Hong Kong,
Kowloon, Hong Kong
{ee124126, eeyan}@cityu.edu.hk
[2]Department of Mathematics, Zhongshan University, Guangzhou, China
stslw@zsu.edu.cn

Abstract. This paper describes a new NURBS-based method for facial modeling and animation. NURBS curves are constructed to correspond with the facial anatomy, and the vertices on the facial model are geometrically associated with these curves. Facial expressions can be simulated by modifying the weights of the control points of the NURBS curves. The overall method is anatomically based and geometrically simple and intuitive.

1   Introduction

Human face modeling and animation can be applied in such diverse areas as low bandwidth teleconferencing, man-machine interface, surgical facial planning, etc. There are five basic kinds of methods for facial modeling and animation: interpolation, muscle-based, parameterization, physics-based, and performance-based.

Interpolation resembles the conventional key-frame approach. It specifies desired expressions at particular points of time and generates intermediate frames using in-between algorithms [1]. This approach is very labor and data-intensive.

Muscle-based approaches simulate various muscle movements using simplified mathematical models. For example, Waters developed 'muscle vectors' to approximate linear, sphincter and sheet muscles [2, 3].

Parameterization uses parameterized surface patches to approximate human faces and utilizes Free-form Deformation (FFDs) for animation [4 - 6]. This approach is one of the most widely used techniques. However, parameterization lacks an accurate anatomical basis and requires the fitting of surface patches to scanned data.

Physics-based approaches generally use Newtonian motion equations on the basis of human facial anatomy and can generate realistic facial expressions [7, 8]. But this approach generally can't achieve real-time performance.

---

[*] Patent pending.

J. Liu et al. (Eds.): AMT 2001, LNCS 2252, pp. 216–223, 2001.

Performance-based animation uses data from real human actions to drive the virtual character [9]. This approach involves motion tracking devices and additional data processing.

In this paper, we propose a novel method for modeling and animating human faces. NURBS curves are built to correspond with facial muscles, and the vertices on the facial model are associated geometrically with these curves. By modifying the NURBS curves, that is, by modifying the weights of their control points, various realistic facial expressions can be simulated. Our method can be broadly considered as an integration of the characteristics of parameterization and muscle-based approaches.

In Section 2, the properties of the NURBS curves related to the facial model are described, as well as NURBS-based modeling. In Section 3, some experiment results are presented. Finally, concluding remarks are presented and future work is suggested in Section 4.

2   NURBS-Based Facial Modeling

2.1   Some Properties of NURBS Curves

A pth-degree NURBS curve can be defined as

$$
\mathbf{C}(u) = \frac{\displaystyle\sum_{i=0}^{n} N_{i,p}(u)\omega_i \mathbf{P}_i}{\displaystyle\sum_{i=0}^{n} N_{i,p}(u)\omega_i} \qquad a \le u \le b,
\tag{1}
$$

where the $\{\omega_i\}$ are the weights, the $\{\mathbf{P}_i\}$ are the control points which form a control polygon, and the $\{N_{i,p}(u)\}$ are the pth-degree B-spline basis functions defined recursively as

$$
N_{i,0}(u) = \begin{cases} 1 & \text{if} \quad u_i \le u < u_{i+1} \\ 0 & \text{otherwise} \end{cases}
$$

$$
N_{i,p}(u) = \frac{u - u_i}{u_{i+p} - u_i} N_{i,p-1}(u) + \frac{u_{i+p+1} - u}{u_{i+p+1} - u_{i+1}} N_{i+1,p-1}(u)
\tag{2}
$$

where $\{u_i\}$ are the knots which form a knot vector

$$
U = \{\underbrace{a,\dots,a}_{p+1}, u_{p+1},\dots,u_{m-p-1}, \underbrace{b,\dots,b}_{p+1}\} .
\tag{3}
$$

Some of the important properties of the NURBS curves are

(a) Localness: Outside the interval $[u_i, u_{i+p+1})$ the control point $\mathbf{P}_i$ has no effect. The control points of the NURBS curve are said to exert the property of localness.

(b) Predictability: Let $\bar{u}$ be a fixed parameter value satisfying $\bar{u} \in [u_k, u_{k+p+1})$, the effect of modifying the value of the weight ω_k is to move the point $\mathbf{C}(\bar{u})$ along a straight line defined by $\mathbf{P}_k$ and the original point $\mathbf{C}(\bar{u})$. As ω_k increases, the curve is pulled towards $\mathbf{P}_k$; as ω_k decreases, the curve is pushed away from $\mathbf{P}_k$. Thus, weight modification has a perspective effect [10].

(c) Continuity: $\mathbf{C}(u)$ is at least $p-k$ times differentiable where k is the multiplicity of a knot.

(d) Affine invariance: applying an affine transformation to the control points is equivalent to applying an affine transformation to the NURBS curve; NURBS curves are also invariant under perspective projections.

2.2 Facial Muscles and Their Simulation Using NURBS

Facial muscles are divided into four groups: the jaw muscles, mouth muscles, eye muscles and brow/neck muscles [11]. There are three types of primary motion muscles:

(a) Linear muscles that move in a linear direction, such as the zygomaticus major and corrugator.

(b) Sphincter muscles that squeeze, such as the orbicularis oris.

(c) Sheet muscles that are like a cluster of linear muscles spread over an area, such as the frontalis.

Based on the properties of NURBS curves summarized in Section 2.1, the NURBS curves can be so constructed that the visual effects of changing weights of control points can closely approximate muscle movements. A NURBS curve can be equivalent to an individual muscle or a group of muscles. Furthermore, changing the weights of different control points can simulate the movement of linear, sphincter, or sheet muscles.

2.3 Implementation

All the NURBS curves in our facial model are cubic since cubic curves have C^0 and C^1 continuity, and higher order curves may introduce unnecessary oscillations and computational complexity. Figure 1 shows the distribution of the NURBS curves in our facial model. The positions of the middle control points approximately represent the locations where the relevant muscles are attached to the skull, but their actual positions are slightly above the skin surface (Figure 2a). The end control points can be either slightly above, or below, the surface of the facial model since the changing of their weights has less effect in curve modification. More importantly, the general shape of a control polygon represents the distribution and affects the surface area of a muscle or a group of muscles in 3D space.

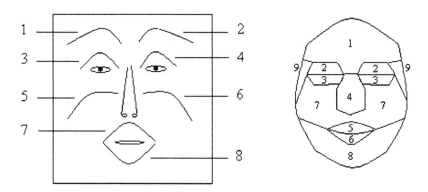

Fig. 1. Distribution of NURBS curves (left) and facial units (right)

All the vertices on the facial model are partitioned into different units. The locations of units are the same as in [8] and is also shown in Figure 1. The association of vertices in these units with the NURBS curves is shown in Table 1. For example, if a vertex V_A is on the upper side of the mouth (unit 5), it is associated with NURBS curve 7, so the movement of curve 7 will affect the position of V_A.

During initialization, a vertex is associated with its connected curve. Each NURBS curve has a number of sample points at intervals of u. A vertex is connected with a sample point based on the minimum distance. Each vertex is associated with a ratio of the movement to its closest sample point on a curve. As shown in Figure 2(b), $A1$ and $A2$ approximately represent the positions where the muscles are attached to the skull, while $B1$ and $B2$ roughly represent the positions where the muscles are embedded into the soft tissue of the skin. $A1$ and $A2$ are also control points of the NURBS curve. V is a vertex and connected to a closest sample point S on a NURBS curve. The ratio r of V to the movement of S is proportional to the distance of V to $A1A2$ if V is between $A1A2$ and $B1B2$, and decreases gradually if V is beyond $B2B2$.

During animation, the curves in Figure 1 are modified by increasing or decreasing their weight(s). The new position of the vertex V is then determined by

$$\overrightarrow{V V'} = r \overrightarrow{S S'} , \qquad (4)$$

where S' is the new position of sample point S, V' is the new position of V.

Table 1. Association of vertices with NURBS curves in Figure 1

Unit No.	Facial Area	Side	Index of Associated Curve
1	forehead	left	1
		right	2
2	upper eyelids	left	3
		right	4
3	lower eyelids	left	N/A
		right	N/A
4	nose		N/A
5	upper mouth	left	7
		right	7
6	lower mouth	left	8
		right	8
7	cheek	left	5
		right	6
8	jaw		N/A
9	sides of head		N/A

3   Experiment Results

Our facial model has been used in generating various facial expressions. First, the weights of all NURBS curves in Figure 1 are set to *1* and the model system is initialized. Then, based on anatomical knowledge, the weights of maximum expressions are stored in arrays. For example, for the expression of surprise, the brows are curved and raised in the upper face. This action is simulated by increasing the weights of several neighboring control points of NURBS curves 1 and 2 respectively. To generate an expression, the curves are first modified using the weights of the maximum expression, then readjusted using linear interpolation.

Since a NURBS curve can represent a group of muscles, changing different weights can simulate movement of the different muscles. For example, the NURBS curve (curve 5 or 6) controlling one side of cheek has seven control points (as in Figure 2b). Increasing the weight of a control point near the nose can simulate the contracting of the levator labii superioris, i.e. the sneering muscle; increasing the weight of a control point near the ear can simulate the contracting of the zygomaticus major, i.e. the smiling muscle. The modifications of NURBS curves are coordinated to simulate certain facial actions. For example, to simulate the downward pull of the lip, which is usually present in the expressions of fear and sadness, the weights of the outer control points of curves 7 are decreased and those of curve 8 are increased.

Our facial modeling system works on a Pentium • PC with a Windows interface, which allows a user to change the expressions using slide bars. Figure 3 shows the results of six primary expressions: surprise, fear, disgust, anger, happiness and sadness.

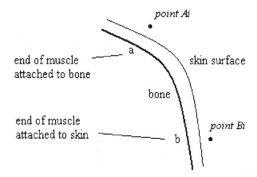

(a)   Side view: positioning of points in (b)

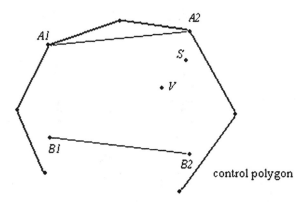

(b)   Front view: NURBS curve control polygon and muscle affected area

Fig. 2. Facial modeling using NURBS curves

4   Discussion and Conclusion

This paper has presented a novel NURBS-based facial modeling method. NURBS curves are constructed to represent facial muscles and their control polygons correspond to the anatomical nature of facial muscles. The vertices on the facial model are associated with these curves. By changing the weights of the NURBS curves, numerous expressions can be simulated. Since NURBS tools are already used in major commercial animation products, our approach can also be easy for animators to

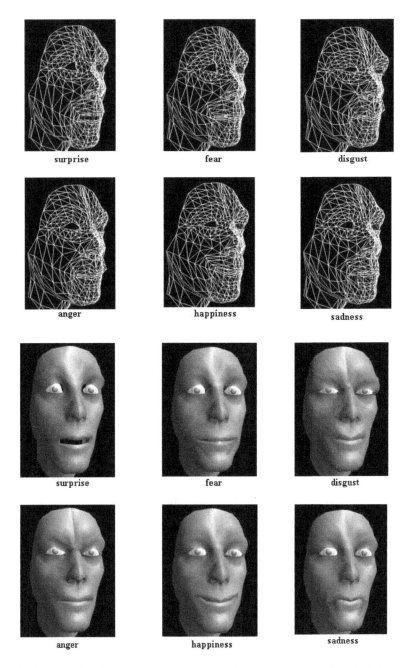

Fig. 3. Simulation of the six primary expressions (vertices and smoothed rendering)

absorb. Compared to previously proposed methods in real-time realistic facial animation, our approach is anatomically based and geometrically simple and intuitive, and doesn't require fitting parameterized patches to scanned data.

We will continue to further develop our method to extend our NURBS-based method to simulate talking heads and other facial features, such as wrinkles.

Acknowledgement. The authors thank the anonymous reviewers for their helpful comments. This project is supported by the Center for Media Technology, City University of Hong Kong. The authors would like to thank Albert Wang for assistance in coding software components. The code source developed by Keith Waters (waters@crl.dec.com) for facial animation has been reused in this project.

References

[1]   F. Pighin, et al, *"Synthesizing Realistic Facial Expressions from Photographs"*, SIGGRAPH '98, Proceedings, 1998, pp. 75-84.

[2]   K. Waters, *"A Muscle Model for Animating Three-Dimensional Facial Expression"*, ACM Computer Graphics, 21(4), 1987, pp. 17 –24.

[3]   K. Waters, *"Modeling Three-Dimensional Facial Expressions"*, Processing Images of Faces, Eds. V. Bruce, M. Burton, Ablex Publishing, Norwood, N.J., 1992, pp. 202 – 227,

[4]   M. Hoch, G. Fleischmann, B. Girod, *"Modeling and Animation of Facial Expressions Based on B-Splines"*, The Visual Computer, vol. 11, 1994, pp. 87-95.

[5]   P. Kalra, A. Mangili, N.M. Thalmann, D. Thalmann, *"Simulation of Facial Muscle Actions Based on Rational Free Form Deformation"*, Eurographics '92, 11(3), 1993, pp. C-59 – C-69.

[6]   L. Moccozet, N.M. Thalmann, *"Dirichlet Free-Form Deformations and their Application on Hand Simulation"*, Proc. Computer Animation '97, IEEE Computer Society, 1997, pp. 93-102.

[7]   Y. Lee, D. Terzopoulos, K. Waters, *"Constructing Physics-based Facial Models of Individuals"*, Proceedings of Graphics Interface '93, pp. 1–8.

[8]   Y. Aoki, S. Hashimoto, *"Physical Modeling of Face using Spring Frame Based on Anatomical Data"*, Proceedings of the International Conference on Multimedia Modeling (MMM '97), 1997, pp. 339-354.

[9]   N.M. Thalmann, P. Kalra, M. Escher, *"Face to Virtual Face"*, Proceedings of the IEEE, 86(5), May, 1998, pp. 870 – 883.

[10]   L. Piegl, W. Tiller, *The NURBS Book (2ⁿᵈ Ed.)*, Springer, Berlin, 1997.

[11]   B. Fleming, D. Dobbs, *Animating Facial Features and Expression*, Charles River Media, Rockland, Mass., 1999.

Evolutionary Negotiation in Agent-Mediated Commerce

Samuel P.M. Choi[1], Jiming Liu[1], and Sheung-Ping Chan[2]

[1]Department of Computer Science, Hong Kong Baptist University, Hong Kong
{samchoi, jiming}@comp.hkbu.edu.hk

[2]Interactive Communication Online Networks, Hong Kong
rickychan@icon.com.hk

Abstract. Automated negotiation has become increasingly important since the advent of electronic commerce. In an efficient market, goods are not necessarily traded in a fixed price, and instead buyers and sellers negotiate among themselves to reach a deal that maximizes the payoffs of both parties. In this paper, a genetic agent-based model for bilateral, multi-issue negotiation is studied. The negotiation agent employs genetic algorithms and attempts to learn its opponent's preferences according to the history of the counter offers based upon the stochastic approximation. We also consider two types of agents: level-0 agents are only concerned with their own interest while level-1 agents consider also their opponents' utility. Our goal is to develop an automated negotiator that guides the negotiation process so as to maximize both parties' payoff.

1 Introduction

The advent of electronic commerce has revolutionized the way that contemporary business operates. Nowadays, online purchasing becomes widely adopted and its selling volume is continuously increasing. Not only electronic commerce reduces the operation cost of a business, but also facilitates a company's service to its customers virtually 24 hours a day. In addition, goods are no longer necessarily traded in a fixed price but based on the market demand (e.g., eBay and priceline). It is expected that in the near future, buyers and sellers can negotiate among themselves so as to reach a deal that maximizes the payoffs of both parties. Hence, it would be interesting to develop autonomous agents that can strive for the best deal on behalf of the traders. In this paper we study how such an autonomous negotiation system can be built based upon agent technologies and genetic algorithms.

1.1 Negotiation

Negotiation is a process of reaching an agreement on the terms (such as price and quantity) of a transaction for two or more parties. The negotiation process typically goes through a number of iterations, and in each iteration one of the parties proposes an offer and sees whether the others accept. If not, other parties can propose their

J. Liu et al. (Eds.): AMT 2001, LNCS 2252, pp. 224–234, 2001.
© Springer-Verlag Berlin Heidelberg 2001

counter-offers and the process repeats until a consensus is reached. For an effective negotiation, it is important that all parties are willing to concede such that the differences among themselves reduce at each round and eventually converge to an agreement. On the other hand, negotiation can also be viewed as a search process in which conflicts among different parties is resolved by finding a feasible alternative. However, negotiation is not just a matter of finding an acceptable deal, but an attempt to maximize all parties' payoffs. In order to achieve this goal, one needs to know the others' utility function. However, the utility functions are usually private and sensitive information. In this paper, we consider how this utility function can be estimated from the history of the opponent's offers.

Negotiation is common in conventional commerce, especially when large and complex business transactions are involved. Negotiation on various terms of a deal offers the potential to yield the involved parties the best payoffs. It also allows the terms of the deal (e.g., price) to be set according to the market demand and supply. However, human-based negotiation could be costly and non-optimal. Automated negotiation is therefore particularly useful due to its relatively low cost. Nevertheless, most existing e-commerce sites still employ fixed-pricing models, or allow only one-side negotiation (e.g., auction sites).

While negotiation is often beneficial to the participants, there are impediments to apply it in the conventional business. The first concern is the time involved. Negotiation is often a time-consuming process because all parties desire to maximize their own payoff while they may have opposite goals. If some of the parties do not concede, it could take forever to reach an agreement. The second is that negotiation requires skillful tactics, and could be difficult for average dealers to bargain effectively on their owns. The third difficulty is that all parties must first get together so as to negotiate. This imposes some restrictions on the customers since e-commerce can be worldwide and often involves people from various time zones.

There exist several types of negotiation models [6]. In this paper, a bilateral, multi-issue negotiation model is studied. Multi-issue negotiation is concerned with reaching an agreement on a deal with multiple terms. The involved parties typically do not want to reveal their underlying utility function and attempt to strive for the best deal through the negotiation process. An important topic for multi-issue negotiation is the question on how to avoid sub-optimal deal; namely, how to avoid an agreement in which one party can modify to obtain better payoff without sacrificing the others. This is also known as pareto-inferior agreement or the problem of "leaving money on the table" [8].

1.2   Previous Work

There have been several approaches to automated negotiation [13]. For multi-issue negotiation, the search space is typically complex and large, and with little information on its structure apriori. One recent research direction is to address such difficult problems with genetic algorithms (GAs) (e.g., [7], [10]). GA [3] is particularly suitable for such tasks due to its efficient searching in a complex and large search space. In Oliver's approach, negotiation strategies are based on simple sequential rules with utility threshold for delimiters. One shortcoming for such representation is the lack of expressiveness. In order to enhance the strategy models, Tu et al. deploys finite state machines for representing simple decision rules. In this paper we are particularly concerned with the learning issues; namely, how to speed up the negotiation by considering the offer history and adaptive mutation rate.

1.3   Agent Technologies

Personal software agents ([12], [4]) are continuously running programs that intimately work with their owners. Agents are proactive, intelligent, capable of understanding their owners' requirements, and therefore can perform tasks on behalf of their owners. Agent technologies have been successfully applied in various domains such as information filtering and job matching. It is natural to extend the agent technology to the automated negotiation tasks. Imagine a picture of our daily life in the near future. Everyone owns at least one agent as a personal assistant. These agents are responsible for various types of personal tasks, ranging from reminding appointments, to handling payments, to scheduling meetings. One task particular interested to electronic business is how agents can be used to deal with online purchasing. Unlike the way we purchase today, agents may negotiate with the sellers on the price among other terms, and even aligns with other buyer agents to bargain for a better deal. Agent negotiation involves three major steps: initiating a negotiation task by proposing an offer, evaluating the opponent's proposal if the offer is not accepted, and suggesting a new counter-proposal. This process is repeated several rounds until an agreement is reached.

    An ideal negotiation system should minimize the involvement of human beings. As noted earlier, software agents are capable of undertaking the task. One reason is that personal agents have the access to their owners' schedule, and thus can infer a deadline for a negotiation. For instance, agents can keep track of the food consumption rate in a refrigerator, and set the negotiation deadline to the date that the food will be exhausted. In addition, agents know their owners' preferences so that the weights can be automatically determined rather than relying on the user input. For instance, if the agent finds that most of the electric appliances of its owner are of brand A, it is plausible to assume that brand A is its owner's favorite. When purchasing other appliances, the agent would give higher priority to that brand. While it is impossible for an agent to know everything about its owner, its ability to anticipate can substantially reduce the required user input. A user's role thus becomes to confirm, rather than to initiate or to specify, a task.

2   Genetic Agent-Based Negotiation System

We propose a framework of automated negotiation systems on the basis of genetic algorithm and agent technology. Our proposed system can be used in conjunction with the electronic marketplace such as [1]. Figure 1 illustrates the idea.

    In our proposed framework, agents proactively predict their owner's needs as well as their requirements. This feature is particular important since need identification is often regarded as the most important stage in the consumer buying behavior (CBB) model. Nevertheless, currently only very primitive event-alerting tools are available at some commercial web sites (e.g., Amazon.com will send an e-mail to its customer if

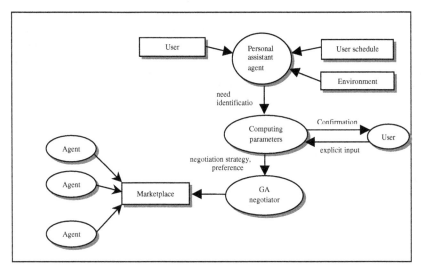

Fig. 1. Genetic agent-based automated negotiation system

there is any new book that may be interested to them), and little research effort has been paid upon this issue. The advent of agent technology now brings a hope in addressing this problem. Alternatively, users may manually initiate a negotiation process. In either case, the agent fills out the default specification according to their owners' profile. It should note that users may modify these specifications and the agent also learns from the feedback.

2.1   The GA Model

Our basic GA negotiation model is based on the one proposed by Krovi et al. [5]. Initially, a negotiation agent identifies itself as either a buyer or a seller and receives an offer from its opponent. If the offer is not satisfactory, the agent generates a counter-offer by the following procedure. The agent first sets up a population of chromosomes, each of which represents a candidate offer for the current round of negotiation. In our experiments, this population contains 90 randomly generated chromosomes and 10 heuristic ones. The heuristic chromosomes includes the counter-offer proposed by the opponent as well as 9 best offers suggested by the agent in the previous round. The inclusion of the counter-offer guides the negotiation process gradually converging to an offer that is acceptable by both parties; the 9 selected offers retain the computation effort in the previous round and thus speed up the whole negotiation process. Nonetheless, this generating process is not sufficient to guarantee efficient searching. To improve the model, one needs to consider two additional constraints for the new population — the retraction and the non-negative constraints. The first constraint restricts that the generated chromosomes cannot be better than their most recent offer while the second ensures that all chromosomes give positive payoff. These constraints are mandatory or otherwise the negotiation process may get into an infinite loop. Now according to the prior concessionary behavior of the opponent, the appropriate value of λ (the parameter for penalizing the opponent, see [5] for the details) can be computed. Then each chromosome is evaluated based on the objective function, and those have larger fitness values are selected to produce offspring through the genetic operators (i.e., crossover and mutation). Finally, the new population replaces the original one and the process continues until the negotiation agents reach a consensus.

2.2   Objective Function

The above GA model is used for proposing counter offers to its opponent. In particular, a user first initiates and assigns a strategy to a negotiation agent. The agent then starts the negotiation process and bargain with its opponent based on the history of proposed offers. The opponent's utility function is assumed of the following product form:

$$u = \prod_i f_i^{w_i},$$

where f_i and w_i corresponds to the utility value and weight (importance) of issue i. Note that this objective function differs from the linear combination formulation that most existing GA negotiation systems employ. We find that our objective function is more general and exhibits some desirable characteristics. For instance, when the weight w_i is 0 (i.e., don't care), $f_i^{w_i}$ is equal to 1. The utility value of f_i thus has no effect on the overall utility u. On the other hand, if a particular issue is very important, a low value on that issue will force the overall utility to be small. Hence, this objective function consists of the joint requirement characteristics and is sensible in many real-world cases.

We also study two levels of negotiation agents. For level-0 agents, opponent's feedbacks are ignored. In other words, the values of w_i are fixed. For level-1 agents, opponent's feedbacks are used to adjust the weights in order to reveal its underlying preferences. This can be achieved by comparing the changes of consecutive offers, namely:

$$R_i = \left| \frac{f_i(t) - f_i(t-1)}{f_i'(t) - f_i'(t-1)} \right|,$$

where $f_i(t)$ and $f_i'(t)$ denotes respectively the user's and the opponent's proposed values for issue i at round t. Note that this ratio reveals the opponent's relative preference compared with the user upon issue i. A large ratio suggests that issue i is more important to the opponent than the user in a quantitative measure. It is now plausible to divide the weight into three rough regions:

Categories	Weight Range
Very important	0.7 to 0.9
Quite mind	0.4 to 0.6
Don't care	0.1 to 0.3

2.3   Data Structure

The implementation details are described as follows. We define an array of structure to represent the population, where each structure contains 6 fields: chromosome, payoff, fitness, crossover point and two fields for pointing to the parents. A chromosome represents the agent's potential offer and is stored into an integer array. As the names suggested, the payoff field records the payoff of the agent while the fitness field keeps the strength of the chromosome. Both fields are dedicated for providing direct access to these frequently referred values so as to reduce the computational time. The crossover point field indicates the chromosome break point for the crossover operator. The parent fields are also maintained for the purpose of efficient chromosome manipulation and for the error checking.

2.4   Experimental Set Up

We study three types of commonly used concession matching tactics suggested by Krovi *et al.* [5]; namely, reciprocal tactic, exploiting tactic and cooperative tactic. Reciprocal tactics is the negotiation strategy that imitates the opponent's concessionary behavior. In other words, if the opponent concedes more, the agent concedes more too. In the exploiting tactic, an agent concedes less when its opponent is cooperative. In the cooperative tactic, an agent concedes generously so as to reach a consensus quickly.

From the implementation perspective, different tactics could result in different range of λ. We therefore define the concession-matching rate as the measure of the concessionary behavior of the opponent against the agent itself. Specifically, the agent x computes the concession-matching rate (c_{xyi}) against the agent y at i^{th} round by the following formula:

$$c_{xyi} = \frac{Y_{i-1} - Y_i}{X_{i-1} - X_i}$$

The value of c_{xyi} specifies the degree that the opponent concedes. When c_{xyi} is equal to zero, it indicates that the opponent has not made any concession. In other words, the agent y is purely competitive orientation. Likewise, when c_{xyi} is equal to or greater than 1, it indicates that the opponent has fully or more than reciprocated concessions. In this case, the agent y is purely cooperation orientation. The relationship between the concession matching behavior of the opponent and λ is defined in the following pseudo-code (Figure 2).

As shown in Figure 2, an agent's tactic determines the value of λ, which is obtained from c_{xyi}. When an agent uses a reciprocal tactic, the range of λ is between 0 and 1. In the exploiting tactic, the range of λ is from 0 to 0.5. For cooperative tactic, the value of λ ranges from 0.5 to 1. It should also note that the concession-matching rate is inverse proportional to λ.

```
double CNeg_ModelDlg::Calculate_Lamda(double Cxy, int index)
    {      double match, lambda;
           if (Cxy >= 1)                    match = 0;
           else if (Cxy >=0)                match = 1.0 - Cxy;

           if (tactics == reciprocate)  lambda = match;
           if (tactics == exploit)      lambda = match/2.0;
           if (tactics == cooperate)    lambda = 0.5 + (match/2.0);
           return lambda;

    }
```

Fig. 2. Pseudo code for computing lambda based on Cxyi

Levels of Goal Difficulty. Intuitively, the level of goal difficulty indicates how ambitious the agent is. If the agent does not satisfy with the current offer, the payoff of that offer will be set to zero. This can be achieved by checking if each field (i.e., price, quantity, processing day and the features of the goods) fulfills the agent's minimum requirement. If all fields are satisfied, the agent's payoff will be computed based on the specified objective function. The fitness value of that offer will therefore always be lower than the ones that fulfill the agent's goal.

Predicting Opponent's Preferences. As discussed earlier, predicting opponent's preferences is important for negotiation. Possessing the knowledge of the opponent not only speeds up the whole negotiation process, but also maximizes one could possibly get from the negotiation. The main idea for predicting opponent's preference is based on the value fluctuation of the opponent's offers. The formula is equivalent to that of the concession matching tactics. The weight for a particular field can now be computed by the following:

Learning Opponent's Preferences. We employ stochastic approximation as a tool for learning opponent's preferences. Stochastic approximation (Wasan 1969) is an online estimation method widely used in machine learning community. It estimates the desired function by obtaining its empirical values over time and gradually adjusts its estimation until convergence.

$$V_i = \alpha \cdot V_{i-1} + (1 - \alpha) \cdot (R_i / 2)$$

```
if (preference == important)  d_weight[index] = 0.7 + (ratio[2]*0.2);
if (preference ==  mind)      d_weight[index] = 0.4 + (ratio[2]*0.2);
if (preference == not_care)   d_weight[index] = 0.1 + (ratio[2]*0.2);
```

Fig. 3. Calculating weight for a particular field

And the weights can now be adjusted by a direct mapping from the prediction value as in the original model, as shown in the following equation:

$$w_i = \beta \cdot w_{i-1} + (1 - \beta) \cdot T_i$$

For the purpose of normalization, the prediction ratio (R_i) is deliberately set between 0 and 2. Note that α and β are the learning rates for the stochastic approximations.

Generation. The population generator does not deviate from the standard one. Our experiments are based on the genetic parameter settings similar to the one described in (DeJong 1980). Specifically, we ran the simulator for 40 generations, with a population size of 50 each, and the length of chromosome was set to 20 bits. The crossover rate is 0.7 and the mutation rate (described below) changes over time according to the responses of the opponent.

Mutation Rate. Unlike the conventional GA models, our agents adapt to their opponents by dynamically adjusting their mutation rate. The rate changes according to the number of generations and the length of the chromosomes. In particular, the mutation rate μ is computed by:

$$\mu = \frac{\log(p)}{g \cdot \sqrt{l}},$$

where p, g and l are respectively the population, goodness and length of the chromosome. This formula suggests that mutation rate should be directly proportional to the log population while inverse proportional to the goodness value. In other words, the higher the goodness value one obtains, the lower mutation rate one should use. This is sensible as mutation is likely to take the current solution away from the local maxima and hence might take longer time to converge. This problem is known as the exploitation and exploration dilemma, and has been studied by different communities. It seems that our proposed formula works in a number of different settings and empirical results verify that this adaptive setting substantially improves the performance of the negotiation agents.

3 Empirical Results

In our experiments, we consider 4 different issues for negotiation: price, quantity, processing days and features. In the first experiment, we first investigate the effects of combining different concession matching strategies on the average negotiation time and the obtained payoff. We set all 4 issues as "quite mind" for the testing purpose. As suggested from Table 1, the exploit strategy in general performs the best in terms of the payoff but takes up the most of the negotiation time. This strategy is suitable for the negotiators who have plenty of time and eager to strive for the maximal payoff. On the contrary, the cooperative strategy can reach an agreement quickly, but obtains the worst payoff. This strategy is appropriate for the one whose time is tight, and thus must sacrifice payoff in order to get the deal in time. Reciprocate strategy tries to make a balance between the two and is good for the conservative negotiators. Nonetheless, the performance of reciprocate strategy largely depends on the strategy of its opponent.

Table 1. Average negotiation time with different concession matching strategies

Seller / Buyer	Reciprocate	Exploit	Cooperative
Reciprocate	Rounds: 42.7 Payoff: 100.5	Rounds: 52.3 Payoff: 123.7	Rounds: 40.6 Payoff: 85.3
Exploit	Rounds: 54.9 Payoff: 126.8	Rounds: 68.5 Payoff: 108.5	Rounds: 40.3 Payoff: 153.3
Cooperative	Rounds: 38.5 Payoff: 92.4	Rounds: 47.2 Payoff: 143.5	Rounds: 34.2 Payoff: 105.7

In our second experiment, we verify the effects of various tactics on the price, and the rest are set to the same tactic. Table 2 shows that if one ranks an issue as important, the negotiation time will take significantly longer. This phenomenon becomes worse as more issues are ranked as important. It is therefore important for the negotiation agent to consider not only the strategy, but also the issues to strive for. It is generally desirable to set the issue weights as needed, in order to attain an agreement faster.

Table 2. Result of experiment 2

Seller's price / Buyer's price	Very Important	Quite Mind	Don't Care
Very Important	Rounds: 90.5 Price: 20.6	Rounds: 47.8 Price: 7.9	Rounds: 44.6 Price: 3.5
Quite Mind	Rounds: 63.3 Price: 21.1	Rounds: 36.3 Price: 19.7	Rounds: 46.3 Price: 12.1
Don't Care	Rounds: 55.6 Price: 29.3	Rounds: 29.2 Price: 26.1	Rounds: 18.5 Price: 3.6

Up to now, we are testing the level-0 agents. In the next experiment, we would like to test on the learning effect of level-1 agent. We use the same experimental setting described above. We notice that level-1 agent yields better payoff and achieve the goal more quickly.

Table 3. Result of experiment 3

Seller's price / Buyer's price	Very Important	Quite Mind	Don't Care
Very Important	Rounds: 83.2 Payoff: 105.5	Rounds: 51.6 Payoff: 131.6	Rounds: 51.7 Payoff: 120.3
Quite Mind	Rounds: 57.3 Payoff: 128.8	Rounds: 43.1 Payoff: 110.3	Rounds: 54.7 Payoff: 157.0
Don't Care	Rounds: 62.5 Payoff: 90.3	Rounds: 69.4 Payoff: 123.5	Rounds: 51.8 Payoff: 106.9

In our last experiment, we verify the effectiveness of the adaptive mutation rate. Figure 8 shows the performance of two different mutation methods. The x-axis is the best fitness value obtained and the y-axis is the number of generations that the GA model goes through. After the first few generations, it is clear that the adaptive approach exhibits more stable and better fitness values. This method significantly speeds up the process for generating counter offers.

4 Conclusion

Automated negotiation has become increasingly important since the advent of electronic commerce. In this paper, we propose a genetic agent-based automated negotiation system for electronic business. Unlike other negotiation systems, our proposed system is able to proactively anticipate the user needs and initiate a purchase process. According to the user's profile and schedule, the agent suggests a set of default parameters and asks its owner for confirmation. This approach thus minimizes the required user input. Given the deadline and the preferences, the negotiation agent is able to select an appropriate negotiation strategy. We describe the implementation details of a GA negotiation agent. Unlike other GA negotiation agents, our agents attempt to learn the opponent's preference by observing the counter offers and adapt to the environment by dynamically modifying its mutation rate. While some parts of our system are still under implementation, we believe that our initial effort has laid a fundamental framework for developing an online automated negotiation system.

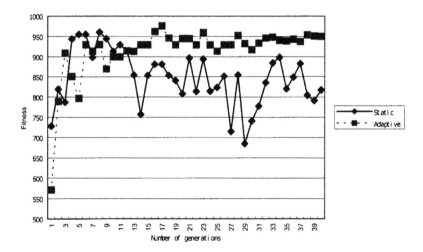

Fig. 3. Static mutation rate versus adaptive mutation rate

References

1. S. P. M. Choi and J. Liu. A Dynamic Mechanism for Time-Constrained Trading. To appear in Proceedings of Fifth International Conference on Autonomous Agents (Agents 2001), Montreal, Quebec, Canada. May 2001.
2. K. DeJong. Adaptive systems design: A genetic approach. IEEE Transaction on Systems, Man and Cybernetics. Vol. SMC-10, pp. 566-574, September 1980.
3. D. E. Goldberg. Genetic Algorithms in Search, Optimization, and Machine Learning. Addison-Wesley, 1989.
4. M. N. Huhns and M. P. Singh. Readings in Agents. Morgan Kaufmann, 1998.
5. R. Krovi and A. C. Graesser. Agent Behaviors in Virtual Negotiation Environments. IEEE Transaction on Systems, Man, and Cybernetics (Part C: Applications and Reviews). Vol. 29, No. 1, February 1999.
6. R. J. Lewicki and J. A. Litterer. Negotiation. Readings, Exercises, and Cases. Homewood, IL, Irwin. 1985.
7. J. R. Oliver. On Artificial Agents for Negotiation in Electronic Commerce. PhD Thesis. The Wharton School, University of Pennsylvania, 1996.
8. H. Raiffa. The Art and Science of Negotiation. Harvard University Press, 1982.
9. T. Sandholm and V. Lesser. Issues in automated negotiation and electronic commerce: Extending the contract net framework. In Proceedings of 1st International Conference on Multiagent Systems, pp.328-335, 1995.
10. M. T. Tu, E. Wolff, and W. Lamersdorf. Genetic Algorithms for Automated Negotiations: A FSM-Based Application Approach. In Proceedings of 11th International Conference on Database and Expert Systems (DEXA 2000), 2000.
11. M. T. Wasan, Stochastic Approximation, Cambridge University Press, 1969.
12. M. J. Wooldridge and N. Jennings. Agent theories, architectures and languages: A survey. The Knowledge Engineering Review, 10(2):115--152, 1995.
13. D. Zeng and K. Sycara. Benefits of learning in negotiation. In Proceedings of the 14th National Conference on Artificial Intelligence, pp.36-41, 1997.

Optimizing Agent-Based Negotiations with Branch-and-Bound

Andy Hon Wai Chun and Rebecca Y.M. Wong

Department of Computer Engineering and Information Technology
City University of Hong Kong, Tat Chee Avenue, Kowloon, Hong Kong SAR
andy.chun@ieee.org & ymwong@ee.cityu.edu.hk

Abstract. This paper presents an algorithm called Nstar (N*) that performs optimizing agent-based negotiation. N* borrows concepts from branch-and-bound and A* optimal search algorithms. The N* negotiation algorithm can be used for a general class of negotiation problems that requires consensus among two or more collaborating agents. N* schedules events through a negotiation protocol that mimics a process of proposing and counter proposing. It makes use of an evaluation function that represents an underestimation of the "global" preference for a particular proposal. This preference is computed based on a user preference model. An optimal solution is found when there is a compromise and the evaluation function is maximized.

1 Introduction

Our N* negotiation algorithm is a type of distributed AI (DAI) algorithm [4, 16]. It was designed to work within a distributed agent-based environment [1]. In such an environment, agents will not have complete knowledge of all the rules, constraints, parameters, and preferences of all other agents. N* was designed to be able to negotiate an optimal solution without this complete knowledge.

Meeting scheduling is a common problem that is modeled as a type of distributed scheduling [10]. Each person is a distributed scheduler that manages its own local resources. A meeting schedule is produced when all these distributed schedulers collaborate to find a solution that satisfies not only their individual constraints and preferences but also the global ones. One form of collaboration is through a generalized contract net protocol [11, 14].

In this paper, we model scheduling as an agent-based process of negotiation. The scheduling of an event is performed by a software agent that negotiates with other agents that need to participate or collaborate in that event. Each agent's prior committed schedule, preferences and constraints are hidden from all other agents. By insulating the negotiation process from details of the user model, we enable our N* negotiation algorithm to work in heterogeneous environments where agents might be built from different agent technologies with different user models and preference strategies. Negotiation in a heterogeneous environment is performed through a well-defined negotiation protocol.

J. Liu et al. (Eds.): AMT 2001, LNCS 2252, pp. 235–243, 2001.
© Springer-Verlag Berlin Heidelberg 2001

Creating a user preference model and designing an algorithm that can perform distributed scheduling without complete knowledge of the individual preference models are the main objectives of our research. This is done through a technique we call "preference estimation," which is similar to underestimations in search evaluation functions combined with dynamic programming.

Our negotiation framework consists of several components (see Fig. 1):

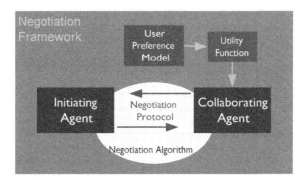

Fig. 1. Key components in our negotiation framework.

User Preference Model - the model encapsulates priorities, preferences and rules related to an individual agent, which might represent a particular user or an organization

Utility Function – the utility functions represent how information stored in the user preference model should be used to evaluate proposals and counter proposals and influence the negotiation process

Initiating Agent – this is the initiator of the event that needs to be negotiated. It also plays the role of a coordinator and manages the whole negotiation process.

Collaborating Agents - the other participants of the event

Negotiation Protocol - the protocol defines the messages that agents may use during negotiation

Negotiation Algorithm - the N* negotiation algorithm makes use of all the previous modules to perform a distributed search for an optimal solution

2   User Preference Model

The N* negotiation algorithms make use of a *user preference model* to evaluate proposals and to determine which counter proposals to make. In simple terms, the user preference model encodes user priorities and preferences as an objective function, which we call the *preference level*. This function evaluates user preferences on proposals and counter proposals made by agents.

A *negotiation problem* is defined by a finite set of fixed attributes, whose values will not change during negotiation, and a finite set of variable attributes, whose values will be negotiated. For example, a person calling a meeting might tell his assistant: "I would like to a hold a project meeting sometime next week, preferably next Wed afternoon, with Tom, Nancy, ..."

In addition, each variable attribute v_i is associated with a domain d_i that defines a finite set of possible values that variable attribute may be assigned. The user preference model allows users to define priorities on *variable attributes* and preferences on their potential values as well as rules on how these priorities and preferences may change due to changes in the environment or decisions that were made.

The importance of a negotiable attribute might be different for different people. For example, the "location" of a meeting might be more important than the "time" to a particular person. The *attribute priority* ap_i of a variable attribute v_i defines its degree of importance. Likewise, he might prefer certain values of these attributes over others. We call the amount of preference for a particular value the *preference value*. For each person, each variable attribute v_j and each potential domain value x_i, there is an associated preference value pv_i.

3   Utility Function

The N* *evaluation function* provides global preference information to the initiating agent to guide the negotiation process or N* search. In our negotiation framework, a potential solution to a negotiation problem is defined as a tuple from $d_1 \times d_2 \times ... \times d_n$ such that the n assignments of values to the problem's variable attributes is to the "satisfaction" of all the collaborating or negotiating agents, i.e., a compromise is found. During the negotiation process, each agent will need to evaluate how "satisfied" it might or might not be with the proposed solution or compromise, using the user preference model. In our framework, each proposed solution to a specified *negotiation problem* is called a *proposal* when offered by the initiating agent, i.e., the agent that initiated the problem to be negotiated, and a *counter proposal* when offered by any other agent involved in the negotiation, i.e, a collaborating agent.

3.1   Preference Level

For example, a proposal/counter proposal P_x might be the tuple $(V_1, V_2, .., V_n)$ where each V_j is a constant value from the domain d_j of variable attribute v_j. If we need to negotiate the "day" and "time" of a meeting, a potential proposal might be the tuple ("Tue", "9am"). In our framework, the result of evaluating how satisfied an agent is with a proposal or counter proposal is called the utility or *preference level* of that proposal. Different agents might of course potentially have a different preference level for the same proposal. For agent i, for a negotiation problem with n variable attributes, the preference level pl_i for a particular proposal/counter proposal P_x is defined as:

$$(Eq.\ 1)\ pl_i(P_x) = \sum_{j=1}^{n} ap_j \times pv \qquad \text{where } pv_{jk} \text{ is the preference value for}$$

the assignment of value V_k to the variable attribute v_j and ap_j is the attribute priority

3.2   Proposal Evaluation Function

The *preference level* only represents the preferences of a particular collaborating agent. The initiating agent that coordinates the negotiation process might need to evaluate the "global" preference of a proposal to determine its negotiation strategy and which proposals to make. In our framework, this global preference is calculated using a *proposal evaluation function*.

Our *proposal evaluation function* is similar to the role of the evaluation function in A* [15] that estimates the total cost of a solution. The evaluation function $f'(n)$ in A* is given by:

$$(Eq.\ 2)\ f'(n) = g(n) + h'(n)$$

where $g(n)$ is the actual cost from start to node n and $h'(n)$ is the estimated minimal cost path from n to goal, i.e., the "underestimated" remaining cost.

For our negotiation algorithm, n is analogous to a particular negotiation cycle. The actual costs are the actual preference levels of the proposals or counter proposals received by the initiating agent from the collaborating agents. The estimated costs are the "estimated" preference levels of new proposals that have not yet been reviewed by the collaborating agents. In our N* algorithm, we use the "current" or "minimum" preference level as the *estimated preference level*. This guarantees that good solutions will not be "overlooked;" since the actual preference level will in fact be lower. This usage of the minimum value is similar to "underestimation" in A* search algorithms.

Only the initiating agent needs to calculate the *proposal evaluation function* and the *estimated preference levels*. For the initiating agent, the estimated preference level $pl'_i(P_x)$ of any proposal/counter proposal P_x of collaborating agent i is defined as:

$$(Eq.\ 3)\ pl'_i(P_x) = \begin{cases} pl_i(P_x), & \text{if } P_x \text{ has already been proposed / counter proposed} \\ \min(pl_i(P_x)|_x) & \text{for all } P_x \text{ proposed / counter proposed} \end{cases}$$

The *estimated preference level* $pl'_i(P_x)$ is equal to the actual $pl_i(P_x)$ if P_x has already been proposed or counter proposed before. Our N* algorithm requires the actual preference level to be passed back from the collaborating agents to the initiating agent during the counter propose step. Otherwise, we will use the minimum preference level received so far from the individual collaborating agent. This is equivalent to the "most recent" preference level, as the value will be decreasing – collaborating agents will always propose the "best" or "most preferred" alternatives first.

Instead of adding the costs, as in A*, our N* proposal evaluation function computes the *average preference level*. With the ability to calculate the $pl'_i(P_x)$ value for every participant and every proposal, the initiating agent can then compute the proposal evaluation function $f(P_x)$, i.e., equivalent to global *average preference level* $apl(P_x)$, for each proposal P_x :

$$(Eq.\ 4)\ f(P_x) = apl(P_x) = \frac{\sum_{i=1}^{n} pl'_i(P_x)}{n}$$

where n is the total number of participants in the event

This *average preference level* provides a "global" indication of how preferred one proposal might be compared with another and hence the chances of it getting accepted. The average preference level $apl(P_x)$ for each proposal is updated once per negotiation cycle to reflect additional preference level information received during the negotiation, i.e., the $pl'_i(P_x)$ value will get more and more precise with each negotiation cycle.

4   N* Algorithm

Our N* algorithm is based on the A* optimal search algorithm. To compare N* with A*, Fig. 2 is the pseudo-code for the A* algorithm. A* performs a best-first search with branch-and-bound using an evaluation function that returns an underestimated total cost. Our N*, on the other hand, performs a best-first negotiation (offering the next "best" proposal with each negotiation cycle) with branch-and-bound using a *proposal evaluation function* that is also represents an underestimated total cost. Fig. 3 is the pseudo-code for our N* negotiation algorithm.

N* tries to propose solutions to the negotiation problem from a sorted list of potential proposals (Fig. 3 – Line 1). The list is sorted according to the *proposal evaluation function* that performs "preference estimation." With each negotiation cycle (Fig. 3 – Line 6), the next "best" proposal (Fig. 3 – Line 8) will be offered/announced to all the collaborating agents (Fig. 3 – Line 9). The definition of "best" may be different for different problem. The N* algorithm allows different negotiation strategies to be implemented simply by redefining "best." For example, a strategy to "minimize negotiation time" can be implemented by defining "best" as the proposal with the maximal number of consenting counter proposals.

Collaborating agents can either accept or reject the proposal in their replies (Fig. 3 – Line 10). If all collaborating agents accept the proposal and the cost (the reverse value of the *proposal evaluation function*) is lower than that of the previous potential solution (Fig. 3 – Line 11), then that proposal becomes the new solution candidate. If no other alternative has a lower cost than the proposal, then it will be returned as the final solution (Fig. 3 – Line 15). Because of branch-and-bound [7] the N* negotiation does not stop, even after a feasible solution has been found, until all other alternatives have lower evaluation function scores.

Otherwise, the counter proposals from all the collaborating agents will be collected and "preference estimations" will be updated (Fig. 3 – Line 18). A collaborating agent that rejects all proposals and has no counter offer means that agent has exhausted all its choices and there is no solution (Fig. 3 – Line 20). The conflict resolution algorithm will be called to resolve this impasse.

```
Line
   1  PROCEDURE Astar (start, goal)
   2  BEGIN
   3    open←{start};                                  // nodes to be expanded
   4    closed←{};                                     // nodes already expanded
   5    solution←NIL;
   6    WHILE (open≠{})
   7    DO BEGIN
   8      node←RemoveFirst(open);                      // best node first
   9      IF (goal∈node & Cost(node)<Cost(solution))   // found potential solution
  10      THEN BEGIN
  11        solution←node;
  12        IF (Min(Cost(open))>=Cost(solution))       // branch-and-bound
  13        THEN RETURN (solution);                    // return optimal solution
  14      END
  15      ELSE BEGIN                                   // else continue search
  16        children←Expand(node);
  17        closed←Insert(node, closed);
  18        children←RemoveLoop(children);             // ignore paths with loops
  19        children←RemoveRedundant(open, children);  // ignore those already in open
  20        children←RemoveRedundant(closed, children);// ignore those that failed before
  21        open←AddFront(open, children);             // update open list
  22        open←Sort(open);                           // sort using underestimated cost
  23      END
  24    END
  25    RETURN (NIL);                                  // no solution
  26  END
```

Fig. 2. Pseudo-code for A* search algorithm

Initially, differences between agents may be great. A proposal that is good for one agent might be bad for another. The N* negotiation process gradually reduces this difference until a common ground or compromise is found. Bui, et. al. [2] offers a different approach to negotiation called *incremental negotiation* where negotiation are performed on meeting attributes in a hierarchical structure. For example, the part of the week (early or late) might first be negotiated, then the day of the week, and then the hour. In other words, individual variable attributes are negotiated one after another in hierarchical fashion. In our negotiation framework, each proposal contains a complete set of proposed variable attribute values and the whole set is negotiated.

5   Applications

The N* negotiation algorithm is a general algorithm that can be used for potentially different types of applications. In this paper, we used an example of agent-based meeting scheduling, which is part of our MAFOA (mobile agents for office automation) environment [17]. MAFOA is a research project to design a comprehensive set of intelligent agents that can support different aspects of office automation, such as purchasing, workflow, meeting scheduling, etc. The main objective is to free people from mundane and routine tasks so that they can concentrate on actual productive work. The MAFOA environment was implemented using Java and the IBM Aglet toolkit [5, 6].

To test our algorithms, we developed a computer simulation test bed to simulate the scheduling and negotiation process involved in scheduling different types of meetings. In our simulation program, we are able to specific a set of simulation

```
Line
   1  PROCEDURE Nstar (proposals)
   2  BEGIN
   3    open←proposals;                                  // proposals to be negotiated
   4    closed←{};                                       // proposals already negotiated
   5    solution←NIL;
   6    WHILE (open≠{})
   7    DO BEGIN
   8      node←RemoveFirst(open);                        // best proposal first
   9      AnnounceProposal*(node);                       // announce proposal
  10      replies←GetReplies*(node);                     // accept/reject proposal
  11      IF (Okay(replies) & Cost(node)<Cost(solution)) // found potential solution
  12      THEN BEGIN
  13        solution←node;
  14        IF (Min(Cost(open))>=Cost(solution))         // branch-and-bound
  15        THEN RETURN (solution);                      // return optimal solution
  16      END
  17      ELSE BEGIN                                     // else continue search
  18        children←GetCounterProposals*(node);         // consolidate counter proposals
  19        closed←Insert(node, closed);
  20        IF (∃x replies[x]={} & children[x]={})       // no reply & no counter proposal
  21        THEN RETURN             (closed);            // try conflict resolution
  22        children←RemoveInfeasible(children);         // ignore infeasible counter proposals
  23        children←RemoveRedundant(closed, children);  // ignore those that failed before
  24        open←UpdateCost(open, children);             // update open w/ new utility est.
  25        open←Sort(open);                             // sort using underestimated cost
  26      END
  27    END
  28    RETURN (NIL);                                    // no solution
  29  END
```

Fig. 3. Pseudo-code for N* search algorithm

parameters, such as the number of simulation cycles, the total number of hours to schedule, the maximum number of participants, the duration of the schedule, the number of hours that have been pre-assigned to other activities, the number of proposals offered in each cycle, the number of counter offers per cycle, etc. Each randomly generated meeting event is defined by a set of attributes – the start-time, end-time, length, participants, host, etc. The computer simulation test bed was used to simulate the scheduling of hundreds of randomly generated meetings. On average, the N* algorithm was able to find the optimal solution within five negotiation cycles for an average meeting group size of six. Details of the simulation test results can be found in [18]. The test bed also allows us to experiment with different variations of the N* algorithm.

The N* negotiation algorithm can also be used for resource allocation problems. For example, we are exploring how N* can be used for airport stand allocation [3]. In this problem, each aircraft arriving at an airport will need to be assigned a stand or gate, in addition to other resources such as baggage handlers, ramp personnel, airline arrival staff, cleaning staff, catering, etc. We represent each aircraft arrival as a *negotiation event*. The participants or collaborating agents are the various service providers and airport resources, such as the physical stand/gate. Besides the airport authority and airline, other agencies or companies might be providing some of the supporting services. Each of these service providers may have their own unique set of preferences and constraints. N* will allow a schedule to be produce that maximizes the business and operational objectives of all the participants.

6 Discussion

In this paper, we presented our distributed negotiation framework and the N* negotiation algorithm. The framework consists of a user preference model and an approach that makes use of the model to evaluate proposals and suggest counter proposals, using a preference level measure. The negotiation process is guided by a proposal evaluation function that evaluates the global preference level for a particular proposal. The N* negotiation algorithm is based on A* and finds the optimal solution that maximizes average preference levels. We have tested our N* algorithm on a classic meeting scheduling problem using a computer simulation test bed that simulates the scheduling of hundreds of randomly generated meetings.

Acknowledgements. This work was supported in part by a Hong Kong RGC Earmarked Grant and a Strategic Research Grant provided by the City University of Hong Kong.

References

[1]   Bradshaw, J.M., (ed.), *Software Agents*, MIT Press, 1997.
[2]   Bui, H.H., Venkatesh, S., Kieronska, D., "A Multi-agent Incremental Negotiation Scheme for Meetings Scheduling," In the *Proceedings of the Third Australian and New Zealand Conference on Intelligent Information Systems*, ANZIIS-95, 1995, pp. 175-180.
[3]   H.W. Chun, Steve Chan, Francis Tsang and Dennis Yeung, "Stand Allocation System (SAS) - A Constraint-Based System Developed with Software Components," *AI Magazine*, Vol. 21, No. 4, Winter 2000, pp.63-74.
[4]   Ferber, J., *Multi-Agent Systems : An Introduction to Distributed Artificial Intelligence*, Addison-Wesley Pub Co, 1999.
[5]   Danny Lange and Mitsuru Oshima, *Programming and Deploying Java Mobile Agents with* Aglets, Addison-Wesley, 1998.
[6]   IBM Japan – Aglets Workbench: http://www.trl.ibm.co.jp/aglets/
[7]   E. L. Lawler and D. W. Wood, "Branch and Bound Methods: A Survey," *Operations Research*, Vol. 14, pp. 699-719, ORSA, 1966.
[8]   Sandip Sen and Edmund H. Durfee, "A Formal Study of Distributed Meeting Scheduling Group Decision and Negotiation," *Group Decision and Negotiation Support System*, Vol. 7, 1998, pp. 265-289.
[9]   Sandip Sen, Thomas Haynes, and Neeraj Arora, "Satisfying User Preferences while negotiating Meetings," *International Journal of Human-Computer Studies*, Vol. 47, 1997 pp. 407-427.
[10]   Sen, S., "Developing an Automated Distributed Meeting Scheduler," *IEEE Expert*, Vol. 12, Issue 4, July-Aug, 1997, pp. 41-45.
[11]   Sandip Sen and Edmund H. Durfee, "A Contracting Model for Flexible Distributed Scheduling," *Annals of Operations Research*, Vol. 65, 1996, pp.195-222.
[12]   Sandip Sen and Edmund H. Durfee, "On the Design of an Adaptive Meeting Scheduler," In *Proceedings of the Tenth IEEE Conference on Artificial Intelligence for Application*, San Antonio, Texas, March, 1994, pp.40-46.
[13]   Sandip Sen and Edmund H. Durfee, "The Role of Commitment in Cooperative Negotiation," *International Journal on Intelligent Cooperative Information Systems*, Vol. 3, No. 1, 1994, pp.67-81.

[14] Smith, Reid G, "The contract net protocol: High-level communication and control in a distributed problem solver," *IEEE Transactions on Computers,* C-29 (12), 1980, pp. 1104-1113.

[15] Stuart C. Shapiro (ed.), *Encyclopedia of Artificial Intelligence,* John Wiley & Sons, 1992.

[16] Weiss, G. (Ed.), *Multiagent Systems: A Modern Approach to Distributed Artificial Intelligence*, MIT Press, 2000.

[17] Rebecca Y. M. Wong, Alex T.T. Ho, Spencer K.L. Fung, and Andy H. W. Chun, "A Model for Resource Negotiation Using Mobile Agents", In *Proceedings of 4th World Multiconference on Systemics, Cybernetics and Informatics* (SCI 2000), Orlando, Florida, July 23-26, 2000.

[18] Rebecca Y. M. Wong, H. W. Chun, "Optimizing User Preferences While Scheduling Meetings", submitted to *International Conference on Enterprise Information Systems 2001,* Setubal, Portugal, July 7-10, 2001.

Engineering Fuzzy Constraint Satisfaction Agents for Multi-user Timetable Scheduling

Chi Kin Chau and Kwang Mong Sim

Department of Information Engineering
The Chinese University of Hong Kong,
Shatin, NT, Hong Kong.
{Ckchau, kmsim}@ie.cuhk.edu.hk

Abstract. This paper explores issues of engineering agents that partially automate some of the activities of timetable scheduling. In particular, it focuses on the incorporation of a more intuitive fuzzy set-based preference model and multi-objective decision-making techniques. The goal of this research is to design an effective preference capturing model and a schedule optimization methodology, to devise fuzzy constraint satisfaction agents (FCSAs) assisting in the automatic scheduling system, and to engineer an agent-based testbed. Experimental results show FCSAs are able to search for and suggest optimum timeslot with a high degree of users' satisfaction.

Keywords: agent, fuzzy constraint satisfaction, multi-user timetabling

1   Introduction

In a fast-paced society, efficient and careful scheduling of business meetings, social events and daily activities is essential for time saving, time management, productivity and even cost saving. The major issues for timetable scheduling include (1) resolving availability and conflict, and (2) searching for time arrangement that matches the preferences of as many attendees' as possible. The challenges encountered by event schedulers include the complexity caused by a multitude of attendees and the inconsistencies of preference profiles. To address the tedious (and sometimes difficult) task of time-tabling, this research has engineered agents that partially automate the tasks of multi-users timetable scheduling.

Objectives: The goal of this research is to engineer a society of fuzzy constraint satisfaction agents that can:

1. translating users' preferences into fuzzy constraints by an intuitive fuzzy set-based preference model,
2. applying multi-objective decision-making techniques to assist users in selecting optimum timeslots fitting those fuzzy constraints.

What distinguishes this research from extant scheduling research work such as Sen [1] and Garrido [2] is that this research explores the issues of a more intuitive

J. Liu et al. (Eds.): AMT 2001, LNCS 2252, pp. 244–254, 2001.
© Springer-Verlag Berlin Heidelberg 2001

preference modeling by fuzzy set (section 2), a fast algorithm to evaluate preferences from the model (section 3) and multi-objective decision making (section 4) to combine with agents (section 5). In section 6, a series of experiments to evaluate the performance is discussed. Methodologies employed in this research are compared with those of related work in section 7.

2   Fuzzy Set-Based Preference Modeling

Since Lotfi Zadeh's seminal literature [3], fuzzy set-based techniques have contributed to a wide range of applications to handle imprecision and vagueness. This research employs a fuzzy model to formalize flexible constraints from human preferences for timetable scheduling.

Preference modeling of timetable scheduling may be viewed as capturing the degree of satisfaction from each attendee about a potential event within a possible event set. Here is a classical approach of fuzzy set-based preference modeling. An event is represented as a 2-tuple:

$$e = (s, d) \text{ where } s \in S, d \in D$$

such that s is the starting time, and d is the event duration with spaces S and D to denote the spaces constraining the values of s and d.

It seems customary to think that meeting times are typically discretized to the nearest minute (eg, 9:00 am) or nearest 5 minutes (eg, 10:05 pm) rather than the nearest second such (eg, 8:58:43 am or 10:03:13 pm). Hence, for ease of formulation but without loss of generality, 5-minute interval discretization is considered here. For instance, let $S_1 = \{s_1, s_2, s_3,...\} = \{9:00 \text{ am}, 9:05 \text{ am}, 9:10 \text{ am},...\}$ be a set of starting times.

Suppose that 5-minute interval discretization is considered, then D denotes a set of possible event durations in terms of number of 5-minute intervals. For instance, let $D_1 = \{d_1, d_2, d_3,...\} = \{6, 7, 8,...\}$, where d_1 denotes 6 5-minute intervals, i.e. 30 minutes. Furthermore, d is bounded as $d_L \leq d \leq d_U$.

χ is used to denote the schedule space of all potential solutions of (s, d). The cardinality of the schedule space: $|\chi| = |S| \times |D|$. If χ is a schedule space that consists of 2 weeks with duration ranging from 60 minutes to 80 minutes, then $|S|$ will be $(2 \times 7 \times 24 \times 12 =)$ 4032, $|D|$ will be $((80-60)/5+1=)$ 5, and $|\chi| = (4032 \times 5 =)$ 20160.

To formalize fuzzy constraints, a membership function, $\mu(e)$, (or called *preference utility*) indicates the fulfillment degree of a potential event e over an attendee's preference.

$$\forall e \in \chi, \mu(e) \begin{cases} = 1 & \text{if } e \text{ completely satisfies the attendee's preference} \\ \in (0,1) & \text{if } e \text{ partially satisfies the attendee's preference} \\ = 0 & \text{if } e \text{ completely violates the attendee's preference} \end{cases}$$

Different attendees (users) have different preferences; hence a different landscape of preference utility space is formed. In timetable scheduling, the task of agents is to identify a suitable e in χ with given a collection of preferences, $\{\mu_i\}|_{i=0...N}$, from N different attendees.

Furthermore,

$$\mu(e) = \mu_{st}(s) \times \mu_d(d)$$

where $\mu_{st}(s)$ and $\mu_d(d)$ represent sub-preference membership functions for the starting time and duration respectively.

This classical approach, however, is unintuitive for an undecided attendee to indicate the exact *preferred starting time* because the decision has not been confirmed yet. Conversely, it seems more intuitive to indicate the desirability of an event *to be happening* at a specific time instead. Using *occurrence preference* at a specific time, in place of starting time, is considered more intuitive. A revised fuzzy set-based preference modeling is formalized as:

$$\mu(s_i, d) = \mu_d(d) \frac{\sum_{\Delta=0}^{d-1} \mu_{oc}(s_{i+\Delta})}{d} \quad\text{..................... Equation (1)}$$

where $\mu_{oc}(s)$ is occurrence preference membership function.

Figure 1 shows an example to illustrate Equation (1):

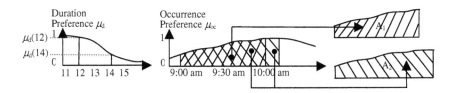

Fig. 1.

$$\mu(9{:}00\ am, 12) = \frac{A_1}{12} \times \mu_d(12) \; ; \; \mu(9{:}00\ am, 14) = \frac{A_2}{14} \times \mu_d(14)$$

where A_1 and A_2 are the respective preference areas (i.e. summed preference) of a event occurring over 12 or 14 intervals starting form 9:00 am.

This revised preference utility becomes a product of the duration preference and the average of the *summed occurrence preference* within duration d and starting from s.

In many instances, users may be undecided about their preferences of time slots. The occurrence membership function provides a more convenient means of capturing human preferences which can involve certain degree of vagueness.

Using the occurrence preference model, preference agents capture users' preferences using a linear combination of occurrence preferences represented as a set of production rules. For example:

If the event is a meeting, use μ_{oc}^{1}

If the event is initiated by the manager, use μ_{oc}^{2}

It is intuitive to produce the occurrence membership function upon a meeting initiated by the manager by linear combination: $\mu_{oc} = \frac{1}{2}\mu_{oc}^{1} + \frac{1}{2}\mu_{oc}^{2}$. Hence, agents can work out appropriate occurrence preferences accordingly.

Using summed occurrence preference seems more convenient to capture humans' intuitive scheduling preference, but appears to be complicated and incurs higher computation cost.

If preference summation is issued by equation (1) only,

The runtime of evaluating preference utility of a single event point, RT(e)

= Θ(Summation of related occurrence preference values)

= $O(d_U)$ (because at most only d_U intervals will be summed, and $d_L \leq d \leq d_U$)

A straightforward approach to find the event point with the maximum preference utility is to visit every exhaustively event point. The computational time of this operation is significant to the overall performance of fuzzy constraint satisfaction.

Hence, the runtime of evaluating preference utilities of all event points exhaustively, RT($e: \forall e \in \chi$)

= $O(d_U |\chi|)$, (for totally $|\chi|$ event points)

3   A Fast Algorithm to Evaluate Summed Occurrence Preference

Directly using preference summation by equation (1) is computationally expensive when the upper bound of duration, d_U, is considerably large. However, it is observed that there are many repetitive computations involved and a faster algorithm can be devised to reuse previous computations and saves more processing time.

Now, let $\lambda(s_i, d) = \sum_{\Delta=0}^{d-1} \mu_{oc}(s_{i+\Delta})$

$\Rightarrow \mu(e) = \mu_d(d)\dfrac{\lambda(s_i, d)}{d}$

$\lambda(s_i, d+1) = \lambda(s_i, d) + \mu_{oc}(s_{i+d})$ .... Equation (2)

$\lambda(s_{i+1}, d) = \lambda(s_i, d+1) - \mu_{oc}(s_i)$ .... Equation (3)

Equations (2) and (3) give the relation among $\lambda(s_i, d)$, $\lambda(s_i, d+1)$, and $\lambda(s_{i+1}, d)$. If $\lambda(s_i, d)$ is given, $\lambda(s_i, d+k)$ and $\lambda(s_{i+n}, d)$ can be evaluated in can be evaluated in a time proportional to k and n. By reusing previous steps in terms of $\lambda(s_i, d-1)$ and $\lambda(s_{i-1}, d)$, some computations are saved without repeating redundant summation of individual occurrence preference values. Hence, a sequential evaluation approach can be enforced in a manner depicted in figure 2. Through the use of a fast sequential evaluation approach, more intuitive occurrence preference can be effectively employed in preference modeling.

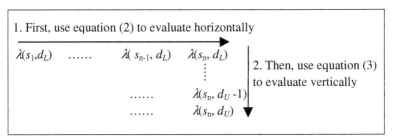

Fig. 2. A Fast Summing Occurrence Preference Approach

To evaluate all the preference utilities from (s_1, d_L) to (s_n, d_U) in search for the maximum value, a fast algorithm is designed to take advantage of equations (2) and (3):

> Given $\lambda(s_1, d_L)$
> For i = 1 to |S|
>   If i > 1 then
>   /* Using equation (3) */
> $\lambda(s_i, d_L) = \lambda(s_{i-1}, d_L+1) - \mu_{oc}(s_{i-1})$
>   End if
>   For $d = d_L$ to d_U
>   If $d > d_L$ then
>   /* Using equation (2) */
> $\lambda(s_i, d) = \lambda(s_i, d-1) + \mu_{oc}(s_{i+d-1})$
>   End if
>
>   /* At this point, $\lambda(s_i, d)$ is determined */
>   Calculate preference utility, $\mu(s_i, d) = \mu_d(d) \dfrac{\lambda(s_i, d)}{d}$
>   End for
> End for

The runtime for the fast algorithm:
RT($e : \forall e \in \chi$) = $O(|\chi|)$ (for totally $|\chi|$ event points)

Comparing with directly using equation (1), the effect of d_U is eliminated.
It can be concluded that: if d_U is considerably large,
RT($e : \forall e \in \chi$ using the fast algorithm) < RT($e : \forall e \in \chi$ directly using equation (1))

In Section 6.1, experiments are carried out to validate the performance of directly using direct equation (1) against of employing the fast algorithm.

4   Multi-objective Decision Making

In timetable scheduling, each attendee's preference is an objective that agents attempt to fulfill, but in many cases, preferences among attendees are not identical and even inconsistent which is a typical multi-objective decision making (MODM) problem. When searching for most suitable timeslot, both the *aggregation approach* [4] *and Pareto-optimal set approach* [5] can be employed.

In the aggregation approach, an aggregation operator is used to aggregate the degree of satisfaction from multiple objectives into a single comparable utility value, which can be used in ranking and prioritizing potential timeslots. This approach can be regarded as mapping a collection of individual preferences into a single group preference. In this research, weighted averaging is used as the aggregation operator. When agents employ aggregated single point search over multi-objective decision making, the potential timeslot with the maximum aggregated utility value will be regarded as the optimum timeslot.

Although aggregation is simple, the preliminary determination of weighting can be difficult. Pareto-optimal set is the set of feasible solutions which are non-dominated; i.e. for each non-dominated solution x there is no other solution x` which is better than x. Pareto-optimal set appears to be a set of plausible potential solutions from which the optimum timeslot can be chose. If Pareto-optimal set search is employed, agent will search for a collection of Pareto-optimal timeslot and users to vote for the optimum timeslot.

5   Agent-Based Testbed

The agent-based framework consists of a society of preference agents and fuzzy constraint satisfaction agents (FCSAs) with blackboard message queues as a communication channel. It is supposed that preference agents act as users' personal assistants residing in PDAs or personal information management software. Preference agents will be connected through the Internet. While preference agents are used to translate human preferences into fuzzy set-based profiles; FCSAs search for optimum timeslot, using the aggregation approach and the Pareto-optimal set approach, and notify the results back. To initiate automatic timetable scheduling, preference agents have to send invitations to all concerned attendees. Attendees' preference agents will be triggered to respond the invitation by loading appropriate preference profiles or consulting the users. Upon all preference profiles are placed in preference queue, FCSAs will carry out fuzzy constraints satisfaction task to resolve for optimum timeslots. Finally, the results will be notified to attendees for confirmations. The agent-based testbed system framework is depicted in figure 3.

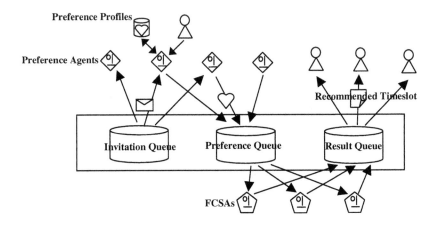

Fig. 3. The Agent-based Testbed

6   Evaluation and Experimentation

To measure the effectiveness of the agent-based testbed, a series of experiments are carried out and the results are reported in following sections.

6.1   Fast Algorithm vs. Directly Applying Equation (1)

The experiment results in figure 4 demonstrate the effectiveness of using the fast summing occurrence preference algorithm from section 3 in contrast to the direct exhaustive computations using equation (1). It was conducted by a series of aggregated single point searches and Pareto-optimal set searches with and without the fast algorithm. Each data point is the median of 30 test data. Four tests were carried under the same condition: $|S|$ as 4032 and $|D|$ as 5. The execution time was measured. In this experiment, the duration upper bound, d_U, was changed from 5 to 19 5-minute intervals. It is evident that the performance of fast algorithm searches remains constant with the increasing value of d_U, but the direct exhaustive searches are severely affected. The results are consistent with:

$$RT(e: \forall e \in \chi \text{ using the fast algorithm) is } O(|\chi|)$$
$$RT(e: \forall e \in \chi \text{ directly using equation (1)) is } O(d_U|\chi|)$$

The difference between performances of aggregated single point searches and Pareto-optimal set searches of directly applying equation (1) is substantial comparing to the one of the fast algorithm. It suggests that the reusing of previous computations by the fast algorithm helps significantly in lowering the processing time. Moreover, the observed performance of the fast algorithm is more efficient.

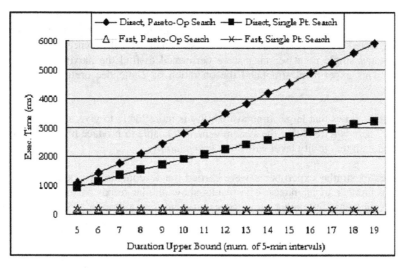

Fig. 4. The Fast Algorithm vs. Direct Summing

6.2   Estimated Timetable Availability

In order to gain a better perception about an attendee's preference profile, the degree of relaxability of fuzzy constraints is assessed. This research defines the estimated timetable availability with respect to a finite schedule space as:

$$availability = \frac{\sum_{\forall e \in \chi} \mu(e)}{|\chi|}$$

Higher value indicates that the constraints might be more relaxed.

In the experiments, the notion of *availability* helps to identify the status of an attendee's preference profile and serves as a rough indicator of a general perception of the schedule space landscape. The tests show general *availability* of ordinal preference profiles is about 0.2 to 0.4. This provides a basic guideline on how random preference profile generations can mimic human preference profiles.

6.3   Timetable Availability vs. User's Satisfaction

The second experiment focuses on the relationship between timetable availability pattern and users' satisfaction. *Availability* defined in previous section is used as an indication of measurement for this purpose. It is hard to show any deterministic relationship. It is due the preference matching heavily depends on the degree of similarity of attendees' preferences. A higher degree of similarity gives a higher degree of user's satisfaction. Nevertheless, this experiment aimed to have a coarse estimation on general preference matching, so that a general assessment can be done on the effectiveness of the preference matching process. Randomly generated preferences are used as test data. Given a sample of random generated 200 attendee preference profiles with different level of *availability*, pairs of preference profiles were selected on the basis that they are lesser than 10% difference of *availability*. Aggregated single point searches were performed to find the maximum preference utility. This experiment simulated the operation of 2-attendee preference matching process.

The result shows that larger time availability is more likely to give higher preference utility. There is a trend that the system generally is able to produce high utility results and maintain that utility level with similar *availability*.

A series of similar experiments were carried out to compare the performance with varying number of attendees. The results show similar trends as the two-attendees case. An increase in number of attendees brought upon a drop in average utility. The results coincide with the intuition of preference matching in real life; when there is a larger number of attendees the chance of find a agreeable schedule favors all attendees is lower. This experiment however shows the system can still maintain average preference utility about 0.3 up to 10 attendees, which proves the applicability of the system is acceptable.

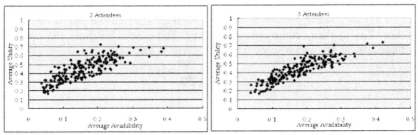

Fig. 6. Two-attendee Case   Fig. 7. Three-attendee Case

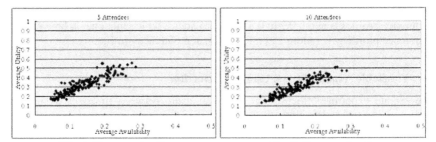

Fig. 8. Five-attendee Case   Fig. 9. Ten-attendee Case

7   Related Work

A number of researchers have proposed different agent frameworks for meeting schedule negotiation such as Sen [1] and Garrido [2]. Garrido's paper focuses on designing a distributed agent communication protocol, and studies the relationship between the degree of revealing privacy and the performance of meeting scheduling. Bearing similar focus, Sen's paper outlines a distributed meeting scheduling model, and suggests heuristic strategies to improve efficiency. Both [1] and [2] employed negotiation agents to search for optimum timeslot, while this research considers using fuzzy constraint satisfaction agent approach. The approach in this research appears more efficient and flexible to solve human preference involved problems such as timetable scheduling. Moreover, both Sen and Garrido ignored crucial human factors issues concerning how to transfer the preferences and constraints of a person into that person's associated scheduling process, an issue that is addressed in this research

Scheduling by fuzzy multiple criteria optimization has been also addressed by Slany [6], but with a focus on application in machine and resource scheduling. Furthermore, Slany's paper does not focus on human preference capturing, and only relies on aggregation method in multi-objective decision making without considering Pareto-optimal set. Both two issues are addressed in this research.

8   Conclusion

This research has presented a preliminary multi-user event scheduling system, which partially solves the preference-based automatic multi-user event-scheduling problem. Despite the preliminary stage of implementation, it already shows value for its test users.

In particular, it is seen that the scheduling system demonstrating a prudent need for an automatic mechanism of agent-based scheduling in daily scheduling. It also shows how an automatic mechanism might be attained in agent-based environment. Experimental results demonstrate that FCSAs are able to locate optimum solution and suggest timeslots with a high degree of users' satisfaction.

Acknowledgement. Portion of this work is supported by Prof. Sim's Direct Research Grant (project code: 2050255) from the Faculty of Engineering at the Chinese University of Hong Kong (CUHK). Both the authors gratefully acknowledge financial support from CUHK.

References

1.   Sen S.and Durfee E. H., A formal study of distributed meeting scheduling. Group Decision and Negotiation Support System, 1998. To appear.

2. Garrido L. and Sycara *K.:* Multi-Agent Meeting Scheduling: Preliminary Experiment Results, *Proceedings of Second International Conference on Multi-Agent Systems(ICMAS-96)*, AAAI Press, pp. 95-102 ,1996.
3. Zadeh L. A., Fuzzy Sets, *Information and Control*, 1965, pp 338-253.
4. Fodor, J. and Roubens M., *Fuzzy Preference Modelling and Multicriteria Decision Support*, Kluwer Academic Pub, pp.107-109, 1994.
5. Dasgupta P., *Multi-objective heuristic search: an introduction to intelligent search methods for multicriteria optimization*, Vieweg, 1999.
6. Slany W., Scheduling as a Fuzzy Multiple Criteria Optimization Problem, *Fuzzy Sets and Systems*, pp. 197-222, March 1996.
7. Slowinski R., and Hapke M., *Scheduling Under Fuzziness*, 2000, Physica-Verlag.

An XML-Based Distance Learning System Capable of Conveying Information on "LECTURE EVENT"

Naoaki Mashita, Hiroshi Shigeno, and Yutaka Matsushita

Keio University, Tokyo, Japan

Abstract. As the demand for lectures without the limitation of time and space, there will be more and more expectations about the implementation of a Distance Learning(DL) System. However, in the present DL system, images related to the actions, reactions and interaction between the teacher and the students are insufficient. In this paper we will emphasize the importance of 'Lecture Event' and suggest description of DL and a DL system which will allow the easy realization of content and make possible a virtual reality experience of real lectures. . . .

1 Introduction

A low birth rate coupled with an aging society will call in the near future for the need to direct the constant improvement in education towards an adult and Life Long Education system. Under these social conditions the advancement in computer and telecommunications technology could be used to offer high quality lecturing and lead to the creation of a state-of-the-art Distance Learning (DL) system. Now the two following types of DL based on a network system are the starting point. Real Time DL and Asynchronous DL. Real time DL means lecture being diffused through telecommunications or broadcasting, a lecturer delivering his teaching simultaneously to a live audience in various remote regions. The ability to effectively open lectures in remote classrooms will translate in a space barrier free classroom lecture education system. As for Asynchronous DL the images and data of the classroom are being stored with the server as an educational content for DL. Using internet one can access and make virtual this educational medium. Given an environment where one could access internet the content of DL could respond to the needs of the students anywhere and at anytime and therefore the classroom lecture would be freed from the limitation of space and time. Recently there have been cases of lectures and images recorded and presented on internet. The lecturer images are simply being reproduced. As the lecture progresses the data of the lecture are being introduced. The link between the images and data is not maintained. As content for Asynchronous DL it is insufficient. In a conventional classroom lecture the elements contributing to the intricate sharing between the lecturer and the students are taken for granted in reason of the following elements.

J. Liu et al. (Eds.): AMT 2001, LNCS 2252, pp. 255–267, 2001.

– Who.
– What is being described.
– What kind of communication is taking place.
– What was the reaction.

Namely, the transmission of information about the lecturer and the student's actions, reactions and interactions is insufficient. It doesn't leave the audience with the impression that it had a classroom virtual reality experience. As previously stated in this paper, the actions, reactions and interactions between the lecturer and the audience in sharing information constitute the definition of a lecture. We will make suggestions as to the way in which a lecture could be stored. Again, the classroom images, voice and data along with the lecture events being stored at real time and afterwards the content being used for Asynchronous DL. We will elaborate about this DL system. The content of the DL based on this system is described as XML. The events of the lecture are used as the axis, the images and lecture data and other type of information are linked. This type of content is called a DL Markup Language Content (a combination of real time and Asynchronous DL). This form of educational content will aim at transmitting the information lacking in a conventional DL system.

2   Proposal for Content of DL Markup Language in a Lecture Event

2.1   The Problems

The Insufficiency of Non-verbal in DL. A lecture is not only structured from the presentation of images, voice and data. It is also structured by a wide range of actions, reactions and interactions. There are also non-verbal elements of which we are not fully conscious. All these elements are compounded and transmit the lecture content to the audience. But generally speaking, at the present, in WBT only the lecture images and data are linked. It can be said that the non-verbal elements information are not efficiently transmitted. We may not be conscious of non-verbal elements but if they are not sufficiently transmitted it prevents from having a real DL virtual reality experience. For the transmission of non-verbal elements in a DL system we have to focus on the asynchronous method.

Classroom lecture: The enormous cost to change the Real Time DL to Asynchronous DL. At this time, generally speaking, in Asynchronous DL in order to show an linked content, the lecture images and data having been stored independently, there is a need for additional content authoring. We then have to take in account the time and the expense of the labor. Judging from the feedback from the DL experiment being carried at present, the management of the images encoding requires just as much time as the lecture itself and the classroom lecture authoring takes several times as much. Therefore to produce series of Asynchronous DL could be very pain staking. This is thought to be the major hurdle to overcome to get university lectures on-line.

2.2   Lecture Event

The problem being brought is the numerous non-verbal information which is unconsciously part of the sharing between the lecturer and the students. They often are born from changes in situation in the course of the sharing . For example, people in the audience picking up a memo. This information is of some importance and it is being shared between the lecturer and the students unconsciously. These non-verbal information elements point to changes in condition. It is possible to describe and also to record them. The changes in condition being unconsciously shared and not readily visible makes it more difficult to extract them and feed them into the system. In this paper we will define each change in condition in lecture events. We will propose to record these lecture events which we may call 5W1H . In this we will be able to reconstitute lecture events by recording these non-verbal elements and changes in condition for Asynchronous DL.

2.3   Combined DL Content

Adding the lecture events to to the classroom lecture, 'Event Markup Language' and 'Document for Study Markup Language' and Note Markup Language, we believe are of real importance.

- Event Markup Language (EML)
- Document for Study Markup Language (DSML)
- Note Markup Language (NML)

which will be defined under the wording XML. The EML which describe the lecture events will be the handler of these events occurring in classroom lecture, under it the lecture data, the blackboard writing and the note taking will be linked. The guideline is illustrated in Figure 1. EML being the axis with reference to NML, DSML describing the content of the DL and which we will define by DL Markup Language under the generic term DLML The following will present a detailed explanation of EML,NML and DSML .

EML generic term used for descriptions of events. EML (Event Markup Language) is a XML based generic term through which are described the lecture events. The DTD (Document Type Definition) of the EML will schematize the important elements as shown in Figure 2. The key words of EML are 'Who' , 'to-Whom' and 'do' basically describing the participants and what was done (events). Plus, it becomes possible to describe more abstract roles. In order to describe the content of one lecture one EML is created and all the events of the classroom lecture are transmitted at real time from beginning to end. In some cases, the content created by the lecture events is described by a 'result' tag linked by an ID. EML doesn't define the way by which the event is being reenacted. Consequently, it is one of the primary merit of XML, it doesn't interfere with the scope of the language being used or the way in which it is expressed thus allowing a high level of freedom.

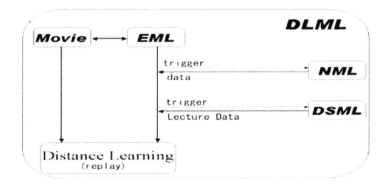

Fig. 1. DLMarkup Language content.

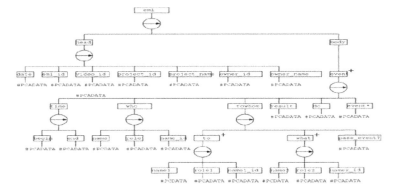

Fig. 2. DTD for EML

DSML Generic term for the description of the data of the lecture.
DSML (Document for Study Markup Language) is the generic use to describe the
data diffused by the lecturer in the lecture. JepaX (Japan Electronics Publishing
Association) is already the leading force in publishing in Japan. This is JepaX
who generally controls electronic publishing in Japan . By having JepaX using
XML we expect it to be a standard as the format for national use. But considering
what JepaX use to describe lecture data, in the course of these data, concerning
wording, phrases and the Figures, important definitions adding to the meaning
are insufficient.To remedy this insufficiency we partly expand JepaX in using
DSML. This paper is leaving out some details.

NML, the generic term for 'Note Markup Language'. (Note Markup
Language) NML is the generic term that focuses on the writing and described
the embellished information of lecture data rendered by the lecturer and the stu-

dents. The DTD of this NML schematize important elements as shown in Figure 3 . NML use the lecture data writing like enclosures, underlines and other markings information as a starting point. These markings point to the importance or questionable aspect by the marking (mean), the annotations about Figure use the marking (src.) . The link information in relation to the markings are also described by the marking 'link'. At this time, because the detailed links to XML content of a lecture data are still confusing, the links becomes the ID of the lecture data and the 'position', the annotations become the way of using the image files. Through NML, the lecturer writing on the blackboard and the students taking of notes, are all linked with NML and can be described through NML linked external instances. In this, the data of the classroom lecture as written on the board by the lecturer can be projected automatically as lecture data to the students. There is no need for the students to write anything down. The things felt and thought are duly recorded and made highly comprehensible. Also the lecturer and the students notes are described collectively by NML making it possible for friends to exchange notes. Plus it makes it possible to share discoveries and ideas, analyzing the notes taken by the lecturer and the students makes it possible to ascertain that the lecturer and students are following the same path and to draw the attention to points difficult to understand or thought to be of high importance.

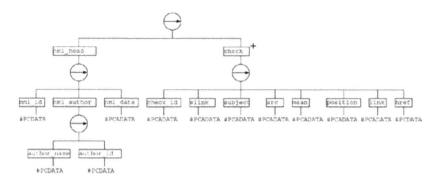

Fig. 3. DTD for NML

2.4   EML, NML, DSML Connection

In the DL Markup Language in order to concentrate on the lecture events the EML becomes the focus of the DSML. The different contents described by NML and DSML are linked in the lecture events described by EML. For example, the scene of a lecturer writing on the blackboard, this lecture event will be described by EML. The information resulting from the board writing will be used through NML, and mutually with the EML, as mentioned previously will be referred an

ID, and the link will take place. In addition, the lecture data described by DSML will be linked with the information described by NML. As well, in order to create DL Markup Language contents, the links are conducted simultaneously with the gathering of information from the classroom lecture. In a conventional lecture, once the lecture is over there is a need for checking the lecture images, the time matching of the lecture images and the lecture data called authoring, in order to get Asynchronous DL it is necessary to consecrate a considerable amount of time. With the DL Markup Language content method (as the lecturer turned a page) this lecture event is being stored, the link is done automatically, Asynchronous DL has been made possible even right after the lecture. Again as EML is being created it is possible to transmit through simulated streaming, at the same time to conduct Real Time DL and the content may also be used for DL Markup Language thus it has become possible to add further flexibility to DL.

3   Implementation of a Prototype

In this chapter we will introduce a new DL system under a DL Markup Language content described by DLML. This system is constituted of the Real Time DL and the Asynchronous DL systems. The guidelines of Real Time DL are presented in Figure 4 and the guidelines of Asynchronous DL are presented in Figure 5. Furthermore, in these figures it appears that NML and EML themselves interchange, this is a guideline Figure, in fact it is the data described by EML and the data described by NML that are interchanged.

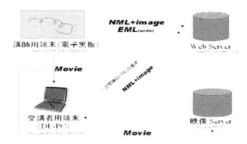

Fig. 4. The Real Time DL

About the environment and equipment of the system.

- Lecturer terminal / Student terminal : Windows NT 4.0 Touch Sensitive Liquid Crystal screen, Internet Explorer 5.0
- Web Server : Sun Spark StationApache web server 1.3.4 Perl5.004 + GD
- Images recording / transmission server : Windows NT 4.0

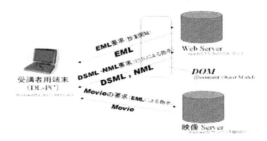

Fig. 5. The Asynchronous DL systems

About the environment in the laboratory on Fast Ethernet, was realized using TCP/IP protocol. The server program mainly described by Perl, the client program by Java and Java Script . EML and NML used Microsoft XML.DOM. Next we will mention about all the necessary parts to realize the system

3.1   Terminal Used by the Audience

The present system is illustrated on a terminal like the one on Figure 8 . This terminal is formed of two displays, the display above is an ordinary liquid crystal display, and below a touch sensitive liquid display is used. The display below can be accessed using a special electronic pen, using the software mouse emulation you can get the same function in the mouse and the pen. This is using the two display liquid crystal Windows NT multi-display function connected to one PC. Further to get this system to work the lecturer and the students both need WindowsNT with OS , Internet Explorer 5.0 or up, a PentiumIII500MHz, more than 128 MB RAM terminal.

3.2   Real Time DL

Extracting Info from Events. We are in the lecture , the lecturer is about to start. The students who are attending the lecture will witness many events. This time, during the prototype the attendants will extract the elements mentioned below.

- Writing. The lecturer and the students are both writing on an electronic blackboard or otherwise on a DL-PC they draw a circle, or a underline or write notes along with the classroom data which appear in relation to what is happening. It all takes place under the system, 'when', 'where' and 'what' (it designs the ID of the NML). It is possible to extract these events.
- The joint blackboard writing. In the event where the students and the lecturer are making use of images for communication they will use the joint blackboard. The things written on this page will be transferred to the system or extracted when the page is changed or when an attendant presses the save button.

Fig. 6. Prototype terminal used by the audience

– Changes in a document (Turning of the page). The lecturer can turn the page by clicking (touching) the scale-down document icon . The system will pick up the event upon the click. When the page is turned the event is extracted.

Lecture event writing to EML. The lecture events that the system extracted automatically and those of the lecturer are transmitted to the WWW server and saved as described by EML. Below is an example of EML.

```
ex.)
  <event seqnum="4" security="public">
    <time><begin>00:08</begin></time>
    <who>
      <name>ENKAKU TAROU</name>
      <role>professor_man</role>
      <name_id>t00001</name_id>
    </who>
    <towhom>
      <to1><role1>all</role1></to1>
      <to2>
        <name2>figure 1</name2>
        <role2>image</role2>
        <name2_id/>
      </to2>
    </towhom>
    <do>important</do>
    <result>NML:a1</result>
  </event>
```

Explanation, a <time> tag shows the time of the event mutually posted in relation to the starting time of the lecture. <who> tag establishes the person or the factor that initiated the event. <towhom> tag establishes the subject of the event. <do> points to the event key word. And <result> to what was created by the event. Namely, in the EML above professor Enkaku Taro makes a point to everybody of the importance of Figure 1 . This type of information will be stored in the system as text file.

3.3   Asynchronous DL System

In this system, the Asynchronous DL can be accessed as DL Markup Language content. As in Figure 1, the event described by EML are used as the key. The information NML and DSML will call the lecture images and the different linked content will be reenacted. The reproduction will be under the DL Markup Language content as event driven . In a classroom lecture, depending on the lecture event many types of contents can be created and using distance learning in relation to the events of a lecture it is made possible to present every type of content, thus our aim is a virtual reality reenactment of a classroom lecture. Also, in order to transmit the non-verbal information that is being shared unconsciously in distance learning we developed the following method of reenaction.

Non-verbal information reenacted by animation. In this system, in order to transmit non-verbal information in distance learning we make use of animation. First, in relation to the lecturer and the students we prepared in advance a variety of images.

- It is important
- Questions, doubts
- Raise hand
- Interesting point
- At work

As for these images, the EML data stored in the last chapter are returned to their original state and at the same time the background color is also changed. In this instance, as shown in the example of Figure 6 and Figure 7 . In Figure 6 the students are showing a feeling that it is of importance and in Figure 7 they are showing that they have trouble in understanding the content. This information about expressions are due to the fact that the description of lecture events related to the students are gathered and managed by EML. For example, in Figure 6 many of the students will use marking because they consider that the data from this part of the lecture are of importance . In this system, if 30% of the students use that particular marking a student character will appear to express 'important' . If more than 70% of the students used the marking to express, 'important', 'question, doubt' or 'interesting', the background color will change to a corresponding color. 'Important' will be the color red, 'question or doubt' will be yellow and 'interesting' will be blue. Through these, while seeing the lecture images the students can get a feling of the atmosphere of the classroom without having to pay too much attention.

Fig. 7. A reenactment of the classroom lecture and animation (an example of the of transmitting the atmosphere of a feeling of importance in the classroom.)

Fig. 8. A reenactment of the classroom lecture and animation (an example of the of transmitting the atmosphere of a feeling of doubt in the classroom).

4   Evaluation of the Prototype

Using the experiment of the prototype in the last chapter we have done this evaluation.

- Answers to the survey from the lecturers point of view, after trying the system.
- Answers to the survey from the students point of view (Asynchronous DL), after trying the system.

Not only about this trial but we also had the students to try WBT and we made a comparative evaluation. In a third grade class of Science and Technology comprising 20 students, we took the level of approval using 1 as the top mark, they answered in a 5 steps evaluation. The results of the survey are shown below
.

4.1   Lecturers Survey about the Use of the System

1. Do you think that the automatic creation of an Asynchronous DL (storing of information) content is convenient?
2. Did the use of Asynchronous DL content give you the impression of using a Real Time DL ?
3. Did you feel psychologically different from a conventional lecture giving the fact that all your actions were being recorded?

Fig. 9. The result of the lecturers survey

4.2   Students Survey about the Use of the System

1. Did you get a deeper understanding with electronic annotations?
2. Did you get an experience of virtual reality class without a feeling of uneasiness?
3. Could you grasp the feeling of an atmosphere of virtual reality?
4. Did you get more information than in a conventional WBT lesson?

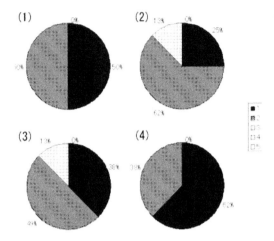

Fig. 10. The result of the students survey

4.3   Observations

Summary of the observations from the survey results.

Using this system just as in a conventional class the lecturer can conduct a classroom lecture without a feeling of uneasiness. Also we found from the survey that the reenacting of DL Markup Language content automatically produced by the storing of info through Asynchronous DL allows to get a sufficient understanding of the class. Further the volume of information surpasses the one that can be gathered in the WBT system and the events occurring in the classroom lecture described by animation characters, and the change in background colors were also appreciated. Therefore , we believe that the non-verbal information can be transmitted in a classroom lecture. The lecture events being extracted and stored at real time means that there is no need for a subsequent cumbersome authoring. We believe that we were able of offering a virtual reality experience of a classroom lecture and realized an Asynchronous DL content.

We know from the result of the survey that the lecturers were able to deliver their lecture without a feeling of uneasiness. But they felt some reluctance about having their every action recorded. Everything recorded in the classroom lecture is being stored and used in Asynchronous DL put them under pressure making them feel that they are not allowed to make any mistake. It has thus become necessary to make a study about the development of a way to submit the Distance Language Markup Language content to some form of correction.

5   Conclusion

This paper has pointed to the insufficiency of non-verbal information in DL and the problems incurred when authoring the Asynchronous DL content. The actions, reactions and interactions of the lecturer and the students are the essence of the definition of a classroom lecture. We suggested the use of the generic term EML for the storage of lecture events and of NML for the storage of writing. Using the lecture images, data and events as an axis we promoted the creation of a DL Markup Language content with events stored at real time and the usage of this stored information in an Asynchronous DL system. The result of an evaluation made after a factual experiment of a prototype.

- The lectures were carried without uneasiness as in a conventional classroom.
- Asynchronous DL content can automatically be created.
- In a DL Markup System the links between the lecture images and the lecture data is realized smoothly.
- In a DL Markup System the non-verbal information can be transmitted to a certain degree.

It is fair to say that the lecture content that was created, namely a DL system using linkage is highly efficient. In the near future, we intend to introduce and evaluate a full-fledged system in a large scale environment.

References

1. Keiko Ookawa, Sayuri Ijyuin, Jun Murai: School of Internet - Internet School on Internet. IPSJ Paper. (1999)
2. Yoshimi Shiraishi: Life-long education and distance Learning Issuing office of Tamagawa University (1990)
3. Abe, Tokuda, Kinoshita, Shiratori: Multimedia Contents authoring. IPSJ paper. (1997) 39-46

An Authoring Tool for Building Adaptive Learning Guidance Systems on the Web

José A. Macías and Pablo Castells

E.T.S. Informática, Universidad Autónoma de Madrid. Campus de Cantoblanco,
28049 Madrid, Spain.
{j.macias,pablo.castells}@uam.es

Abstract. In the field of guided learning on the Internet we present, in this paper, an interactive tool for designing intelligent tutoring systems on the web. Our tool makes easier the creation of an ontology describing the content model for a given course. Such ontology contains information about classes and instances, reflecting the structure and components for the later creation of an adaptive course, using our web-based runtime course manager system. Our authoring tool generates XML code to improve course understanding as well as transportability and processing by our runtime system, which means that the generated code will reflect, in an easier way, the course structure and contents, being readable for most of users and course designers.

1 Introduction

The rapid development of the Internet in the last decade has given rise to new research in web-based educational technology for the creation of Intelligent Tutoring Systems (ITS) that support user adaptation and guidance. ITS's are computer-based instructional systems that have separate data bases, or knowledge bases, for instructional content (specifying what to teach), and for teaching strategies (specifying how to teach), and attempt to use inferences about a student's mastery of topics to dynamically adapt instruction [9]. Most of the efforts in this field are focused on providing intelligence on the web by means of Adaptive Hypermedia Systems (AHS). An Adaptive Hypermedia System or engine may change the content and presentation of hypermedia nodes and may alter the link structure or annotate links, based on a user model [5].

On the other hand, creating and manipulating web applications is, in general terms, an awkward task for non-expert users. In fact, nowadays there is a growing need for ITS authoring tools [10]. However few approaches exist for evaluation and generalisation because they are very difficult and expensive to build. The development of these tools is always driven by pragmatics and usability issues. In this direction, some authoring tools try to make easier the way of coding and processing course and educational information on the web, using an ontology for structuring contents and presentation. An ontology is an explicit specification of a shared conceptualisation. Its usefulness for information presentation, information integration and system development has been demonstrated recently [12].

J. Liu et al. (Eds.): AMT 2001, LNCS 2252, pp. 268–278, 2001.
© Springer-Verlag Berlin Heidelberg 2001

The main goal of our work is to provide an authoring tool, called PERSEUS, used to defined an ontological representation of course domain and model. Such tool allows the designer to create adaptive educational applications based on PEGASUS (Presentation modelling Environment for Generic Adaptive hypermedia Support Systems), our generic runtime system for developing adaptive hypermedia presentations in the Internet. The objective of PEGASUS is to provide course designers with a simple specification paradigm for defining non-trivial aspects of adaptive presentation independently from contents [6,7]. PERSEUS provides an object-oriented user interface for PEGASUS, improving generality and usability for building courses in different domains.

2   Related Work

The development of web-based strategies for creating adaptive software has yield considerable advancements in the adaptive hypermedia context over the last few years, with systems like DCG [14,15], ELM-ART [16], Interbook [1] and TANGOW [2]. ELM-ART and DCG use an explicit representation of domain concepts, interrelated in a prerequisite graph. DCG includes a planner that guides the student along a path to reach goal concepts starting from already-known concepts. ELM-ART uses a sophisticated system to estimate the knowledge acquired by the user in relation to a concept map of the course, according to which the system dynamically proposes the student a path to follow at each moment. While in ELM-ART and DCG the structure of courses is fixed, being the student itinerary what varies, TANGOW generates the course structure at runtime. TANGOW models student activity in the form of a hierarchy of tasks that represent didactic units that the student can perform. ATLAS [8] allows the fully interactive construction of courses that adapt automatically to the student's characteristics and her/his behaviour while taking the course. The designer interacts with the tool by using an intuitive visual language based on the direct manipulation of elements involved in the course. The tool takes care of the transition between a teacher's understanding of the course and the representation model of the underlying system.

The systems mentioned above lack an authoring tool that provides design support, except TANGOW, which uses ATLAS as an authoring tool for course design. ATLAS works over a fixed ontology (the TANGOW model), while PERSEUS, as a continuation of our previous work in ATLAS, allows the designer to build his/her own ontologies. In PERSEUS, course construction is achieved by defining a content model, by means of an intuitive user interface that allows the course designer to build general objects and class ontologies as basic tools for the design of the educational system.

Some systems, like KA2 [12], and Eon ITS [11], are focused on ontology engineering. KA2 has been conceived for semantic knowledge retrieval from the web, building on knowledge created in the knowledge-acquisition community. To structure knowledge, an ontology has been built in an international collaboration of researchers. The ontology constitutes the basis to annotate WWW documents of the knowledge acquisition community in order to enable intelligent access to these documents and to infer implicit knowledge from explicitly stated facts and rules from the ontology. the EON ITS uses an ontology to define the types of topics and topic links allowed in a semantic net representation of the tutor's knowledge called the "Topic Network". Here, the ontologies are not specific to the domain, but appropriate for a class of domains. The ontologies specify a number of other things, such as topic properties (e.g. difficulty, importance), and allowed values in the student model. Knowledge is structured in EON using several mechanisms. The first is the hierarchy of basic objects: Lessons, Topics, Topic Levels, and Presentations. The second method consists of allowing arbitrary classifications of Topics and Topic links in the topic network. Given the right ontology, all the hierarchies, lattices and networks can be represented with topic networks. The third mechanism is the Topic Levels themselves. In PERSEUS, the underlying knowledge presentation is similar in many respects to EON. Our tool has only a few fixed classes previously defined. This way, each designer completes or builds his/her own class hierarchy depending on the content model of the course, or presentation, to be designed.

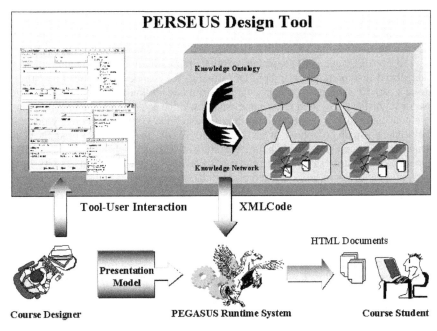

Fig. 1. A general view of our adaptive educational system, where PERSEUS is integrated as an authoring tool for developing course contents. Both the domain model and the presentation model will be provided to PEGASUS for generating the appropriate course feedback to the final user

3   PERSEUS as a Design Tool

PERSEUS (Presentation ontology buildER for cuStom lEarning sUpport Systems) is an interactive tool for designing web-based adaptive courses. The PERSEUS interface allows designers to model courses by defining and creating an ontology of objects that are used to build adaptive presentations for the educational context (Figure 1).

This tool can generate XML code from ontologies created by the designer in the PERSEUS environment. Such XML code will be processed by PEGASUS, our runtime management system used to execute the right sequence of steps in order for any given course to be presented to the final user.

The steps needed for creating a content model are, to begin with, the creation of a class hierarchy, and, in the second place, the creation of objects that are instances of the previously defined classes. To achieve this, we just have to provide the right values for attributes and relations used to specify a certain course [6,7].

3.1 Creating a Knowledge Ontology

We can create any class hierarchy by just opening the class edition windows. PERSEUS provides a few predefined classes: *DomainObject, Topic, Fragment* and *AtomicFragment*. New classes can be defined by providing a class name, and the parent class from which the relevant attributes and relations are inherited. This way, we can build a whole hierarchy for a given domain. For each class, we can create class attributes, by just giving a name and an attribute type (string, number, or boolean). Later, a presentation model can be defined by associating a presentation to each class of the hierarchy.

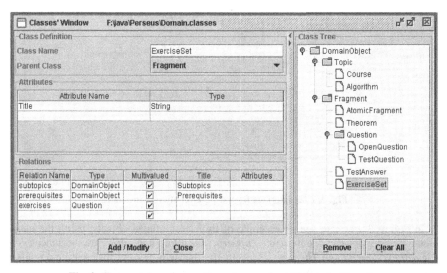

Fig. 2. Class ontology for creating a lesson about Dijkstra's Algorithm

In order to relate a class to others, we can create class relations. A class relation has a name, a given type (corresponding to the related class type), a relation title, and a boolean value to indicate whether the relation is multi-valued or not. In addition, relations can have attributes that are defined interactively by clicking on the appropriate table cell (see Figure 2) and filling-in text fields in a pop-up dialog, where we specify the attribute name, type (string, number, or boolean), and a default value for each attribute.

The result of creating classes is a personalised tree-view of the hierarchy (right panel in Figure 2), where we can navigate by clicking on every node and deleting, if we want, the selected information. We show on Figure 2 a real example of a class ontology for creating a lesson about Dijkstra's Algorithm. In this Figure, we can see how some kinds of classes: *Algorithm, Course, Question,* and so forth, have been defined, starting from the default hierarchy mentioned previously. This ontology will be used for instantiating a course about graph theory, as we describe next.

3.2   Creating a Knowledge Network

Once a class hierarchy has been defined, specific objects or class instances can be created. The interface to achieve this task is shown in Figure 3, where the user can create objects from a specific class hierarchy.

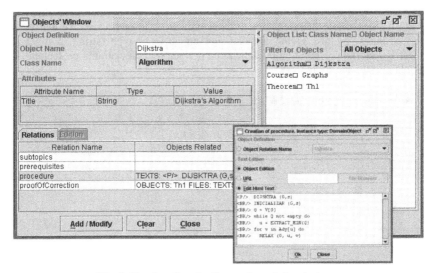

Fig. 3. User interface for the creation of class instances

In Figure 3, one can see an example of three instantiated objects, using the class hierarchy previously mentioned. *Dijkstra, Graphs,* and *th1,* are instances of *Algorithm, Course,* and *Theorem,* respectively, that will be used for creating a course about graph algorithms. As showed, each object has its own relations, based on the previously created class hierarchy. If we look at the *procedure* relation defined for the *Dijkstra* object (from the *Algorithm* class), we can see that an atomic fragment has been defined (right window of Figure 3), containing the algorithm pseudocode written in HTML. This way, we can create objects and relate them to each other in order to build different structures for a given lesson or a complete course.

3.3 Generating XML Code

After creating class instances and relations between them, the next step is to generate XML code from the complete design. By clicking on the *Generate XML Code* menu command, PERSEUS automatically generates and saves into a file the XML information about the design. In Figure 4 we can see the XML code generated for the previously created Dijkstra's Algorithm object.

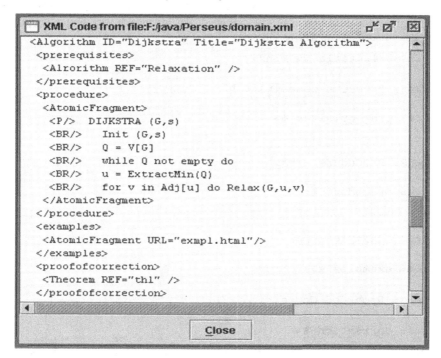

Fig. 4. Window showing the generated XML code for the *Dijkstra´s Algorithm* course object

Since the design information is directly generated in XML, the course information is highly portable. In particular, this makes it easy for any kind of user to read and understand, in a very simple way, the objects and the relations between them.

3.4 Post-processing of XML Code in PEGASUS

Finally, PEGASUS will create dynamically all course pages after reading the XML code from PERSEUS. This will be the last step for completing the final presentation.

PEGASUS allows associating a presentation model to ontology classes. The PEGASUS presentation model consists of presentation templates and presentation rules. Presentation templates define what parts (attributes and relations) of a knowledge item must be included in its presentation and in what order, their visual appearance and layout. Presentation rules are responsible for generating adaptive presentation constructs, involving relations between domain objects from very succinct high-level descriptions given in templates.

PEGASUS templates are defined by using an extension of HTML based on JavaServer Pages™ (JSP) [13], that allows inserting control statements (between `<%` and `%>`) and Java expressions (between `<%=` and `%>`) in the HTML code. In these templates, the designer can use all the presentation constructs of the HTML language (lists, tables, frames, links, forms, etc.), and insert, using very simple Java expressions, the domain items to be presented. For instance, a very simple template for class *Algorithm* could be as follows:

```
<h2> <%= title %> </h2>

<h3> Previous concepts </h3>

<%= prerequisites %>


<h3> Procedure </h3>

<%= procedure %>


<h3> Examples </h3>

<%= examples %>

<h3> Proof of Correction </h3>

<%= correction %>
```

In these templates the presentation author only needs to refer to attributes and relations of the presented class (shown in bold in the example). The presentation system takes care internally of aspects like automatically handling lists (multivalued relations like the examples of an algorithm), or recursively applying templates to referenced objects according to their class (e.g. the proof-of-correction *Theorem*'s of an algorithm). The resulting page for Dijkstra's algorithm with this presentation template can be seen in Figure 5, where HTML elements surrounding the algorithm presentation (frame structure with contextual index on the left and *Previous / Next* buttons at the bottom) come from the presentation template for the root class *KnowledgeUnit*.

The template definition language supports the introduction of adaptive elements by using conditionals. For instance, in the preceding example, the presented information could be conditioned to the student's level of expertise, including all available examples when the student is a beginner, and a single example for more advanced students, showing the proof of correction only if it is relevant and not too difficult for the student:

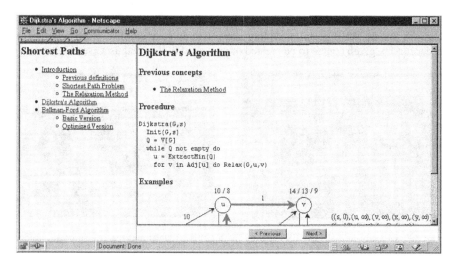

Fig. 5. Generated web page for a topic of type *Algorithm*

```
<% if (user.expertise < 0.5) { %> <%= examples %>  <% }
%>

<% else { %> <%= examples.upto(1) %> <% } %>

<% if (correction.relevant && correction.difficulty <
user.expertise) { %>

<h3> Proof of Correction </h3> <%= correction %> <% }
%>
```

The expression language for templates includes other facilities that allow, for instance, cutting down, filtering or sorting lists according to an arbitrary comparison function, generating trees and linked lists by traversing a relation, or forcing the generation of hypermedia links. The basic template language allows the specification of a wide set of non-trivial presentations by using a very simple syntax. However the designer can write arbitrarily complex Java code inside the templates themselves.

4 Putting All Together into HADES

As we described previously, the main goal of our work is to build a complete adaptive system in which any given course can be presented to the final user. Up to now we have described different parts of the technology used to build adaptive presentations, however a certain mechanism is required to integrate the PERSEUS design tool and the PEGASUS runtime system for creating and managing available courses.

For this purpose, we have developed HADES (Hypermedia ADaptive Educational Server), a main WEB portal providing users with an easy and fast WEB interface in order for any given course to be created or presented to the final user (see Figure 6).

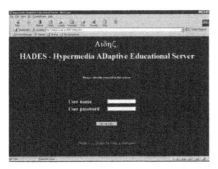 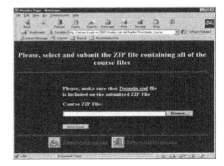

Fig. 6. Two snapshots of HADES showing the login page (left) and the course creation page (right)

Users are registered into HADES by completing an initial form. Once the user is registered and logged to HADES, the system automatically captures the main characteristics of the user platform (e.g. language, screen resolution, navigator type and version, and so on). Moreover, each user can have one o more specific roles in the system (student, course designer, or administrator). HADES stores and reads all this information from a distributed data base management system, and it updates the user model in response to actions performed by the user in the system. HADES also has specific administration options for advanced users in order to manage users, roles and general system configuration.

To add a new course, the designer has to create a ZIP file, containing all the files required for the course construction (the XML domain file built with PERSEUS as described in previous sections, HTML fragments, JPG images, presentation templates and rules, etc.). Then the system will store and organise automatically all courseware elements, updating the HADES database of available courses for later delivery (see Figure 7).

HADES integrates PEGASUS as a runtime system for running all courses and presentations requested by any connected user. An overview of the global architecture of the system can be seen in Figure 7, where we can see PERSEUS, PEGASUS and the HADES portal resulting in a complete system for the generation and support of WEB presentations.

5   Conclusions

In the context of web-based adaptive learning, PERSEUS, an interactive authoring tool for building adaptive tutoring systems, has been introduced. Our tool allows the course designer to model course information under an object-oriented paradigm, creating an appropriated ontology to define courses. Course information is translated into XML code, which makes easier the course post-processing and portability to

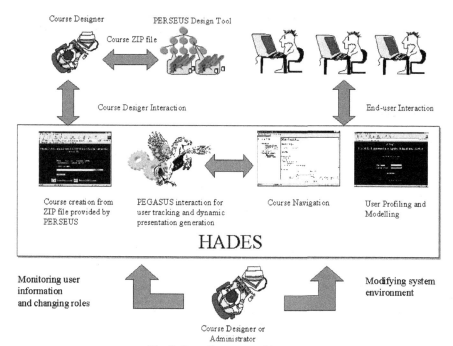

Fig. 7. Overall system architecture

other runtime systems like PEGASUS, our adaptive course management system. PEGASUS generates the course presentation from a presentation model defined using templates coded using JSP technology.

In addition to a tool like PERSEUS to build domain models for representing course contents, another kind of tool for creating PEGASUS presentation models is needed. The main idea of a presentation design tool is to be able, for course designers, to specify the way that the course information generated by PERSEUS will be showed to the final user. In this direction, we are currently working on a tool that infers changes to how course pages are generated, by allowing users to edit system-supplied pages directly with a basic tool like Netscape Composer. This means making it possible to infer changes, in a automatic way, on course presentation. Since such tool operates as an automatic inference system, it will get information from user actions, a modified course page in this case, and will produce adaptive changes on saved course information. The tool will be based on the programming by example paradigm [3,4] and will be integrated into HADES.

PERSEUS, PEGASUS and HADES, are being developed in Java™ (JDK 1.3), using XLM/JDOM. PEGASUS and HADES use JavaServer Pages™ [13] for dynamic page generation. A version of PERSEUS is available from http://astreo.ii.uam.es/~atlas/perseus/perseus.html. HADES can be accessed at http://astreo.ii.uam.es:8081.

Acknowledgements. The work reported in this paper is being partially supported by the Spanish Interdepartmental Commission of Science and Technology (CICYT), project number TEL1999-0181.

References

1. Brusilovsky, P., Eklund, J., Schwarz, E.: Web-based Education for all: a Tool for the Development of Adaptive Courseware. Computer Networks and ISDN Systems, 30, pp. 1-7, 1998.
2. Carro, R.M., Pulido, E., Rodríguez, P.: Dynamic generation of adaptive Internet-based courses. Journal of Network and Computer Applications, v. 22, pp. 249-257, 1999.
3.. Castells, P. and Szekely, P.: Presentation Models by Example. In Design, Specification and Verification of Interactive Systems '99, D.J. Duke and A. Puerta (eds.), pp. 100-116. Springer-Verlag, Viena 1999.
4. Cypher, A. (ed.): Watch What I Do: Programming by Demonstration. The MIT Press, 1993.
5.. De Bra, Paul.: Design Issues in Adaptive Web-Site Development. Proceedings of the Second Workshop on Adaptive Systems and User Modeling on the World Wide Web. pp. 29-39 Toronto 1999.
6. Macías. J.A. and Castells, P..: Adaptive Hypermedia Presentation Modeling for Domain Ontologies. To appear in Proceedings of 10th International Conference on Human-Computer Interaction (HCII '2001). New Orleans (Louisiana), August 2001.
7. Macías, J.A. and Castells, P.: A Generic Presentation Modeling System for Adaptive Web-based Instructional Applications. To appear in Proceedings of ACM Conference on Human Factors in Computing Systems (CHI'2001), Extended Abstracts. Seattle (Washington), April 2001.
8. Macías, J.A. and Castells, P..: Interactive Design of Adaptive Courses. 2° Simposio Internacional de Informática Educativa (SIIE'2000). Puertollano (Ciudad Real), 2000.
9. Murray, T. : Authoring Intelligent Tutoring Systems: An analysis of the state of the art. International Journal of Artificial Intelligence in Education, Vol. 10, pp. 89-129, 1999.
10. Murray, T.: Authoring Knowledge Based Tutors: Tools for Content, Instructional Strategy, Student Model, and Interface Design. Journal of the Learning Sciences, Vol. 7, No. 1, pp. 5-64, 1998.
11. Murray, T.: Special Purpose Ontologies and the Representation of Pedagogical Knowledge. In Proceedings of International Conference for the Learning Sciences (ICLS-96), Evanston, IL, 1996. AACE: Charlottesville, VA. 1996.
12. Staab, S. et all. Semantic Community Web Portals. Proceedings of the Ninth International World Wide Web Conference. Amsterdam, May 15-19, 2000.
13. Sun Microsystems, Inc.: Java Server Pages™ Technology. http://java.sun.com/products/jsp.
14. Vassileva, J.: Dynamic Courseware Generation: at the Cross Point of CAL, ITS and Authoring. Proceedings of International Conference on Computers in Education (ICCE'95). Singapoore, pp. 290-297. 1995
15. Vassileva, J.: Dynamic Courseware Generation on the WWW. Proceedings 8th World Conference of the AIED Society. Kobe, pp. 498-505, Japan, 1997.
16. Weber, G. and Specht, M.: User modeling and Adaptive Navigation Support in WWW-based Tutoring Systems. Proceedings 6th International Conference on User Modeling (UM97). Sardinia, Italy, 1997.

A Framework of Caring Interaction by a Network Model of Client's Concepts Based on a Nursing Theory and Naive Psychological Approaches

Akira Notsu, Osamu Katai, and Hiroshi Kawakami

Kyoto University, Sakyo-ku, kyoto 606-8501, JAPAN,
katai@i.kyoto-u.ac.jp,
http://www.symlab.sys.i.kyoto-u.ac.jp/

Abstract. A framework of "caring interaction" via network model representation of client's concepts on a Nursing Theory and Naive Psychological approaches is introduced. The main gist in this research is a sophisticated network organization of various messages from clients and pieces of knowledge in the related field some of which may be issued from the persons who care them. As the bases of this network modeling, a famous theory of nursing, the Roy Adaptation model, and also Heider's theory of Perceptual Balance based on his Naive Psychology are introduced. Heider's theory provides us with a method to analyze the perceptual consistencies ("perceptual balance") among the messages and the pieces of knowledge. This analysis is carried out by detecting these inconsistencies involved in the network model, where the detection can be done automatically. These inconsistencies are then related to various "modes of caring interaction" via the Roy Adaptation model of nursing. Hence, this network model is expected as an agent framework which provides us with an effective way of "caring interaction".

Keywords. Nursing Theory, Caring, Perceptual Balance, Naive Psychology, Agent

1 Introduction

In this paper, we will propose a framework of caring interaction based on a Nursing Theory and an Interpersonal Psychological approach referred to as Naive Psychology. The essential point here is the way to organize various messages from clients and pieces of knowledge on the related fields. In this paper, we adopted as these frameworks, a famous theory of nursing, the Roy Adaptation model, and also Heider's theory on Cognitive Balance based on his Naive Psychology. These bases provide us with a sophisticated way of organizing messages and pieces of knowledge to derive effective caring interactions with clients. In Section 2, a brief survey of nursing theories in shown, and then Roy's theory of nursing is introduced. In Section 3, Heider's theory of Naive Psychology and the notion of

J. Liu et al. (Eds.): AMT 2001, LNCS 2252, pp. 279–290, 2001.

Perceptual (Cognitive) Balance are introduced. In Section 4, these methods are integrated into a novel network modeling of clients suitable for effective Caring Interaction.

2   Nursing Theories and the Roy Adaptation Model

2.1   General Aspects on Nursing Theories

Nursing theories are concerned with inventing and discovering various focal concepts and methods of nursing by examining various events and their relevance in nursing interventions with the purpose of describing, explaining and prescribing caring processes. They provide us with basic frameworks and aspects for organizing various pieces of knowledge, information and events in nursing processes. The monumental book "Notes on Nursing: What It Is and What Is It not" by Florence Nightingale had not been noticed for many years. After 1950 [1], various theories motivated by the Notes have been developed. These theories can be categorized into four groups: Environmental Theories, Need-Oriented Theories, System Theories, and Interaction-Oriented Theories [2]. Among these, we will employ the Roy Adaptation Model that belongs to the System Theories.

2.2   The Roy Adaptation Model[3][4][5]

The "Roy Adaptation Model" of nursing regards a human being as an adaptation system. The clients' adaptive behavior is regarded as the products of four kinds of "Adaptive Modes" (Fig. 1): Physiological Mode, Self-concept Mode, Role Function Mode, Interdependence Mode.

Thus, environments are regarded to consist of stimuli that are inputs to yield clients' responses in the Roy Adaptation Model. Nurses modify stimuli to promote the clients adaptation in these adaptation modes.

Fig. 1. Human being as an adaptation system

According to her definition, whether a client action being adaptive or not is given as it being effective or not for attaining the goal of the client such as survival, development and maturation. These adaptation modes are regarded to be adaptive response systems of human being by processing various stimuli under various environmental changes.

2.3   Self-Concept Mode

"Self-concept" by Roy's definition is the product of various mediations and affections on oneself. This is given through examining own internal perceptions and also responses of other persons. As shown in Fig. 2, it consists of 'Physical self' and "Personal self". The physical self consists of corporal senses and body images. Corporal senses mean one's own direct perception of one's body such as "tired", "cheerful", etc. Body images are the way how one's appearance is regarded by oneself such as being fat, slender, attractive, etc. Personal self consists of three components as follows: Self-consistency, Self-ideal, Moral-ethical Self.

In this Self-concept Mode, clients' behavior is examined and assessed by referring to these factors, and the relevant stimuli to clients are assessed by categorizing them into those related to cognition, development, learning, others' responses, maturity crisis and coping control, by which the goal of nursing can be derived.

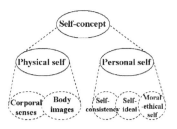

Fig. 2. Self-concept and its constituents

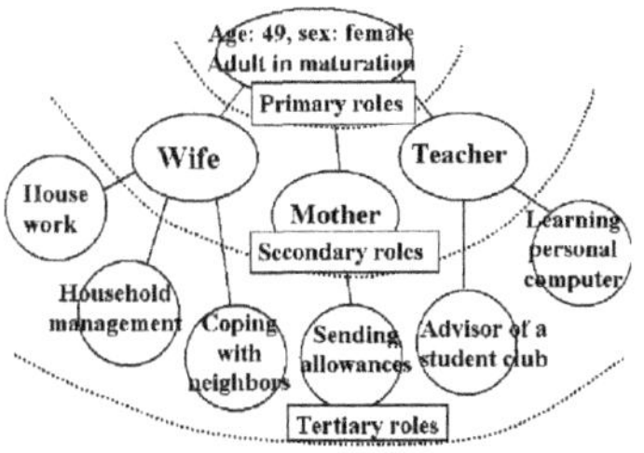

Fig. 3. Classification of roles in Role Function Mode

2.4   Role Function Mode

Role is a unit of social function and is classified into Primary, Secondary and Tertiary Roles as depicted in Fig.3. A primary role is given by one's age, sex, and developmental state mainly prescribed by one's age such as "a boy before entering primary school with age five" and "a girl in young age with the age of sixteen" are examples of the primary role. A secondary role is related to pursing specified social roles and hence is usually fixed such as being a "father", "parent", "mechanical", etc. A tertiary role, on the other hand, is freely chosen and is temporally set such as being a coach of junior football, being a member of a student club, etc. that will not affect other roles.

2.5   Interdependence Mode

By "interdependence" we mean a highly intimate interpersonal relationship, and the "Interdependence Mode" is used to maintain appropriateness and social wholeness of a client, which consists of dependent and independent actions. Everyone needs to be loved, supported, evaluated and respected by others and also to respond to others. The important thing is to balance dependence against independence. The key point here is interactions between the clients and others, while in Physiological Adaptation mode and Self-concept mode the key points are on the clients' side solely.

Usually, the important and related persons are called "Significant Others" or "Support Systems", and the mutual satisfaction of needs at both sides are sought for by developing proper interactions and interrelationships, i.e., by balancing the dependence with the independence.

To cope with these needs, following various Modes of Adaptation may take place:

1. Support-seeking mode: These actions are used to attain certain goals by satisfying affective needs that may be proper or improper.
2. Attention-seeking mode: This mode is popular in children. For example, to speak loudly, to wear showy cloths and to play a practical joke develops to this mode.
3. Affection-seeking mode: This mode of adaptation is used to enhance and to build interrelationship with significant others in order to heal, guard or permit oneself.

2.6   Nursing Processes

As mentioned before, nursing processes in the Roy Adaptation Model focus on the four adaptation modes, and the Roy Adaptation Model consists of the following six steps:

1. Action assessment
2. Stimulus assessment
3. Nursing diagnosis
4. Goal setting
5. Nursing intervention
6. Evaluation

In this model, nurses use these six steps with respect to the four adaptation modes, i.e., the Physiological Mode, the Self-concept Mode, the Role Function Mode, and the Interdependence Mode. To repeat these steps until the goals of nursing are attained, that is, the clients can do proper actions. At any step, if necessary, the assessment of intervention is done to obtain precise indication of nursing and also of altering the stimuli.

3 Naive Psychology and Perceptual Balance

3.1 Naive Psychology and the Notion of Perceptual Balance

In the application of the nursing method in Section 2 with the aid of a Communication Message Board, we have to have a method to analyze the content of messages and the interrelationship among them. For this purpose, we will refer to the Naive Psychology or Common-Sense Psychology proposed by F. Heider [6]. He is famous for his Theory of Perceptual Balance or Cognitive Balance, usually referred to as P-O-X Theory. [7]-[11]

He analyzed words for expressing situations of a person ("Word Analysis"), and also situations ("Situation Analysis"), based on the Naive Psychology. He arrived at the basic underlying concepts for analyzing situations as follows: Relation Types:

1. Relations of experiencing or being affected
2. Relations of causing
3. Relations of can (being able to)
4. Relations of trying
5. Relations of wanting
6. Relations of belonging
7. Relations of ought and may
8. Sentiment Relations

Relations (1)-(7) other than Sentiment Relations (8) are called "Unit Formation Relations". All these kinds of relations are categorized into as being positive or negative, i.e., into (1)+, (1)−, (2)+, (2)−, ..., (8)+ and (8)−.

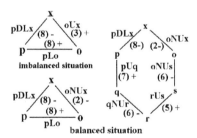

Fig. 4. Heider's perceptual balanced and unbalanced situation

He focused his attention to the consistency of these relations in very localized setting of situations, that is, the perceptual or cognitive balance of a person (noted as "p") with other person ("o") concerning an entity ("x"). For example, let us consider the case where

- P likes o (we have denoted as pLo: positive Sentiment Relation)
- O made a record cabinet (x) (oUx: positive Unit Formation Relation)
- P thinks that the record cabinet is poorly made (pDLx: negative Sentiment Relation)

This situation is shown in Fig. 4 and is regarded to be "imbalanced" or "unbalanced". The balance of this triangular system is defined as the sign of the product of the signs of these three arcs being (+). In this case, we have $(+)x(+)x(-) = (-)$, so the situation is imbalanced. The balanced situation can be accepted by p without "stress", while the imbalanced or unbalanced situation make p feel stressful and uncomfortable. The theory of Perceptual Balance by Heider says that an imbalanced state (situation) is altered to restore the balance of the system (situation). Fig. 5 depicts possible alterations of relations between the three entities, p, o and x, to restore balance.

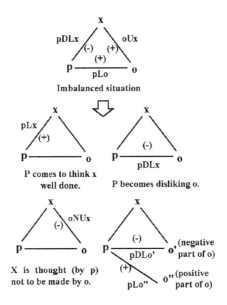

Fig. 5. Restoration of imbalanced situation

Even though this localized analysis reflects essential part of perceptual balance and hence provides the basis of various theories on cognitive or social balance, the situations to be analyzed is too localized and simple to cope with "Caring Communication" through message boards, where each mode corresponds not only to persons or entities, but also various messages on the boards. The balance in the message board is defined as each cycle in the graph structure of a message board having positive sign (+), when the sign is defined as the product of the signs in the cycle. [7][8][10][11]

4   Network Modeling of Clients

Based on the Roy Adaptation Model on nursing, it is expected to enhance the Adaptation Mode, particularly, in Self-concept Mode, Role function Mode and Interdependence Mode. As shown in Fig. 2, the Self-concept consists of Physical self and Personal self, and Personal self is of primal importance in this case. In the Interdependence Mode, three major adaptation modes, i.e., Support-seeking mode, Attention-seeking mode and Affection-seeking mode will be considered as mentioned in Section 2-B-c. The interesting point here is that the Direction of enhancement or intervention can be considerably dependent on the relation types. Roughly speaking, we can readily see the following correspondence between the relation types (in the Naive Psychology) and the basic notions in the Roy Adaptation Model:

1. Relation (message) of experiencing or being affected ⇔ Attention-seeking mode (Interdependence mode) Affection-seeking mode (Interdependent mode)
2. Relation (message) of causing ⇔ Support-seeking mode (Interdependent mode)
3. Relation (message) of can ⇔ Role function
4. Relation (message) of trying ⇔ Role function mode
5. Relation (message) of wanting ⇔ Self ideal mode (Self-concept)
6. Relation (message) of belonging ⇔ Role function mode
7. Relation (message) of ought and may ⇔ Moral-ethical self mode (Self- concept)
8. Sentiment Relation (sentiment message) ⇔ Self-consistency (Self-concept)

By the use of these message types, we can organize network model of clients based of the framework of the Roy adaptation model.

On this network models, we will incorporate "signs" ("+" or "-") to the links (arcs) by which we can regard these models as "signed graphs". The basic links in the conceptualization of adaptation modes such as self-concept mode, role mode and interdependence mode are given such as the ones shown in Fig. 6. We can see that these links should be associated with the positive sign (+). This is because these links basically stand for "is-a" links (class-subclass links), that is, upper nodes are more general concepts than the lower nodes, or equivalently, the lower nodes are more concrete than upper ones. The links bridging over the hierarchies of self-concept, Roe and Interdependence may have negative signs (-) depending on the real content of the relations between the nodes (concepts) bridged by the links. If the nodes are positively (negatively) related, the links are given with the positive (negative) sign "+" ("-"). This decision may be done by referring to the related social commonsense or by the judgment of the clients to be modeled.

In this network modeling, appropriate location and linking of nodes should be taken into account. This can be cone by taking note of contents of nodes which may necessitate manual commitment.

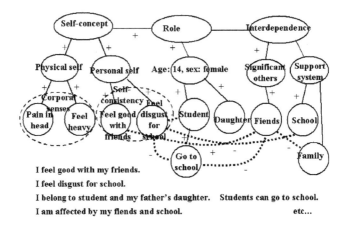

Fig. 6. Network model of the concepts on a client

5   Five Styles of Caring Interaction

These signed graphs (network) are usually of complex structures and may involve imbalanced cycles. The existence of imbalanced cycles corresponds to an occurrence of conflict that causes an adaptive behavior reducing the person's stress. For example, suppose that a person has said, "I want to play game more. But I have to study more." Then, we will have the network structure shown in Fig. 7. In the figure, the area encircled by broken lines shows the "focused" area. That is, the person focuses himself (herself) to the area in his mind. This area involves an imbalanced cycle. Hence, it is imbalanced.

5.1   Horizontal Shifting

The stress caused by this imbalance may be resolved by focusing on another area, which does not involve imbalanced cycles. Another way of resolution is to alter the judgment of means or objective form negative to positive or vice versa. For example, the following conversation between two persons, say A and B, goes along this line of resolution.

　　A: "I hate going to school."
　　B: "why?"
　　A: "I feel disgust for school."
　　B: "you feel good with your friends, don't you?"
　　Or B: "Really? School is enjoyable!"
　　By this "focus shifting", we can restore or maintain our balance and reduce mental stress. Fig. 8 shows this focus shifting. Let us consider a way of "caring interaction" by taking note of an imbalanced cycle in the focused area. Suppose that a "caring agent" is now communicating with a client, and the agent has constructed client's model by the use of above method of message analyses. The

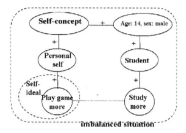

Fig. 7. An imbalanced state (cycle)

agent first search for the area of focus by the client and detect the imbalance in that area. This can be easily dose by analyzing the signed graph structure of the network model of the client.

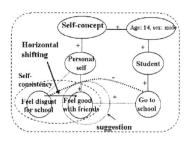

Fig. 8. Horizontal shifting for resolving imbalance

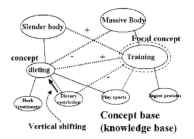

Fig. 9. Hierarchal network organization of concepts in the general knowledge on related fields

Then the agent searches for an appropriate way of "focus shifting" ("horizontal shifting") by moving the focused area apart from the imbalanced cycles.

5.2 Vertical Shifting

Also, the agent has to examine the linkage relations between the "hierarchies" of concepts in the related fields (Fig. 9). this "Concept base" is given by referring to the general conceptual hierarchies and by incorporating linkage relations into the hierarchies. These hierarchies are usually derived by "ontological" analysis of concepts [12][13]. These linkage relations are given with positive (+) signs or negative (−) signs depending on the effectiveness or the harmfulness of a concept (such as an objective) on another concept (such as a mean). By "vertically" shifting from a node (concept) to another node (concept), the sign change of linkage relations take place yielding restoration of balance in imbalanced focused area.

By the use of above resolving algorithm, we can implement caring interaction mechanism of agents.

5.3   Sign Alteration of Links

Another way for restoring balance is to directly change the sign of a link involved in an imbalanced cycle. This can only be done by interacting the client with communicating to persuade that he (or she) should alter the sign of the link by changing his way of evaluating or judging this relation.

In searching for the links whose sign should be altered, the notion of the Minimal Balancing Process [10][11] is important, by which efficient restoration of balance can be attained. In some cases, this efficient restoration is done by referring to the notion of dual graph of systems and the algorithm to derive minimal balancing. This algorithmic approach can easily be implemented by using agent-based approach.

5.4   Introduction of Other Concepts

The final way of restoration is to introduce alter nodes (concepts) into the network of concepts by referring to relevant concepts in the concept case in Fig. 9. This augmentation of the network has similar effects to the vertical shifting.

5.5   Passing to Direct Nursing Intervention

When this mechanization of caring interaction is difficult, the agent can pass the "core information" on the client to the person who will care the client. The core information in this case is the main cause ("mode") of the imbalance in the focused area. When we arrive, for instance, at the Role function mode, we use the nursing intervention in the Roy's Adaptation model. First the primary roles of a client are elucidated, and then we proceed to the secondary and the tertiary roles with assessing their importance. More precisely, the following steps are used:

1. Clarify the primary role of a client.
2. Specify proper developmental state of the client according to his primary role.
3. Specify the developmental tasks and the secondary roles for pursuing the tasks.
4. Gather relevant information on the primary and the secondary roles for pursuing the developmental tasks by referring to the self-concept adaptation mode and the interdependence mode of the client.
5. Compare the actual behavior with the role of the client by referring to social norms and constraints.
6. Assess the derived improper behaviors (that are outside the norms or constraints) by referring to the self-concept adaptation mode and the interdependence mode of the client.

7. Select the primary and the secondary roles as the relevant stimuli or factors that are related to the elucidated problems.

In the above procedure, it is of course important to reflect the explicit and the implicit meaning contained in the messages by which the inconsistency of relation type (3) or (6) (Role function mode) is caused.

6 Conclusion

We have introduced a framework of caring interaction that incorporates five kinds of interaction from (1) to (5). That is, (1) horizontal shifting and (2) vertical shifting of focused area in the network of key concepts prescribing the mental situation of clients and (3) sign alteration of links among the concepts, and also (4) introduction of other concepts related to the mental situation of the clients by referring to the hierarchical general structure of relevant concepts that are stored in the agent as its knowledgebase. The find interaction is (5) to rely on a person (say, a nurse) to make nursing commitment by passing her (him) relevant information on this commitment such as the key concepts or the linkage relation between the concepts that caused the imbalance of the clients' mental state.

The design concept of this caring interaction is still under construction. This is because we should be careful and serious enough to assess and predict various possible effects of introducing this kind of interactionmechanisms into practice.

References

1. Florence N. Nightingale: Note on nursing: What it is and what it is not (Com. Ed.). Philadelphia: Lippincott. (Original publication 1895).
2. J.B. George (ed.): NURSING THEORIES: The Basis for Professional Nursing Practice, Appleton & Lange, 1995.
3. M. Sloper and C. Thompson: Roy Adaptation Model Nursing Assessment Guides, Mount St. Mary's College, 1991.
4. Sister Callista Roy and H. A. Anderson: The Roy Adaptation Model, 2nd Eds. Appleton & Lange, 1999.
5. H. A. Andrews and Sister Callista Roy: Essentials of the Roy Adaptation Model, Appleton-Century-Crofts, 1986.
6. F. Heider: The Psychology of Interpersonal Relations, John Wiley, 1958.
7. F. Harary: A Structural Analysis of Situation in the Middle East in 1961; J. Conflict Resolution, Vol. 5, No. 2, pp. 167–178, 1961.
8. D. Cartwright and F. Harary: Structural Balance; a Generalization of Heider's Theory; Psychological Review, 63, pp.167–293, 1956.
9. T. M. Newcomb: An Approach to the Study of Communicative Acts; Psychological Review, 60, pp. 393–404,1953.
10. O. Katai and S. Iwai: Studies on the Balancing, the Minimal Balancing, and the Minimum Balancing Processes for Social Groups with Planar and Nonplanar Graph Structures; J. Math. Psychol., Vol. 18, No. 2, pp. 141–176, 1978.

11. O. Katai and S. Iwai: On the Characterization of Balancing Processes of Social Systems and the Derivation of the Minimal Balancing Processes; IEEE Trans., Vol. SMC-8, No.5, pp. 337–348, 1978.
12. R. Mizoguchi: Ontology for Modeling the world from Problem Solving Perspectives, proc. of IJCAI-95 Workshop on Basic Ontological Issues in Knowledge Sharing, pp.1–12, 1995.
13. J. Sowa: knowledge representation: logical, philosophical and computational joundation, PWS Publishing Comp, Boston (to be published in 1999)

Parallel Design Based on Neural Network

Shaobai Zhang, Xiefeng Cheng, and Zhiquan Feng

School of Information Science and Engineering, Jinan University
No.106, Jiwei Road, Jinan 250022, P.R.China
zhangsb123@263.net

Abstract. This paper, first, analyzes the problem about alternative models in parallel process; Secondly, present a neural network architecture and learning algorithm; Finally, discuss parallel software design method based on multi-layered neural network model and object-oriented techniques. An object-oriented approach to the initial analysis and design of a solution model provided the benefits of data abstraction and encapsulation which aided in the identification and modeling of the parallelism inherent in the problem domain.

1 Introduction

There is a widespread belief that the general acceptance of parallel computation is being hampered by the lack of appropriate software engineering tools and techniques the hardware technology exists but is not being adequately exploited. Many software applications require the use of exploiting parallel programming techniques in order to meet their specification. Parallelism is needed to exploit the processing power of multiprocessor systems in order to achieve high performance, to provide fault-tolerance and reliability in safety-critical and real-time system, and to deal with physically distributed computing resources. Difficulties arise both in the portion of existing applications and the development of new software system for parallel machines. Currently the construction of parallel software is perceived as a demanding and time-consuming task. Although considerable research effort has gone into specific aspects of parallel software design and implementation, there is still a need for coherent methodologies, techniques and tools to support the development process. Our objectives in this paper are to consider some issues involved in a parallel design model of artificial neural network and solve optimization problem that it is given in software design method for parallel systems.

2 Neural Architecture and Motion Equation

For parallel systems it can be argued that questions of correctness are more important than for sequential systems because of their nature: many parallel systems are characterized by infinite/unbounded and non-deterministic behavior, which renders the construction of sufficiently thorough testing programs impossible. In addition they are frequently used in safety critical situations. In standard systems it is accepted that system specification does not involve the use of operational models but

J. Liu et al. (Eds.): AMT 2001, LNCS 2252, pp. 291–296, 2001.
© Springer-Verlag Berlin Heidelberg 2001

is based on the description of system behavior in logical terms. The absence of adequate logical models has led to the use of operational models. On a more practical level, problem with the use of parallel system arise not only from perceived difficulty in learning these techniques but also in the provision of quality tools to handle realistically sized system. Because of the complexity issues involved in the analysis of large systems, many of the current automated support systems are insufficiently powerful to be used for this task. Therefore, we will focus on the use of neural network models in the development of parallel software systems.

The mathematical model of the artificial neural network consists of two components: the first part specifies the motion equation of a neuron: for say neuron j,

$$\frac{du_i}{dt} = f_j(v_i \ldots v_n)$$

where v_i is governed by i_f. The second part specifies the output of a neuron: $v_j = g_j$ (u_j). The function g_j is normally a sigmoid function. For a conventional neuron f_j is the linear summation of output signals, i.e.:

$$f_j = \sum_{i=1}^{n} w_{i\,j}\, v_i\, \theta_j.$$

The modified neuron simply extends the f_j from a linear function to a more general form. The convergence property of a neural network can be best described by a scalar function known as the energy function E. This function has two important properties: E is bounded below and $\frac{dE}{dt} \leq 0$. The second property means that E will decrease or remain the same as time progresses, since E is bounded below. The energy will eventually converge to a local minimum, which is a stable equilibrium point of the neural network. This concept indicates that a neural network can be used to solve an optimization problem if its energy function represents a measurement of optimality of the solution.

In general, it is very difficult to determine the architecture of a neural network, such as the number of layers and the number of internal nodes. However, the optimization neural network is completely determined by the energy function. Once the energy function is obtained, the exact optimization neural network can be derived. The following procedure shows the steps for obtaining a neural network for optimization problems form an energy function:

1)   Introduce a set of variables $\{v_1, v_2, \ldots v_n\}$ to represent the quantities to be optimized.

2)   Determine an energy function E $(v_1, v_2, \ldots v_n)$ as a measurement of optimality, The function should be bounded below and its minima should correspond to the desired solutions of the optimization problem.

3)   Employ n neurons whose outputs are $v_1, v_2, \ldots v_n$ and whose activations are $u_1, u_2, \ldots u_n$.

4)   Define the motion equation of neuron i as

$$\frac{du_i}{dt} = f_i(v_1, v_2, \ldots v_n) = \frac{\partial E(v_1, v_2, \ldots v_n)}{\partial v_i}$$

5)   Define the output of neuron i as: $V_i = g(u_i)$

Where g is a monotone increasing function.

6)   Construct the network accordingly.

Where E is bounded. By choosing $\dfrac{du_i}{dt} = -\dfrac{\partial E}{\partial v_i}$ we can show that $\dfrac{dE}{d} \leq 0$.

Thus, the neural networks constructed in this way will always coverage to a local minimal-energy state. In this neural network for optimization problems, the set $\{v_1, v_2, \ldots.. v_n\}$ serves as the output. Initially the v_i will be assigned to random values. Once the network is running, internal dynamics will change the value of v_i and force the network to converge to the minimal-energy state. When the network reaches the steady state, the value of v_i are exactly the solution of the problem and thus can be treated as the outputs.

Because of the complexity of the optimization problem, it is difficult to obtain an energy function with exactly on global minimum. It may contain certain undesired local minima, which correspond to suboptimal or even invalid solutions. In this case, we may need to apply relaxation mechanisms, such as simulated a needling to escape from these local minima.

3   Energy Function the Parallel Design

The goal of the artificial neural network for solving optimization problems is to minimize the fabricated computational energy function E. The energy function not only determines how many neurons should be used in the system but also the strength of the synapse links between neurons. It is constructed by considering the necessary and sufficient constraints and/or the cost function from the given problem. It is usually easier to build the motion equation than the energy function. The energy E can be obtained: $E = f_x + k \times f_{ij}$

Where the value f_x is indicated by below the equation:

$$f_x = \frac{1}{\displaystyle\sum_{i,j}^{N} f(v_i, v_j) - g(f(v_i), f(v_j)) + 1}$$

and, N is the numbers of neurons in neural network distributed.

$$f(v_i, v_j) = \begin{cases} 1 & v_i \text{ link } v_j \\ 0 & v_i \text{ unlink } v_j \end{cases} \qquad g(f(v_i), f(v_j)) = \begin{cases} 1 & f(v_i) = f(v_j) \\ 0 & f(v_i) \neq f(v_j) \end{cases}$$

The artificial neural network provides a parallel gradient descent method to minimize the fabricated energy function E.

4 Learning Algorithm and Parallel Software Design

Artificial neural network models have been studied for many years. The most prominent learning algorithms, which are based on sigma-pi unit back propagation, have the following serious problems:

1) It is usually very difficult to determine a multi-layered neural architecture, for example how many hidden layers should be used, how many neurons in each hidden layer are required and what interconnections between neurons should be made;

2) There are possibilities of sub optimal convergence during the sigma-pi back propagation process;

3) It is possible that convergence will require prohibitively much iteration during each learning trial;

4) There is no guarantee that sigma-pi back propagation units are sufficiently general to reflect all learning situations.

In order to precludes the above problems that occur in the existing feed forward multi-layered neural networks, a new statistical learning model called the multinomial conjunction will be used. Multinomial conjunctions are based on a well-developed statistical decision theory framework, which guarantees that conjunction learning will converge to optimal stales over learning trials and the learning will be fast during learning trials.

For the parallel software design based on neural network architecture, there is still a need for design methodologies. The majority of existing parallel software design methodologies have evolved from their well understood and widely used sequential counterparts. Data flow diagrams have perhaps proved the most influential in this respect, forming the foundation of a number of approaches including the Large-Grain Data Flow (LGDF) technique, DARTS (Design Approach for Real-Time Systems) with the related ADARTS and CODARTS, and the transformational schema approach.

The LGDF technique is an attempt to exploit flow diagrams in designing parallel programs. It views a hierarchical collection of data activated processes, which share a common memory area. Access to shared data is managed in a data flow-like manner using different types of arrow symbols to denote write access, read-only access and destructive read access. When the data flow design is complete, a number of steps are outlined to transform the design into a parallel implementation. To this end, a set of data flow operations are defined which facilitate the direct implementation of the data dependencies in the design. The data flow operations are actually macros that are expended into the program execution control statements for a given architecture at compile time. This approach provides source code portability across diverse parallel architectures simply by re-implementing the data flow operations. With object-oriented techniques, each module or object in a design directly models an object or class of object in the problem domain. Objects in design can be designated as sequential objects, blocking objects and concurrent objects. Sequential objects are passive objects whose semantics are only guaranteed in systems with a single thread of control. Therefore sequential objects are not useful in decomposing a system into parallel process into a number of cooperating objects. Both blocking objects and concurrent objects are guaranteed to preserve their semantics in the presence of multiple threads of control. Blocking objects are passive, representing servers that are operated upon by active concurrent objects. Booch further categorizes active objects as either actors or agents. Actors use the services of other objects, but do not offer services for other objects to use. Agents both use the services of other objects and offer services to other objects. Agents usually exist to perform some work on the behalf of other actor or agent objects.

5 Conclusion

An object-oriented approach to the initial analysis and design of a solution model provided the benefits of data abstraction and encapsulation which aided in the identification and modeling of the parallelism inherent in the problem domain. For a many-to-one or one-to-many relationship between object classes in the object model, we can expediently control using neural network architecture. During each learning cycle the experience segment receives prior/learning data and sends them to the parameter estimators. Which in turn send current parameter estimates to the performance segment. Parallel algorithm based on the neural network is designed for multi-layer or singer-layer channel where the channel area must be minimized. The goal of the parallel algorithm is to find a near-optimum routing solution for the given interconnections in a short time. It has many advantages e.g. it can be easily modified for accommodating more than multi-layer channel routing problems, it runs not only on a sequential but also on a parallel machine with maximally $n \times m \times 2$ processors, and the program size is very small, Additionally, the possibility of utilizing object-oriented approaches when designing-architecture dependencies solutions could be investigated. Such architecture dependencies introduce further refinement steps into the design and provide potential for a change in emphasis of the development process from a simple top-down refinement approach to a more involved simultaneous up down and bottom-up approach. This could include an investigation into the use of object-oriented approaches in providing an optimal process allocation, which is traditionally seen as a difficult and time-consuming stage of any parallel software implementation.

In conclusion, this work has demonstrated that neural network architecture and object-orientation has the potential to play a useful role in the difficult task of developing parallel software solutions. Therefore, for developing parallel message processing, it is important using neural network model and object-oriented analysis and design techniques.

References

1.   J.J. Hopfield, "Neurons with Graded Response Have Collective Computational Properties like Those of Two-state Neurons", proc. of the National Academy of Science USA,81, 1984.
2.   Mcclelland J.L., Rummelhart D.E., and the PDP Research Group, "parallel Distributed Processing" Vol. I and Vol. II, MIT Press, 1986.

3.   Corradi, A and Leonardi, L "Concurrency within objects: Layered approach" Inform. Software Technology. Vol.33 No.6, 1997.
4.   Booch. G "Object-oriented development" IEEE Trans. Software Eng. Vol. SE-12, NO.2 , 1996.
5.   Funabiki N. and Takefuli Y., " a parallel algorithm for channel routing problems", IEEE Trans, on CAD. 10,12.1991.
6.   Tan Ran, Xue shengjun, "An Autonomous Agent and Recognition Based on Self-organizing Neural Architecture", Proceedings of International Workshop on CSCW in Design, 1996
7.   G.C.Fox & J.G. Koller,"Code Generation by a Generalized Neural Network: General Principles and Elementary Examples", J. of Parallel and Distributed Computing 6,1989.
8.   P.P.chu, " On Neural Networks for Solving Optimization Problems". Proc. of the 4th ISMM Int. Conf. on Parallel and Distributed Computing and Systems, Washington, D.C. 1999.
9.   J.J.Hopfield & D.W.Tank"Neural Computation of Decisions in Optimization Problem", Biological Cybernetics,52,1985.

Fair Play Protocol

Tak-Ming Law

Hong Kong Institute of Vocational Education (Morrison Hill)
Department of Computing, 6 Oi Kwan Road, Wan Chai, Hong Kong.
Email: tmlaw@vtc.edu.hk

Abstract. Fair-Play protocol enables the fairness between two parties on any continuous sequence transaction, which leads to a final decision, or game activities, such as chess competition or video conferencing augmentation. In order to avoid disputes and achieve fairness, the steps of the game should be traceable (i.e. provable that the current step is originated from the first step of the game) and public verifiable and audible. Therefore, the goal of Fair-Play protocol is to achieve fairness, tractability of the process from the beginning step until the final decision, and provability of success.

Keywords: fairness, disputes, tractability

1 Introduction

Fair exchange protocols [1,2,3,4,5] were proposed for protecting the privacy, rights and benefits of both the sender and recipient during and after the transaction. While gambling protocols were intended for fair gambling deals. For any kinds of gamble, the reputation of fairness must be maintained; otherwise, nobody will participate in the gamble or the end results of the bet will be invalid.

One of the gambling tools is chess or checkers contest (for amateur leisure time with small amount of money gambling) on Internet web pages. Even though the gambling amount may be small (e.g. USD 5.00 per contest paid by the loser to the winner), the fairness within the contest has to be maintained; otherwise, the contest game will not be popular. There is an Agent (Trusted Third Party i.e. **TTP**) involved being the arbiter and host for interested people to join the contest. The Agent actually is a web page providing the game service to the public and charge for the service fee of 5% from the winner. After the contest finished, the Agent also guarantees the payment will be transferred from the loser to the winner within a specific period.

The Public Fair Play Protocol (**PFPP**) should have the following features:
1. Any two players can hold chess contest fairly at any time and any place.
2. In order to avoid disputes and achieve fairness, the steps of the game should be traceable (i.e. provable that the current step is originated from the first step of the game) and public verifiable and audible.
3. The exchange of challenges (steps) is continuous until a successful check is

J. Liu et al. (Eds.): AMT 2001, LNCS 2252, pp. 297–301, 2001.

made. This concept can be applied in videoconference protocol, which hash-chain up and digest all the previous messages exchanged until a final conclusion has been made. The conclusion of the game can be finally digested into a *"token"* and kept by the winner of the game. The *token* is win-or-loss evidence that can be placed into a public directory for everyone to verify (by auditing the hash chain of the steps digested from beginning of the game and check that if the last digest of the hash chain equals to the given *token*).

2 Notation

A and B	: Two players of the chess contest.
W	: Winner of the contest (it is the substitution for either A or B).
TTP	: Trusted Third Party
x_A	:Secret key of player A.
x_B	:Secret key of player B.
g	:A generator of a finite group.
g^{xA}	:Public key of A (i.e. $y^A = g^{xA} \bmod p$)
g^{xB}	:Public key of B (i.e. $y^B = g^{xB} \bmod p$).
p	:Large prime and which is public.
K_{AB}	:Symmetric session key between player A and B.
S_A	:Signature of A.
S_B	:Signature of B.
M_1, M_2	:Concatenation of M_1 and M_2.
$Move$	:The ith Message (chess movement information) communicate between A and B. $Move_{pre}$ and $Move_{cur}$ denote previous (received) and current (sending) movements respectively. And $Move_0$ and $Move_{last}$ denote the 1st step movement and last step movement (checked) of the game.
N_x	A cryptographic nonce generated by the party x at the current time of sending.
H	:Cryptographic one-way hash function.
h_{pre}, h_{cur}	: hash digest (hash chains) of previous and current accumulated step movements respectively.

3 The Protocol

1. $A \rightarrow B : g^{xA}$

     Then B performs $K_{AB} = (g^{xA})^{xB}$

2. $B \rightarrow A : g^{xB}$

     Then A performs $K_{AB} = (g^{xB})^{xA}$ and $h_{pre} = H(Move_0, N_A)$

3. $A \rightarrow B$ $: S_A(\{Move_0\} K_{AB}, h_{pre})$

While (Not (*Checked*))
Begin
4. $B \rightarrow A$: $S_B (\{Move_{cur}\} K_{AB}, h_{cur}=H(h_{pre}, Move_{cur}, N_B))$
IF A gives up **THEN** *abort* **ELSE**
A prepares a new message $Move_{cur}$ for step 5 (to send over to B) and
$h_{pre}= h_{cur}$. (i.e. h_{pre} in step 5 = h_{cur} in step 4)

5. $A \rightarrow B$: $S_A (\{Move_{cur}\} K_{AB}, h_{cur}=H(h_{pre}, Move_{cur}, N_A))$
IF B gives up **THEN** *abort* **ELSE**
B prepares a new message $Move_{cur}$ for step 4 (to send over to A) and
$h_{pre}= h_{cur}$. (i.e. h_{pre} in step 4 = h_{cur} in step 5)
End

The player has been challenged and without response (say) for over 10 minutes will be treated as "gives-up". The Winner will forward the details of "gives-up" information and current step (hash chain) of the game, before the other side "give-up", to the *TTP* as the evidence. The "give-up" information consists of the environmental information, which proves the other side indeed "gives-up". The time difference intervals of each step made can be measured by the timeliness of nonce between A and B which can be verified by the hash chain h_{cur}. Afterwards, *TTP* will send a token of credit to the winner for future redemption (in terms of monetary value or prize credits).

The *abort* sub-protocol is as follows.
1. $W \rightarrow TTP$: h_{cur}, *gives-up*, $S_W(h_{cur}$, *gives-up*)
2. $TTP \rightarrow W$:$Token_{credit}$

The *Checked* sub-protocol is as follows.
1. $W \rightarrow TTP$: h_{cur}, $Move_{last}$, $S_W(h_{cur}, Move_{last})$
2. $TTP \rightarrow W$:$Token_{credit}$

4 Elaboration

Step 1 and 2 indicate that the establishment of session key K_{AB} between A and B.

In step 3, A starts the game by passing the decision of the first move $Move_0$ to B along with the hash $h_{pre}=H(Move_0, N_A)$ and the message is signed by A. Since the hash contains a nonce, the result can be trace back in case verification is requested either side.

Step 4 and 5 will be performed iterately until the check is made (i.e. the end of the game) or either side "gives up" the game. In step 4, B sends the current move $Move_{cur}$, which is encrypted by the session key K_{AB}, and the hash chain $h_{cur}=H(h_{pre}, Move_{cur}, N_B)$ to A and the message is signed by B. After receipted the response from B, A prepares a new message $Move_{cur}$, which will be sending over to B in step 5, and update the hash chain by $h_{pre}= h_{cur}$. In step 5, A responses to B by performing almost the same procedures as B. During step 4 and 5, as either side (A or B) receipts the *gives-up* information, the *abort* sub-protocol will be invoked and the opposite side (*A* or *B*) will automatically become the Winner *W*.

Within the *abort* sub-protocol, the Winner *W* will send the most up-to-date hash chain h_{cur} and the information of *gives-up* along with its signature $S_W(h_{cur}, gives\text{-}up)$ to *TTP* as a proof of victory. Afterwards, *TTP* will send a token of credit $Token_{credit}$ to the winner for future redemption (in terms of monetary value or prize credits).

If the current move $Move_{cur}$ is classified as Checked, the *Checked* sub-protocol will be invoked. As the side (either *A* or *B*) made the last $Move_{cur}$ and which is classified as Checked, then he becomes the Winner *W*. Just like the *abort* sub-protocol, the Winner *W* will send the most up-to-date hash chain h_{cur} and the last move $Move_{last}$ (which is $Move_{last} = Move_{cur}$) along with its signature $S_W(h_{cur}, Move_{last})$ to *TTP*. Afterwards, *TTP* will send a token of credit $Token_{credit}$ to the winner for future redemption (in terms of monetary value or prize credits).

5 Some Remarks

The notion of Fair-Play protocol is originated from fair exchange protocols. By adopting the requirements for fair exchange, which were formulated in [3], more insights for Fair-Play protocol can be revealed. Fair-Play protocol is designed to meet the following requirements.

- *Effectiveness.*   If two parties behave honestly and correctly, they will receive the expected items without any involvement of the *TTP*. They can create some simple protocols to verify the hash chains on each step for mutual authentication.

- *Fairness.*   After completion of a protocol run, the win-or-loss evidence $Token_{credit}$ is non-repudiated. Either each party cannot deny the final result of $Token_{credit}$, which is sent by *TTP* in the sub-protocol of *Checked*.

- *Timeliness.*   At any time during a protocol run, each party can unilaterally choose to terminate the protocol without losing fairness.

- *Verifiability of Third Party.*   If the third party misbehaves, resulting in the loss of fairness for a party, the victim can prove the fact in a dispute by verifying the hash chain h_{cur} from the sub-protocol *Checked*.

6 Conclusion

The goal of Fair-Play protocol is to achieve fairness, tractability of the process from the beginning step until the final decision, and provability of success. Its application is not only on game play, but also on any continuous sequence augmentation type transaction, which leads to a final decision, such as price biding and Internet public law court. Future development will be focus on finding more application areas on the concept of Fair-Play protocol.

Reference

1. M. Ben-Or, O. Goldreich, S. Micali And R. Rivest.   A Fair Protocol For Signing Contracts.   Ieee Transactions On Information Theory, It-36(1), (1990) 40-46.
2. N. Asokan, M. Schunter And M. Waidner.   Optimistic Protocols For Fair Exchange. Proceedings Of 4th Acm Conference On Computer And Communications Security, Zurich, Switzerland, (1997), 7-17.
3. N. Asokan, V. Shoup And M. Waidner.   Asynchronous Protocols For Optimistic Fair Exchange.   Proceedings Of 1998 Ieee Symposium On Security And Privacy, Oakland, California, (1998) 86-99.
4. F. Bao, R. H. Deng And W. Mao.   Efficient And Practical Fair Exchange Protocols With Off-Line Ttp.   Proceedings Of 1998 Ieee Symposium On Security And Privacy, Oakland, California, (1998) 77-85.
5. Jianying Zhou, Robert Deng And Feng Bao.   Some Remarks On A Fair Exchange Protocol.   Proceedings Of 2000 Third International Workshop On Practice And Theory In Public Key Cryptography, Melbourne, Victoria, Australia, (2000) 46-57.

Collaborative Filtering Methods for Binary Market Basket Data Analysis

Andreas Mild[1] and Thomas Reutterer[2]

[1] Vienna University of Economics and B.A.,
Pappenheimgasse 35/5, 1200 Vienna, Austria
andreas.mild@wu-wien.ac.at
[2] Simon, Kucher & Partners,
Kaerntner Strasse 7, 1010 Vienna, Austria
treutterer@simon-kucher.com

Abstract. Retail managers have been interested in learning about cross-category purchase behavior of their customers for a fairly long time. More recently, the task of inferring cross-category relationship patterns among retail assortments is gaining attraction due to its promotional potential within recommender systems used in online environments. Collaborative Filtering algorithms are frequently used in such settings for the prediction of choices, preferences and/or ratings of online users. The fundamental assumption of such algorithms resides in the available similarity information between a specific active user and a database of all other users. We study the effects of different similarity measures, available data points per user and the number of items to be recommended on the relative predictive performance in an experiment using market basket data collected from a grocery retailer. Using various measures for evaluation of the predictive ability, we derive some clues to the proper parameterization of such systems.

1 Introduction

Consumers are permanently involved in multi-category decision making, such as grocery shopping trips, mail-order purchasing, or financial portfolio choice. In a retailing context, the result of such multi-category decision processes leads to the formation of shopping or market baskets which comprise the set of categories (or items) that individual consumers purchase on one and the same purchase occasion. Retailers are traditionally interested in understanding the composition of their customers' market baskets, since valuable insights for designing micro-marketing and/or targeted cross-selling programs can be derived.

Conventional analyses of market basket data can be classified into explanatory and exploratory approaches to measuring cross-category dependencies. Models of the former type focus on the identification and quantification of complementary cross-category effects (in terms of choice, inter-purchase timing, etc.) of some marketing variables under managerial control, such as price, promotions, or featuring (see, e.g., [18,24,21,7,12,17]). Exploratory approaches

J. Liu et al. (Eds.): AMT 2001, LNCS 2252, pp. 302–313, 2001.

try to discover and to condense the complex interdependency structures typically observed among multiple categories in a managerially meaningful manner. This can be accomplished using (pairwise) association measures (e.g., [4,8,14]) leading to a priori aggregated representations of product category proximities or, e.g., via quantization of vector similarities for disaggregated market basket data (see [23]). Another prominent stream of research in this direction utilizes data mining techniques in order to generate association rules among subsets of product categories (see, e.g., [1,6,11]).

More recently, the emerging rise of in-store scanning technologies and especially the availability of customers' navigation and clicking information through online environments like the web makes mass-customization of both content (i.e., information, products, or product categories offered to web-site visitors at specific prices and conditions) and design via electronic media eminently possible. As a consequence, the analysis of (online) market basket data for fine-tuning the bundles of a company's offerings at the individual user level is (re-)attracting the interest of marketing researchers. Online firms, such as Amazon.com or barnesandnoble.com, are using recommendation systems that suggest products to their customers based on so-called Collaborative Filtering (CF) methods. These methods use data from users with similar preferences or actual choices in order to determine a specific (active) customer's or user's preferences and the subsequent recommendation of new items that are deemed to fit these preferences.

In the following sections of this paper, we investigate the performance of such CF methods using market basket data across 55 product categories. The data are representing 9835 retail transactions (i.e., customers' purchases of multiple product categories) that have been collected from the point-of-purchase scanning devices of a grocery retail outlet over a one-month period. The remainder of the paper is organized as follows. First, we outline inherent basic assumptions and alternative variants of the CF methodology. Next, we examine the relative predictive performance of competing model specifications by experimentally varying external (data-related) conditions and model parameters that are hypothesized to be crucial for the accuracy of CF-based recommendations. Finally, we draw conclusions and discuss the practical significance of our results.

2   Collaborative Filtering Methods

For a given number of n customers included in the database, memory-based CF algorithms calculate the predictive value $p_{a,j}$ for a user a and a specific item j on the basis of a weighted sum of votes of other similar users; in our subsequent empirical application the term 'item' corresponds to product category and 'vote' to a consumer's choice $[0;1]$ among a predefined set of catagories. We use a modified version of the function proposed in [5]:

$$p_{a,j} = \kappa \sum_{i=1}^{n} w(a,i) c_{ij} \tag{1}$$

The propensity of a user a to purchase an item j thus depends on the similarity $w(a, i)$ between the user a and each user i and the actual purchasing behavior c_{ij} of each user i. κ ensures that the absolute values of the weights sum to unity. Most studies on collaborative filtering are restricted to the use of Pearson's correlation coefficient [20] or a measure of vector similarity [22] based on the cosine of the angle between two vectors for the calculation of the similarity between users. We introduce two additional measures for the calculation of the weights, namely the so-called Jaccard or Tanimoto coefficient and the Hamming distance (for a brief description of the used proximity measures, see, e.g., [2,15,16]). In contrast to the correlation coefficient, both measures cannot take on negative values. The Tanimoto similarity between two users a and i is defined as

$$w(a, i) = \frac{n(c_a \cap c_i)}{n(c_a \cup c_i)} = \frac{n(c_a \cap c_i)}{n(c_a) + n(c_i) - n(c_a \cap c_i)} \qquad (2)$$

where $n(X)$ represents the number of elements in the customer basket (or item-set) X. As is obvious from the above description, the Tanimoto coefficient ignores the number of coinciding non-chosen elements (i.e., zeros). Since there is only very limited variance to be expected in similarities (using, e.g., correlational measures) constructed for sparse data sets, this might be advantageous in the case of extremely asymmetric distributed or sparse data vectors. The Hamming distance is the most trivial measure of dissimilarity between code representations. It is simply defined as the number of different bits in sequences of equal length:

$$d_h(a, i) = \text{bitcount}\{(\hat{c_{aj}} \wedge c_{ij}) \vee (c_{aj} \wedge \hat{c_{ij}}) \forall j = 1, ..., J\} \qquad (3)$$

with $\hat{c_{aj}}$ as the logic negation of c_{aj}. $\vee$ denotes the logical sum, whereas $\wedge$ denotes the logical product. The function bitcount$\{X\}$ determines the number of elements in the set X with the logical value 1. For direct application, we normalize d_h to a range between 0 and 1 and calculate the similarity as

$$w(a, i) = 1 - \text{norm}(d_h(a, i)) \qquad (4)$$

Naturally, there is an almost endless catalogue of proximity coefficients presented in the literature so far (for an overview see, e.g., [10,2,13,15]). The vast majority, however, can be closely related to one of the measures included in our subsequent experiment.

3   Design of the Simulation Study and Evaluation Criteria

The choice of a specific proximity measure used for similarity matching of customers' choice patterns represents one of the (probably most important) technical features that might impact the predictive accuracy of CF techniques. However, there are several other data-related factors, such as the amount of information available from a person, that are reported to affect the performance of CF-based recommender systems (see, e.g., [5,3]). In order to separate the effects outlined in the subsequent section and to evaluate their relative importance when designing an appropriate recommender system for (binary) market basket analysis, we conduct an extensive simulation study by systematically varying some hypothesized experimental design factors.

3.1 Experimental Design and Related Hypotheses

The experiment consists of two stages, with both stages being part of a simulation study. In the first stage, for each customer-item combination a value for expression (1) is calculated for each cell of a complete factorial design. In the second step, TOP-N recommendations are formulated based on the following rationale: We first calculate the median predictive value for each item across all available customers, i.e., median($p_{.j}$). Then, for each customer i we calculate the difference between the predictive value for each item and the median predictor, i.e., diff(i, j) = p_{ij}−median($p_{.j}$). Finally, the Top-N list of potential item recommendations for each customer i is generated using the N largest values for diff($i, .$). Table 1 shows a summary of the treatment variables and their respective levels that are combined in a full-factorial design. The corresponding hypotheses to be tested can be briefly commented as follows:

Table 1. Experimental design variables

Factor	Levels	Used in stage
Proximity measure (1)	Correlation Tanimoto Hamming	1,2
Number of given items (2)	54 44 34	1,2
Sparsity of item list (3)	8 10 12	1,2
Number of item recommendations	5 10 15	2

As a consequence of our above discussion on similarity concepts frequently used by CF and related matching techniques and the expected impact on the predictive performance, the first experimental factor represents the proximity function used for calculation of the similarities between customers. This leads to the formulation of our first hypothesis:

> *H1: The choice of the proximity measure used for the calculation of weights $w(a, i)$ affects the predictive accuracy of the CF algorithm.*

The second factor — the number of given items — is synonymous with the length of the vector c_{ij}, i.e., the number of categories, used for similarity calculation between an active customer and the database. Since the length of the item vectors used are indicativ for the amount of data available from a customer and more information about a person's choice pattern is expected to be beneficial for the algorithm's predictive performance, we posit:

> H2: The number of given items positively impact the predictive accuracy of the CF algorithm.

Whereas the number of given items is designed to test whether there is a trade-off between predictive accuracy and the amount of data collected per person, the third experimental factor determines the degree of sparsity of the available item list in terms of the minimum size (i.e., number of items) per shopping basket included in the database of our simulation study. For example, if a minimum size of 8 items is required, only shopping baskets containing at least 8 different purchased items are used. Thus, a smaller minimum basket size increases the sparsity of the data matrix used and forces the weights to be based on few common items. To test this relationship, we posit:

> H3: The sparsity of the available item lists (minimum number of items per shopping basket) negatively effects the predictive accuracy of CF.

In addition, in stage 2 of our experiment we vary the number of recommended items as a result of our Top-N recommendation procedure as described. While the probability of recommending 'correct' items (i.e., recommended items that are actually chosen) is expected to increase with an increasing size of Top-N recommendations, the 'quality' of recommendations might decrease due to smaller distances between the respective votes and the median. This suggests:

> H4: The number of Top-N recommendations per user influences the predictive accuracy of the CF algorithm.

Next, we discuss the evaluation of the predictive performance of the various CF specifications according to the outcomes of our simulation experiment.

3.2   Performance Measures

For the evaluation of the first stage of our simulation experiment, we use the Mean Absolute Deviation ($MAD = \sum(|\text{predicted value - choice}(0,1)|)/\text{number}$ of observations) between the prediction and the actual choice or non-choice. In real-world applications with practical importance, however, the analyst is especially interested in the accuracy of predictions for actually chosen items. Thus, we calculate the MAD for those items which had been chosen by a respective user, defined as $MAD_1 = \sum(|\text{predicted value} - \text{choice}(1)|)/\text{number of observations}$. To measure the predictive accuracy of our Top-N recommendations in the second stage of our experiment, we proceed as follows:

Table 2. Contingency table of chosen vs. recommended items

item j	recommended		
	1	0	
chosen 1	a	b	a+b
0	c	d	c+d
	a+c	b+d	e=a+b+c+d

Analogous to the well-known construction framework used for proximity measures based on binary data (see, e.g., [2,13,15]), for each cell of the full-factorial design, we evaluate the simulation outcome based on the association of chosen versus recommended items as given in the 2-by-2 contingency table 2: The cell denoted as a, for instance, contains the number of users that choose a specific item j which is also included in the list of Top-N recommendations for the respective users. Hence, cell e corresponds to the total number of users. Based on this cross-classification scheme, we define the following performance measures:

$$\text{Simple matching coefficient (SM)} = \frac{a + d}{a + b + c + d} \tag{5}$$

Here, the SM coefficient measures the fraction of correctly predicted items. Using this measure, actually chosen items that were recommended and non chosen items not displayed on the Top-N list are equally weighted. However, correctly predicted items that are actually chosen are more important. Therefore, we derive two components of the Tanimoto similarity measure to account for the practically important difference between true positives and false negatives:

$$\text{HR1} = \frac{a}{a + c} \quad \text{and} \quad \text{HR2} = \frac{a}{a + b} \tag{6}$$

Hit rate 1 (HR1) represents the fraction of correctly predicted choices and all predicted choices, whereas hit rate 2 (HR2) expresses the fraction of correctly predicted choices and all actual choices.

4   Simulation Results and Hypothesis Tests

After running the simulations for the above described full-factorial experimental design using a total number of 9835 grocery retail transactions each covering binary (choice/non-choice) market basket data across 55 different product categories, we can test the posited hypotheses and study the relative impact of the design factors. With respect to the first stage of the experiment, the results of an analysis of variance (ANOVA) of the performance measure MAD depending on the individual treatment factors used (i.e., proximity measure, number of items given, and sparsity of the item list), the choice variable as well as first-order interactions among them are summarized in table 3. The choice variable was introduced in order to capture the performance differences for all other potential (unobserved) factors between actually chosen and non-chosen items.

Table 3. Experimental stage 1 ANOVA results for MAD depending on treatment factors, actual choice, and first-order interactions show significant impacts of the proximity measure used and item list sparsity on the predictive accuracy. The latter is also negatively affected if only actually chosen items are to be predicted. The same applies to first-order combinations between the three factors.

Factor	df	F-value
Constant	1	746603*
Proximity measure (1)	2	17.5*
Number of given items (2)	2	.6
Sparsity of item list (3)	2	140*
Actual Choice (4)	1	227136*
First-order interactions:		
Factors 1 × 2	4	.483
Factors 1 × 3	4	.442
Factors 1 × 4	2	129.546*
Factors 2 × 3	4	.170
Factors 2 × 4	2	1.946
Factors 3 × 4	2	2057.929*

R-squared=.474
* indicates significance at the 95% confidence level

Given the above results, all but the number of given items (factor 2) main effects are significant at the 0.95 level, thus supporting our hypothesis *H1* and *H3*. The small F-ratio[1] for factor 2 level variations does not suceed to reject the null hypothesis of group means equality at the 95% confidence level, thus hypothesis *H2* can not be supported by our experimental results. This gives rise for the interesting conclusion that (at least for binary data) CF algorithms seem to behave relatively robust with respect to the amount of data collected from each person and that the predictive performance remains unaffected even if a considerable rate of information is missing.

The major impact on the predictive accuracy, however, is represented by the factor 'actual choice', i.e., whether only actually chosen or non-chosen items

---

[1] The F-values represent the ratio of the sample variance estimated from the group means of the respective factor levels used and that estimated within these groups. Hence, large F-values are indicative for substantial performance differences between factor levels. Furthermore, they can serve as a score for statistically testing the null hypothesis that the group means (of factor levels) are equal in the population of simulation runs at a pre-specified confidence level and for a given number of degrees of freedom (df).

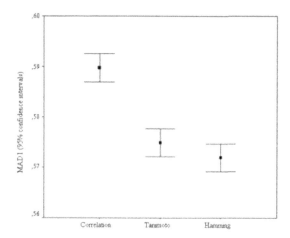

Fig. 1. The significant differences of performance measure MAD_1 means (95% confidence intervals indicated as bars) indicate that both the Tanimoto similarity and Hamming distance outperform the use of a correlation coeffient for CF of binary data.

are investigated. The huge difference between the MAD for actually non-chosen ($MAD = 0.15$) and chosen items ($MAD_1 = 0.58$) impressively reflects the problems of correctly predicting chosen items. We focus our further presentation of results on the analysis of chosen item-customer combinations. Interestingly, we find significant first-order interactions between the proximity measure used and the choice dummy (factors 1×4) as well as between the minimum basket size (item list sparsity) and the choice variable (3×4). Figures 1 and 2 show the corresponding results (factor level means and 95% confidence intervals). Even though absolute differences are relatively small, it can be seen from Figure 1 that both the Tanimoto and the Hamming measure outperform the correlation coefficient in terms of MAD_1 indicating that the frequently proposed correlation coefficient is not adequate for the calculation of similarities for the relatively sparse binary data as typically observed in market basket data analysis. Figure 2 shows a positive impact on the MAD_1 measure of predictive accuracy when the minimum basket size included for predictions is increased, thus supporting hypothesis *H3*. This phenomenon can be explained by the decreasing sparsity of the database and puts emphasis on the sensitiveness of the CF technique with respect to the correct specification of customer data with a minimum number of (common) items in order to achieve acceptable levels of prediction accuracy.

Let us now turn to the results derived from stage 2 (Top-N recommendations) of our experiment. Table 4 shows the results of separate ANOVAs on all 3 defined performance measures using the different numbers — namely 5, 10, and 15 Top-N — of recommendations as factor levels (means and standard deviations indicated in brackets). While both hit rates HR1 and HR2 show larger

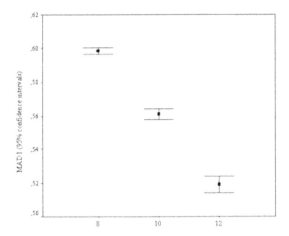

Fig. 2. The distinctive discrepancies of MAD_1 performance measure means and relatively tight 95% confidence bars for three alternative levels of minimum basket size (8, 10, and items) prove the sensitiveness of CF techniques on data density.

ratios with an increasing number of recommendations, SM decreases. The declining SM values clearly reflect the increasing risk of miss-predictions with larger recommendation sets. However, augmented HR2-ratios show the increasing exploitation of the constant cross-selling potential, since it can also be interpreted as the fraction of realized cross-selling opportunities. Hit rate HR1, in contrast, reflects the accuracy of the recommendations since $1 - HR1$ represents the fraction of recommendations which did not satisfy the customer needs. Thus, with the exception of the insignificant impact of the number of Top-N recommendations on HR1, hypothesis H4 is supported by our findings.

Table 4. Experimental stage 2 ANOVA results for measures of predictive accuracy (simple matching and hit rates) depending on three different levels of number of Top-N recommendations.

Rec.	SM	HR1	HR2
5	.726 (.221)	.156 (.208)	.062 (.082)
10	.675 (.203)	.165 (.212)	.124 (.124)
15	.616 (.178)	.170 (.213)	.183 (.152)
F-value (2 df)	110.6*	1.5	356.7*
* indicates significance at the 95% confidence level			

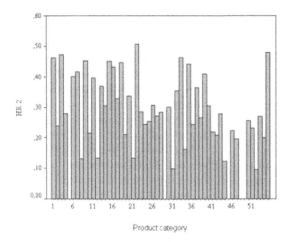

Fig. 3. Hit rate HR2 (the fraction of actually chosen items that were correctly recommended) significantly varies across product categories.

Finally, figure 3 shows HR2 across various product categories for an optimal combination of the design factors. It can be seen that HR2 ratios strongly vary across product categories. Notice, that values of zero do not necessarily mean that all predictions were wrong but that this category has no entries. Hence, in practical applications, the marketing analyst who wishes to utilize CF technology based recommendation systems is advised to focus on the categories with considerably high HR2 values.

5   Summary and Concluding Remarks

The paper presented documents the findings from an extensive simulation study applying the collaborative filtering (CF) methodology to the prediction of consumers' choices among product categories using binary market basket data collected from a grocery retailer. The simulation experiment is conducted by systematically varying some hypothesized experimental design factors that are frequently reported to crucially affect the predictive accuracy of recommendations. Our findings suggest the following conclusions: For similarity matching, the often proposed correlation coefficient is, though not dramatically, outperformed by the Tanimoto coefficient as well as the Hamming distance measure. This result is not very surprising, since the presence of binary data clearly questions the suitability of correlation measures. With respect to the adequate design of CF techniques for qualitative data, however, further research should be encouraged to investigate other candidate similarity concepts. A particularly interesting stream of research is represented by the 'fuzzy similarity' concept as introduced by Zadeh

[25] and successfully applied in models for case-based reasoning (see, e.g., [19, 9]. As an important result from our simulation study, we can provide evidence that CF performance is clearly harmed by an increasing sparsity of the database, which should draw the analyst's attention to the proper determination of useful customer data with a minimum number of (common) items in order to achieve acceptable levels of prediction accuracy. On the other hand, CF algorithms are behaving relatively robust with respect to the amount of data collected from a single person; the predictive performance remains almost unaffected even if a considerable rate of information is missing. Furthermore, considerable differences in predictive performance can be observed depending on whether actual choices or non-choices are to be predicted. Since the former is typically the primary objective in most practical applications, this observation gives rise to handle the raw predictive scores or votes delivered from CF algorithms with caution. Consequently, our findings encourage further investigations into the effects of some more reasonable algorithmic modifications and/or manipulations of the predictive output before deriving final recommendations. Finally, it should be noted that our simulation study is based on one single real binary data set only. Further research should aim at different data sets originating from various (preferably online) data sources.

References

1. Agrawal, R., Srikant, R.: Fast algorithms for mining association rules. Proceedings of the 20th VLDB Conference, Santiago, Chile (1994)
2. Anderberg, M.R.: Cluster Analysis for Applications. Academic Press, New York San Francisco London (1973)
3. Ansari, A., Essegaier, S., Kohli, R.: Internet Recommendation Systems. Journal of Marketing Research **37** (2000) 363–375
4. Boecker, F.: Die Bestimmung der Kaufverbundenheit von Produkten, Duncker & Humblot, Berlin (1978)
5. Breese, J.S., Heckerman, D., Kadie, C.: Empirical Analysis of Predictive Algorithms for Collaborative Filtering. Proceedings of the Fourteenth Conference on Uncertainty in Artificial Intelligence, Morgan Kaufmann Publisher, Madison, WI, (1998)
6. Buechter, O., Wirth, R.: Discovery of association rules over ordinal data: A new and faster algorithm and its application to basket analysis. In: Wu, X., R. Kotagiri, Korb, K.B. (eds.): Research and Development in Knowledge Discovery and Data Mining. Second Pacific-Asia Conference, PAKDD-98, Melbourne, Australia. Springer-Verlag, Berlin Heidelberg New York (1998) 36–47
7. Chintagunta, P.K., Haldar, S.: Investigating Purchase Timing Behavior in Two Related Product Categories. Journal of Marketing Research **35** (1998) 43–53
8. Dickinson, R., Harris, F., Sircar, S.: Merchandise compatibility: An exploratory study of its measurement and effect on department store performance. International Review of Retail, Distribution and Consumer Research (1992) 351–379
9. Dubois, D., Esteva, F., Garcia, P., Godo, L., Lopez de Mantaras, R., Prade, H.: Fuzzy sets-based models in case-based reasoning. Lecture Notes in Artificial Intelligence, Vol. 1266. Springer-Verlag, Berlin Heidelberg New York (1997) 599–610

10. Gower, J.C.: A general coefficient of similarity and some of its properties. Biometrics **27** (1971) 857–871
11. Hilderman, R.J., Carter, C.L., Hamilton, H.J., Cercone, N.: Mining Market Basket Data Using Share Measures and Characterized Itemsets. In: Wu, X., R. Kotagiri, Korb, K.B. (eds.): Research and Development in Knowledge Discovery and Data Mining. Second Pacific-Asia Conference, PAKDD-98, Melbourne, Australia. Springer-Verlag, Berlin Heidelberg New York (1998) 159–173
12. Hruschka, H., Lukanowicz, M., Buchta, Ch.: Cross-category sales promotion effects. Journal of Retailing and Consumer Services, **6** (1999) 99–105
13. Hubalek, Z.: Coefficients of association and similarity, based on binary (presence-absence) data: An evaluation. Biological Review **57** (1982) 669–689
14. Julander, C.-R. Basket Analysis. A new way of analyzing scanner data. International Journal of Retail and Distribution Management **20** (1992) 10–18
15. Kaufman, L., Rousseeuw, P.J.: Finding Groups in Data. An Introduction to Cluster Analysis. John Wiley & Sons, New York Chichester Brisbane Toronto Singapore (1990)
16. Kohonen, T.: Self-Organizing Maps. Springer-Verlag, Berlin Heidelberg New York (1997)
17. Manchanda, P., Ansari, A., Gupta, S.: The "shopping basket": A model for multi-category purchase incidence decisions. Marketing Science **18** (1999) 95–114
18. Mulhern, F.J., Leone, R.P.: Implicit price bundling of retail products: A multi-product approach to maximizing store profitability. Journal of Marketing **55** (1991) 63–76
19. Plaza, E., Esteva, F., Garcia, P., Godo, L., Lopez de Mantaras, R.: A Logical Approach to Case-Based Reasoning Using Similarity Relations. International Journal of Information Sciences **106** (1996) 105–122
20. Resnick, P., Iacovou, N., Suchak, M., Bergstrom, P., Riedl, J.: Grouplens: An open architecture for collaborative filtering of netnews. Proceedings of the ACM 1994 Conference on Computer Supported Cooperative Work. Anaheim, CA (1994) 219–231
21. Russell, G.J., Kamakura, W.A.: Modeling multiple category brand preference with household basket data. Journal of Retailing **73** (1997) 439–461
22. Sarwar, B., Karypis, G., Konstan, J., Riedl, J.: Analysis of Recommendation Algorithms for E-commerce. Proceedings of the EC'00, Minneapolis, Minnesota (2000)
23. Schnedlitz, P., Reutterer, T., Joos, W.: Data-Mining und Sortimentsverbundanalyse im Einzelhandel. In: Hippner, H., Kuesters, U., Meyer, M., Wilde, K. (eds.): Handbuch Data Mining im Marketing. Knowledge Discovery in Marketing Databases. Vieweg Verlag, Wiesbaden (2001) 951–970
24. Walters, R.G.: Assessing the impact of retail promotions on product substitution, complementary purchase, and inter-store sales displacement. Journal of Marketing **55** (1991) 17–28
25. Zadeh, L.A.: Similarity relations and fuzzy orderings. Information Sciences **3** (1971) 177–200

An Implementation and Design of COMOR System for OOM Reuse

Young-Jun Kim

Department of Secretarial Studies, Cheonan College of Foreign Studies,
393, Anseo-dong, Cheonan, Chungnam, Korea
yjkim@mail.cheonan-c.ac.kr

Abstract. This study is to design a system of object-oriented model (OOM) re-use. This enhance the efficiency of software reuse through expressing object model utilizing cases, retrieving object model which is reused and developing ob-ject modeling procedure. We developed object model reuse system by case-based reasoning, called case-based object model reuse system (COMOR System). This system consists of four subsystems: the graphic user interface to interact with end-user, the object-oriented model management system to build a new object model, the case base to store the past object models, and the knowledge base to store object-oriented modeling and reusing knowledge.

1 Introduction

Source code reuse contains many limits in the process of improving the productivity and quality of software development using software reuse. Owing to this problem, researchers' interests are concentrated on how to reuse the outputs in the system analy-sis phase rather than source code reuse itself (7). As object-oriented model (OOM) method is gradually developed, which has been discussed in good earnest since the late 1980s, some researches claiming this technology can maximize the reusing effi-ciency in the analysis phase are given. Now, the researches on software reuse utilizing case-based reasoning have been shown as well; and it is the time when more active researches that can apply them should be accomplished (3). This study is, in the sys-tem analysis phase, to design and implementation a system of OOM reuse.

2 Model Reuse Method

Software reuse has some merits that can reduce the efforts, cost and time for software development and make software management efficient. Computer-Aided Prototyping System (CAPS) is the system that reuse software component on the basis of a con-structed specification. The Intelligent Design Aid (IDeA), as the knowledge-base tool supporting the specification in the analysis phase, helps the specification demanded by

J. Liu et al. (Eds.): AMT 2001, LNCS 2252, pp. 314–320, 2001.
© Springer-Verlag Berlin Heidelberg 2001

a user to be consistently maintained. Reuse Based Object-Oriented Techniques (REBOOT), as the system expressing the process of component reuse in detail, shows the process of software component reuse that is based on object-oriented approach; and its ultimate goal is to reuse outputs from OOM method (2).

2.1 OOM Reuse Method

The productivity and quality of software development depends upon effective reusing outputs in the of analysis phase. The study related to OOM method is the most remarkable field, notwithstanding the fundamental solution for the matter mentioned above has not been offered yet. OOM method, unlike the existing other ones, attracts researchers' attention because this technology can keep consistency in the software development whole phase, and use it again (5). In order to reuse the outputs of analysis phase, we are to identify objects and the attributes of them in the given problem domain, and to express the association and inheritance among the identified objects.

2.2 CBR Reuse Method

Case-based reasoning (CBR) is the method that means a reuse for solving new problems through modifying the solutions used in the past (6). For this reason, many researchers become very interested in CBR as a good alternative that can surmount the problems in knowledge acquisition. The cases are expressed by object and are stored in case-base. OOM management system, which can manage object is expressed, and knowledge-base is designed, which has the OOM rules and reuse rules. While CBR is a systematic effort for reusing the similar past experiences in order to solve new problems, software reuse is a systematic one for reusing the experiences and knowledge software development in the past for the purpose of new software development.

2.3 OOM Reuse Rules

The rules for OOM reuse are as following: the similarity rule, the rule for retrieving a similar OOM, the rule for a retrieved OOM reuse, the rule for modifying model and the maintenance rule for adding model to case-base and so on. The class, attribute and operation can be shown as several terms with similar meanings in OOM. A problem object model means the OOM given by a user. A case object model means the arbitrary OOM in case-base, which is selected for measuring the similarity between problem object model and it. A retrieved object model means the OOM that is the most similar to problem object model among case object models. An initial object model means the new OOM generated by applying reuse rules. A final object model means the OOM finally completed through modifying.

Reuse rules are applied when the initial object model is generated OOM reuse by retrieval rules. If it discovers the class of problem object model that is similar to the specific class of retrieval object model, using class similarity value calculated by this rules, it can combine two classes into one. Modification rules mean the rules for modifying the part of model that users are not satisfied with OOM. A partial algorithm of reuse and modification rule is displayed under. These rules are basically applied for the specific class or association in OOM. Maintenance rules mean the rules for adding the completed OOM to case-base by applying retrieval, reuse and modification rules.

```
Procedure Generate_rules(Case_Base)
Reuse_Rule_Set = ;
Modification_Rule_Set = ;
For I = 1 To Case_Number -1
   Problem = Case_Base(i)
    For J = I + 1 To Case_Number
      Target = Case_Base(j)
      Diff = Calculate_DiffofAttributes (Problem, Target)
      If Diff <= Threshold Then
        Single_Rule = Make_ Reuse_Rule (Problem, Target)
        Modification_Rule = Single_Rule U Retrival_Rule
    End If
Next J
Next I

Refine_Reuse_Rules(Reuse_Rule_Set)
```

3 Design of System

We will design case-based object model reuse system (COMOR System) applying several rules. This system supports the process of OOM reuse, utilizing retrieval, reuse, modification and maintenance rules of CBR. This system offers graphic user interface and minimize the time and efforts adding cases to case-base for the effective OOM reuse. This is composed as followings: graphic user interface is expressed a UML class (1). OOM management system has the function of reasoning and management and generates the OOM using case-base and knowledge-base.

This system generates initial object model by applying retrieval, reuse and modification rules, if problem object model is input by the user. In the next step, modification rules for initial object model are applied again, or final object model complete through a direct modification by the user. The user inputs OOM about the related work specification through graphic user interface. This OOM can exist as various forms in accordance with the degree of users' experience and efforts for modeling.

This system can generate initial object model with applying reuse rules in knowledge-base. If the user isn't satisfied with initial object model, he can require modification after he chose a part of initial object model; OOM management system here will retrieve whether there is the similar object among OOM or not, and offers the user the object as an alternative, which has similarity value beyond the specific standard.

4   Implementation of System

A case for COMOR system is 'Sales management of the company MS', and its work specification is as followings. The items treated by the head office are the goods (*i.e.* computer, fax machine, copy machine... *etc.*), office supplies and parts. All goods are kept
in local warehouse, when the stock of goods is below the specific standard, the head
office gives an order for goods to the deliverer. The transaction between the head
office and customers is divided into selling the goods and office supplies, lending the
goods and the service for consumers.

4.1 Input of Problem Object Model

This system supporting the object modeling of the company MS through this work
specification stores the OOM in various fields such as transaction, order and membership managements. The initial object model of this system is generated on the basis of
problem object model. it can be extended by modification rules and final object model
is completed through this processing. First of all, the user inputs class (customer, delivery, employee, goods, lending, ordering, sales, service and warehouse) attribute and
operation through graphic user interface, which are identified from the specification of
the company MS.

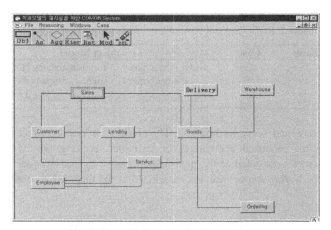

Fig. 1. Generation of initial object model

4.2   Generation of Initial Object Model

The user required generating initial object model using the problem object model in
fig. 1. The OOM management system retrieved object model 'Order management of
furniture agency NY', which is the most similar case in case-base like table 1.

The OOM management system generated the extended initial object model through reuse rules using knowledge-base and retrieval object model (Order management of furniture agency NY) like fig. 2. The modifying objects in this initial object model are classes and associations such as 'goods-warehouse', 'employee-lending-goods', 'customer-service' and so on. The table 2 is the modified alternative for'customer-service-goods',

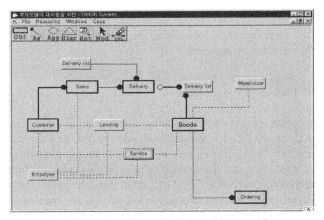

Fig. 2. Generation of extended initial object model

Table 1. Retrieval result of similarity case using problem object model

Rank	Case	Object Model
1	2	Order management of furniture agency NY
2	1	Book management of lending company JY
3	5	Customer management of electronics SW

'employee-sales' and 'service-employee'. The association 'customer-reception-goods' is selected as the modified alternative for 'customer-service-goods'. The association 'person-contract' is selected as the modified alternative for 'employee-sales'. Finally, 'employee-service worker-service treatment' is selected as the modified alternative for 'service-employee'.

Table 2. Modified alternative for customer, employee, service

Association	Modified alternative association
customer-service-goods	customer-reception-goods
employee-sales	person-contract
service-employee	employee-service workers -service treatment

4.3 Completion of Final Object Model

This process is repeated until all the modified objects are satisfied or system can't generate the modified alternative. Initial object model that the user wants is gradually developed as a completed OOM through this repetition.

In accordance with the result of the completed initial object model, class 'reception' and 'receptionist' are changed into each 'service reception' and 'salesman'. The associations 'transaction-service reception', 'employee-transaction' and transaction-delivery' are added. Redundant 'customer-sales', 'customer-lending' and so on are deleted. The final object model of company MS is completed by repeating in process like fig. 3.

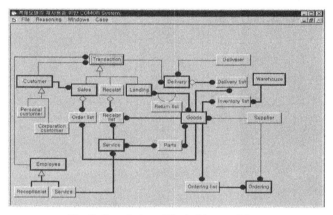

Fig. 3. Completion of final object model

5 Discussion

We developed the methods and procedures of OOM on the basis of CBR, and propose how to express the case of OOM with it. Moreover, this study expresses both the rules for retrieving the past object models needed for reuse and the rules for modifying OOM in accordance with the new problems.

This study extended the domain of software reuse from source code to the system analysis phase. If you use this system, you can get over the problems of knowledge acquisition, which exists for analyzed outputs reuse. This system bring about the effects of reducing the efforts and cost, which are expected on account of shortening the time required for software reuse. This system, offering graphic user interface which expresses the outputs in the system analysis phase, enables object modeling to be easier than source code reuse.

References

1. Booch, G., I. Jacobson, Rumbaugh, J.,: UML version 1.0, Rational Software (1997)
2. Faget, J., Morel, J. M.,: The REBOOT Environment, In Proceeding 2nd International Workshop on Software Reusability, Lucca Italy March (1993)
3. Joshi, R., McMillan, W.,: Case Based Reasoning Approach to creating user interface components, Pro. in Conference on human factors in computing systems (1997) 81-82
4. Kim, Y. J., Kim, C. T.,: Design of Software Reuse System using Object Model in System Analysis, Proceedings of the 2000 IEEE ICMIT, Singapore Nov. (2000) 556-560
5. Prieto-Diaz, R.,: Status Report: Software Reusability, IEEE Software, May (1998) 61-66
6. Riesbeck, C. K., Schank, R. L.,: Inside Case -Based Reasoning, Hillsdale NJ Lawrence Erlbaum Associates (1989)
7. Yourdon, E.,: Object-Oriented System Design: An Integrated Approach, Prentice-Hall Englewood Cliffs, NJ (1994)

Automatic Aircraft Recognition Using Maximum Likelihood Ratio Test

Wei Yi

Signal Processing Division, Dept. of Electrical & Electronic Engineering, University of
Strathclyde, 204 George Street, G1 1XW, Glasgow, UK
Weiyi@spd.eee.strath.ac.uk

Abstract. The automatic aircraft recognition in aerial images has been a topic
receiving the maximum attention in the literature for more than two decades
due to its practical value. Since the original images may be obtained in various
uncertain environment, defects such as noise/background clutter, skewness,
partial occlusion and blue may affect the image quality which lead to high
environment dependence of some existing aircraft detection systems/
algorithms. This paper proposes a novel approach based on the Maximum
Likelihood Ratio Test (MLRT) to extract different aircraft from the real aerial
images. Objects in the tested images are corrupted randomly by the various
defects. Without any extra information, the successful detection rate of the
aircraft reaches 96% and that of the nonplane objects reaches 100% when only
six aircraft references are chosen. The experiments are carried out to test
sensitivity of the proposed method to the noise and partial occlusion. The
comparisons with the Moment Fourier Descriptors (MFD) are also given.

1 Introduction

Photo interpretation (PI) or intelligent data extraction from images, especially from
the aerial images has been one of the important topics in the image understanding
field. Among all objects in the aerial images, the recognition of the aircraft receives
the maximum attention in the literature. However, in many real applications, the aerial
images are often obtained in uncertain environment, which may pollute their objects
randomly with the noise/background clutter, skewness, blur and partial occlusion. On
the other hand, the low-level image processing techniques cannot always produce an
edge image meeting the high-level recognition requirement. Some existing aircraft
detection systems/algorithms either crucially depend on the image quality, or rely on
the additional information such as one-dimensional radar signals and CAD models.

In general, a shape recognition system is a four-step process. They are the image
obtaining, preprocessing, feature extraction and shape classification. The source
images used for this research are more than a dozen 2700*2700 original gray-level
aerial images. No qualitative or quantitative information is available on the image
quality. The preprocessing step includes the object segmentation, noise reduction and
edge detection. Only common techniques are adopted since the preprocessing is not
our main focus. The feature extraction stage uses the Principal Component Analysis
(PCA) to complete the translation, rotation and scale normalisation of an unknown

J. Liu et al. (Eds.): AMT 2001, LNCS 2252, pp. 321–326, 2001.

object and the calculation of its statistical characteristics. Detailed algorithm can refer to [4].

This paper puts its emphasis on the last step. Based on the Maximum Likelihood Ratio Test (MLRT), it proposes a novel approach to make plane/nonplane decisions. A statistical variable named Maximum Likelihood Ratio (MLR) is constructed through comparing the features of an unknown object and a model aircraft. The decision making is based on whether the MLR of the unknown object is less than or equal to the threshold.

This paper is organised as follows: the second part introduces the algorithm design. The third part gives the detailed experimental results and analysis. The fourth part draws the conclusions.

2   Algorithm Design

Although various types of aircraft appear in different sizes and shapes, they all share some common features, such as two fuselages, one nose and one tail etc. If all edge pixels or centralised edge pixels of an aircraft are considered as a set of observation data, the skewness and kurtosis of the data can be calculated. Based on the experiments on the different kinds of the aircraft, the average skewness and kurtosis of an aircraft fulfill the requirement of the asymptotic normal distribution. Therefore the normal distribution is adopted here to model the edge pixels of an aircraft.

Given an unknown object has already undergone the geometric normalisation. The coordinates of all edge pixels in a vector format is $P = (T, Z)^T$ with $\overline{P}$ as its expectation and D_p as its variance.

The null hypothesis H_0 is : the unknown object is an aircraft. That is, $D_p = D_0$, where D_0 is the variance of an aircraft model.

The alternative hypothesis H_1 is : the unknown object is not an aircraft. That is, $D_p > D_0$.

Applying the two-dimensional joint normal distribution $N_2(\mu, D)$, the MLR of the unknown object can be written as

$$\lambda_\omega = \frac{F(P; \overline{P}, D_0)}{F(P; \overline{P}, D_p)} \tag{1}$$

where

$$F(P; \overline{P}, D_0) = \frac{1}{(2\pi)^n |D_0|^{n/2}} \exp\left\{-\frac{1}{2}(P - \overline{P})^T D_0^{-1}(P - \overline{P})\right\} \tag{2}$$

$$F(P; \overline{P}, D_p) = \frac{1}{(2\pi)^n |D_p|^{n/2}} \exp\left\{-\frac{1}{2}(P - \overline{P})^T D_p^{-1}(P - \overline{P})\right\} \tag{3}$$

Applying (2) and (3) to (1), the MLR is finally defined as

$$-2 \ln \lambda_\omega = n \times [tr(D_p D_0^{-1}) - \ln|D_p D_0^{-1}| - 2] \tag{4}$$

where n is the number of edge pixels.

In order to obtain the suitable value of the threshold C_0, the distribution properties of $-2\ln\lambda_\omega$ need to be known. In fact, when the number of edge pixels n is large, $-2\ln\lambda_\omega$ is asymptotically distributed as χ_α^2 with 3 degrees as freedom. Choosing the confidence $\alpha = 0.003, C_0 = \chi_{0.003}^2(3) = 15.0$ according to the statistical table.

The criterion for decision making is that when $-2\ln\lambda_\omega \geq 15.0$, the unknown object is declared not an aircraft and vice versa.

3   Experimental Analysis

3.1 Experimental Results

Based on the algorithm design introduced in part 2, this paper conducted experiments on an object database containing 53 objects. Most of these objects originate from the original aerial images. The final goal is to separate all the aircraft in the database from other objects. To this end, firstly 5 scenarios are classified here to group all objects according to their qualities. They are good quality (G), skewness (S), noise and background clutter (N), partial occlusion (O) and blur (B). Fig. 1 contains 10 images from each group. By choosing only six aircraft as the references, six MLRs of each unknown object can be obtained. Only when all the MLRs are beyond the threshold 15.0, can we declare the unknown object is not a plane. Fig. 1 also shows the MLR of each edge image compared with one reference aircraft $D_0 = \begin{bmatrix} 1976.4 & 0 \\ 0 & 538.3 \end{bmatrix}$.

(a) G	(b) G	(c) N	(d) N	(e) O
$-2\ln\lambda_\omega = 0.41$	$-2\ln\lambda_\omega = 6.0$	$-2\ln\lambda_\omega = 14.0$	$-2\ln\lambda_\omega = 2.0$	$-2\ln\lambda_\omega = 2.07$

(f) O	(g) B	(h) B	(I) S	(j) S
$-2\ln\lambda_\omega = 2.0$	$-2\ln\lambda_\omega = 96.0$	$-2\ln\lambda_\omega = 49.0$	$-2\ln\lambda_\omega = 3.0$	$-2\ln\lambda_\omega = 10.0$

Fig. 1. 10 original image segments with different qualities

As can be seen from Fig.1, the MLRs of nonplane objects are far beyond the threshold. The overall experiments are conducted to each unknown object in the database. With six aircraft as the references, the successful detection rate of the aircraft is 96% and that of the nonplane object is 100%.

3.2 Performance Analysis

3.2.1 Simulation of Noise

The noise and background clutter are two of the major factors affecting the edge quality. To study how robust the proposed algorithm to overcome the noise, a simulation program is run by adding the noise created by the software to some good quality images. The critical level which each image can achieve is recorded. An example of the simulation is shown in Fig. 2.

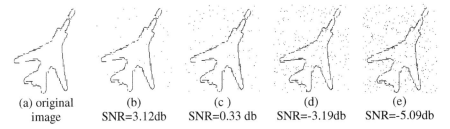

| (a) original image | (b) SNR=3.12db | (c) SNR=0.33 db | (d) SNR=-3.19db | (e) SNR=-5.09db |

Fig. 2. Simulation experiment on noise

Firstly the definition of the Signal-to-Noise Ratio (SNR) is given below

$$SNR = \frac{P_s}{P_N} = \frac{P_s}{P_s' - P_s} = \frac{\sum v_{ti}^2 + \sum v_{ui}^2}{\sum v_{ti}'^2 + \sum v_{ui}'^2 - \sum v_{ti}^2 - \sum v_{ui}^2} \tag{5}$$

$$SNR(db) = 10*logSNR \tag{6}$$

where v_{ti} and v_{ui} are the centralised coordinate of the original edge images, and v_{ti}' and v_{ui}' are the centralised coordinate of the polluted images.

In Fig.2, (a) is the original image, (b)-(f) are corrupted images which can still be detected. (f) shows the critical SNR(db) that the algorithm can achieve. (g) shows the critical SNR(db) that the algorithm just fail.

The simulation on all good quality images are implemented and the results show that the algorithm can still work well when SNR(db) reaches –4.43db.

3.2.2 Simulation on Partial Occlusion

Another factor directly affects the decision making is the partial occlusion. In real applications, the partial occlusion may happen on the different parts of the objects and to different levels. Therefore it is not realistic to build a huge reference database especially for the detection of partially occluded objects.

A simulation program is run to test the robustness of the proposed method to overcome the partial occlusion problems when the same reference aircraft are used. Several good quality aircraft images are chosen here and obscured a set of percentage of the aircraft to simulate the partial occlusion. Fig. 3 is an example.

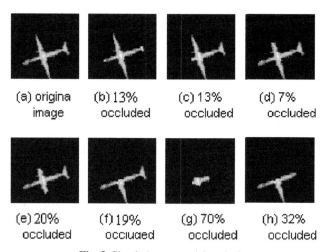

(a) original image
(b) 13% occluded
(c) 13% occluded
(d) 7% occluded
(e) 20% occluded
(f) 19% occluded
(g) 70% occluded
(h) 32% occluded

Fig. 3. Simulation on partial occlusion

In Fig.3, (a) is the original image. (b) is the symmetric occlusion along the major axis. (c) and (d) are the asymmetric occlusion along the nose and tail. (e) and (f) are symmetric and asymmetric occlusion along the minor axis. (g) and (h) are symmetric and asymmetric occlusion along both major and minor axes.

The above experiments show that the algorithm is more robust in detection when the occlusion happens symmetrically along the major or (and) minor axis.

3.3 Comparisons with the Moment Fourier Descriptors (MFD)

The MFD was proposed by Wang[1] in 1994 and used to recognise the complicated shapes without requiring a closed region. Based on the recognition principles addressed in [1], a program is developed to extract the aircraft from the same database. Also choose six aircraft as the references, the comparison of the MFD with the proposed method is shown in Table 1.

Table 1. Comparisons of the MFD with the MLRT based approach

MFD			MLRT based approach		
Original Results	Pla ne	non-plane	Original Results	Plane	non-plane
Plane	96 %	62%	Plane	96%	0%
Nonpla-ne	4%	38%	Non-plane	4%	100%
Average processing time for each object is 15s			Average processing time for each object is 6s		

4   Conclusions

This paper adopts the Maximum Likelihood Ratio Test to extract the aircraft based on their statistical features with geometric invariance. It has the following strengths over some existing methods:

(1) Fast speed and no extra requirement for the computer resources. The application of the MLRT transfers a pattern classification problem into the judgement of one inequality;

(2) Accurate recognition. From the experimental results, the MLRs of the nonplane objects are far beyond the threshold. Therefore the algorithm makes clear decisions with a very wide margin between the aircraft and nonplane.

(3) High performance against the image defects. Most of the objects are segmented from the original images and affected randomly by one or some of the image defects. Generally no prior information related to these defects is available. The application of the MLRT can minimise these negative effects while preserve the maximum information of the shape.

References

1. S. S. Wang, P. C. Chen and W. G. Lin, Invariant Pattern Recognition by Moment Fourier Descriptors, vol. 27, No. 12, Pattern Recognition, (1994),1735-1742
2. B. S. Everitt and G. Dunn, Applied Multivariate Data Analysis, Edward Arnold, (1991)
3. Z. Q. Bian and X. G. Zhang, Pattern Recognition, Tsinghua University Press, (2000).
4. Y. Wei and S. Marshall, Principal Component Analysis in Application to Object Orientation, Vol. 3, \no.3, Geo-spatial Information Science, (2000), 76-78

A Machine Learning Algorithm Based on Supervised Clustering and Classification

Nong Ye and Xiangyang Li

P. O. Box 875906, Department of Industrial Engineering, Arizona State University, Tempe, Arizona, 85287, USA
{nongye, xyli}@asu.edu

Abstract. In this paper a novel data mining technique – Clustering and Classification Algorithm-Supervised (CCA-S)[1] is introduced. CCA-S supports incremental learning and non-hierarchical clustering, and is scalable for processing large data sets. CCA-S incorporates the class information in making clustering decisions, and uses the resulting clusters to classify new data records. We apply and test CCA-S on several common data sets for classification problems. The testing results show that the classification performance of CCA-S is comparable to the other classification algorithms such as decision trees, artificial neural networks and discriminant analysis.

1 Introduction

The development of modern computing and information technologies has enabled the collection of large amounts of data in engineering fields. Data mining techniques are required in these application fields to discover patterns and useful information from large amounts of data. Classification is an important area of data mining. A number of techniques can be applied to solving classification problems, including discriminant analysis, decision trees, artificial neural networks, instance-based classification and so on [1, 8]. The following criteria are often used to evaluate a classification technique: the classification precision, the training and classification speed, the scalability on large data sets, the robustness to noises, and the incremental learning ability. The scalability and the incremental learning ability become increasingly important with the collection of large amounts of data enabled by the development of modern information technologies. In many industrial processes, large volumes of data are produced every day. The patterns embedded in such data may change over time. Ideally, a data mining technique should have the incremental learning ability to update the existing patterns with the collection of new data and be scalable to processing large amounts of data.

This paper presents a novel classification technique to support scalability and incremental learning ability, called Clustering and Classification Algorithm – Supervised (CCA-S). CCA-S is developed from two existing data mining approaches - clustering and instance-based classification. However, CCA-S differs from the

---

[1] A US and international patent on this algorithm has been filed, and is currently pending with ASU Case No. M1-015.

J. Liu et al. (Eds.): AMT 2001, LNCS 2252, pp. 327–334, 2001.

existing clustering techniques by using the class information to supervise a non-hierarchical clustering procedure. The resulting clusters and instance-based classification are then used to classify new data for reducing the impact of possible noise and outliers in the training data and improving the prediction precision.

2   Clustering and Instance-Based Classification

2.1   Clustering

Let S be a set of N data points - generally data points in a p-dimensional space, where this space may have a well-defined distance metric. A partition of S into K sets, $C1$, $C2$, ..., Ck, is called a K-clustering, and Ci is a cluster. The distance or dissimilarity between two data points can be defined through a function that does not necessarily satisfy the triangle inequality. Cluster analysis finds the clusters of data points by optimizing a given criterion or simply using certain heuristics.

The well-known heuristic algorithms are hierarchical and partitioning clustering algorithms [4]. The hierarchical clustering algorithm uses a nested sequence of partitions. A typical partitioning algorithm, K-means method, groups data points into K clusters to minimize some criterion on produced clusters. Both the hierarchical and partitioning clustering algorithms require a complete pair-wise distance matrix of all the data points before the clustering can proceed. This creates the difficulty in supporting incremental learning when new data points become available to update the clusters.

Incremental learning incorporates the new training data points into the existing models. Several methods have been developed to improve the scalability and the incremental learning ability using the concept of the local neighborhood region.

Grid-based clustering. A method for finding the regions of high density in the data space is based on the cell densities of a grid. In this method a histogram is constructed by partitioning the data space into a number of non-overlapping regions or grids, and approximately describes the density of the data points in each cell.

Density-based clustering. Density-based clustering uses a local cluster criterion. It requires that from one data point in a cluster there exist a given number of points within a given radius. Hence, the density-based clustering approach considers the clusters as the regions in which the data points are dense.

Subspace clustering. Subspace clustering is a kind of grid-based clustering. It is a bottom-up approach to finding the dense units and merging them to find the dense clusters in the higher dimensional subspaces. The rational is that if a dense cell exists in k dimensions then all its projections to a subset of the k dimensions are also dense.

Some incremental or scalable algorithms have been developed in recent years based on the above concepts. BIRCH uses a hierarchical data structure, called CF-tree, to incrementally and dynamically cluster the incoming data points [10]. DBSCAN is a clustering technique [2] based on the concept of density. WaveCluster is a density-based and grid-based technique that applies the wavelet transformation to the feature space of the data points [9]. MAFIA is a subspace clustering technique that uses adaptive grid size to improve clustering quality [3]. Among these algorithms BIRCH and DBSCAN have incremental learning ability. All these algorithms have the approximate computation complexity of $O(N)$ with regard to N points in a data set.

All the above clustering algorithms perform unsupervised clustering. Domain knowledge is usually required either during clustering to determine the parameters in these algorithms or after clustering to interpret the clustering results. For example, the hierarchical clustering approach produces a hierarchical clustering tree. Given different distance thresholds, this hierarchical clustering tree produces different sets of clusters. For another example, the size and number of the grid cells in the grid-based clustering approach and the radius in the density-based approach are critical to the clustering result and performance. These parameters depend on domain knowledge, and likely require trial-and-error experimentation to choose appropriate values. In this paper, we investigate and develop a supervised clustering algorithm that uses the class information rather than arbitrary parameters to guide the clustering procedure.

2.2 Instance-Based Classification

Instance-based Classification is based on the assumption that the classification of an instance is most similar to the classification of other instances that are close to this instance. Instance-based classification is a straightforward method using similar cases to classify a new data point. Using the class information of its neighbors, the new data point is classified into the dominant class of these neighbors. The k-nearest-neighbor methods have been very successful in many practical applications [1]. Despite the success of the k-nearest-neighbor methods for classification, there are problems with their practical application on large and complex data sets. When the original data points are used, the classification performance is impacted by noises and outliers to a certain extent. Clustering can be used to group the data points and represent their underlying patterns. Using the clusters rather than the original data points can improve the classification performance as well as the scalability. The number of clusters is generally much smaller than the number of the original data points, thus requiring less storage space and enabling a more efficient search for the nearest neighbors.

3   Clustering and Classification Algorithm – Supervised (CCA-S)

Let each data record be a $(p+1)$-tuple with the predictor variable vector X in p dimensions, $X = (X_1, X_2, \ldots X_p)$, and the target variable Y representing the class of each data record. Each data record is as a data point in a p-dimensional space. Each predictor variable is either numeric or nominal. Y can be a binary variable with the value of 0 or 1, or a multi-category nominal variable. The Y value is given for each data record in the training data. The Y value for each data record in the testing data must be determined from the values of the predictor variables through classification. In this paper, we describe CCA-S for only the numeric predictor variables and the binary target variable. Variations of CCA-S for dealing with other types of the predictor variables and the target variable will be presented in future reports.

3.1 Training – Supervised Clustering

In training there are two steps to incrementally group the N data points in the training data set into clusters.

Step 1. Scan the training data and compute the parameters.
This step calculates the squared correlation coefficient between each predictor variable X_i and the target variable Y to determine how relevant each predictor variable is for classifying the target class in the target variable. The squared correlation coefficient r_{iY} can be incrementally computed as in [5].

A dummy cluster is created for each target class with the centroid coordinates { X_{k1}, X_{k2},..., X_{kp} } being the mean vector of the predictor variables for that target class as follows.

$$X_{ki} = \frac{\sum_{n=1}^{N_k} X_{i,n}}{N_k}, \qquad k = 0,1 \ and \ i = 1,2,..., p. \tag{1}$$

where N_0 is the number of the data points with the target class of 0, N_1 is the number of the data points with the target class of 1. The two dummy clusters for the two target classes (0 and 1) respectively are assigned with the same target class (e.g., 2) which is different from the target classes of 0 and 1. The dummy cluster for a given class (0 or 1) is used in the clustering procedure to let the clusters for this class spread over the entire space of the data population for this class rather than congest around the centroid location of the space.

Step 2. Incrementally group each data point in the training data set into clusters.
1. For a new data point X, find the nearest cluster L to this data point using the distance measure, $d(X,L)$, weighted by the squared correlation coefficient of each predictor variable. The centroid coordinates of L are denoted by $(L_1, L_2, ..., L_p)$. Different distance measures [5] may be used. Here we give the weighted Canberra distance.

$$d(X,L) = \sum_{i=1}^{P} \frac{|X_i - L_i|}{X_i + L_i} r_{iY}^2. \tag{2}$$

where X_i and L_i are the coordinates of the data point X and the cluster L's centroid on the ith dimension.
2. If L has the same target class label as that of X, combine X into L, and update the centroid coordinates of L and the number of the data points (N_L) in this cluster.
3. Otherwise, create a new cluster with this data point as the centroid. The number of the data points in the new cluster is 1, and the target class of the new cluster is the target class of this data point.
4. Repeat 1 to 3 until no data point in the training data set is left.

Hence, CCA-S performs a non-hierarchical clustering procedure based on the distance information as well as the target class information of the data points in the training data set.

3.2 Testing – Classification

In testing, the clusters produced from the training phase are used to classify the data points in the testing data set by determining their values of the target variable. Based on instance-based classification, we assign the distance-weighted average of the target values of the k nearest clusters, L_1, ..., L_k, to the target value of the data point X as follows:

$$W_j = \frac{1}{d^2(X, L_j)} \qquad (3)$$

$$Y = \frac{\sum_{j=1}^{k} Y_j W_j}{\sum_{j=1}^{k} W_j}$$

where L_j is the centroid coordinates of the jth nearest cluster, W_j is the weight for the cluster j; the target class of this cluster is Y_j and the target class of the X data point is Y. The class value Y of this data point falls in the range of $[0,1]$ to describe the closeness of this data point to the two target classes of 0 and 1.

3.3 Incremental Learning Capability of CCA-S

CCA-S supports the incremental update of the clusters with new training data. The parameters from the previous training phase, including the correlation coefficient for each prediction variable, the centroid coordinates of each cluster, and the number of the data points in each cluster, are kept all the time and thus can be updated incrementally with each record in the new training data by repeating the steps in training.

3.4 Computation Complexity

Given the N data points, the computational complexity of CCA-S is O(N) because each data point in the training data set is scanned only once in training. CCA-S does not require the pair-wise distance matrix as in the hierarchical clustering approach. If we take into account the effect of other factors on the computational complexity, the upper bound of the computational complexity of CCA-S is $O(pNM)$, where M is the total number of the clusters produced from the training phase. The computational complexity of classifying a data point in the testing data set is $O(pM)$.

4   Testing

CCA-S is tested on several data sets that are commonly used for evaluating the classification performance of a data mining technique. These data sets are obtained from the University of California, Irvine, Repository of Machine Learning Database (http://www.ics.uci.edu/~mlearn/MLRepository.html). Three data sets are selected from this repository based on the level of classification difficulty. The three data sets are *bcw* (Wisconsin Breast Cancer), *pid* (PIMA Indian Diabetes) and *bld* (BUPA Liver Disorders) in the order from the easiest to the most difficult [6]. All of the three data sets have numeric predictor variables, and the binary target variable as required by this version of CCA-S. The data records with missing values of the predictor variables are removed from the data sets because this version of CCA-S does not deal with missing values.

4.1   Description of the Data Sets

The data set *bcw* is used to predict whether a tissue sample of a patient's breast is malignant or benign [7]. It has nine integer attributes, and 683 data records. The attributes as the predictor variables include such as certain measures on tissue cells.

The data set *pid* is collected on females at least twenty-one years old of Pima Indian heritage living near Phoenix, Arizona, USA. The classification problem is to predict whether a patient would test positive for diabetes given some physiological measurements and medical test results. The data set has seven numeric attributes and 532 data records.

For the data set *bld*, the classification problem is to predict whether a male patient has a liver disorder given blood tests and alcohol consumption. There are six numeric attributes, and 345 data records.

4.2   Testing and Error Rate Estimation

In testing, CCA-S uses the weighted Canberra distance in formula (2). The classification is based on formula (3) to calculate the target value of a data record as the distance-weighted average of the target values of all the clusters produced from the training stage. Since the target variable is binary, the class value falls into [0,1]. The classification threshold is set as 0.5. If the class value is greater than 0.5, it is considered as class 1, otherwise it is considered as class 0.

The classification error rate of CCA-S is determined through a ten-fold cross-validation. That is, each data set is divided evenly into ten non-overlapping subsets. The data records with different target classes are chosen in proportion. A classifier is built for each subset using the data records in the other nine subsets as the training data. Then the classifier is tested on the data in this subset as the testing data to obtain the error rate on this subset. The cross-validation error rate for the entire data set is computed as the average of the ten error rates.

4.3 Result Analysis

Among the techniques in [6] are the decision tree algorithms including C&RT, S-Plus tree, C4.5, FACT, QUEST, IND, OC1, LMDT, CAL5, T1, discriminant analysis algorithms including LDA, QDA, NN, LOG, FDA, PDA, and MDA, a regression algorithm – POL, artificial neural network techniques including LVQ and RBF, and other data mining techniques. There are a total of 33 techniques reported in [6]. The error rates for these techniques are also determined using the ten-fold cross-validation method. The error rates of CCA-S and these algorithms are shown in Table 1. In the report by Lim, Loh, & Shih [6], only the minimum and maximum error rates of these algorithms on each of the three data sets are provided.

Table 1. Error rate s of CCA-S and other data mining algorithms on the three data sets

		bcw	pid	bld
CCA-S		.035	.235	.446
Other	Min	.03	.22	.28
algorithms	Max	.09	.31	.43

As can be seen from Table 1, the classification performance of CCA-S is comparable to those other classification algorithms in [6]. For the classification problems in *bcw* and *pid*, CCA-S produces the error rates close to the best performance of the other classification algorithms. For the data set *bld*, CCA-S yields the performance similar to the worst one of the other classification algorithms. The performance of CCA-S on *bld* is the worst among the three data sets, which is also the case for the other classification algorithms as can be seen in Table 1.

5 Conclusions

This paper presents the novel data mining algorithm CCA-S based on supervised clustering and instance-based classification. We demonstrate the comparable performance of CCA-S to that of many other existing data mining techniques for classification problems. The advantages of CCA-S lie in its scalability and its ability to support incremental learning. These two advantages are critical to the successful application of any data mining techniques to the increasing number of large-scale, dynamically changing data sets. CCA-S can be applied to many classification problems, such as those for statistical quality control to detect anomalous patterns of a manufacturing process, group technology, shop floor control, and so on, where computers are used to constantly collect large amounts of process data. In our future reports, we will present variations of CCA-S for dealing with a wide variety of variable types, the post-refinement of the clusters from the training phase, and other issues.

Acknowledgement. This work is sponsored in part by the Air Force Office of Scientific Research (AFOSR) under grant number F49620-99-1-001. The U.S. government is authorized to reproduce and distribute reprints for governmental purposes notwithstanding any copyright annotation thereon. The views and conclusions contained herein are those of the authors and should not be interpreted as necessarily representing the official policies or endorsements, either express or implied, of, AFOSR, or the U.S. Government.

References

1. Cherkassky, V., Mulier, F.: Learning from Data. John Wiley & Sons, Inc. (1998)
2. Ester, M., Kriegel H.P., Sander, J., Wimmer, M., Xu, X.: Incremental Clustering for Mining in a data Warehousing Environment. Proceedings of 24th VLDB Conference. New York (1998)
3. Harsha, S.G., Choudhary, A.: Parallel Subspace Clustering for Very Large Data Sets. Techinical Report No. CPDC-TR-9906-010. Northwestern University (1999)
4. Jain, A. K., Dubes, R. C.: Algorithms for Clustering Data. Prentice Hall, New Jersey (1988)
5. Johnson, R. A., Wichern, D. W.: Applied multivariate Statistical Analysis. Prentice Hall, New Jersey (1998)
6. Lim, T., Loh, W., Shih, Y.: A Comparison of Prediction Accuracy, Complexity, and Training Time of Thirty-three Old and New Classification Algorithms. Machine Learning, Vol. 40. (2000) 203-228
7. Mangasarian, O. L., Wolberg, W. H.: Cancer Diagnosis via Linear Programming. SIAM News, Vol. 23(5). (1990) 1-18.
8. Mitchell, T.: Machine Learning. WCB/McGraw-Hill. (1997)
9. Sheikholeslami, G., Chatterjee, S., Zhang, A.: WaveCluster: A Multi-Resolution Clustering Approach for Very Large Spatial Databases. Proceedings of 24th VLDB Conference. New York (1998)
10. Zhang, T.: Data Clustering For Very Large Datasets Plus Applications. Ph.D. Thesis, Dept. of Computer Science, University of Wisconsin – Madison (1997)

Visualization of a Parallel Genetic Algorithm in Real Time

Xiaodong Li

School of Computer Science and Information Technology, RMIT University
GPO Box 2476v, Melbourne 3001,Victoria Australia
Xiaodong@cs.rmit.edu.au

Abstract. Parallel Genetic Algorithms (PGA) have been implemented in the past largely on parallel computers, and more recently on serial PCs. PGAs have been used successfully in solving many difficult optimization tasks. To gain further insight into the state and progress of the algorithm, we often need to extract useful information from the large amount of data generated from a PGA run, but this can be a difficult task. Many of the current PGA implementations often have no capability of visualizing an evolving GA population dynamically during execution time. In this paper, we describe an implementation of a fine-grained parallel GA using Swarm, a multi-agent simulation tool originally developed at the Santa Fe institute. The PGA model developed is capable of visualizing dynamically the performance of an evolving GA population with plotted graphs on model parameter values in real time. This implementation also allows modification of some model parameter values during an optimization run, therefore offers advantages over many existing PGA implementations. We demonstrate the usefulness of the visualization techniques used in this PGA implementation using two optimization examples.

1 Introduction

Genetic algorithms were introduced by Holland [1], and they have gained immense popularity because of its efficiency in solving difficult optimization problems. With the increasing advancement and availability of various parallel computers, there have been many efforts in implementing GAs on parallel computers [2], [3]. Parallel GA takes its inspiration from nature, where interactions among species occur in a parallel manner and are normally confined within an individual's local environment. In a PGA often there is no global control on how individuals should interact with each other. The parallel implementation of GA allows us to make use of features such as local interactions that are non-existent in a conventional GA. One of the challenging tasks in implementing a PGA is that, in order to gain a good insight into the evolutionary progress in a PGA population during an optimization run, how we can extract useful information from the vast amount of data produced. There has been a number of visualization methods developed to cater for this need [4], [5]. Pohlheim proposed

J. Liu et al. (Eds.): AMT 2001, LNCS 2252, pp. 335–346, 2001.

a set of standard visualization techniques for different data types of a Genetic Algorithm [5]. These data types and techniques can be used to gain an instant impression of the evolutionary algorithm's progress and the actual state of the individuals of the population. The techniques can be summarized in two categories. The first category includes methods used for displaying data produced over many generations, therefore providing a picture of the progress of the evolutionary algorithm. The second category contains techniques to visualize data produced at every generation, thus presenting a picture of the current state of the GA population.

In this research our focus is to look at how to extend the existing visualization features to allow dynamic displaying of the data produced during a PGA run. We developed a Parallel GA model that allows visualization of variable value changes occurring in a PGA population at run time (with dynamically plotted graphs). In particular, the dynamic changes of the spatial structure of the PGA population can be visualized. These dynamically generated plotted graphs (as animation sequences) can offer greater advantages over the static plotted graphs such as those proposed so far by Pohlheim [5]. With the use of dynamically plotted graphs visualizing various model parameter values at run time, we might be able to gain further insights that otherwise might be missed out from studying the dynamics of an evolving GA population. Another feature of this particular PGA implementation is that it allows certain degree of interaction between a user and the model during an optimization run. The user can pause the model run and then modify the values of some parameters before resuming the run (using *probes*). The visualization features such as dynamic display and interaction described here can be useful in analyzing the progress and states of an evolving PGA population.

In the following sections, we start with an overview on Swarm, as the proposed PGA (i.e. a fine-grained Parallel GA) is developed using Swarm. This is followed by a description of the use of parallelism and scheduling in Swarm, which makes such a parallel GA implementation possible and at ease on a serial machine (rather than a parallel machine). We then describe more specifically how parallelism and scheduling can be applied to the parallel implementation of a GA. We also present two examples of optimization problem solving so that the visualization features offered by this specific PGA implementation can be demonstrated. Finally we finish with a conclusion.

2   Simulation Using Swarm

Swarm is a general-purpose simulation package that provides a set of standard and reliable tools for simulating and analyzing a wide variety of distributed complex systems. Swarm provides libraries that allow users to construct simulations where a collection of independent agents interacts through discrete events [6]. Since its first release in 1995, simulation models based on Swarm have been developed in such diverse areas as economics, biology, ecology, social and political sciences [7].

2.1 An Overview on Swarm

Swarm is written in Objective-C, a pure object-oriented programming language and a superset of C. Swarm uses the *Tcl* scripting language and *Tk* widget set to implement batch-oriented and graphical interfaces (e.g., graphs, buttons and windows for user input). Swarm was initially written only for Unix workstations running X-windows, but now is available on Windows NT/98 and Linux as well.

The primary objective of Swarm is to save complexity researchers from having to deal with the issues involved in the implementation of concurrent, distributed artificial world. In order to achieve this, the Swarm system provides a wide range of generic artificial worlds populated with generic agents, a large library of design and analysis tools, and a kernel to drive the simulation. Researchers are then free to customize Swarm's general-purpose objects to model system according to their own domains.

Table 1. Mappings from model to Swarm.

Complex systems model	Swarm Implementation
Nested swarms	Nested zones + schedules
Agents	Objects
Events	Messages
Observers	Display and logging objects
Instruments and probes	Probe objects
Statistical tools	Analysis objects

Table 1 shows that a model designer can map a complex system model to Swarm with relative ease. The task of mapping Swarm formalism to a low-level computer implementation is taken care of by Swarm itself, therefore the model designer can concentrate on mapping the logical model to Swarm without worrying about implementation details.

A typical Swarm program (as shown in Fig. 1) consists of a collection of agents with a schedule of events over those agents [8]. A schedule consists of a sequence of actions to be performed. An action consists of three parts, a message to send, an agent or collection of agents to send the message to, and a time to send the message. Agents interact by sending messages to one to another requesting for actions or data. *Swarm* can also be nested, in which case an agent itself can be a swarm of agents. *Interface* objects are responsible for collecting information for graphical display, whereas *Model* abstraction objects may do some house keeping for the artificial world.

2.2 Parallelism and Scheduling in Swarm

Parallel-distributed architecture is an essential attribute in many complex systems. Swarm has been designed specifically to serve this need. The Swarm *Space Library* contains many classes that can be used for building objects representing artificial world environments where agent interactions occur.

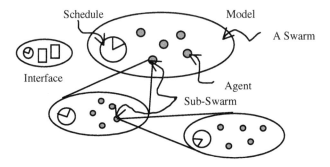

Fig. 1. Simulation components in Swarm.

As for scheduling activities, Swarm allows the model designer to treat event scheduling just like objects. Swarm has an *Activity Library* by which the model designer can schedule periodic events and create groups of events that can be executed at periodic intervals or triggered dynamically. Swarm provides a number of methods named as *ActionGroup* for ordering the constituent actions of an activity structure, i.e., a collection of actions that are assumed to execute either in linear sequence or at the same time. Different *ActionGroups* can be collected together in *Schedules,* which are triggered at specific intervals. Internal model events and external updating of graphs and outputs can be either invoked simultaneously or separated at different interval [9].

3   Description of the Parallel GA Algorithm

The parallel implementation of GA adopted here is a fine-grained parallel algorithm. In this implementation, we basically parallelize a conventional GA onto a 2-dimensional grid. Each individual chromosome of the current population occupies one spot on the grid. Interactions among individuals (i.e., selection, mating and mutation) are restricted to the adjacent neighbourhoods on the grid (as seen in Fig. 2), therefore interactions depends only on local information, compared with the use of global information in a conventional GA. There are many possible designs for local interaction here. In this implementation, we allow each individual to choose the fittest individual from the immediate neighbouring ones. If there are more than one individual that has the best fitness value, then we randomly choose one out of all the best individuals. Fig. 3 shows the outline of the PGA implementation.

The selection at each generation is based on the fitness value of each individual. A culling rate $C\%$ is applied to a current population of N individuals. This culling leads to elimination of $C\%$ less fit individuals within the current population. After culling, C number of spots on the 2d grid will be vacant. The coordinates of these vacant spots

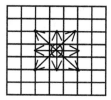

Fig. 2. Neighbourhood size of 1 of an individual (in the centre) from a GA population mapped onto a 2-dimensional grid.

Procedure **Parallel Genetic Algorithm**
Begin
 Initialisation: randomly generates an initial population of N individuals and mapped them onto a 2d grid;
 Evaluation: compute the fitness of each individual, and rank the fitness values and save them in a list.
 REPEAT:
  culling: eliminate the $C\%$ less fit individuals and save the remaining fitter individuals in the intermediate population. Keep a list of the coordinates (x, y) of the eliminated individuals;
  For i=1 to $N - C$ do
   randomly select two individuals among the remaining fitter $(N - C)\%$ of the population;
   select the best of the two and place it in the intermediate population with i-th (x, y) location (from the saved coordinate list);
  For j=1 to N do
   mate j-th individual with its neighbouring individuals with a mating probability; Search for a best-fit individual from neighbourhood; If there is more than one best-fit ones, then randomly choose one out of all the best ones;
   perform mutation with a mutation probability on the offspring;
   place the offspring in the new population with the coordinate (x, y) of the j-th individual;
  update: update the current population with the new population;
  evaluation: compute the fitness of individuals in the population;
  plotting graph: generate the fitness graph;
  generation step: generation counter + 1.
 UNTIL <stop criteria>
 End

Fig. 3. Outline of the PGA algorithm.

are saved to a list. These coordinates are used for placing newly generated individuals onto the 2d grid. The vacant spots are filled by randomly selected copies of the remaining fitter individuals in the current population. A tournament selection scheme is employed in this process. For example, if two individuals are randomly selected from the remaining fitter individuals, then only the best of the two is then placed in the intermediate population before mating. This process of randomly selecting two individuals from the remaining population (after culling) and placing the best in the intermediate population is repeated until the intermediate population is full. After the selection stage, mating, mutation, and evaluation can then occur in parallel. The PGA model can be formally described by:

$$PGA = (P_0, N, L, S, C, \Gamma, \Delta, E, \Theta) \tag{1}$$

where P_0 is the initial random population, N is the population size, L the local neighbourhood size, S the shape of the neighbourhood, C the culling threshold, Γ the mating operator, Δ the mutation operator, E the fitness evaluation function, and Θ a termination criterion.

4   Implementation of a Parallel GA in Swarm

In general, a Swarm program consists of following types of object [6]:

Model Controller: Perform tasks such as creating instances of agents and schedules to execute periodic events.
Interface Objects: Collect information for graphic display, send data to the screen and interact with the user.
Agents: Actors in the artificial world and possibly auxiliary objects which control agent behavior.
Model Abstractions: Objects which may collect information and respond to inquires from the agents or perform other tasks in the artificial world.

The first two types of objects are fairly standard across different simulation programs, however the other two types may require a fair amount of new code.

Fig. 4 shows the structure of the simulation model for the PGA. The above mentioned objects will be described in detail in the following paragraphs.

Model Controllers: The simulation first creates an instance of *ModelSwarm* and *ObserverSwarm*, which control the initialization of the model, event scheduling and output control. The *ModelSwarm* is the core of the simulation model, while the *ObserverSwarm* takes care of the graphic display (Fig. 4). The *ModelSwarm* first initializes parameters (or accept them from a GUI probe object), and creates instances of the individual chromosomes for the GA population. An instance of *FitSpace* and *World* (of a 2-dimensional grid object type) are created. The individuals created here should know the *World* they live in. The *FitSpace* object is used for storing the fitness values of individuals. *PopList* is a collection object containing all the individuals in the population. It can be used later when the model broadcasts to every individual of the population. Individuals are then connected to one *ActionGroup* and *Schedule* instances where the main event loop of the model is defined.

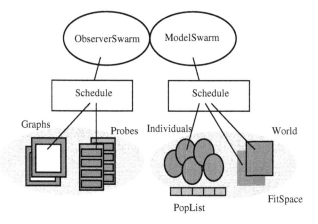

Fig. 4. Structure of the PGA model using Swarm.

Interface Objects: The graphical interface is initialized and controlled by *OberverSwarm*. A *ProbeMap* is created, then a number of *Probes* are created and added to the *ProbeMap*. *Probes* allow a user to dynamically interact with the objects in the model such as reading or setting instance variables as well as dynamically generating method calls. The main advantage is that these interactions may occur through the provided GUI, rather than hardwired in the code. In Fig. 5 we can see that *Probes* are used for accepting user commands such as "start", "stop" or step through the simulation. A user can also alter the initial values of a number of parameters shown on the *ProbeMap* such as "initPopSize", "generations", and "useDisaster". For example, if at some generation step, the user decides to apply disasters to the evolving GA population, this can be done simply by pause the optimization run, and then set the "useDisaster" to 1 (instead of the 0 as shown in Fig. 5) before resuming the run. We will present such an example in section 6.2. A separate *Probe* is also created to allow the user to choose how frequently the GUI is updated. An instance of *EZGraph* is created to display the minimum, average and maximum fitness values at each generation. This information is collected and calculated dynamically by calls to *ModelSwarm* which are passed on through the collection object *PopList* to the individuals. The GUI runs on a separate event loop controlled by one *ActionGroup* and *Schedule* containing instructions for calling the graphs and probes.

Agents: Individual chromosomes are the agents in this model. They are defined by the class *BinChromosome*. A protocol containing various GA operators such as "mate", "duplicate", "clone" and "swap" has been used as part of *BinChromosome*, therefore an individual knows how to perform these tasks when interacting with another individual.

Model Abstraction: 2-dimensional discrete space objects *FitSpace* and *World* are created. *FitSpace* contains fitness values of all individuals, and *World* stores all the individuals as objects placed on this 2-dimensional world. All individuals have access to these two objects. These two space objects are updated at each generation, so that they reflect the most up-to-date fitness values of individuals and their status in the *World*.

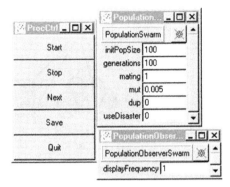

Fig. 5. Interface objects, a ControlPanel object containing command options, two ProbeMap objects containing a list of probes for a number of model variables. Note that parameter values displayed in the two ProbeMap can be modified during a system run.

5   Examples

The objevtive of presenting the following examples is to illustrate the features that a user can explore with this PGA implementation. No performance comparisons of this PGA with others are given. We describe two examples used with this PGA. In the first example, we use the PGA to optimize the number of ones in a 32-bit string. In the second example we use De Jong's test function F5 [10]. F5 is a multi-modal function with many steep peaks. The function has been inverted for this example, so it becomes a maximization problem with the optimal of 500. We adopt an approach of applying "disasters" to the GA population in this case [11]. Disaster is also a phenomenon that can be found in nature as a way of introducing novelty to the current population gene make-up. The goal of using disasters is similar to using mutation, but it is only applicable to a PGA, because of the properties of spatial structure introduced by such a PGA population.

5.1   Optimizing a 32-Bit String

A simple optimization problem is used as a demonstration here, in which the PGA needs to optimize the number of ones in a 32-bit string. In this experiment, we choose a population size of 100, crossover rate of 1.0 (which means each individual has to crossover with one of its neighbor), and mutation rate of 0.005. Once we press the "start" button, the model start running. Fig. 6 shows the fitness values of 100 individuals at generation 1, 10, 25 and 50 respectively.

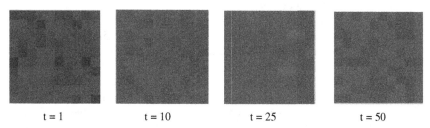

| t = 1 | t = 10 | t = 25 | t = 50 |

Fig. 6. The fitness values of 100 individuals in a PGA population displayed at generation 1, 10, 25 and 50 respectively. The degree of redness is proportional to the fitness value of an individual. The green squares are the optimal solutions found.

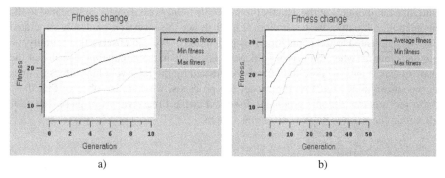

Fig. 7. The average, minimum and maximum fitness values for the population as plotted when the model run proceeds to: a) generation 10; b) generation 50.

Note that a few optimal solutions are found at generation 25 (green-colored squares in Fig. 6), as optimization run proceeds to generation 50, many more optimal solutions are found. The model can be run step by step by pressing successfully the "Next" button (see Fig. 5). Fig. 7 a) and b) are the snapshots of plotted fitness values at generation 10 and 50 respectively. These graphical displays are generated dynamically as we run the model. The average, minimum and maximum fitness values shown in the Fig. 7 a) and b) show the performance of the current PGA population at each time step.

5.2 Applying Disasters

In this example we used De Jong's test function F5, which is a multi-modal function with many steep optimal peaks. De Jong's F5 function as shown below is a highly multi-modal [10]:

$$f_5(x_i)=0.002+\sum_{j=1}^{25}\cfrac{1}{j+\sum_{i=1}^{2}(x_i-a_{ij})^6}, \qquad -65.536\leq x_i \leq 65.536 \qquad (2)$$

We applied "disaster" to a GA population in order to maintain diversity in such a population. This is necessary in solving many GA-hard problems. We use a population size of 225, a crossover rate of 1.0, and mutation rate of 0.003. First we let the model run until the population reaches an average fitness that becomes stagnant, then from that point onwards, we apply disasters over a number of generations. As shown in Fig. 8 a), a disaster with neighborhood size of 1 is allocated to the population at generation 160. The fitness values of individuals and their spatial structure changes can be seen in Fig. 9. The location of the disaster in the population is randomly chosen (see Fig. 9 a)). The disaster site is made up of the 9 cells on the 2d grid if the disaster size of 1 is chosen. This site is then replaced with a group of 9 randomly initialized individuals at the exactly the same site. Only one disaster is allocated to the population at a particular generation. Fig. 9 shows in succession randomly generated disasters allocated to the population in 4 generations. We can observe that initially the big dark square (where a disaster is located) is visible in the population, because of the poor fitness values of these individuals contrasted by the relatively high fitness values in the surrounding area. As the model run proceeds, we can also observe that these "disaster" squares become gradually dissolved as the fitness values of these individuals within the squares improve over generations.

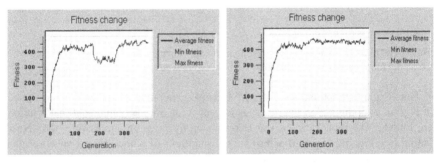

Fig. 8. a) Applying disasters to a population at generation 160, and then stopped applying disasters at generation 260; b) Result of a simulation run without applying disasters to the population.

Note that in Fig.8, because of the use of scale for the fitness values (lie between 0 to 500), the maximum and minimum fitness values at each generation do not seem to change much. This indicates that during an optimization run, a few individuals in the PGA population was able to quickly identify good solutions (with values around 499.2), very close to the optima of 500, even at the beginning of the run. At the meantime, there were also individuals with very low fitness values in the population throughout the run. These individuals' fitness values did not improve much over time. However we can see the average fitness value over the whole population first shows a very sharp increase, and then a slow increase over generations, until it becomes stagnant with a value about 450. This indicates that more individuals in the population were able to locate good solutions after some generation steps. PGA shows a better performance especially in dealing with problems with multiple optima.

It can be also noted in Fig. 8 a) that when disasters were applied, there was a sharp drop in the average fitness of the population. However such a drop stopped and then was even reversed when disasters were not being applied to the population. We also had a run of the model without applying the disasters to the population. The result can be seen from Fig. 8 b). As we can observe in Fig. 8 b), the final average fitness value of the population after 400 generations is slightly lower than the one found in Fig. 8 a). This finding shows the usefulness of applying disasters to a PGA population in improving its performance.

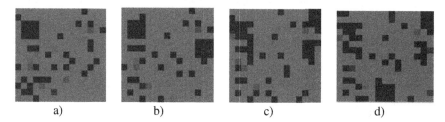

a)   b)   c)   d)

Fig. 9. An example of applying disasters in succession to the GA population in 4 generations. The green squares show solutions with fitness value over 490. The big dark squares (each containing 9 sites) visible in the population represent the randomly generated disasters allocated to the population. a) and b) show a disaster applied to the population at left-top corner, and near the right edge of the population respectively. c) and d) show that areas being occupied by disasters become gradually dissolved as the individuals' fitness in these areas have improved.

6 Conclusion

In this paper the implementation of a fine-grained parallel GA using a multi-agent framework Swarm has been described. This PGA provides the visualization features showing dynamically the changes occurring in an evolving GA population in real time. The dynamic change occurring in fitness values over the spatially distributed PGA population can be visualized via a sequence of raster images, which are generated during an execution run. We believe that an evolutionary process is a time-dependant process, therefore these dynamically generated graphs can offer greater advantages over the static plotted graphs such as those proposed by Pohlheim (1999). This PGA model also allows some degree of user interaction. For example, a user can pause the model run and then modify the model parameter values before resuming the run. For an evolutionary process running over many thousands of steps, we could use this feature to intervene the evolving process. For example, if the population becomes stagnant (i.e., pre-mature convergence) as observed during a run, we could increase the value of mutation rate at that particular generation step we have just reached, then resume the evolving run again.

References

1. Holland, J.H. (1975) Adaptation in Natural and Artificial Systems, University of Michigan Press, Ann Arbor, MI.
2. Grefenstette, J.J., (ed.,) (1987) Genetic Algorithms and Their Applications: Proceedings of the Second International Conference on Genetic Algorithms, Lawrence Erlbaum Associates, Cambridge, MA, July 28-31, 1987.
3. Cantu-Paz E. (1997) "A Survey of Parallel Genetic Algorithms", IlliGAL Report No. 97003, May 1997, Illinois Genetic Algorithms Laboratory, University of Illinois, Urbana-Champaign.
4. Routen, T.W. (1994). Techniques for the Visualization of Genetic Algorithms. In Proceedings of The First IEEE Conference on Evolutionary Computation, Piscataway, New Jersey, USA: IEEE Service Center, Vol. II, pp.846-851.
5. Pohlheim, H. (1999). Visualization of Evolutionary Algorithms – Set of Standard Techniques and Multidimentional Visualization. In Proceedings of the Genetic and Evolutionary Computation Conference (GECCO'99). San Francisco, CA: Morgan Kaufmann Publishers, pp.533-540.
6. Stefansson, B. (1997) "Swarm: An Object Oriented Simulation Platform Applied to Markets and Organizations", Evolutionary Programming VI, Lecture Notes in Computer Science, edited by Angeline, P., Reynolds, R., and Eberhart, R.Vol.1213, Springer-Verlag, New York.
7. Minar, N., Burkhart, R., Langton, C., and Askenazi, M. (1996) "The Swarm Simulation System – A Toolkit for Building Multi-Agent Systems, Santa Fe Institute Working Paper 96-06-042, Santa Fe, NM.
8. Stefansson, B.(1998) "Agent Based Modeling in Swarm", Lecture notes, UCLA Political Science.
9. Burkhart, R. (1997) "Schedules of Activity in the Swarm Simulation System", Position Paper for OOPSLA's 97 Wrokshop on OO Behavioral Semantics.
10. Goldberg, D. (1989) *Genetic Algorithms in Search, Optimization and Machine Learning*, Addison-Wesley, Reading, MA.
11. Kirley, M., Li, X. and Green, D.G. (1998) "An investigation of a Cellular Genetic Algorithm that mimics evolution in a landscape", *Lecture Notes in Artificial Intelligence*, edited by B. McKay, *et al.*, **vol**: 1585.
12. Merelo, J.J., GeNeura and Swarm Teams (1997) "Breeder user's and programmer's Manual", Technical report, http://www.swarm.org/community-contrib.html.

The Rise and Fall of Napster – An Evolutionary Approach

Bengt Carlsson and Rune Gustavsson

Blekinge Institute of Technology,371 25 Ronneby, Sweden
{bengt.carlsson, rune.gustavsson}@bth.se

Abstract. The paper addresses dynamics in information ecosystems due to competition between selfish agents to get control of protectable resources. In our case study we investigate the first arms race on Internet triggered by the Napster introduction of an easy to use service for sharing files with music content among users. We set up a model for investigation of possible scenarios emerging from the Napster and Gnutella peer-to-peer tools for information sharing. We also introduce a formal model for analyzing the Napster scenario in the cases of selfish or altruistic users. The prediction provided by our model is in line with what really happened in the Napster case. The model also shows that the outcome was indeed unavoidable if we have selfish users.

1   Introducing Napster and Gnutella. Setting the Scene

The file format MP3 introduced the possibility to compress large audio files into more easy to handle files. For music lovers it became possible to store lots of MP3 files on computers or share them with others, using an Internet connection and file transfer protocols. Napster introduced a peer-to-peer (P2P) environment providing easy mechanisms for connecting different users (peers) and their MP3 file resources. Each of the peers (users) could use a lookup service provided by Napster to find out where to retrieve wanted MP3 files, and also provide their own files. That is, Napster provided a centralized register of locations of files but the files themselves remained at the individual users. Napster quickly became a tremendous success with almost a hundred million of users downloading MP3 music for free. Of course Napster simultaneously become a threat against traditional business models supported by the record companies.

The fight initiated by Napster and taken up by Recording Industry Association of America (RIAA) was about ownership of content and enforcement of copyright laws. At the start Napster concentrated its efforts on providing easy MP3 file sharing among users willing to share their files with others. So, in a sense Napster itself did not 'copy' any files, it only provided easy means for others to share content between each other. After some heated debate about 'freedom on the net' and 'rights to content' there were in the beginning of March 2001 a court order forcing Napster to protect copyright, of music from being shared using its centralized lookup service. The mechanism for protection was to introduce filtering of the lookup service. Users, groups of users or others who of different reasons wanted to protect 'freedom on the

J. Liu et al. (Eds.): AMT 2001, LNCS 2252, pp. 347–354, 2001.
© Springer-Verlag Berlin Heidelberg 2001

Net' quickly circumvented the first simple filters. In short the first information *war* on the web become a reality, including an *arms race* concerning the control of distributed and valuable content.

The following figure captures the principal players and issues of the battlefield.

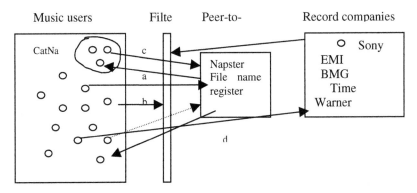

Fig. 1. Information warfare in a Napster clone

CatNap is a local proxy server that uses letter shifting (cryptography) of all data sent to the Napster server. The filters on Napster´s servers no longer recognize the filenames. The drawback is that users only find files of other CatNap users on the Napster network.

In Figure 1 we have indicated participants of the 'content war' as users, arms providers, e.g., CatNap, and record companies which all form alliances and create new weapons to win the war. In this paper we will model the situation as an information ecosystem of competing agents or groups of agents. The dynamics of the 'content war' is interesting to model for several reasons. Firstly, we know at the time of the publishing of the paper, the outcome. Napster has, at least temporarily, closed down. Could there have been other outcomes? Secondly, what can we learn from this example in order to design information ecosystems with desirable properties.

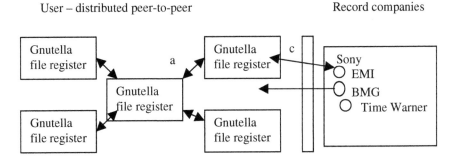

Fig. 2. Information warfare in a Gnutella clone

During the war other P2P providers for content sharing appeared. The best example is Gnutella. Gnutella does not have a central file register as Napster. The RIAA weapon against Napster, enforcing a filter at the Napster site was not applicable in the Gnutella case. Figure 2 captures the battlefield at Gnutella.

The Gnutella based 'content war' is different due to the distribution of the lookup services. We will compare these two P2P systems, e.g., what would have happened if Napster had had a distributed lookup service? What would have been a proper first RIAA counterattack?

The rest of the paper is organized as follows. In the next section we discuss the characteristics of the two types of warfare described above. The following section gives a short description of the actors in the warfare. The warfare is modeled as a competition between selfish agents. We have elsewhere addressed other issues of this model (Carlsson 2001). A formal model for analyzing and prediction a Napster type of 'content war' is proposed. We conclude the paper with a summary and some open questions.

2   Discussion of the Napster and Gnutella Warfare

Napster and Gnutella exemplifies a centralized and a distributed method for information exchange. Both systems have been involved in an arms race within information warfare. In figure 1 the centralized Napster clones are examined and in figure 2 the distributed Gnutella clones. Both systems presuppose societies of selfish actors, but the success of an agent as part of an antagonistic group is dependent on the degree of cooperation within the group.

The "main battle" in figure 1 is about the filtering function. There are several possible scenarios following the introduction of the filtering function.

1. The users copyrighted files are filtered out, making Napster a music distributor respecting copyright laws. If users continue using Napster and if the filtering function is working properly the record companies will be the winners against the users. If users are leaving Napster for other P2P tools, such as Gnutella, Napster will be the loser. Record companies and users will in that case continue an arms race without Napster´s de facto standard of P2P tools.

2. The users try to dupe the filtering function in a conscious or unconscious way. This alternative presumes a cooperative behavior among users, because a user will benefit from the activity of others. A too widespread altering of file names will probably make the filtering function more alert. The arms race concerning the filtering function will probably reach a dead end. The record companies have a leaky filter and the users have an incomplete MP3 record register. Both sides may find better alternatives.

3. A subgroup of users encrypts their MP3 files. CatNap dupes the filter and uses the Napster serves as if no filter existed. This will be a victory for the users, if the Napster server remains unaffected. With an analogy to biology, CatNap will live as a parasite. If a parasite kills its host, the breeding-ground will disappear. Why should Napster keep its server if all users join the CatNap? In reality, CatNap disappeared during the first month of a filtered Napster community.

4. The users join the record companies music sites to pay for downloaded copyrighted music. Record companies have the opportunity to offer additional (non digital) materials, concert schedules for the artists or introducing free downloadable music from new artists (lowering their commercial introduction costs).

Due to our formal analysis of section 3, we do not think other centralized P2Ps will take over Napster´s position; neither will encryption tools be more dominating. RIAA will sue imitations of Napster and the filtering function should limit the spread of encrypted files for the great majority of people. A sub-community of music sites with unfiltered files will keep the arms race alive.

Since Napster´s filters was introduced half a year ago, other unfiltered MP3 tools have grown enormously- MusicCity, a hybrid between Napster and Gnutella, has grown more than forty-fold now reaching more than one million users a day. During one week more than 1.500.000 copies of MusicCity were downloaded compared to less than 10.000 for Napster.

Figure 2 shows how a single user is connected to, at most, several thousand other users within a distributed P2P tool. There will be an indirect battle between the users and record companies in the Gnutella case because of the lack of centralized P2P servers. There are at least three perceivable battle zones.

1. Distributed P2P means heavily increased network loads. This "bandwidth stealing" may cause an arms race against net traffic suppliers. In the future more efficient search methods or methods for scaling up the number of nodes may be expected. The search improvement may use agent technology and the scaling up improvement may use a client/server system where clients are hidden behind reflectors.
2. Being part of a file sharing system implies a lot of trust towards other users. In fact virus attacks have happened among Gnutella users. An arms race is supposed to occur where it is in the interest of the record companies to be the bad guys supporting the intruders.
3. Anyone may join the open P2P society, not just ordinary users. It is in the interest of record companies and other commercial companies to introduce improved P2P tools with spyware facilities included. These tools log the users' habits and may use the information for commercial or security interests. An arms race is already ongoing with anti-spywares detecting the spywares.

If Napster and RIAA block downloading, a distributed P2P file transfer is favored. We do not think any of these tools may fully replace Napster because of the increased net loads. Instead of being sued by RIAA, the net traffic suppliers may react against a too successful distributed P2P system.

A *robust* Information Ecosystem may evolve as a result of arms race situations as in the Napster/Gnutella cases. The advantage of participating in an arms race is not a permanent but a time-extended robustness; to be able to download an MP3 file before the filtering agent observes it or, to avoid a virus attack because of a new anti-virus tool being available. Agents who fail will be culled or have to improve their robustness in relation to mainstream agents. Within Information Ecosystems those parts under attack may improve, making future attacks less successful due to arms race.

Viruses and spywares are tools that may infiltrate or attack the Information Ecosystem. Firewalls against virus attacks (and maybe against spywares in the future) will increase the protection. Anti-virus and anti-spywares increase the ability for the intruders to be detected and the response of being weakened. An arms race will occur when countermeasures are taken by the intruding part.

3   Actors in the Content Wars

We will in this section describe three actors within Information Ecosystem. Two of them, the record companies and the music listeners are each forming an antagonistic part of the ecosystem. The P2P providers may form coalitions with both the record companies and the music listening users from time to time.

The main goal for the record companies is to have users pay for downloading copyright protected music. If users download for free they will probably not buy records. This seems as an obvious position taken by the record companies, but there are objections for the record companies to defeat Napster as a source of illegal distributor:

- Napster makes it possible for the record companies to reach millions of presumptive customers for introducing new artists or promote new releases.
- Napster is a (at least partly) loyal site towards the record companies, which is shown by the alliance with Bertelmann AG, one of the big record companies.
- It is probably impossible to lock out all copyrighted music from the Napster servers, because of insufficient technical solutions and improved efforts from users to outwit the server.
- If Napster shuts down or becomes a pay-for site, a lot of other P2P sites with a more hostile attitude against the record companies may take over.

If consumers are not willing to pay for downloading music, they will still have a lot of opportunities with or without Napster. Some record companies and artists realize a risk of losing control if Napster disappears, while other regard Napster as the root of all evil. This dynamic determines the actions of the recording industry.

The main interest from the users' point of view is to download free music as simply as possible. Unlike the big economic interests from RIAA, there is no essential question binding users together. So why should users cooperate with other users?

Within sociobiology one kind of cooperative behavior is explained as "if you scratch my back, I scratch yours", or expressed differently; I can do you a favor if it does not cost too much and if I can expect something in return. Within the Napster domain we ask whether it is possible for distributed rules to appear within file sharing systems, without any obvious advantages for the user giving this service. As a group the users should keep together but a single user should try to keep the advantage of file sharing without giving services back, if there is a risk involved.

Users should be aware of the risk of connecting to other users, because they are actually sharing file systems located inside a user's computer. There is a risk of having a virus attack or being exploited by spywares..

Napster initiated a P2P information exchange revolution at the same level as Netscape and later on Microsoft Explorer browsers did within Internet. Unlike the major Internet browser tools, it is not sure Napster will put an industrial standard to the P2P area. Napster is not holding a monopoly over a specific computer service; it has rival clones and options, which may quickly take over if things go wrong. With

P2P tools, the files stay on the client machine, never passing through the server. Napster clones provides the ability to search for particular file names on one or more servers before initiating a direct transfer between the clients. Gnutella clones have a real P2P connection and do not store any information at central servers.

4   A Formal Framework of Content War

We restrict our discussion to 'content war' of the Napster type. We model the arms race as a discrete set of events. At time t_n, M_n denotes the number of copyright protected files at Napster, N_n denotes the number of files protected by the filter at the same time. The protection rate, P_n, at the same time is given by:

$$p_n = \frac{N_n}{M_n} \tag{1}$$

where $P_n < 1$, and the users can download $U_n = M_n - N_n$ files.

From (1) it follows that we have total protection of the copyrighted material if and only if $\lim_{n \to \infty} p_n = 1$

The arms race is modeled as two potentially infinite sequences. The defense sequence $D = \{M_1, M_2, ..., \}$ and the attack sequence $A = \{U_1, U_2, ..., \}$ The arms race will continue only if it is worthwhile to use the lookup service at Napster to download files during any given protection rate. At any time t_n the attackers will develop new tools to penetrate the filter of the t_n generation protecting M_n that will enable users to access extra files during the time interval up to time t_{n+1}, when the arms race have produced the next generation of filter mechanisms.

The *incentive* for users to use the lookup service at Napster in the time interval $[t_n, t_{n+1}]$ is:

$$I_n = (U_n + q_n M_n)/M_n, \tag{2}$$

where $0 < q_n < 1$, and $q_n M_n$ is a measure of the gain the users will have due to better attack tools between the generation updates of the protective defense.

A continuous arms race presupposes that the incentive for *selfish* users to visit Napster is always positive during the arms race, i.e.,

$$\lim_{n \to \infty} = a > 0 \tag{3}$$

From (1) and (3) we derive $\lim_{n \to \infty} = a$, and we have the asymptotic behavior of the downloaded files by an eager and selfish agent

$$U_{n+1} = U_1 + \sum_{k=1}^{n} q_k M_k \qquad (4)$$

From this asymptotic behavior we can deduce the following inequality:

$$n \leq K (M - U_1)/ aM_1, \qquad (5)$$

where K is a constant and M is the maximum number of copyrighted files.

From this upper bound estimate of n we thus conclude that the arms race *eventually will cease due to lack of incentive* to continue using the services for the users *even if* total protection of copyrighted material has not been achieved, i.e, we can not have (3). We also can conclude that in the case of unselfish agents, e.g., $a = 0$ in (3), n can be unbounded and hence we can an indefinite arms race. This means that users will continue to use the services even if there are no personal gains after a while. The reason could be altruistic, e.g., to contribute to the development of total copyright protection on the web.

We thus can predict that a Napster type of 'content war' eventually will end with a loss for Napster in the sense that selfish users will lose interest in the Napster services! Compare with the scenarios of Section 2. This prediction is in line what really happened to Napster.

5   Conclusions

One of the most interesting events, which have occurred during the last year on the web, is the Napster-Gnutella introduction of peer-to-peer based information sharing tools. The response from the music industry started the first 'content war' on the net triggered by a court law forcing Napster to install filtering protections for copyrighted music files. The countermeasures, i.e., tools to circumvent the installed filters quickly appeared followed by improved filtering mechanisms. We have in fact witnessed an arms race on the Internet.

The Napster content war will undoubtedly be followed by other similar conflicts and emergent behaviors in Information Ecosystem. By now, we know the outcome of the war, Napster has (temporary) lost. We introduce in the paper a formal model of arms race in Information Ecosystems in order to analyze the Napster case and to allow more general conclusions.

We use an evolutionary model based on natural selection, i.e. measuring the "fitness" of the individual agents to explain long-term adaptations, e.g., hardening of protection mechanisms, in the Information Ecosystem.

We regard the hardening of protection mechanisms of assets to be the result of an arms race where protection measures are followed by sharper weapons of attack in an escalation model. In order to model an ongoing escalation we introduce selfish and eager attacking agents and eager defending agents.

Our theoretical model shows that during these assumptions the arms race will end with a loss for the attacking side, as in the Napster case. If the attacking agent is not selfish but only eager, we can have an infinite arms race. Our model is in fact more general than the Napster case. A Gnutella type of 'content war' could be modeled in the same way.

In reality a Napster war ends earlier than the model predicts simple due to the fact that there appear other options, which means that a selfish agent might decide to leave Napster for that reason. This is in fact what has happened on the web.

One should observe that in the 'content war' mentioned the only service, which could be effectively blocked by the music industry, was the centralized Napster service. We could foresee that in future Information Ecosystems more and more of the services will be 'hardened' to protect 'content ownership' and thus enable 'download' by payment only. What our formal model predict in these cases, since the 'free alternatives' will be scare or non-existent, is that selfish agents eventually will pay for their downloads than continue the arms race for free down loading of copyrighted material. That is, we will have a situation with an emerging worldwide price war on content on the net.

An interesting future work is to further elaborate these issues by extending the model to open Information Ecosystems.

We furthermore believe that an approach using methods of investigation similar to a biological ecosystem will be necessary in the future of the Information Ecosystem.

Acknowledgements. Besides the anonymous reviewers we also want to thank Martin Hylerstedt for proof-reading.

References

Carlsson, B. The Tragedy of the Commons - Arms Race within Peer-to-Peer Tools. To appear in the proceedings of the *2nd International Workshop Engineering Societies in the Agents' World*. ed. Omicini, A., Petta, P., and Tolksdorf, R. *Lecture Notes in Artificial Intelligence 2203,* Springer-Verlag (2001)

Carlsson, B. and Davidsson, P. A Biological View on Information Ecosystems. To appear in the proceedings of the *Second Conference on Intelligent Agent Technology*, World Scientific (2001)

Carlsson, B. and Gustavsson, R. Arms Race Within Information Ecosystems. To appear in the proceedings of the *Fifth International Workshop Cooperative Information Agents*, Springer-Verlag. (2001)

Dunbar, R., Grooming, Gossip and the Evolution of Language, Faber & Faber Ltd (1996)

Sandholm,T.W., and Lesser, V.R., Coalitions among computationally bounded agents, Artificial Intelligence, 94(1) (1997) 99-137

Wellman, M., A computational market model for distributed configuration design, Proc. 12th National Conference on Artificial Intelligence (AAAI-94), Seattle, WA (1994) 401-407

Williams, G. C., Adaptation and natural selection, Princeton University Press (1966)

Wilson, E. O., Sociobiology-The abridged edition, Belknap Press (1980)

On the Elaboration of Hand-Drawn Sketches

Saul Simhon and Gregory Dudek

Centre for Intelligent Machines
McGill University
3480 University St, Montreal, Canada H3A 2A7
{saul, dudek}@cim.mcgill.ca

Abstract. This work considers an approach for artificially enhancing the richness and level of detail of graphical scenes. In particular, we examine a method for automatically generating high-resolution novel curves from manually sketched drawings of those curves. The essential idea is to augment the hand-drawn curves using prior knowledge to produce a more elaborated picture. Our method uses multi-scale analysis of a class of training data to capture statistical properties of the set. These properties are then conditioned at a coarse scale by the hand-drawn curve to *steers* the synthesis according to the overall shape of the curve. Given an approximation sketch, the algorithm generates the most likely scene by propagating probabilities over a Markov Chain. Users without artistic capabilities can then describe scenes in a more natural way to build impressive graphics.

1 Introduction

In this paper we consider the manually guided synthesis of detailed curves from very rudimentary steering information. Our goal is to provide a quick and easy way for users to draw elaborate drawings. We present a method to automatically synthesize the elements of a drawing that are too difficult or time consuming to manually draw while maintaining the overall shape of the drawing. In most cases, users do not have difficulty outlining the overall shape of drawings at a course scale. There may be some deviation in the proportion and placements of elements but the main difficulties arises at low scales and high variation areas. Developing a method to help reconstruct those intricate details is an integral step towards more sophisticated systems for elaborating complex images from much simpler high-level specifications.

The approach we take consists of learning statistical properties of a class of *a priori* data over multiple scales. We calculate probabilities using a Non-Stationary Markov Model over the curves' arc-lengths. By learning the statistical relationships between consecutive elements and between a curve and a smoother hand-drawn facsimile, we can later exploit these relationships to synthesis the high-resolution details. Further, since a non-deterministic approach is taken, various instances of the same illustration can be generated simply by random sampling over the regions of maximum likelihood.

J. Liu et al. (Eds.): AMT 2001, LNCS 2252, pp. 355–364, 2001.
© Springer-Verlag Berlin Heidelberg 2001

Preliminary application to this framework uses a class of parametric curves for coastline synthesis but the frame work can be applied to any data class where high-resolution detail is a function of overall shape. Providing the techniques we describe below can assist in many applications such as: 3-D modeling where curves are used to specify object boundaries and deformations; key-frame animation where curves specify trajectories of objects; pen-and-ink illustrations where curves are the main elements of the design. This work can also be extend to applications for surfaces and textures.

2   Background

One of the most widely used methods to draw curves and surfaces consists of specifying a set of vertices and using an interpolating function that defines the geometry between the vertices. Commonly, tensor product NURBS [5] are used since they provide local control of the curve segments with up to second degree parametric continuity. However, in order to represent surfaces of arbitrary topology, the model must be partitioned into a collection of patches and explicitly stitched together [3]. A large number of parameters are introduced to stitch adjacent patches using geometric continuity conditions. Subdivision curves and surfaces offer a better alternative by repeatedly refining an initial control mesh [1]. DeRose *et al.* present a general subdivision model for reconstructing piecewise smooth surface models from scattered control points [10]. Their work describes subdivision rules that model sharp features while maintaining the smooth areas by relaxing continuity conditions across labeled edges and modifying subdivision masks based on label type. Although subdivision surfaces are used often in state of the art computer graphics applications, they still require highly-skilled users, especially in scenes that are over-refined where editing becomes very cumbersome and details are very intricate.

Another difficulty in traditional curve and surface fitting techniques is that there is no attempt to preserve higher resolution detail when editing at a broader region. Work by Forsey and Bartels [6] addressed this problem by developing hierarchical B-splines. Large- or small-scale changes to the surface can be made by manipulating control points at the corresponding levels in the hierarchy. Some of the drawbacks in their work imposed users to manually design the hierarchical network. Further, the surface points and derivatives were no longer linear functions of the control points, introducing computational complexities and non-unique solutions. Later work [7] automated the process by recursively fitting surfaces at a coarse scale and refining areas with large residuals. In other work, Salesin *et al.* [12] [4] describe a multi-scale curve representation based on wavelets that produced unique solutions for given shapes. Curves may be modified at multiple levels of detail, such as changing the overall form of the curve while preserving its detail or vise versa.

Although these and other similar methods provide multi-scale editing, they lack in representing the connection between overall shape and high-resolution detail. The goal is to disassociate the scales, providing independent control for each level of detail. While this is desirable for certain applications, it does not allow users to fully describe a curve directly from coarse data. Our method, analogous to wavelet transform, captures statistical relationships over varying scales, recognizing that a change in the overall shape should affect the high-resolution features. The main premise is that a good way to interpret an incomplete specification is based on previously seen data.

The approach we take in synthesizing curves is similar to and inspired by stochastic methods of texture synthesis [14] [11] [2]. Work by Efros and Leung [2] describe a method of learning statistical properties of a texture sample and extrapolating these properties to generate the pattern. A texture is modeled as a Markov Random Field where the probability distribution for the value of a pixel is dependent on only its neighboring pixels. A new pixel is synthesized by choosing the value that is most probable based on a neighborhood match with the sample texture. Wei and Levoy [13] combined this method with a pyramid-based filter [9] to maintain large-scale structure. They also apply their method in the temporal domain, producing movies such as ocean waves and fire. A strong assumption in these approaches is that of a local and stationary random process. Such assumptions are not necessarily valid when dealing with the syntheses of arbitrary scenes. Further, there is no way of controlling and steering the growth of textures. In our work, presented in the next section, we use a non-stationary transition probabilities and adopt a controlling component to steer the synthesis process.

3   Curve Synthesis: Markov Steering

We treat the user as a stochastic process, generating a sequence of random measurements over some time interval (a random experiment). Let us suppose that at each point in time we observe a measurement x. This measurement corresponds to a sample point described by the entire function $X(t)$. Let $X_s(t)$ represent a stochastic process for a class of sample curves s over a time interval T. A single sequence of observations for a particular sample set s is called the realization of the stochastic process, corresponding to an instance of the user's curve description. We assume the sequence has an nth order Markov property, i.e. a Markov Process:

$$p\{x_s(t+1)|x_s(t), x_s(t-1) .. x_s(t-n+1)\} = p\{x_s(t+1)|x_s(t), x_s(t-1) .. x_s(0)\}$$

Let α represent a closed curve (the method will still work for curves that are not closed but the Markov chain is not homogeneous). The curve has a parametric representation $(x(t), y(t))$ where t is the arc-length of the curve from $0 <= t <= T$. We denote the absolute angle of the tangent of α at point t by $\theta(t)$. We denote $\phi(t)$ as the steering component of the curve $\theta(t)$ corresponding to a level of abstraction:

$$\phi(t) = \psi(\theta(t)) \tag{1}$$

where ψ is some function that maps the high-resolution curve to one that the operator is more apt to sketch. That is, $\phi(t)$ is considered as the input curve used to maneuver the Markov Process. In principle, this controlling component can consist of any function of the high-resolution curve; there is no geometric requirement as it can even be a mapping to a language symbol space. However, to maintain the Markov property and real time execution, we transform the state space using a time-invariant causal linear filter [8]. We consider a linear transformation such that Equation 1 can be represented in matrix form:

$$\Phi = \Psi\Theta \qquad (2)$$

where Θ is a state vector consisting of n sample points (discrete version of $\theta(t)$), Ψ is a $n \times m$ low-pass filter matrix and Φ is a state vector with m sample points (discrete version of $\psi(t)$). By removing the high-frequency components, we provide the user with a control curve that is easier to hand-draw and requires less sampling points to model. Such a transformation loses information and is not invertible.

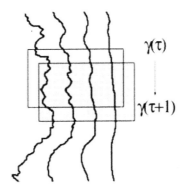

Fig. 1. Extracting the next state given the previous ones. Each state is a multi-scale/multi-order representation of the curve.

Multi-scale analysis is performed by repeatedly filtering the training curves using a low-pass filter. This results a multi-scale curves where the controlling component lies near one of the coarse levels. We then define a state space as an $OxSxA$ dimensional space Γ, where O is the order (history) and S is the scale and A is the dimension of the curve attributes that are used (in our case, $A = 1$, the tangent angle θ).

We define the stochastic model as a first order homogeneous Markov Process for the multi-dimensional states $\gamma(t)$ over the state space Γ. Note that although we use a first order Markov Model, higher order history of a curve is encoded within a single state (Figure 1). Statistical properties of *a priori* data are learned by calculating the transition probabilities $p(\gamma(t+1)|\gamma(t))$.

A Markov Chain with non-stationary transition probabilities is used to reconstruct the curve:

$$P_\gamma(t+1) = M_\gamma(t)P_\gamma(t) \tag{3}$$

Where $P_\gamma(t)$ is the probability state vector at sample t and $M_\gamma(t)$ is the transition matrix at sample t. Similar to texture synthesis techniques, given a seed $(\phi(0), \theta(0))$, we can extrapolate a curve by statistically sampling over $P_\gamma(t)$. This generates a new curve that is based on the statistical properties of the training data. We don't explicitly construct the transition matrix since the data is very sparse and the state-space it too large. Instead we store the probabilities in a linked list, which requires searching at each iteration (space-time tradeoffs).

Transition probabilities for a multi-scale/multi-order state $\gamma(t)$ are calculated by first comparing $\gamma(t)$ with all states $\gamma(t)'$ in the training data using a similarity measure. We then associate the transition probability to the next state $\gamma(t+1)$ by summing up values and normalizing. The similarity measure is calculated as follows:

$$D(\gamma(t), \gamma(t)') = \frac{\sum_\tau \sum_s w(s,\tau)G(\gamma(t,s,\tau) - \gamma(t,s,\tau)')}{\sum_\tau \sum_S w(s,\tau)} \tag{4}$$

where G is a Gaussian function and W is a weight matrix that associates the importance of matches over scale and history. We integrate over the region defined by the state space Γ, (i.e. $\tau: 0-> O, s: 0-> S$).

We configure the weight matrix to maintain consistency over both high resolution details early in the history and overall shape. Further, for training sets that exhibit some stationarity, the search space does not have to be restricted by t but can consist of any location in the training data that has similar statistical response. In fact, one might want to search over a range Δt about t to provide additional tolerance for the hand-drawn curve.

The probability of the next state is calculated by first propagating the probabilities of the previous states using the transition probabilities calculated above and then conditioning the result by the user input ϕ_{in}. The conditioned probability for the i'th state is given by:

$$p_i^{conditioned} = p_i^{predicted}G(\phi_{in} - \theta_{s,i}) \tag{5}$$

where $\theta_{s,i}$ is the current angle extracted from the ith state at a pre-determined scale s. The variance of the Gaussian G sets the influence the input has over the prediction. Large variances depict low user confidence while small variances such as a delta function only pick close/exact matches. A sample point is instantiated using the value of maximum probability, providing an interactive environment where users can see the resulting deblurred curve. For efficiency, a threshold is set to maintaining only the top few candidates.

A summary of the algorithm is outlined as follows:

- Initialize the probability vector by assigning equal probabilities to each $\gamma(0)$ in the training example
- Condition the probability vector using the hand-drawn sketch point $\phi(0)$.
- Threshold the probability vector

- For each sample point from the hand-drawn sketch:
  - Compute the transition probabilities from time t to $t+1$.
  - Given the probability vector at time t, predict the next one using the computed transition probabilities.
  - Condition and threshold the probability vector

3.1   Experimental Results

We have implemented the algorithm and provided a graphical user interface where users can draw curves and see the results. The interface also allows to set parameters, such as scales, orders, weights and variances, and to load and save curves and training data. This is advantageous when users with to add newly synthesized curve to the training set. For our experiments, we used 40 curves of world country borders for training, a 5 scale 20'th order state space and a uniform average filter. Figure 2 shows some samples of the training set. Experiments were done on a 1 GHz P3 processor with real time response.

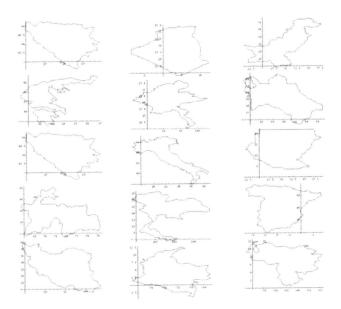

Fig. 2. Some examples of curves used in training.

Figure 3 and 4 show some sample runs with both the hand-drawn curves and the resulting synthesized curves. Most of the curves generated are *novel* ones, never seen in the training set. They maintain the statistical properties of the training set and the overall shape of the hand-drawn curve. The resulting curves

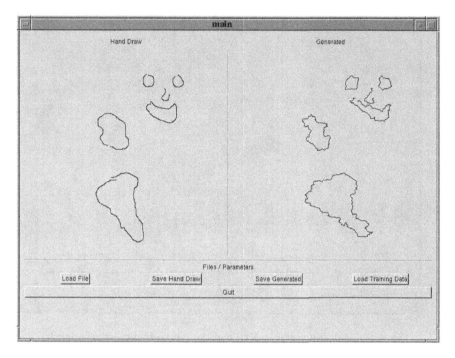

Fig. 3. Hand drawn sketches (left) and the synthesized coastline (right).

look like coastlines. There are some issues with curve closures and intersections which are primarily due to accumulated errors and the stochastic nature of the algorithm. A possible extension to this work can consist of imposing additional constraints to maintain properties such as closure.

The algorithm produces good results for data classes that sustain structure over local regions. This forms a good framework for applications such as texture mixing but limits the application to data types where global structure prevails. Further, data types with large scale structure usually have features that are well localized in time. As much as the filters blur this time localization, a single offset in the hand-drawn curve might steer the synthesis in a drastically different path. Such mis-synchronization can be seen in figure 6. Figure 5 show some samples of a training set we used that exhibits large-scale properties. The set consisted of 14 leaf outlines. Figure 6 shows the results using this set. One example produced an exact reconstruction for the training set, another example shows a mixture of the training data that is locally consistent but not globally and a third example shows a case where there is no close match found in the training data due to mis-synchronization of global features.

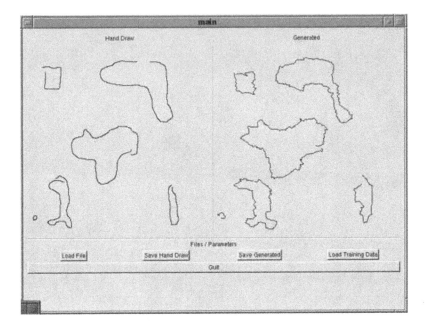

Fig. 4. Hand drawn sketches (left) and the synthesized coastline (right).

Fig. 5. Samples taken from the training set.

4   Future Work

This paper describes a new approach in generating graphics. The idea can be extended for various applications. Primarily, we will investigate methods to extend this work to data that requires consistency over large scales. This may include imposing global function over the curve such as an energy based regularization method. Such methods can also refine the curve by locking on to the right segment or minimizing mixtures. Future direction also includes dealing with multiple curves, automatic classification and segmentation for a better synthesis. We also plan on extending the application to textures and motion signals.

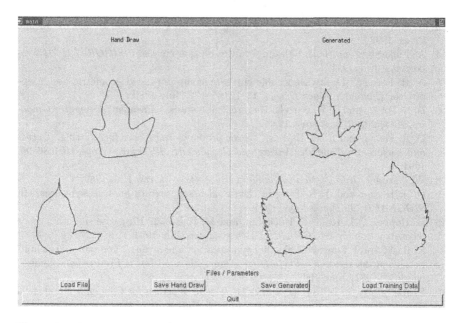

Fig. 6. Hand drawn sketches (left) and the synthesized leaves (right). The top center shows an exact reconstruction; bottom left shows a reconstruction consisting of several samples from training that is globally inconsistent; bottom right shows a reconstruction where the control curve reaches the top of the leaf too early and the training data is not rich enough to properly adjust the synthetic curve.

5 Conclusion

This work presents a step towards a method for elaborating hand-drawn curves in real time. The method consists of using *a-priori* data to automatically generate the details for a coarse hand-drawn curve. We model the curves as multi-scale stochastic signals over time. We then propagate uncertainties over a Markov Chain and condition the resulting probability vector by the hand-drawn curve. It was show that the method generates curves well for coastlines which posses only local properties while for data with large scale structure the method did not maintain those properties. The method allows users to construct libraries and generate new curves that are similar to the class of libraries used.

References

1. E. Cohen, T. Lyche, and R. Riesenfeld. Discrete b-splines and subdivision techniques in computer-aided geometric design and computer graphics. CGIP, 14(2): 87–111, October 1980.
2. A. A. Efros and T. K. Leung. Texture synthesis by non-parametric sampling. *International Conference on Computer Vision*, September 1999.

3. G. Farin. *Curves and Surfaces for Computer Aided Geometric Design.* Academic Press, 1992.
4. A. Finkelstein and D.H. Salesin. Multiresolution curves. In*SIGGRAPH '94 Proceedings*, July 1994.
5. A. R. Forrest. The twisted cubic curve: A computer-aided geometric design approach. *Computer Aided Design*, 12(4):165–172, July 1980.
6. D. R. Forsey and R. H. Bartels. Hierarchical b-spline refinement. *Computer Graphics*, 22(4):205–212, August 1988.
7. D. R. Forsey and R. H. Bartels. Tensor products and hierarchical fitting. *Curves and Surfaces in Computer Vision and Graphics II, SPIE proceedings*, 1610:86–96, 1991.
8. W. Gardner. *Introduction to Random Processes.* McGraw-Hill, 1989.
9. D. J. Heeger and J. R. Bergen. Pyramid-based texture analysis/synthesis. In *SIGGRAPH '95 Proceedings*, 1995.
10. H. Hoppe, T. DeRose, T. Duchanm, and M. Halstead. Piecewise smooth surface reconstruction. In *SIGGRAPH '94 Proceedings*, July 1994.
11. R. Paget and I. Longstaff. Texture synthesis via a non-causal non-parametric multiscale markov random field. In *IEEE Transactions on Image Processing*, volume 7, pages 925–931, June 1997.
12. E. J. Stollnitz, T. D. DeRose, and D. H. Salesin. *Wavelets for Computer Graphics: a Primer.* Number Technical Report 94-09-11. University of Washington, Computer Science and Engineering, September 1994.
13. Li-Yi Wei and M. Levoy. Fast texture synthesis using tree-structured vector quantization. In *SIGGRAPH 2000 Proceedings*, 2000.
14. S. Zhu, Y. Wu, and D. Mumford. Filters, random fields and maximum entropy, towards a unified theory for texture modeling. *International Journal of Computer Vision*, 27(2):107–126, 1998.

The Introduction of Three Methods Generating Stereoscopic Image[1]

Guoying Zhao and Xinyuan Huang

The CAD Center, North China Univ. of Tech., 100041, Shijingshan District, Beijing, China
zgy@ncut.edu.cn; hxy@ncut.edu.cn

Abstract. In the virtual reality technology, the vision display system must settle the problem of stereoscopic display and stereoscopic image resource to build up the immersion sense of VR. This paper introduces three methods of generating stereoscopic image: moving flatly, cylindrical transform and spherical transform, simply compares these three methods and gets the conclusion that the cylindrical transform and the spherical transform can get the better effect.

Keywords: virtual reality (VR); stereoscopic; moving flatly; cylindrical transform; spherical transform

1 Introduction

Following the multimedia, Virtual Reality technology is a second hotspot of research and application. VR not only makes people feel supernatural and great in the digital world which gathers the image, voice and text, it but also takes people into another *true* world built by computers. VR technology includes: computer graphics, multimedia technology, artificial intelligence, man-machine interface technology, sensor technology, highly collateral real time computing technology and so on. VR converge a series of high and fresh technology.

VR has been thought much once having come out. Some experts think: the 80th age is PCs age, the 90th age is multimedia age, and the beginning of the 21st century is VR technology era. Especially practice VR technology facing application is very important for technology revolution and market economy. The vision display system of VR can be approximately divided into three kinds: armet display screen, high resolution CRT system and three dimension stereoglasses connected with traditional display. But no matter which system, we must settle the problem of stereoscopic display and stereoscopic image resource.

There are many reasons of why Stereoscopic TV program did not prevail abroad, but the uppermost reasons have three: the first is TV hardware refurbish frequency is

---

[1] This study has gotten the imbursement of the national 863 high-tech item fund (the item is *Applied VR technology* and the number of the item is *863-306-ZT03-08-1*) and ministry of education item.

J. Liu et al. (Eds.): AMT 2001, LNCS 2252, pp. 365–376, 2001.
© Springer-Verlag Berlin Heidelberg 2001

not enough, so flicker is severe; the second is the quality of stereoglasses is not stable; the third is Stereoscopic TV program is limit, and nice program is so lack. Along with the development of hardware technology, the refurbish frequency of TV and computer improve quickly, and the performance of components is more stable. The first and second problem can be naturally solved, so Stereoscopic TV program is limit will be the uppermost reason restricting the Stereoscopic TV application.

Stereoscopic display technology (namely stereoscopic technology, parallax technology) is named comparing with traditional display technology. It mostly uses human vision principle for reference, and make the plan image have the true stereoscopic impression, that is to say, make the plan image have depth of field sense according to the parallax of two eyes. We will introduce and compare three stereoscopy generating technologies.

2   The Introduction and Comparison of Three Methods Generating Stereoscopic Image

The distance of human two eyes is about 6~7cm. When observing a special point, two eyes will focus the aim point. The angle of two lines of sight changes with the distance between aim points. The human eyes and brain determine this distance according to the difference of two images. The difference of these two images is named stereography. Eyes can regard the object as three dimension according to the measured distance. Our brain gets the information based on small difference and explains the information details to make us have the depth sense. So, when two images have appropriate distance, we will have the stereographic sense. This is the theory of getting the stereographic image, and is the basic of our study.

2.1 Moving Flatly

Now the common method is simply moving flatly to generate stereoscopic image pairs. For an image, we regard the odd rows as right channel and even rows as left channel. Moving the pixels of left channel to right and the pixels of right channel to left to form the images with a little difference in two eyes, we can get depth sense. But for this method, the camera is horizontal, the light axes is parallel, so it simulates the case that depth is far-forth bigger than the excursion distance and two eyes observe infinite beyond and have no focus, as shown in figure 1. This case has difference with the fact, so the effect is not good. When observe position moves flatly, or head turns, eyes can not focus right. So the camera will be assembled and the field of vision will be overlapped in the handy object, like the following cylindrical transform or spherical transform.

2.2 Cylindrical Transform

We project a plan image to half cylinder through two eyes and combine the two images generated by projection to form stereoscopic image, as shown in figure 2. For

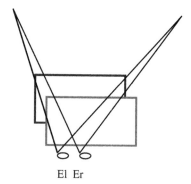

Fig. 1. Moving flatly to form the stereoscopic image pairs

this method, the light axes are not parallel, but are intersected a point in front of or behind the screen. Compared with moving flatly, this method makes the overlapped field for two eyes observe. The stereoscopic image generating by this method has the focus point when people view. If people wear the stereoglasses and observe the combined image, they will see the image plane extrude from or concave the screen.

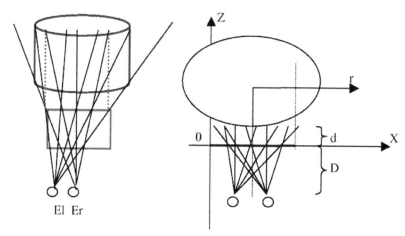

Fig. 2. People will see the stereoscopic image

Fig. 3. Concrete implementation of cylindrical plane projection

In the concrete implementation, we often suppose the observe position is parallel with the projection plane and imaging plane, so we may not consider the effect of height in the stereoscopic imaging: y=i, 0<=i<height, thereinto, *height* is the imaging plane height, as shown in figure 3 we suppose that the leftlower of the image is the origin, so the projection cylinder equation in the *xoz* plane is:

$$(x - \frac{width}{2})^2 + (z - d - r)^2 = r^2 . \tag{1}$$

Thereinto *width* is imaging width, *r* is the radius of cylinder cross section.
The equation of imaging plane is:

$$\begin{cases} x=i \ (0<=i<width) ; \\ z=0 . \end{cases} \tag{2}$$

Two eyes coordinate: left eye:

$$\begin{cases} Xl = \frac{width}{2} - \frac{pz}{2} ; \\ z= -D . \end{cases} \tag{3}$$

Right eye:

$$\begin{cases} Xr = \frac{width}{2} + \frac{pz}{2} ; \\ z= -D . \end{cases} \tag{4}$$

pz is the distance of two eyes.

Firstly, we see the solution of pixel of one row projection point by the left eye:

Left eye projects a point(h,0) (0<=h<width), to the cylindrical plane, the equation of the beeline which through the left eye and the point is:

$$z + D = \frac{D(x - Xl)}{h - Xl} \quad (h<>Xl) . \tag{5}$$

The equation (5) expresses the beeline through the left eye and the point (h,0).

Apply this beeline equation to equation(1), and we can get the point of intersection of the beeline and the cylindrical plane:

Due to (5), we can get:

$$z = \frac{D(x - h)}{h - Xl} \quad (h<>Xl) \tag{6}$$

Apply (6) to (1) and we can get:

$$((h - Xl)^2 + D^2)x^2 - ((h - Xl)^2 * width + 2D^2h + 2D(h - Xl)(d + r))x$$
$$+ (\frac{width^2}{4} + d^2 + 2dr)(h - Xl)^2 + D^2h^2 + 2D(h - Xl)(d + r)h = 0 \tag{7}$$

Equation (7) is a unary quadratic, there into,

$$\begin{cases} a = (h - Xl)^2 + D^2 \ ; \\ -b = (h - Xl)^2 * width + 2D^2 h + 2D(h - Xl)(d + r) \ ; \\ c = (\dfrac{width^2}{4} + d^2 + 2dr)(h - Xl)^2 + D^2 h^2 + 2D(h - Xl)(d + r)h \ . \end{cases} \qquad (8)$$

According to the solution formula of the unary quadratic $ax^2 + bx + c = 0$:
$x = \dfrac{-b \pm \sqrt{b^2 - 4ac}}{2a}$, we can get the projection point coordinate in the cylindrical plane.

When $h <= Xl$, the formula chooses **+**, when $h > Xl$, chooses **-**.

Also, we can get the image projection to the cylinder by the right eye. Then we respectively take the odd and even rows of the two images to combine, and we can get the stereoscopic image.

In fact, when people observe, the observe position is not fixed. People maybe from one position to another or turn their heads. When people move flatly, the image can still be projected to the half cylinder, because cylinder always has tangent plane. As shown in figure 4, when observe position moving flatly, the image can be right projected to the cylindrical plane; but when the head turns, image only can be projected to spherical plane because the upright distance of two eyes is not zero.

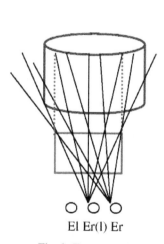

Fig. 4. Eyes move flatly

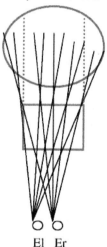

Fig. 5. Spherical projection

2.3 Spherical Transform

We project a plan image to half sphere through two eyes and combine the two images generated by projection to form stereoscopic image, as shown in figure 5.

The concrete implementation using spherical flat projection to generate the stereoscopic image is similar to the cylindrical projection. But the equation of the spherical plane is:

$$(x - \frac{width}{2})^2 + (y - \frac{height}{2})^2 + (z - d - r)^2 = r^2 \tag{9}$$

Thereinto *width* is imaging width, *height* is imaging height , *r* is the radius of sphere.

The equation of imaging plane is:

$$\begin{cases} x=i \ (0<=i<width) \ ; \\ y=j \ (0<=j<height) \ ; \\ z=0 \ . \end{cases} \tag{10}$$

Two eyes coordinate: left eye:

$$\begin{cases} Xl = \frac{width}{2} - \frac{pz}{2} \ ; \\ y=y0 \ ; \\ z= -D \ . \end{cases} \tag{11}$$

right eye:

$$\begin{cases} Xr = \frac{width}{2} + \frac{pz}{2} \ ; \\ y=y0 \ ; \\ z= -D \ . \end{cases} \tag{12}$$

pz is the distance of two eyes: y0 is y coordinate of the imaging plane pixel.

Firstly, we see the solution of pixels of one row y=w (0<=w<height) projection points by the left eye:

Left eye projects a point(h,w,0) (0<=h<width), to the sphere, and the beeline equation of *xoz* plane is:

$$z + D = \frac{D(x - Xl)}{h - Xl} \quad (h<>Xl) \ . \tag{13}$$

The equation (13) expresses the beeline through the left eye and the point(h,w,0) .

Apply this beeline equation to equation (9), and we can get the point of intersection of the beeline and the spherical plane:

Due to (13), we can get

$$z = \frac{D(x - h)}{h - Xl} \quad (h<>Xl) \ . \tag{14}$$

Apply (14) to (9) , we get equation (15):

$$((h-Xl)^2+D^2)x^2-((h-Xl)^2 * width+2D^2h+2D(h-Xl)(d+r))x$$

$$+(\frac{width^2}{4}+\frac{height^2}{4}+w^2-width*w+d^2+2dr)(h-Xl)^2 \tag{15}$$

$$+D^2h^2+2D(h-Xl)(d+r)h=0$$

Equation (15) is a unary quadratic, thereinto,

$$\begin{cases} a=(h-Xl)^2+D^2; \\ -b=(h-Xl)^2 * width+2D^2h+2D(h-Xl)(d+r); \\ c=(\frac{width^2}{4}+\frac{height^2}{4}+w^2-width*w+d^2+2dr)(h-Xl)^2 \\ \quad +D^2h^2+2D(h-Xl)(d+r)h \end{cases} \tag{16}$$

According to the solution formula of the unary quadratic $ax^2+bx+c=0$:

$x=\dfrac{-b\pm\sqrt{b^2-4ac}}{2a}$, we can get the projection point coordinate in the spherical plane.

When $h<=Xl$, the formula chooses +, when $h>Xl$, chooses -.

Also, we can get the image projection to the sphere by the right eye. Then we respectively take the odd and even rows of the two images to combine, and we can get the stereoscopic image.

When people observe, the image will focus on the plane in front of or behind the screen. If people moved, or turned their head, though two eyes are not in the same horizontal plane, image is still focused on the spherical plane and people can observe the true and right stereoscopic image.

In the case that two eyes are not in the same horizontal plane, the spherical plane equation is same to (9). We suppose that the angle between two eyes line and xoz plane is a, the coordinate of two eyes is:

Left eye:

$$\begin{cases} Xl=\dfrac{width}{2}-\dfrac{pz}{2}\cos\partial; \\ Yl=\dfrac{height}{2}+\dfrac{pz}{2}\sin\partial; \\ Z=-D. \end{cases} \tag{17}$$

Right eye:

$$
\begin{cases}
\text{Xr}=\dfrac{width}{2}+\dfrac{pz}{2}\cos\partial\,; \\[2mm]
\text{Yr}=\dfrac{height}{2}-\dfrac{pz}{2}\sin\partial\,; \\[2mm]
\text{Z}=\text{-D}\,.
\end{cases}
\tag{18}
$$

Also, we firstly see the solution to the left eye projection to a row pixels y=w (0<=w<height):

The line of left sight projects a pixel (h,w,0) (0<=h<width), into the spherical plane, and the beeline equation is:

$$
\frac{x-h}{h-Xl}=\frac{y-w}{w-Yl}=\frac{z}{D}\quad(h<>Xl)
\tag{19}
$$

The equation (19) expresses the beeline through the left eye and the point (h,w,0) ;

Apply this beeline equation to equation (9), and we can get the point of intersection of the beeline and the spherical plane:

Due to (19), we get:

$$
\begin{cases}
y=\dfrac{(w-Yl)x-w*Xl+h*Yl}{h-Xl} \\[3mm]
z=\dfrac{D(x-h)}{h-Xl}
\end{cases}
;\quad(h<>Xl);
\tag{20}
$$

Apply (20) to (9), and we can get a unary quadratic similar to $ax^2+bx+c=0$ there into:

$$
\begin{cases}
a=(h-Xl)^2+(w-Yl)^2+D^2\,; \\[2mm]
-b=(h-Xl)^2*width+2D^2h+2D(h-Xl)(d+r) \\[2mm]
\quad+2(w-Yl)(w*Xl-h*Yl) \\[2mm]
c=(\dfrac{width^2}{4}+\dfrac{height^2}{4}+d^2+2dr)(h-Xl)^2+D^2h^2
\end{cases}
\tag{21}
$$
$$
+2D(h-Xl)(d+r)h+(w*Xl-h*Yl)^2\qquad.
$$
$$
+height*(h-Xl)(w*Xl-h*Yl)
$$

According to the solution formula of the unary quadratic $ax^2+bx+c=0$:

$$x = \frac{-b \pm \sqrt{b^2 - 4ac}}{2a},$$ we can get the projection point coordinate in the spherical plane.

When h<=Xl, the formula choose +, when h>Xl, choose -. Apply the solution x to (18), we can get the corresponding y.

If h=Xl, x coordinate of the projection point is Xl, and beeline through the left eye and the point(h,w,0) is:

$$\begin{cases} z(w - Yl) = D(y - w) \\ x = Xl \end{cases} \tag{22}$$

Apply it to (9), we can get a unary quadratic about y: $ay^2 + by + c = 0$, thereinto:

$$\begin{cases} a = (w - Yl)^2 + D^2 ; \\ -b = (w - Yl)^2 * height + 2D^2 w + 2D(w - Yl)(d + r) ; \\ c = (\frac{width^2}{4} + \frac{height^2}{4} + d^2 + 2dr + Xl^2 - width * Xl)(w - Yl)^2 \end{cases} \tag{23}$$
$$+ D^2 w^2 + 2D(w - Yl)(d + r)w.$$

We can get the projection point coordinate in the spherical plane: (Xl, y).

When w<=Yl, the formula chooses -. When w<Yl, chooses +.

Also, we can get the image projection to the sphere by the right eye. Then we respectively take the odd and even rows of the two images to combine, and we can get the stereoscopic image.

2.4 Comparison

For computing, the method of moving flatly is most simple. Cylindrical transform is in the next place. It only needs to compute the projection position of each pixel by two eyes once, and store these positions, so we only need take out the pixel in the position after that; Computing of spherical transform is most complex. It must compute each point pixel value after projection. When two eyes are not in the same horizontal plane, we will consider the upright distance of projection.

For impression, moving flatly only simulates that two eyes observe the infinite beyond and have no focus. Its impression is not as good as cylindrical plane and spherical plane transform. Cylindrical plane transform only simulates the case that two eyes observe flatly. Spherical plane transform also can simulate the case that two eyes are not in the same horizontal plane. The following figure 7 is the generated stereoscopic image when the odd and even rows respectively move right and left 17 pixels. The figure 8 is generated by cylindrical projection when   width=r=320, pz=240, D=1600 and d=80. Figure 9 is generated by spherical projection when width=320, r=2*width, height=240, pz=60, D=800, d=175.

Fig. 7. Stereoscopic image generated by moving flatly

Fig. 8. Stereoscopic image generated by cylindrical projection

3 Conclusion

These three methods can produce depth sense, cylindrical plane and spherical transform also can simulate and solve the case that people observe horizontally and

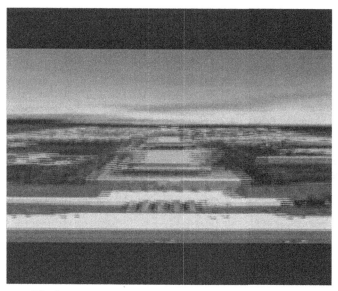

Fig. 9. Stereoscopic image generated by spherical projection

non-horizontally, but the latter two methods, especially the spherical plane transform, their computing is very complex, almost each pixel must be complexly computed. And the spherical plane transform must consider the abandon and filling up of the margin and the middle pixels. These three methods all process the whole image, so when we wear the appropriate stereoglasses, we feel the whole scene be pushed far or pulled near, this is not match the fact. In fact, we feel that each object has different depth, for example, in the classroom, the blackboard is farthest, the desks are in front of the blackboard and so on. So the process to the separate object in the scene is requested to form the different level depth sense. We can adopt the object segmentation to take out each object in the scene, set different depth for each object according to the request, and use the above methods to get the better stereoscopic image and simulate the reality more actually.

References

1. Zheng Zhuying. Information process of two eyes solid vision. Beijing: Science publishing company, 1998
2. Written by Kenneth.R.Castleman, translated by Zhu Zhigang. Digital image process. Beijing: electron industry publishing company, 1998
3. Peng Qunsheng, Bao Hujun, Jin Xiaogang. Arithmetic foundation of computer third dimension graphics. Beijing: Science publishing company, 1999
4. Tang Rongxi, Wang Jiaye, Peng Qunsheng. Computer graphics tutorial. Beijing: Science publishing company, 2000
5. Zeng Fenfang. Virtual Reality technology. Shanghai: Traffic university publishing company, 1997

6.   Byron J.Pierce, Karl Frederick Arrington, Miguel A.Moreno. Motion and stereoscopic tilt perception. Journal of the SID,1999, 7(3):P177-182
7.   Mel Siegel, Yoshikazu Tobinaga, Takeo Akiya. Kinder Gentler Stereo. Stereoscopic Displays and Virtual Reality Systems VI, IS&T/SPIE Conference on Stereoscopic Displays and Applications X, 1999: P18-27
8.   Yasser A.Ahmed, Hossam Afifi, G.Rubino. New Stereo Matching Algorithm. Stereoscopic Displays and Virtual Reality Systems VI, IS&T/SPIE Conference on Stereoscopic Displays and Applications X, 1999: P170-177
9.   Janusz Konrad. Enhancement of viewer comfort in stereoscopic viewing:parallax adjustment. Stereoscopic Displays and Virtual Reality Systems VI.   IS&T/SPIE Conference on Stereoscopic Displays and Applications X, 1999:P179-190
10. Yasser A.Ahmed, Hossam Afifi. New stereoscopic system. Stereoscopic Displays and Virtual Reality Systems VI, IS&T/SPIE Conference on Stereoscopic Displays and Applications X, 1999: P321-328
11. Li Bin. Analyse and design of stereoscopic system. TV technology, 2000, 3:P10-13

Kansei-Oriented Image Retrieval

Shangfei Wang, Enhong Chen, Jing Hu, and Xufa Wang

Artificial Intelligence Lab.
Department of Computer Science and Technology of USTC
Hefei, P.R.China, 230027
sfwang@mail.ustc.edu.cn

Abstract. In the design of multimedia database system, one of the important issues is how to deal with kansei of human beings. A kansei-oriented image retrieval has been proposed in this paper. Human kansei includes two aspects: common kansei and individual kansei. Our approach also consists of common kansei retrieval and individual kansei retrieval. First, avoiding the dependence on the method of selecting impression words, factor analysis is applied to construct an orthogonal psychological space based on common human kansei. After that, a radial basis function neural network is used for learning and memorizing the common kansei, then automatically evaluates and annotates each image with adjective words in the orthogonal psychological space. Furthermore interactive evolution computation is presented to realize individual kansei retrieval. Last an interesting experimental result is shown.

1 Introduction

As technology in computer hardware and software advances, efficient information retrieval from multimedia database gets highly demanded. Recently content-based image retrieval method has been studied as core technique[1]. It can be applied to digital library, media management system, home shopping, and so on. Several working systems have already been developed, for example, QBIS system of IBM, Photobook of MIT and Chubot of Berkley. But what current computer vision techniques can automatically extract from images are mainly low-level features which has little relevancy to human intuition and emotion, while the ultimate end use of an image retrieval is human who tent to use high-level concepts in everyday life. Therefore the study of human perception of image content from a psychophysical level is crucial. This paper has provided a kansei-oriented image retrieval.

Kansei is a Japanese word [2], which is the total concept of intuition, emotion, preference, subjectivity, sensation, perception, cognition, and other psychological processing function. Human kansei involves two factors [3]: common kansei and individual kansei. Common kansei is an average or objective kansei, which means that a certain number of people might agree to some extent-not everyone would agree but most of them would agree, while individual kansei reflects the difference between each other. In this paper, we provide a kansei-oriented image retrieval consisting of common kansei retrieval and individual kansei retrieval. By kansei-oriented, it means that the user is at the center of our approach sensitive to and

J. Liu et al. (Eds.): AMT 2001, LNCS 2252, pp. 377–388, 2001.

actively using his/her cognitive abilities as well as his /her sensitivity. Our frame consists of four essential components: 1) Image processing kernel which extract color and shape features from images as kansei features .2) An orthogonal psychological space constructed by using factor analysis. 3) Learning unit consisting of a Radial Basis Function Neural Networks (RBFNN), which memorizes the "objective" or "average" human kansei and indexes images based on "average" human kansei. 4) Dynamic and interactive kansei image retrieval model using Interactive Evolution Computation (IEC) which takes into consideration the differences between users' Kansei.

This paper is organized as follows: Section 2 describes our approach in detail; Section 3 shows the performance by computer experiments; Section 4 gives the conclusion.

2   Kansei-Oriented Image Retrieval

Fig.1 shows the overview of our Kansei-oriented Image Retrieval (KIR) framework. It consists of four components: Image processing kernel, an orthogonal psychological space, learning unit consisting of a RBFNN and dynamical and interactive kansei image retrieval.

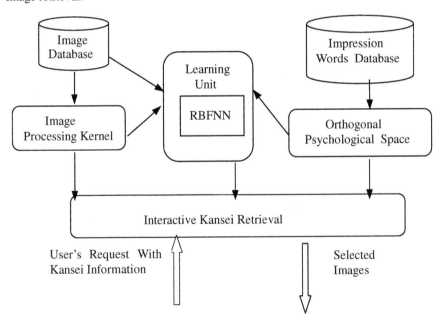

Fig. 1. Overview of Kansei-oriented Image Retrieval (KIR)

2.1 Image Processing Kernel

We define color and shape features as the kansei feature which express the characteristic elements of images.

2.1.1 Extraction of Color Feature

Concerning the color feature, we analyze compositions, which are very important when human beings impressed from images [4][5]. The system uses four basic composition templates: vertical, horizontal, circular and radiation division, which are showed in Fig.2. These templates divide the image into several regions, and the average RGB colors are calculated in each region.

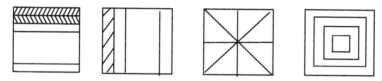

Fig. 2. Four composition templates

2.1.2 Extraction of Shape Feature

Shape features are based on graphical features in Digital Safari Guidebook. [4]. First, the RGB data are converted to brightness from equation (1) :

$$\text{Brightness} = 0.299 \times R + 0.587 \times G + 0.114 \times B \qquad (1)$$

Then, brightness is converted to binary, based on the threshold value, which is set on the average value of brightness. This binary image is divided into 8 by 8 blocks, and the number of black pixels on each region is counted. The numbers on each region are defined as the shape features. The dimension of the shape feature is 64.

2.2 Orthogonal Psychological Space

In order to avoid dependence on the methods of selecting adjective words, we make use of orthogonal psychological space. In this section we examine the constructional process of psychological space in details[6], which includes the careful selection of adjectives, psychological experiment and factor analysis.

We first carefully consider N ($N = 23$) adjectives listed in table 1 (These adjectives are originally written in Chinese), then K ($K = 16$) male graduate students in their 20s are asked to evaluate M ($M = 58$) images using these adjectives varied in 5-degree scores. For example, for the adjective beautiful, a student should give a five-degree score from "not at all" to "very much" as shown in Fig.3, thus the emotion data $\{z_{mnk}, m = 1,..., M ; n = 1,..., N ; k = 1, ... , K \}$ are gathered.

Table 1. Adjective words

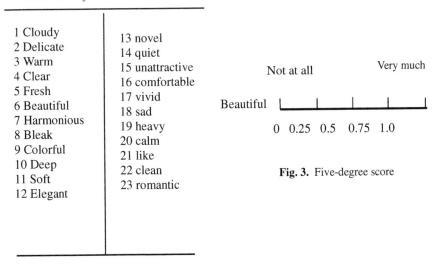

1 Cloudy	13 novel
2 Delicate	14 quiet
3 Warm	15 unattractive
4 Clear	16 comfortable
5 Fresh	17 vivid
6 Beautiful	18 sad
7 Harmonious	19 heavy
8 Bleak	20 calm
9 Colorful	21 like
10 Deep	22 clean
11 Soft	23 romantic
12 Elegant	

Fig. 3. Five-degree score

First, we average the emotion data according to Eq.2.

$$y_{mn} = \frac{1}{K}\sum_{k=1}^{K} z_{mnk}$$

(2)

Then, standardize $\{y_{mn}\}$ with respect to objects $m = 1, 2, \ldots, M$:

$$x_{mn} = \frac{y_{mn} - \overline{y_n}}{s_n}$$

(3)

Where

$$\overline{y_n} = \frac{1}{M}\sum_{m=1}^{M} y_{mn} \quad , \quad s_n^2 = \sum_{m=1}^{M}\left(y_{mn} - \overline{y_n}\right)^2$$

Define an $M \times N$ data matrix:

$$X = \begin{pmatrix} x_{11} & \cdots & x_{1N} \\ \vdots & \ddots & \vdots \\ x_{M1} & \cdots & x_{MN} \end{pmatrix}$$

The purpose of factor analysis[3] is to resolve X into the following forms:

$$X = FA' + UD$$

(4)

Each matrix is explained as follows:

F is the factor score matrix:

$$F = \begin{pmatrix} f_{11} & \cdots & f_{1L} \\ \vdots & \ddots & \vdots \\ f_{M1} & \cdots & f_{ML} \end{pmatrix}$$

where $l = 1, 2, \ldots, L$ are common factors and $L < N$. the m-th row of F: $f_m = (f_{m1}, f_{m2}, \ldots, f_{mL})$ indicates the coordinate of object m in the factor space.
A is the factor loading matrix:

$$A = \begin{pmatrix} a_{11} & \cdots & a_{1L} \\ \vdots & \ddots & \vdots \\ a_{N1} & \cdots & a_{NL} \end{pmatrix}$$

The n-th row of A: $a_m = (a_{m1}, a_{m2}, \ldots, a_{mL})$ corresponds of word n in the factor space.
U is the unique factor score matrix, and D is the weighting matrix:

$$U = \begin{pmatrix} u_{11} & \cdots & u_{1N} \\ \vdots & \ddots & \vdots \\ u_{M1} & \cdots & u_{MN} \end{pmatrix} \qquad D = \begin{pmatrix} d_1 & \cdots & 0 \\ \vdots & \ddots & \vdots \\ 0 & \cdots & d_N \end{pmatrix}$$

Here PCA is used to obtain the factor score and factor-loading matrix. Since PCA is an orthogonal transformation, which means the distances in L-space are preserved. In other words, by PCA and FA, each adjective can be regarded as a vector in the first L main factor space and the distances between adjectives also can be measured in the same space. Furthermore, through PCA the original N dimension space is reduced into L dimension orthogonal space, which means each image also has L dimension corresponding values in this orthogonal psychological space. This $M \times L$ factor score matrix F will be used as training data for RBFNN.

It is assumed in this section that usual emotion concepts consist of linear combination of several basic concepts.

2.3 Learning Unit

The learning unit provides the following functionality:
1) Define the relationship between impression words and the kansei features of images;
2) Memorize user's common kansei
3) Automatically annotate each image based on the common kansei
In order to realize these functionalities, we use RBFNN, which is a forward neural network of three layers. The mapping function of the network is:

$$f(X_i) = \lambda_0 + \sum_{k=1}^{K} \lambda_k \exp\left(-\frac{\|X_i - C_k\|^2}{2\sigma_k^2}\right) \qquad (5)$$

In Eq.5: C_k is the center of the kth hidden unit, σ_k is the width, K is the number of the hidden units; λ_0 is the bias; λ_k is the weight between the out unit and the kth hidden unit; X_i is the input vector; $f(X_i)$ is the output of the network.

. Here the kansei features of an image are used as the input of the networks and the corresponding values in the eight-dimensional orthogonal psychological space is the output the networks. After training, the weights of the networks represent the relationship between impression words and images kansei features, thus the network memorizes the common kansei. Then we can get the common kansei of each image by inputting its kansei features to the RBFNN, In other words, the image is automatically annotated by the RBFNN with eight values in the orthogonal psychological space. Thus we can retrieval an image just by indexing its common kansei.

2.4 Dynamic and Interactive Retrieval Model

Because human kansei consists of common kansei and individual kansei, the dynamic and interactive retrieval model includes two retrieval methods: common kansei retrieval and individual kansei retrieval.

2.4.1 Common Kansei Retrieval

The flowchart of the common kansei retrieval is shown in Fig. 4. The user input an impression word, which is stored in the impression database, and then the retrieval system indexes the common kansei of each image and display top 8 images with the closest Euclid distance from the inputted impression word.

This method provides general image retrieval capabilities. However, as this method is based upon the objective or average human kansei stored in the learning unit, the retrieved images may not suit the user's taste-they are an informed average, not a "custom fit". So a dynamic interactive adapting retrieval mechanism according to individual variation and improving accuracy of the retrieval results is very important. Here we use interactive evolution computation to overcome this problem.

2.4.2 Individual Kansei Retrieval

Interactive evolution computation[7] is the optimization technology that uses human evaluation. Simply stated, the interactive EC is an EC whose fitness function is replace by human. The human operator evaluates the output of the target system according to the distance between the goal and the system output in psychological space, while the EC searches in the feature parameter space based on the human evaluation.

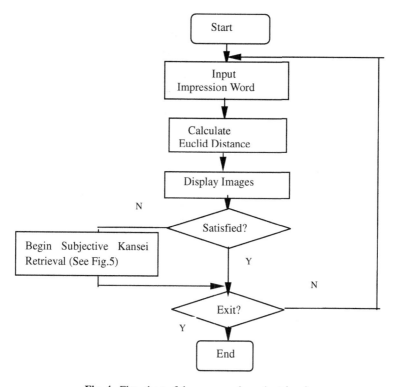

Fig. 4. Flowchart of the common kansei retrieval

In our system, the user first uses common kansei retrieval to get the images what he wants. If the retrieval results are not satisfactory, the individual kansei retrieval is started. The result images of the common kansei retrieval will be used as initial population. User decides the fitness of images based on the similarity of what he/she wants, and the system creates and displays the next generation images with evolution computing (Selection and Crossover). The procedure is repeated until the user obtains the image that is most similar to what he has in mind.

3   Experiment Results

The system is written with PHP and C and the size of image database is 200. Fig. 6 shows the user interface of the system. A user chose the adjective from the list, and then the system begins to retrieval.

3.1 The Result of Psychological Space

Table 2 gives the factor loadings, here $m = 8$.

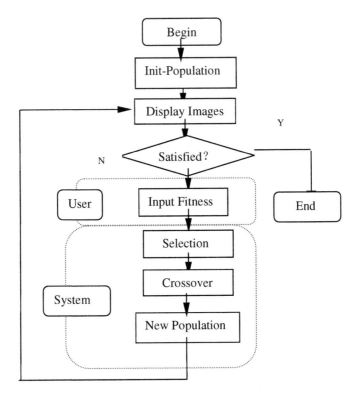

Fig. 5. Flowchart of the individual kansei retrieval

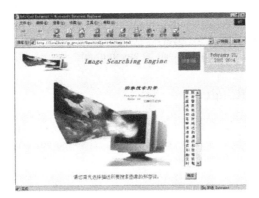

Fig. 6. Interface of Kansei-oriented Image retrieval

Table 2. Result of FA

	1	2	3	4	5	6	7	8
1	0.096	0.179	-0.151	-0.190	-0.266	0.583	0.328	-0.201
2	-0.088	0.227	-0.085	-0.067	0.152	-0.130	0.035	-0.270
3	-0.121	-0.169	0.426	-0.150	0.228	0.342	0.111	0.380
4	0.154	0.089	-0.698	0.072	-0.261	-0.011	0.417	0.206
5	-0.546	-1.041	-0.066	-0.262	-0.308	0.164	-0.102	-0.136
6	0.150	-0.111	-0.022	0.371	-0.012	-0.149	-0.249	0.204
7	0.028	-0.112	0.229	-0.135	0.061	-0.256	0.210	0.092
8	0.966	0.519	-0.266	0.504	0.136	0.007	-0.051	0.018
9	0.026	0.344	-0.239	-0.030	0.010	0.205	-0.253	0.067
10	0.667	0.746	0.594	-0.331	0.178	0.033	0.163	-0.241
11	-0.115	0.304	0.092	-0.011	-0.193	0.009	0.038	0.212
12	-0.047	0.220	0.387	-0.170	0.120	0.147	-0.203	0.034
13	-1.214	0.666	0.099	-0.133	-0.447	-0.417	0.011	-0.093
14	-0.064	0.327	-0.342	-0.049	-0.073	0.234	0.104	-0.009
15	-0.263	-0.335	0.395	0.714	-0.182	0.251	0.030	-0.129
16	-0.149	-0.215	-0.081	-0.567	0.341	0.043	-0.041	0.077
17	-1.090	0.010	-0.446	0.078	0.574	-0.002	0.009	-0.189
18	-0.150	-0.274	0.090	-0.056	-0.097	-0.090	0.156	0.011
19	0.668	-0.458	0.005	0.078	0.245	-0.182	0.430	0.035
20	0.324	-0.310	-0.017	0.228	0.100	0.036	-0.019	-0.420
21	0.313	-0.395	-0.140	-0.114	0.112	-0.144	-0.145	0.002
22	0.050	0.267	0.215	-0.063	-0.028	0.293	-0.336	0.053
23	1.443	-0.238	-0.180	-0.386	-0.341	-0.157	-0.223	-0.112

Though FA, the original 23-dimension space has been reduced to 8-dimension orthogonal space. Each adjective and image can be seen as a vector in this orthogonal psychological space. Thus we can just index image in the emotional space.

3.2 Common Kansei Retrieval

To evaluate the performance of common kansei retrieval, we requested 10 out of 16 male graduate students who have done the sense experiment in section 2.2 to search "brilliant"," clear" and "romantic" images. If the number of images, which the user is satisfied with, is larger than five out of eight, we consider the experimental result is good. Four is normal and less than three is bad. The test result is shown in table 3.

Table 3. Test result for common image retrieval

	Brilliant	Clear	Romantic
Good	5	4	8
Normal	3	3	1
Not good	2	3	1
Total	10	10	10

In this test, above 70 percent of the subjects are satisfied with the retrieved images. Fig.7 shows the common kansei retrieval result for "brilliant".

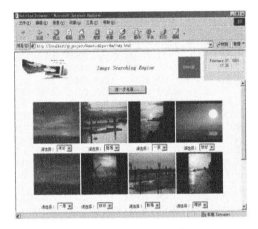

Fig. 7. Common kansei retrieval for "brilliant"

3.3 Individual Kansei Retrieval

Fig 8 is an individual kansei retrieval result for "brilliant" of a male graduate student after three trials of interaction. The student thinks all of the eight images are satisfiable.

Fig. 8. Individual kansei retrieval for "brilliant"

To evaluate the performance of common kansei retrieval, we requested 10 male and 10 female graduate students in their twenties to search "brilliant", "clear" and "romantic" images. If the number of images, which the user is satisfied with, is larger than six out of eight, the interactive individual kansei retrieval process is stopped. Table 4 shows the average number of trials to obtain the satisfied images for these three adjectives.

Table 4. Test result for individual image retrieval

	Brilliant	Clear	Romantic
Male	3	4	2
Female	5	5	6

In this test, we can see that the female needs more interaction than male to find their satisfied images, maybe because the orthogonal psychological space and learning unit base on the sense experimental data of 16 male students. In the future research, we will establish learning units for each group of users according to their age, sex etc.

4 Conclusion

How to deal with human kansei is an important issue in designing multimedia database system. Human kansei includes two aspects: common kansei and individual kansei. Common kansei is an "average" or "objective" kansei of a certain number of people, while individual kansei reflects the difference between each other. This paper provides a kansei-oriented image retrieval consisting of common kansei retrieval and individual kansei retrieval. First, avoiding the dependence on the method of selecting impression words, factor analysis is applied to construct an orthogonal psychological space based on common human kansei. After that, a radial basis function neural network is used for learning and memorizing the common kansei, then automatically evaluates and annotates each image with adjective words in the orthogonal psychological space. Furthermore interactive evolution computation is presented to realize individual kansei retrieval. The experimental results demonstrate the effectiveness of our approach. However, our system provides 23 adjective words for users, next we will do some research on the mechanism of adding new adjectives. In addition, we will divide users into several groups according to their age sex etc, and establish learning units for each group.

Acknowledgement. This research is supported by National 973 Project of P.R.China.

References

[1] Arnold W.M. Smeulders, Marcel Worring, Simone Santini et al, Content-based Image Retrieval at the End of the Early Years, IEEE Trans. On Pattern Analysis and Machine Intelligence, Vol. 22, No. 12, December 2000 pp.1349-1380
[2] Takagi H., Interactive Evolutionary Computation–Cooperation of computational intelligence and human KANSEI, Proceedings of IIZUKA'98, pp.41-50
[3] Norihiko M., Yasuo N., Hideo J. et al, Talking of the Dreams of "Engineering of Impression", Impression'98
[4] Takashi H., Masafumi H., Image Query by Impression Words-The IQI System, IEEE Trans. on Consumer Electronics, Vol.44, No.2, May, 1998, pp.347-352

[5] Iwaoka T., Kobayashi H., Ota S., Digital Safari Guidebook. With image retrieval, Proceedings of the 1999 6th International Conference on Multimedia Computing and Systems, pp.1011-1012

[6] Wang Shangfei, Enhong Chen, Image Retrieval Based on An Artificial Emotion Model, admitted by ICONIP2001

[7] J.Y. Lee, S.B. Cho, Interactive Genetic Algorithm for Content-based Image Retrieval, Proc. of Asian Fuzzy Systems Symposium, Masan, Korea, June 1998, pp.279-484

ICSPACE – An Internet Cultural Space

T.A. Tavares, A.S. Araújo, and G.L. Souza Filho

NatalNet Lab
DIMAp - Computer Science and Applied Mathematics Department
UFRN - Federal University of the Rio Grande do Norte
Campus Universitário - Lagoa Nova - 59072-970, Natal - RN - Brasil

Abstract. This work describes the structure and the functionality of ICSPACE - an Internet Cultural Space. ICSpace provides for the artist community the possibility to build an open and dynamic environment in the Internet. In our approach, the computer is used as a knowledge supplier expanding the human artistic expression. ICSPACE structures the exhibition of the artist's works in thematic rooms implemented with VRML. The thematic rooms are seen as independent and correlated cells. The association of a set of rooms provides a complex formation that defines the own cultural center. The cells are based on a spatial metaphor. The idea is to allow that authors to choose the best position to expose theirs works in ICSpace "virtual reality environment". ICSPACE implementation requires the integration of technologies like human computer interaction, cooperative work, virtual reality, hypermedia systems and dynamic art. The main goal of the ICSPACE is to provide a space to promote cultural exchange through the Internet, removing barriers between people and artists.

Keywords: Virtual Reality, Hypermedia Systems, Dynamic Art, VRML, Web Applications.

1 Introduction

In the last years, the evolution of Telecommunications and Computer Networks areas makes possible the use of computers to help people to communicate, interact, get informed and interchange knowledge with other computers and people [3]. So, we can go beyond and say that the computer now is characterized as an instrument used as a human interaction mediator. The computer can simulate sophisticated environments that bring the real world into a simple monitor.

The association of recent concepts like Virtual reality [1, 5, 6] and multimedia portal [4, 7] have provided the combination of different medias as sound and video to offer advanced services thought the Internet. These concepts turn usual services more attractive to users. A simple query like look for a book, for example, can be more interesting if the user could visit the library rooms, take the book and open it.

This paper presents ICSpace, a virtual cultural space that combines several technologies to develop an open cultural space in the Internet. Initially we will

J. Liu et al. (Eds.): AMT 2001, LNCS 2252, pp. 389–399, 2001.

provide an overview of the ICSPace. The next step is to point out the related concepts that define the system's architecture and how this system deals with users and the available work of arts. At the end we present the initial results obtained with the system implementation.

2   Related Works

Now it is possible to visit a great number of museums and libraries through the Internet. Museums such as the Louvre [10] in Paris, Van Gogh [11] in Amsterdam and Museum of Contemporary Art of Chicago [12] are some examples. The information contained in those culture centers is decentralized and popularized through the net. In accordance with Talagala et al [13], museums use the Web as an extension of their walls, and this fact increases the exhibition capacity and the scope of those institutions.

For example, with the Atlantic Modern Art Center [14] that have published its collection in the Internet. One of the great advantages pointed by the users of this service is the possibility to visit exhibitions which are no longer active in the real museum through the on-line collection. In this site, HTML pages basically link text and image media and represent each segment of the center through a color scheme.

The Virtual Music Museum "Virtuella Musik Musset" [15] makes a metaphor of the reality when it creates its own virtual space based on a real model of a medieval castle. In that space, existing only in the computer, several musical instruments may be appreciated, information about them can be read and the sound produced by each instrument can be listened. Figure 1-a illustrates one of the environments of the museum, where text, image and audio medias are displayed in a virtual reality environment implemented using VRML.

The virtuality of the Pygoya Museum is not restricted to the exhibition space only. It is extended with work of arts that only appear at the virtual museum. The so called cyberart or digital art is an artistic manifestation created and transmitted through the Internet that is based in images generated by a computer. The Pygoya Museum makes its digital art collection available through virtual worlds in VRML as shown in the Figure 1-b.

All the museums and cultural centers presented here have a common characteristic: they are informative applications, that is, media presentation environments. In this case, the interaction resources are quite restricted and the user is limited to the visualization of a collection formed by a pre-determined number of works made available by the museum. In this point the Chicago Contemporary Art Museum [12] is quite innovative because, despite working with a defined collection, it enables the user to organize the exhibition space. When entering the virtual museum the user faces an empty environment and then he/she may choose which works will be exhibited and the location of each work. This facility is called virtual trusteeship.

The works presented in this section illustrate the state of the art in applications of the museums and cultural centers implementations. These tools share

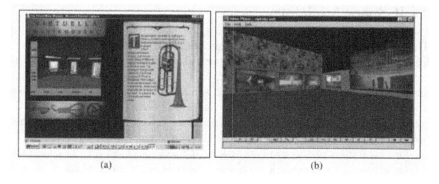

Fig. 1. (a) Music Virtual Museum. (b) Pygoya Museum – CyberArt

some features and present particularities that define their positive and negative aspects.

Table 1. Virtual Museums Comparison.

	Atlântico Modern Art Center	Music Virtual Museum	Pygoya Museum	Chicago Contemporary Art Museum
Media	📄 🖼	📄 🖼 🔊	📄 🖼 🔊	📄 🖼
Presentation Environment	HTML	VRML + HTML	VRML	VRML + HTML
Conceptual model	Real	Virtual	Virtual	Real
Interactivity	☆	☆☆	☆☆	☆☆☆

Legend: 📄 = text   🖼 = image   🔊 = audio

Table 1 presents a comparative approach of the application based on the following parameters: media handled, presentation environment, conceptual model and interactivity. The first parameter defines which media are being used in the representation of the works. The presentation environment specifies what technologies are used to the site implementation. The conceptual model describes if there is a link with reality or not, a real conceptual model defines sites of museums that exist physically and a virtual conceptual model specifies spaces that only exist in the computers. The interactivity measures the available options the user has to interact with the museum site. For example, implementations using virtual reality favor the interactivity, since they facilitate interaction forms, as the navigation in depth and moving.

3   ICSpace Modeling

This session will present ICSPace conceptual model. We used use cases diagrams from UML to represent this model. Figure 2 shows the application context. This model defines the real world metaphor, which provide the basis for the whole application. This metaphor is based on a real cultural space operation where artists expose their work of arts for the visitors. The visitors can circulate in the space, look to the exposed works, notice other visitors' presence, express their opinion and, eventually, communicate with each other.

The exhibition of the work of arts at ICSpace is based on the concept of thematic rooms. The thematic rooms are the cells of the cultural space, that is, they constitute independent and correlated modules. The modules have autonomy for administrate processes and information. The association of a group of thematic rooms creates a complex formation that defines the cultural space.

Cultural Center Use-Case Diagram – Application Context Description

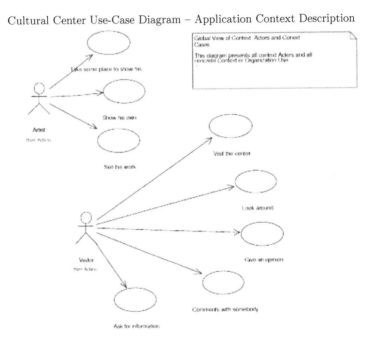

Fig. 2. Use Case Diagram.

The users interact with ICSpace assuming one among two roles, represent by different avatars: author or visitor. As an author the user visits the space to choose the most appropriate position to expose his work of art. As a visitor the user can walk through the thematic rooms, observe the exposed works and interact with other visitors or authors. So, the first thing the user do when he begins to visit the ICSpace is to choose the avatar that will represent him. During the visit the user notices other visitors' presence by way of their respective avatars and can send messages or invite the other users to a chat. The visitors can also to record critics about the exposed works. The critics are arranged to the authors and other visitors.

4   ICSpace Structural Organization

As aforementioned, the structural organization of ICSpace is based on thematic rooms. The rooms can be seen as small portals. These portals are responsible for the information distribution, presentation and management. Therefore, the thematic rooms define ICSpace in structural level and also represent the system functional kernel.

Figure 3 shows the ICSpace structure. In this picture we can see the users' roles (author and visitor), the ICSpace user interface, the thematic rooms (video, music, digital art and literature cells) and the repositories of work of arts and applications.

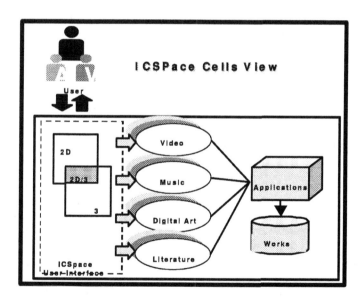

Fig. 3. ICSPace Cells View.

4.1 ICSPace User Interface

ICSpace user interface was developed using the model proposed in [9]. The interface is based on two models: a 3D and a 2D. This way, the users have three options of access:

- *"Virtual"* – based on virtual reality that provides a virtual presentation environment for each thematic room. Figure 4-a presents a panoramic view of the ICSpace VRML model.
- *"Web"* – based on Web pages that provide HTML files that link the thematic rooms and the exposed works.
- *"Mix"* – an hybrid way, which mixes virtual reality and the Web model into web pages with frames, which present a virtual world and HTML text to users [8].

As an example we will describe in more details the video cell. These cells are based on two virtual environments. The first is used to present the available collection, that is, to show to the visitors a room where they can see posters with information about the movies that are exposed (Figure 4-b). When the user decide to see a particular video, he can watch to the video in a second virtual environment (Figure 3-c) where the video appears integrated into the virtual environment, projected in a simulation of a cinema. There is an other option were the visitor watches to the movie through a video player, that is, a plug in that exhibits the video in an external area (or external window). In this case, VRML just activate the exhibition of the video that is done in a new window generated by the player.

4.2 Thematic Rooms

The thematic rooms are structures that contain the work of arts published in the cultural space. Initially we intend have the following rooms:

- *Literature.* In these rooms the authors publish works in text format that will be presented as HTML pages.
- *Image.* They are spaces for image exhibition. The images can be paintings or digital compositions in different formats, as GIF, JPEG or BMP.
- *Music.* The music rooms will accommodate the authors' musical compositions. Other mechanisms can be incorporated to these rooms, as videoconference services where visitors can appreciate live performances and interact with the own authors.
- *Video.* The operation of the video rooms is be based on Video on Demand technology, bringing the visitors to a virtual environment inside the ICSPace where they can access the available video collection.

The ICSPace cells are based on a spatial metaphor. The idea is to allow that the authors choose the best position to expose their work of arts inside the "virtual" space. Each work fill a space in the cell. When the occupation of a cell

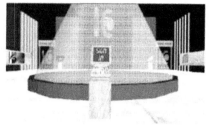

(a) Area View.

(b) Main Hall.

(c) Projection Room.

Fig. 4. ICSPace Views

reaches the maximum level, the cell divides itself, starting a process of structural reorganization of the cultural space. Figure 7 illustrates this process. The main criterion to establish that reorganization is a proximity function that considers, fundamentally, the space metaphor. Besides, other criteria can be established in agreement with the defined attributes of each work. Figure 5 illustrates this process.

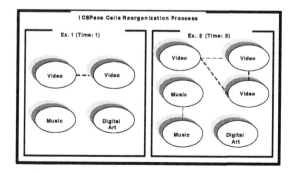

Fig. 5. ICSPace Cells reorganization.

The implementation of the thematic rooms include objects that improve the ICSPace services, providing visualization and navigation tools. However, it still remains to consider an important point: the integration among those users. For so much, we intend to dispose tools that promote the communication among the people that visit the center. Those tools, or mechanisms, can be implemented through groupware technologies. The idea is to provide chat rooms, discussion lists and on-line conferences. This way, the room visit can be monitored and visitors can communicate with other visitors that are visiting the same room at the same time.

4.3   ICSpace Users

Once inside ICSpace an avatar identifies the user. The avatars representation allow users to notice others users in the space. Besides, the use of different profiles, author and visitor, designates functionalities for each one of those profiles.

When logging in ICSpace, the user choose an avatar and, optionally, provides other data identifying itself. The avatar must agree with the access way: visitor or author. After that, the user can navigate through the center, visit rooms, publish work of arts, look for work of arts and communicate with other users.

4.4   ICSpace Collection

ICSPace collection is defined by the set of available work of arts. The process of insert works begins in the submission process. In order to submit a new work the author should get in ICSPace, go to the insertion module, fill some information in a form and submit it. By the way, the author chooses the place where he wants to expose his work in the cultural space. This is done using the 2D ICSpace map. Figure 6 shows the insertion forms and the 2D view of the video room. Once approved, the submitted work is made available to the visitors of the cultural space.

ICSpace uses two strategies to store the work of arts. In the first option, the works are accommodated in repositories of the cultural space. In the other option, the author takes the storage responsibility and ICSpace just maintains a pointer (link) to the work of art. ICSpace storage capacity virtual building area is limited to control the complexity of the navigation through the center. Therefore it is necessary to employ a substitution politics for maintaining the collection. This politics defines the life cycle of each work considering aspects like time of permanence, visits number and critics.

5   ICSpace Implementation Strategy

ICSPace implementation strategy is based on the prototype and the incremental evolution paradigms. Therefore a politics of versions was adopted, so the prototypes are been constructed focusing the final product. The strategy includes the following implementation phases:

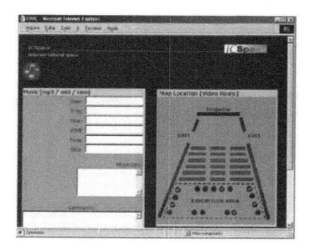

Fig. 6. ICSPace Forms for Inserting Work of Arts.

Phase I. Interface Design. During this phase, ICSpace interface (VRML and HTML) was developed. Also, some basic functional features were implemented too. The focus was the ICSpace repositories. That is, the implementation of the metadata server, the media server and some retrieval mechanisms. There are two base forms for the media exhibition: integrated with the VRML interface and dissociated, which uses external players to present the media content. At this moment, the work's insertion is an ICSpace administrator task. The basic features of the users repositories are also implemented, like the functions for inserting and excluding data. Some queries mechanisms are still under development.

Phase II. Database Implementation. In this phase the work's exhibition rooms creation process is automated using a database. In accordance to the ICSpace reorganization politics, when a room reaches its maximum capacity of works it can be divided, originating other exhibition rooms. To implement these politics, we used a generic structure for each room type stored and handled using a database oriented application. Figure 7 illustrates the dynamic rooms creation. In this process, triggers implemented associated to the database, automatically create the rooms. We have defined a set of constraints, when these constraints are satisfied the trigger activates the room creation process.

Phase III. Communication Tools. In this stage the focus is to provide new functions for the ICSpace users. The basic idea is to improve communication tools. Also, representation and perception techniques will be incorporated to the cultural space implementation. This way, will be possible to know the users skills, their characteristics and their preferences. The works insertion becomes an user activity. Another goal is to provide communication mechanisms among the users, using avatars. The use of an avatar makes possible the user representation in the ICSpace using interface objects like 3D graphics and so, users may communicate and be noted by other ones.

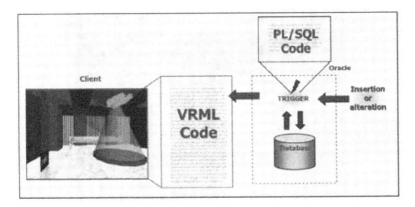

Fig. 7. ICSPace Dynamic Rooms Creation.

In the current stage of this project we already concluded the Phase I and are working in the Phase II. The different technologies that will be used were analyzed and defined. For example, in the phase I we have used VRML and HTML to develop the interface and Oracle 8.0.4 to implement the database application. During phase II we are using the Oracle native language (PL/SQL language) and the servlet technology including Java language. Also, we explored JDBC for communication between Oracle Database and Servlets. For the Phase III we are will implement a VRML multi-user server to support to the avatars implementation and groupware technologies to improve communication features.

6   Conclusions

This work have presented the structure and the functionality of ICSPACE – an Internet Cultural Space that provides for artists' community the possibility to build an opened and dynamic environment into the net. In our approach computer is used as a knowledge supplier expanding the human artistic expression. ICSPACE design guidelines structure the exhibition of the artist's works in thematic rooms. The thematic rooms are seen as independent and correlated cells. The association of a set of rooms provides a much more complex formation that defines the own cultural center. These cells are based on a spatial metaphor. The idea is to allow that authors choose the best position to expose theirs works in the space "virtual reality environment". Users interact with ICSPACE assuming one amongst two profiles: author or visitor. As author, users visit the center to choose the most adequate position to expose his work. Besides, users can take a walk on the rooms, interact with other visitors and authors. In the beginning of a visit, the user chooses an avatar that will represent him. During the visit the user notes the presence of other visitors through their respective avatars and can send messages or invite them to talk. The visitors can also register critics relative to the exposed work of arts. The number of exposed works in ICSPACE is limited, basically by the available storage space and for the complexity of its building, which is proportional to the number of exposed works of art. So, to solve this problem, ICSPACE uses different strategies to control the substitution of the exposed works of art. ICSPACE implementation addresses different technologies like human computer interaction, cooperative work, virtual reality, hypermedia systems and dynamic art. ICSpace prototype is already implemented. We have video and audio cells operational. The module that deals with the insertion of the work of arts is also implemented with CGI forms. We are now working in the development of the groupware tools to promote cooperation among users. The idea is to open the ICSpace to the artists community as soon as possible, our target date is August 2001. We intend that ICSPACE becomes a space to promote cultural exchange through the Internet, integrating people and artists breaking spatial barriers.

References

[1] AMES, A., NADEAU, D., MORELAND,J. (1995) VRML Sourcebook. John Wiley & Sons, Inc. http://www.wiley.com /compbooks/k26.html
[2] Anonymous-4 (1996). The VRML 2.0 Specification. http://vrml.sgi.com/moving-worlds/spec/
[3] BERGER, J.E. et al. (1994) NVR: A System for Network Virtual REALITY. Proceedings of IEEE Conference on Multimedia Computing Systems.
[4] CECILIO, Edmundo L. & RODRIGUES, Rogério (1996). Vídeo Sob Demanda. Relatório Técnico TM 10, Laboratório Telemídia, Depto. de Informática, PUC-Rio. 60p.
[5] ELLIS, S.R. What are Virtual Environments? (1994) IEEE Computer Graphics & Applications, 14(1):17-22, Jan. 1994.
[6] ISDALE, Jerry. "What is Virtual Reality? – A homebrew Introduction and Information Resource List".
http://sunee.uwaterloo.ca /pub/vr/documents/WHATISVR.TXT.
[7] PRAJA, Ramesh Jain. (1999) Multimedia Portals. In: IEEE Media Visions.
[8] RAGGETT, David. (1997) Extending the WWW to Support Platform Independent Virtual Reality. http://vag.vrml.org/www-vrml/concepts/raggett.html
[9] TAVARES, T. A; LEITE, J. C; & SOUZA FILHO, G. L. (2000) Design da Interface do Sistema de Vídeo Sob Demanda da Rede NatalNet. In: Vi Simpósio Brasileiro de Sistemas Multimídia e Hipermídia - SBMídia, 2000, Natal. Anais do VI Simpósio Brasileiro de Sistemas Multimídia e Hipermídia. 2000. p.141-157.
[10] Louvre Museum Website –
http://www.culture.fr/louvre/louvrea.htm (10/04/2001)
[11] Van Gohh Museum Website – http://www.vangoghmuseum.nl (10/04/2001)
[12] Chicago Museum Website – http://www.mcachicago.org/ (10/04/2001)
[13] Atlântico Art Center Website – (http://www.caam.net/en/index.htm)
[14] Virtuella Musik Musset Museum Website – http://www.musiknet.se/ musikmuseum/ sve/index.html
[15] Pygoya Museum Website – http://digitalartmuseum.com/march/pygoya/

Author Index

Arafa, Yasmine   113
Araújo, A.S.   389

Beard, Simon   90, 101

Cappi, Juan   57
Carlsson, Bengt   347
Castells, Pablo   268
Chan, Sheung-Ping   224
Chau, Chi Kin   244
Chau, Chun Keung   134
Chen, Chun   191
Chen, Enhong   377
Cheng, Samuel   5
Cheng, Xiefeng   291
Choi, Samuel P.M.   224
Chun, Hon Wai A.   235

Drogoul, Alexis   165
Dudek, Gregory   355

El-Bakry, Hazem M.   205
Esichaikul, Vatcharaporn   36

Feng, Zhiquan   291
Fish, Robert S.   5
Fortier, Andres   57
Fu, Xiaodong   83
Fukuda, Toshio   1

Garcia, Francilene Procpio   77
Gelman, Alexander   5
Goderis, Sofie   57
Gu, Erdan   191
Gustavsson, Rune   347

Ham, HoSang   171
Ho, Kelvin Yuen-Hin   144
Horiguchi, Yukio   24
Hu, Jing   377
Huang, Ding   216
Huang, Runhe   45
Huang, Xinyuan   365
Huynh, Quoc   90
Hwang, ChongSun   171

Ishida, Toru   2

Jin, Qun   45

Kanade, Takeo   3
Kang, YunHee   171
Katai, Osamu   182, 279
Kawakami, Hiroshi   182, 279
Khatib, Oussama   4
Kim, Young-Jun   314
Kong, Xiangyang   5

Lai, Chak Shun   134
Lam, Stephen Wang-Cheung   144
Law, Tak-Ming   297
Li, Weihua   83
Li, Xiangyang   327
Li, Xiaodong   335
Li, Xingshan   199
Lin, Wei   216
Liu, Jiming   224

Ma, Jianhua   45
Macías, José A.   268
Mamdani, Abe   113
Marriott, Andrew   90
Mashita, Naoaki   255
Matsushita, Yutaka   255
Mild, Andreas   302
de Moraes Filho, Carlos
    Alberto Odorico   77
Muñoz-Meléndez, Angélica   165
Murugesan, San   65

Notsu, Akira   279

Ramanathan, Annamalai   65
Reid, Donald   101
Reutterer, Thomas   302
Rossi, Gustavo   57

Sae-Tang, Suwimol   36
Sawaragi, Tetsuo   24
Schwabe, Daniel   57
Shepherdson, Russel   101
Shi, Bertram Emil   134
Shigeno, Hiroshi   255

Sim, Kwang Mong   153, 244
Simhon, Saul   355
Souza Filho, G.L.   389
Stallo, John   90
Sun, Weng Hong   153

Takahashi, Hiroto   17
Tavares, T.A.   389
Toda, Kentaro   182

Wang, Shangfei   377
Wang, Xufa   377
Wong, Rebecca Y.M.   235

Xu, Duanqing   191

Yan, Hong   216
Ye, Nong   327
Yi, Wei   321
Yin, Peng   5
Yonezawa, Yasuo   17
Yu, Hong Heather   5
Yuan, Chunwei   199

Zhang, Shaobai   291
Zhao, Guoying   365

Lecture Notes in Computer Science

For information about Vols. 1–2179
please contact your bookseller or Springer-Verlag

Vol. 2005: W. Ziarko, Y. Yao (Eds.), Rough Sets and Current Trends in Computing. Proceedings, 2000. XV, 670 pages. 2001. (Subseries LNAI).

Vol. 2063: T. Marsland, I. Frank (Eds.), Computers and Games. Proceedings, 2000. XIII, 443 pages. 2001.

Vol. 2128: H. Ehrig, G. Juhás, J. Padberg, G. Rozenberg (Eds.), Unifying Petri Nets. VIII, 485 pages. 2001.

Vol. 2180: J. Welch (Ed.), Distributed Computing. Proceedings, 2001. X, 343 pages. 2001.

Vol. 2181: C. Y. Westort (Ed.), Digital Earth Moving. Proceedings, 2001. XII, 117 pages. 2001.

Vol. 2182: M. Klusch, F. Zambonelli (Eds.), Cooperative Information Agents V. Proceedings, 2001. XII, 288 pages. 2001. (Subseries LNAI).

Vol. 2183: R. Kahle, P. Schroeder-Heister, R. Stärk (Eds.), Proof Theory in Computer Science. Proceedings, 2001. IX, 239 pages. 2001.

Vol. 2184: M. Tucci (Ed.), Multimedia Databases and Image Communication. Proceedings, 2001. X, 225 pages. 2001.

Vol. 2185: M. Gogolla, C. Kobryn (Eds.), «UML» 2001 – The Unified Modeling Language. Proceedings, 2001. XIV, 510 pages. 2001.

Vol. 2186: J. Bosch (Ed.), Generative and Component-Based Software Engineering. Proceedings, 2001. VIII, 177 pages. 2001.

Vol. 2187: U. Voges (Ed.), Computer Safety, Reliability and Security. Proceedings, 2001. XVI, 249 pages. 2001.

Vol. 2188: F. Bomarius, S. Komi-Sirviö (Eds.), Product Focused Software Process Improvement. Proceedings, 2001. XI, 382 pages. 2001.

Vol. 2189: F. Hoffmann, D.J. Hand, N. Adams, D. Fisher, G. Guimaraes (Eds.), Advances in Intelligent Data Analysis. Proceedings, 2001. XII, 384 pages. 2001.

Vol. 2190: A. de Antonio, R. Aylett, D. Ballin (Eds.), Intelligent Virtual Agents. Proceedings, 2001. VIII, 245 pages. 2001. (Subseries LNAI).

Vol. 2191: B. Radig, S. Florczyk (Eds.), Pattern Recognition. Proceedings, 2001. XVI, 452 pages. 2001.

Vol. 2192: A. Yonezawa, S. Matsuoka (Eds.), Metalevel Architectures and Separation of Crosscutting Concerns. Proceedings, 2001. XI, 283 pages. 2001.

Vol. 2193: F. Casati, D. Georgakopoulos, M.-C. Shan (Eds.), Technologies for E-Services. Proceedings, 2001. X, 213 pages. 2001.

Vol. 2194: A.K. Datta, T. Herman (Eds.), Self-Stabilizing Systems. Proceedings, 2001. VII, 229 pages. 2001.

Vol. 2195: H.-Y. Shum, M. Liao, S.-F. Chang (Eds.), Advances in Multimedia Information Processing – PCM 2001. Proceedings, 2001. XX, 1149 pages. 2001.

Vol. 2196: W. Taha (Ed.), Semantics, Applications, and Implementation of Program Generation. Proceedings, 2001. X, 219 pages. 2001.

Vol. 2197: O. Balet, G. Subsol, P. Torguet (Eds.), Virtual Storytelling. Proceedings, 2001. XI, 213 pages. 2001.

Vol. 2198: N. Zhong, Y. Yao, J. Liu, S. Ohsuga (Eds.), Web Intelligence: Research and Development. Proceedings, 2001. XVI, 615 pages. 2001. (Subseries LNAI).

Vol. 2199: J. Crespo, V. Maojo, F. Martin (Eds.), Medical Data Analysis. Proceedings, 2001. X, 311 pages. 2001.

Vol. 2200: G.I. Davida, Y. Frankel (Eds.), Information Security. Proceedings, 2001. XIII, 554 pages. 2001.

Vol. 2201: G.D. Abowd, B. Brumitt, S. Shafer (Eds.), Ubicomp 2001: Ubiquitous Computing. Proceedings, 2001. XIII, 372 pages. 2001.

Vol. 2202: A. Restivo, S. Ronchi Della Rocca, L. Roversi (Eds.), Theoretical Computer Science. Proceedings, 2001. XI, 440 pages. 2001.

Vol. 2203: A. Omicini, P. Petta, R. Tolksdorf (Eds.), Engineering Societies in the Agents World II. Proceedings, 2001. XI, 195 pages. 2001. (Subseries LNAI).

Vol. 2204: A. Brandstädt, V.B. Le (Eds.), Graph-Theoretic Concepts in Computer Science. Proceedings, 2001. X, 329 pages. 2001.

Vol. 2205: D.R. Montello (Ed.), Spatial Information Theory. Proceedings, 2001. XIV, 503 pages. 2001.

Vol. 2206: B. Reusch (Ed.), Computational Intelligence. Proceedings, 2001. XVII, 1003 pages. 2001.

Vol. 2207: I.W. Marshall, S. Nettles, N. Wakamiya (Eds.), Active Networks. Proceedings, 2001. IX, 165 pages. 2001.

Vol. 2208: W.J. Niessen, M.A. Viergever (Eds.), Medical Image Computing and Computer-Assisted Intervention – MICCAI 2001. Proceedings, 2001. XXXV, 1446 pages. 2001.

Vol. 2209: W. Jonker (Ed.), Databases in Telecommunications II. Proceedings, 2001. VII, 179 pages. 2001.

Vol. 2210: Y. Liu, K. Tanaka, M. Iwata, T. Higuchi, M. Yasunaga (Eds.), Evolvable Systems: From Biology to Hardware. Proceedings, 2001. XI, 341 pages. 2001.

Vol. 2211: T.A. Henzinger, C.M. Kirsch (Eds.), Embedded Software. Proceedings, 2001. IX, 504 pages. 2001.

Vol. 2212: W. Lee, L. Mé, A. Wespi (Eds.), Recent Advances in Intrusion Detection. Proceedings, 2001. X, 205 pages. 2001.

Vol. 2213: M.J. van Sinderen, L.J.M. Nieuwenhuis (Eds.), Protocols for Multimedia Systems. Proceedings, 2001. XII, 239 pages. 2001.

Vol. 2214: O. Boldt, H. Jürgensen (Eds.), Automata Implementation. Proceedings, 1999. VIII, 183 pages. 2001.

Vol. 2215: N. Kobayashi, B.C. Pierce (Eds.), Theoretical Aspects of Computer Software. Proceedings, 2001. XV, 561 pages. 2001.

Vol. 2216: E.S. Al-Shaer, G. Pacifici (Eds.), Management of Multimedia on the Internet. Proceedings, 2001. XIV, 373 pages. 2001.

Vol. 2217: T. Gomi (Ed.), Evolutionary Robotics. Proceedings, 2001. XI, 139 pages. 2001.

Vol. 2218: R. Guerraoui (Ed.), Middleware 2001. Proceedings, 2001. XIII, 395 pages. 2001.

Vol. 2219: S.T. Taft, R.A. Duff, R.L. Brukardt, E. Ploedereder (Eds.), Consolidated Ada Reference Manual. XXV, 560 pages. 2001.

Vol. 2220: C. Johnson (Ed.), Interactive Systems. Proceedings, 2001. XII, 219 pages. 2001.

Vol. 2221: D.G. Feitelson, L. Rudolph (Eds.), Job Scheduling Strategies for Parallel Processing. Proceedings, 2001. VII, 207 pages. 2001.

Vol. 2223: P. Eades, T. Takaoka (Eds.), Algorithms and Computation. Proceedings, 2001. XIV, 780 pages. 2001.

Vol. 2224: H.S. Kunii, S. Jajodia, A. Sølvberg (Eds.), Conceptual Modeling – ER 2001. Proceedings, 2001. XIX, 614 pages. 2001.

Vol. 2225: N. Abe, R. Khardon, T. Zeugmann (Eds.), Algorithmic Learning Theory. Proceedings, 2001. XI, 379 pages. 2001. (Subseries LNAI).

Vol. 2226: K.P. Jantke, A. Shinohara (Eds.), Discovery Science. Proceedings, 2001. XII, 494 pages. 2001. (Subseries LNAI).

Vol. 2227: S. Boztaş, I.E. Shparlinski (Eds.), Applied Algebra, Algebraic Algorithms and Error-Correcting Codes. Proceedings, 2001. XII, 398 pages. 2001.

Vol. 2228: B. Monien, V.K. Prasanna, S. Vajapeyam (Eds.), High Performance Computing – HiPC 2001. Proceedings, 2001. XVIII, 438 pages. 2001.

Vol. 2229: S. Qing, T. Okamoto, J. Zhou (Eds.), Information and Communications Security. Proceedings, 2001. XIV, 504 pages. 2001.

Vol. 2230: T. Katila, I.E. Magnin, P. Clarysse, J. Montagnat, J. Nenonen (Eds.), Functional Imaging and Modeling of the Heart. Proceedings, 2001. XI, 158 pages. 2001.

Vol. 2232: L. Fiege, G. Mühl, U. Wilhelm (Eds.), Electronic Commerce. Proceedings, 2001. X, 233 pages. 2001.

Vol. 2233: J. Crowcroft, M. Hofmann (Eds.), Networked Group Communication. Proceedings, 2001. X, 205 pages. 2001.

Vol. 2234: L. Pacholski, P. Ružička (Eds.), SOFSEM 2001: Theory and Practice of Informatics. Proceedings, 2001. XI, 347 pages. 2001.

Vol. 2235: C.S. Calude, G. Păun, G. Rozenberg, A. Salomaa (Eds.), Multiset Processing. VIII, 359 pages. 2001.

Vol. 2236: K. Drira, A. Martelli, T. Villemur (Eds.), Cooperative Environments for Distributed Systems Engineering. IX, 281 pages. 2001.

Vol. 2237: P. Codognet (Ed.), Logic Programming. Proceedings, 2001. XI, 365 pages. 2001.

Vol. 2239: T. Walsh (Ed.), Principles and Practice of Constraint Programming – CP 2001. Proceedings, 2001. XIV, 788 pages. 2001.

Vol. 2240: G.P. Picco (Ed.), Mobile Agents. Proceedings, 2001. XIII, 277 pages. 2001.

Vol. 2241: M. Jünger, D. Naddef (Eds.), Computational Combinatorial Optimization. IX, 305 pages. 2001.

Vol. 2242: C.A. Lee (Ed.), Grid Computing – GRID 2001. Proceedings, 2001. XII, 185 pages. 2001.

Vol. 2243: G. Bertrand, A. Imiya, R. Klette (Eds.), Digital and Image Geometry. VII, 455 pages. 2001.

Vol. 2244: D. Bjørner, M. Broy, A.V. Zamulin (Eds.), Perspectives of System Informatics. Proceedings, 2001. XIII, 548 pages. 2001.

Vol. 2245: R. Hariharan, M. Mukund, V. Vinay (Eds.), FST TCS 2001: Foundations of Software Technology and Theoretical Computer Science. Proceedings, 2001. XI, 347 pages. 2001.

Vol. 2246: R. Falcone, M. Singh, Y.-H. Tan (Eds.), Trust in Cyber-societies. VIII, 195 pages. 2001. (Subseries LNAI).

Vol. 2247: C. P. Rangan, C. Ding (Eds.), Progress in Cryptology – INDOCRYPT 2001. Proceedings, 2001. XIII, 351 pages. 2001.

Vol. 2248: C. Boyd (Ed.), Advances in Cryptology – ASIACRYPT 2001. Proceedings, 2001. XI, 603 pages. 2001.

Vol. 2249: K. Nagi, Transactional Agents. XVI, 205 pages. 2001.

Vol. 2250: R. Nieuwenhuis, A. Voronkov (Eds.), Logic for Programming, Artificial Intelligence, and Reasoning. Proceedings, 2001. XV, 738 pages. 2001. (Subseries LNAI).

Vol. 2251: Y.Y. Tang, V. Wickerhauser, P.C. Yuen, C.Li (Eds.), Wavelet Analysis and Its Applications. Proceedings, 2001. XIII, 450 pages. 2001.

Vol. 2252: J. Liu, P.C. Yuen, C. Li, J. Ng, T. Ishida (Eds.), Active Media Technology. Proceedings, 2001. XII, 402 pages. 2001.

Vol. 2253: T. Terano, T. Nishida, A. Namatame, S. Tsumoto, Y. Ohsawa, T. Washio (Eds.), New Frontiers in Artificial Intelligence. Proceedings, 2001. XXVII, 553 pages. 2001. (Subseries LNAI).

Vol. 2254: M.R. Little, L. Nigay (Eds.), Engineering for Human-Computer Interaction. Proceedings, 2001. XI, 359 pages. 2001.

Vol. 2256: M. Stumptner, D. Corbett, M. Brooks (Eds.), AI 2001: Advances in Artificial Intelligence. Proceedings, 2001. XII, 666 pages. 2001. (Subseries LNAI).

Vol. 2258: P. Brazdil, A. Jorge (Eds.), Progress in Artificial Intelligence. Proceedings, 2001. XII, 418 pages. 2001. (Subseries LNAI).

Vol. 2259: S. Vaudenay, A.M. Youssef (Eds.), Selected Areas in Cryptography. Proceedings, 2001. XI, 359 pages. 2001.

Vol. 2260: B. Honary (Ed.), Cryptography and Coding. Proceedings, 2001. IX, 416 pages. 2001.

Vol. 2264: K. Steinhöfel (Ed.), Stochastic Algorithms: Foundations and Applications. Proceedings, 2001. VIII, 203 pages. 2001.